Setting the Table for Julia Child

Setting the Table for Julia Child

Gourmet Dining in America, 1934–1961

DAVID STRAUSS

The Johns Hopkins University Press

Baltimore

The Johns Hopkins University Press
2715 North Charles Street
Baltimore, Maryland 21218-4363
www.press.jhu.edu

Library of Congress Cataloging-in-Publication Data

Strauss, David, 1937–
   Setting the table for Julia Child : gourmet dining in America, 1934–1961 /
David Strauss.
      p. cm.
   Includes bibliographical references and index.
   ISBN-13: 978-0-8018-9773-3 (hardcover : alk. paper)
   ISBN-10: 0-8018-9773-4 (hardcover : alk. paper)
    1. Dinners and dining—United States—History—20th century.
2. Gourmets—United States—History—20th century. 3. Food habits—
United States—History—20th century. 4. Food—Social aspects—United
States—History—20th century. 5. Gourmet. 6. Cookery, American—
History—20th century. 7. United States—Social life and customs—
1918–1945. 8. United States—Social life and customs—1945–1970. I. Title.
   GT2853.U5S77 2011
   394.1'20973—dc22   2010015272

A catalog record for this book is available from the British Library.

Frontispiece: Carving a suckling pig, La Confrérie des Chevaliers du Tastevin
dinner, Chateau Clos de Vougeot, France, from *La Confrérie des Chevaliers du
Tastevin* (Paris: Éditions E.P.I.C., 1950), p. 81. La Confrérie des Chevaliers du
Tastevin

*Special discounts are available for bulk purchases of this book. For more information,
please contact Special Sales at 410-516-6936 or specialsales@press.jhu.edu.*

The Johns Hopkins University Press uses environmentally friendly book
materials, including recycled text paper that is composed of at least 30 percent
post-consumer waste, whenever possible. All of our book papers are acid-free,
and our jackets and covers are printed on paper with recycled content.

To my gourmet heirs:
Ben and Monique, Jesse, Annie and Guillermo, Leah and Matt
Bon Appetit!

CONTENTS

Conclusion   248

Color illustrations follow page 128

Nearly half a century ago, well before food studies became a respectable academic discipline, Richard Hofstadter recounted his culinary adventures at Le Pavillon in New York to perplexed students in his Columbia University graduate history seminar. As it turned out, this was a pleasant, but not a frivolous, departure from the assigned topic. Asserting that there was no such thing as an American cuisine, Hofstadter sparked a spontaneous debate over whether hot dogs, hamburgers, and steaks met the criteria for such a culinary regime. That debate, which has been percolating in my brain and whetting my appetite ever since, planted the seed from which this book has grown. It addresses, as our seminar did, the contrast between the relatively unstable foodways of the United States and the more highly articulated French dining regime. Further, it calls to mind the many ways, small and large, that Richard Hofstadter's innovative spirit continues to shape the writing of history.

While no one can recreate the taste of past gourmet dinners, observers' accounts, menus, recipes, and catalogues of specialty food and wine stores, as well as the papers of leading food writers, publishers, and activists in gourmet societies, provide useful information about those occasions. The following institutions have generously opened their collections of such documents to me: Les Amis d'Escoffier (Boston, Chicago, and New York chapters); the *Boston Globe* Library; Bowling Green State University; the Chicago History Museum; La Confrérie des Chevaliers du Tastevin (New Orleans, New York, and Washington, D.C., chapters); the Enoch Pratt Free Library; Houghton Library; the International Wine and Food Society (Boston, Chicago, London, and New York chapters); Iowa State University; the John Hartman Center at Duke University; Kalamazoo College; the Kalamazoo Public Library; the Michigan State University Library; the Missouri Historical Society; Oklahoma State University Library; Princeton University Library; the Schlesinger Library; the Smith College Library; the Society of

Medical Friends of Wine; the Stanford University Library; the Straus Historical Society; the University of California Libraries at Berkeley, Davis, and Los Angeles; the University of Pennsylvania Library; the University of Texas Library; Western Michigan University Archives; and the Williams Research Center, New Orleans.

Much of the material for writing a history of gourmet dining is in the hands and minds of individuals who have been active in gourmet dining societies, in writing about food and wine, or in maintaining collections of useful materials. I am grateful to the following for providing recollections and documents on different aspects of the topic: Victor Atkins, Edwin James Blair, Cameron Brown, Sharon Carlson, Narcisse Chamberlain, Jacques Chevignard, Louis-Marc Chevignard, Christine Crawford-Oppenheimer, John Danza, Lynn Eaton, Rebecca Gray, James Hammond, Louis Hatchett, William Hoffmann, Sarah Hutcheon, Marilyn Mellowes, Martin Olliff, Joan Reardon, Ruth Slechta, Dan Strehl, Charles Turgeon, Gail Unzelman, Barbara Ketcham Wheaton, and Julius Wile. (For telephone interviews, see the "Essay on Sources.")

Special thanks go to Lee Langan, archivist of the San Francisco Wine and Food Society, who initially shared with me his digital record of the Society's menus and later scanned selected items from the collection to be reproduced in the color gallery.

At Kalamazoo College, Kathryn Lightcap scanned a number of images for the manuscript; Marigene Arnold, Gail Griffin, Franklin Presler, and Bob Stauffer have shared their thoughts in ongoing conversations about the changing American dietary regime, while David Barclay and Charlene Boyer-Lewis have made helpful suggestions for revising the manuscript. Special thanks to Paul Smithson, who sharpened my grasp of fine printing, and to Billie Fischer for interpreting Italian Renaissance motifs. For his reflections on the conceptual issues underlying the treatment of gourmet dining, I am grateful to Bob Stauffer.

Scholars in the burgeoning field of food history have also read one or more chapters of the manuscript. Thanks to Amy Bentley, Jan Langone, Harvey Levenstein, Anne Mendelson, Jessamyn Neuhaus, Thomas Pinney, Laura Shapiro, and Amy Trubek for their helpful advice. Christopher Endy's critique of chapter 6 has helped me to understand the influence of *Gourmet* guidebooks on post–World War II tourism.

At the Johns Hopkins University Press, thanks to Debby Bors, Bob Brugger, Jeremy Horsefield, and Josh Tong, whose careful reading of the manuscript much improved it.

I have drawn inspiration from two conferences on food history that have reflected on current and future directions for research in the field: "Food and Drink in Consumer Societies" (Hagley Museum and Library, November 1999) and "Women, Men, and Food: Putting Gender on the Table" (Radcliffe Institute for Advanced Study, April 2007). It is a pleasure, as well, to acknowledge the Radcliffe Institute for Advanced Studies for awarding me a Schlesinger Library Research Support Grant.

Two individuals have supported my project from the outset and have read every word of the manuscript in its entirety at least once. John Lankford has been unstinting in his support of my efforts to chart new territory in the history of food, while insisting that the story be told in a clear and lively fashion. My wife, Dhera, has purged early drafts of egregious errors, assisted me in selecting the illustrations for the text, and supplied the title for the book. Equally important, she has provided a steady flow of gourmet cooking to fuel the project and inspire the imagination.

Recipes and menus written in French or Italian, as well as other expressions in these languages, appear in italics. In cases where the name of a dish has been written in English and French, I have not altered the original version.

Setting the Table for Julia Child

Introduction

I magine for the moment a typical day's food itinerary in the lives of Jane and John Hale, both working for a law firm in a large American city in 2011. They rise to a light breakfast of orange juice followed by croissants, which they have purchased from a local bakery and warmed in their microwave; while devouring the croissants, they sip Sumatra coffee brewed from beans purchased at a nearby Starbucks and freshly ground. During the lunch hour, the two meet at a small French restaurant near their law office to dine on a leek and mushroom quiche, accompanied by a glass of California merlot, and field greens dressed in oil and vinegar. On their way home in the evening, they stop at the local supermarket to purchase a filet of flounder, which they poach in a California sauvignon blanc and serve with rice pilaf, brussels sprouts, and slices of baguette from their bakery. After finishing the bottle of sauvignon with the meal, they divide a serving of grapes and munch on artisanal chocolates as they savor a strong cup of decaf, home-brewed espresso.

This culinary scenario, which the Hales take for granted, would, in fact, have been unimaginable without a remarkable revolution in American foodways. Among the notable changes are the appearance of artisanal food enterprises, a greater variety of ethnic cuisines, and a class of consumers—mainly urban professionals and managers—whose palates are attuned to the new flavors and foods now available. To the extent that the beneficiaries are aware of these changes, they often credit them to Julia Child, who looms larger than life over the American culinary scene despite her death in 2003. Julia's 1961 cookbook, *Mastering the Art of French Cooking*, and the ensuing 1963 television show, *The French Chef*, were instrumental in popularizing gourmet dining in the United States. In the process, she became a much-respected and beloved authority whose influence continues to this day.

Julia's celebrity, however, has obscured the work of her predecessors from the repeal of Prohibition to the appearance of her first book. As a result, scholars have ignored the creation of gourmet dining societies in the 1930s and have only touched on the founding of *Gourmet: The Magazine of Good Living*, fully twenty years before the appearance of Julia's masterpiece. It is important to recover this past in order to properly assess the contributions of her predecessors and to understand the foundation on which she built. Only in this way is it possible to identify the accomplishments for which she was primarily responsible. In writing this book, I have recreated the context for Julia's work in order to give a clearer account of the roles she and her predecessors played in the rise of gourmet dining in America.

No small task at the outset, however, is to understand what "gourmet dining" means. As Julia wisely noted, Americans have so overused the term "gourmet" that it has become virtually meaningless. Once a noun identifying a connoisseur of fine dining, gourmet is now routinely used as an adjective that is even attached to restaurants at Disney World and frozen dinners.[1]

In France, *gourmet* originally signified a connoisseur of wines. To identify a connoisseur of fine dining (including wines), as well as a gluttonous individual, the French have preferred the terms *gastronomer* and *gourmand*. Indeed, the founding father of food writing, Jean Anthelme Brillat-Savarin, used *gourmand* to mean *connoisseur*, as did Julia Child and her French collaborators, who were "heartily sick of gourmets" and thus named their cooking school "L'École des Trois Gourmandes." Aside from its overuse, *gourmet* was objectionable to Julia because it connoted someone who was a refined, perhaps even a picky, eater. A gourmand, by contrast, enjoyed satisfying a lusty appetite while appreciating fine dinners. Thus, diners identified as gourmands would exercise their appetites without abandoning the rules of gastronomy that structured the consumption of food and wine.[2]

Despite their efforts, *gourmet* became the preferred term for a connoisseur of food and wine in the United States. As early as 1890, the art critic Theodore Child described the gourmet as someone who was both knowledgeable about the flavors of various ingredients and moderate in his appetite. Forty years later, F. Gray Griswold, a member of "The Kittens" dinner club in New York, seemed to agree with Theodore. He defined the gourmet as a "man with refined and appreciative taste for all things that are perfect in the way of food to eat and wine to drink." Both authors, worried about the digestive problems as well as dulled brains that followed from overindulgence, thus preferred "gourmet" to "gourmand." Other food writers of the 1930s generally followed their usage, and so the term gourmet came to identify fine diners in the United States. Following that usage, I consider those individuals who know fine food and wines, even when they have lusty appetites, as gourmets. It should be clear as well that Americans borrowed not only the terminology from France but also the cuisine. At least until 1961, gourmet dining for Americans usually meant some variation of French cuisine.[3]

In recent decades, however, "gourmet" has been used more frequently as an adjective to describe certain occasions, products, and processes such as "gourmet dining" or "gourmet food." In its noun form, "gourmet" identified an individual who possessed an enduring capacity for recognizing good food and wine and exercised it continuously. Indeed, as André Simon, founder of the Wine and Food Society, insisted, the art of good living requires "giving daily" as much thought to food as to clothes. Once users labeled products and occasions as "gourmet," however, they created a divide between the gourmet and everyday realms. Furthermore, under the new regime it was tempting to judge the book by the cover. Most Americans now identify individuals who attend the right occasions and shop at the right places as gourmets whether or not they are discerning diners. This is a case of putting the cart before the horse. The true gourmet would first determine the quality of the food and wine at these shops and dinners before patronizing them.[4]

Despite these conceptual confusions, the influence of French cuisine in America has been significant. Yet the story of its dissemination beyond a small elite must begin with the launching of a gourmet dining movement in America following the repeal of Prohibition. And it must take account of the complexities of French cuisine that include both the production and consumption of fine food and wine for a variety of different events. A gourmet dinner runs the gamut from intimate occasions for family and friends prepared by a home cook to more elaborate and formal restaurant events presided over by professional chefs. The events are only the superstructure; the services and products provided by grocers, wine dealers, cookbook writers, and cooking schools constitute the foundation of this practice. And one of the distinguishing characteristics of the gourmet enterprise has been an ongoing written dialogue among practitioners in cookbooks, restaurant guides, travel books, society newsletters, and magazine articles, all of which helps to define practices and locate gourmet dining in the larger cultural life of the country.

Treated as a sociocultural phenomenon, gourmet dining illuminates the rise of luxury consumption of which it is an integral part. In this sense, it is a close relative of the high-end women's fashions and interior decorating patronized by wealthy elites. Gourmet dining, like the women's fashion industry, appealed to potential consumers by virtue of its status as a foreign import that limited its access initially to Americans who could afford a tour of France. The purveyors of both fine dining and women's fashions relied heavily on articles and advertisements in luxury lifestyle magazines to promote their wares to affluent Americans.

Thorstein Veblen was among the first critics to consider the social significance of upper-class consumerism in his pioneering study, *The Theory of the Leisure Class*. Not coincidentally, he gravitated to this subject in the gilded age, when newly rich American industrialists were indulging themselves in expensive clothing, more lavish interior decoration, and the kind of fine dining they experienced on their travels in Europe. Veblen not only documented the extravagant consumption of the wealthy but attempted to explain and condemn it as well by labeling various practices as "conspicuous consumption" and "conspicuous leisure." These concepts approximate what Pierre Bourdieu has recently called "cultural capital," focusing, as they do, on matters of style, knowledge, and the grasp of language, which are closely correlated to an individual's position within the class hierarchy.[5]

Veblen's critics among contemporary scholars have rightly dismissed his overly simplistic account of the motives of luxury consumers; even so, he was surely right in thinking that many buyers sought to enhance their social standing through the right purchases, while those below them in the social order often aped their "betters" to improve their own status. However, it is also true that Veblen erred in virtually ignoring the sensual pleasure that consumers experienced in viewing beautiful paintings or enjoying the flavors and textures of well-prepared food, whether they were part of the upper class or lower in the social hierarchy. And he ignored evidence that cultural dissemination sometimes proceeded from the bottom up.[6]

Nonetheless, Veblen's book remains an instructive text on the history of luxury consumption. Among other things, it establishes the unequal interest among affluent Americans in different realms of consumption. From Veblen's examples, it is clear that fashionable clothing and refined house decorations were far more interesting to the gilded-age rich than was fine dining. No doubt, this discrepancy had much to do with the country's Puritan heritage, which regarded any luxury consumption with suspicion but tolerated fashion and home decoration, which engaged the visual sense, more readily than cuisine. Food was not only ephemeral, but after a dinner, its history was one of digestion and excretion, subjects that were inappropriate for public discussion. Accordingly, Veblen's virtual silence on the pleasures of the table suggests that he shared the inhibitions of the nouveaux riches, whose social practices he usually criticized, although his illicit love affairs indicate that he felt otherwise about the pleasures of the bedroom.[7]

Veblen was certainly perceptive in discerning one of the prime strategies of the leisure class in assuring its ascendancy. In an era of mass-produced, standardized, and inexpensive goods, socially ambitious consumers, who wished to distinguish themselves from the masses, favored the purchase of handcrafted items that were one of a kind and unaffordable to less affluent individuals. As an illustration of this strategy, one can see that, by offering original dishes "designed" by a chef, the early restaurants enabled wealthy consumers to put on display their connoisseurship. In recent years, the increasing standardization of the food industry has made it all the easier for high-end restaurants to appeal to well-heeled patrons with artisanal food. In contrast to the mass-produced items in fast-food venues, the quality of the restaurant's signature dishes stands out clearly.[8]

Among Veblen's most important legacies was his methodology, which required a systematic cataloguing of clothing styles and objects of house decoration, as well as the rituals and behavior of luxury consumers of that era, to demonstrate the consumption patterns of the leisure class and their cultural implications. In my study of gourmet diners of the mid-twentieth century, some of whom were the heirs of Veblen's leisure class, I have approximated Veblen's practice by documenting the menu choices of gourmet societies, the restaurants they elected to dine in, along with the dress codes and rituals of the societies, to provide insights into the values and behavior of the dining societies and their members. The recipes published in *Gourmet*, along with restaurant reviews and travel advice that specify options available to readers, who wished to discover the pleasures of the table, offer similar insights. In addition, the commentary in various gourmet society newsletters, quarterlies, and histories contains material that illuminates the way dining societies wrestled with the problems of creating French cuisine in an American setting.

Some 250 years before Veblen's polemic, the court of Louis XIV and the French nobility were developing a highly articulated dining code that incorporated many of the elements of what we now consider gourmet dining. That code spread gradually to the French bourgeoisie in Paris through the invention of the restaurant and the elaboration of carefully constructed menus in the years before and during the French Revolution. From the beginning, a dialogue about culinary principles, the diner's behavior at the table, the environment in which dinners were served, and the implications of these activities for life beyond the table accompanied the serving of fine dinners. Regarding these implications, Brillat-Savarin claimed in his classic tome, *The Physiology of Taste*, that a dinner properly prepared and served to diners from different professions and social backgrounds would raise the level of intellectual interchange between them and bring about a state of social conviviality. Much like the rite of communion, a gourmet dinner offered material substances that, when properly consumed, would elevate the spiritual condition of the diners.[9]

The French dialogue about culinary practices and principles in the early nineteenth century gave birth to a dining culture that helped to define the national identity; once word of this dining culture spread beyond French borders, foreigners increasingly visited France to experience the distinctive pleasures of the table. To exploit the opportunities opened to them by the popularity of their cuisine after 1850, the French created an informal culinary empire in Europe and America by exporting well-trained chefs. In sharp contrast to the angry European criticism of America's global fast-food empire in recent years, few Americans commented on this earlier chapter of culinary imperialism.[10]

As a foreign import, gourmet dining in America competed with existing dining practices in an alien social and cultural environment. A borrowed institution of this sort quite naturally offended those mainstream Americans, especially middle-class women, who preferred to live by utilitarian values and appealed almost exclusively to the few Americans who had experienced French cuisine in France. They were familiar with the great repertoire of dishes and wines available in French restaurants, valued the aesthetics of fine dining, and enjoyed the lively conversations that often accompanied these dinners. Thus, even though the United States was a more egalitarian country than France, gender and class factors played an important role in shaping dining practices.

Despite the wealth and power of those Americans who appreciated fine dining, it was impossible to reproduce French cuisine in the United States in all its manifestations. Aside from the absence of certain ingredients and the initial scarcity of French chefs, gourmet dining was neither rooted in the history of the country nor a central component of the national identity. After all, Americans were busy settling the interior of a vast continent at the moment when the French discovered a frontier in the new dining practices, recipes, and cooking techniques that spread from the court to the bourgeoisie. Through cookbooks designed for homemakers, this culinary culture was soon accessible to middle-class homemakers in France. While there were distinctions between home and restaurant cuisine, common cooking processes, fresh ingredients, and the use of similar sauces and stocks underlay kitchen practices in both settings. Not all Frenchmen dined well in the nineteenth century, but a broadly accepted culinary culture was in place by 1900 to support the preparation of dinners of greater or lesser refinement.[11]

Because of the predominantly utilitarian approach to dining in America, the introduction of French cuisine would challenge the ingenuity of its borrowers. They would have to locate proper ingredients and find or train chefs who could prepare French dishes from recipes in cookbooks or by memory. In addition, recruiting diners who were interested in trying new dishes with different flavors and textures and instructing them in the art of matching these dishes with appropriate wines would require time and effort. Of course, as Veblen pointed out, the scarcity of gourmet diners in America would become an advantage for the American leisure class. The work, money, and knowledge required to produce and consume refined dinners would lend prestige to producers and consumers alike, in addition to the pleasure they might experience from dining on dishes that had passed muster with connoisseurs in France.

For these reasons, French dining in America became the practice of a small, moneyed, and well-traveled elite that was effectively isolated from mainstream America. One of its early practitioners, Thomas Jefferson, a member of the planter elite, perfectly illustrates this link between gourmet dining and elevated social status. While serving as minister to France in the 1780s, Jefferson developed a taste for French cuisine and culture just as the first restaurants were opening their doors in Paris. During his stay there, Jefferson collected French cookbooks and wines that were shipped back to his home at Monticello, where he served French dinners to his distinguished guests. In the early nineteenth century, such elegant dining was limited to planters like Jefferson, merchants in America's growing cities, and French expatriates, all of whom could afford to import French wines and hire knowledgeable chefs, but rarely dined in public.

Following Jefferson's example in the late nineteenth century, the newly rich industrialists were in a somewhat better position to dine in the French fashion. After all, the transatlantic steamship brought Paris restaurants just a week's voyage away from the eastern seaboard and facilitated the importation of French wines. Wealthy Americans could also take advantage of restaurants that immigrant French chefs had established in the years following Jefferson's travels. Most notable were Delmonico's (1830) in New York, Antoine's (1840) in New Orleans, and Au Poulet d'Or (known as Poodle Dog) in San Francisco (1849), where Americans could enjoy a variant of French cuisine without visiting Europe. Men's clubs in large American cities, which often hired French chefs and stocked extensive wine cellars, offered other opportunities to experience French cuisine. In the private realm, a few affluent industrialists enlisted French chefs to prepare their favorite French dishes on a regular basis at home.[12]

Like social class, gender was a barrier to gourmet dining in both countries, although American women experienced this barrier even more forcefully than their French counterparts. To be sure, French gastronomers assumed an unbridgeable gap between the male professional chef, who produced *haute cuisine* in a restaurant kitchen, and the amateur housewife or her cook preparing *cuisine bourgeoise* at home. In fact, the French culinary culture shared by chefs and cooks, based on the belief that dining should be a pleasurable and healthful activity, transcended that divide. In America, however, twentieth-century food writers in women's magazines, who were, in turn, supported by food-processing firms and nutritionists, challenged this core principle. They urged American home cooks to make health virtually the sole consideration in planning meals. In following this prescription, compliant home cooks distanced themselves and their families from the essential elements of French cuisine, especially the use of fresh ingredients transformed through the cooking process into tasty meals. In effect, the gender gap in America reinforced the divide between social classes and assured that interested members of the upper class would be the principal practitioners of gourmet dining.[13]

As it turned out, many upper- and upper-middle-class women, no doubt conflicted by the tension between class and gender, found class the more powerful influence. Representative of this group were women food writers for the luxury lifestyle magazines who eloquently promoted the gourmet dining tradition and blazed a trail for Julia Child. In recruiting thousands of upper-middle-class women to the gourmet movement as home cooks, Julia contributed to changing the composition of the gourmet movement to reflect important changes in the class structure and gender relations after World War II.

Beyond class and gender, the prevailing utilitarian ethos in America, which prescribed hard work to assure basic food, clothing, and shelter, reinforced the barriers to the widespread practice of gourmet dining. One manifestation of this ethos was a reluctance among many Americans to embrace sensual experience. Observers have often noted that the population of Catholic countries, where church services incorporate rituals, ceremonies, and imagery as key elements of the faith, is more readily disposed to enjoy sensual experiences in other dimensions of their lives. The reverse is generally true of citizens in Protestant countries and even more so where Calvinist traditions have prevailed. For this reason, most old-stock, middle-class Americans in the nineteenth century were unreceptive to the pleasures of gourmet dining. By contrast, their upper-class compatriots gravitated more readily toward sensual experiences as long stays in Europe and affiliation with the Episcopalian or Catholic churches socialized them to European ways.[14]

For many Americans, the gratification of the senses remained a questionable activity through much of the early twentieth century. Indeed, the fear of sensual pleasure was one factor that motivated many supporters of the Prohibition amendment. Ironically, the debacle of that policy and the rise of speakeasies eventually convinced some of these supporters to change course, question their so-called Victorian values, and repudiate the Prohibition amendment. Repeal was certainly a big step toward lowering the barriers that society had erected to protect individuals from the dangers of sensual experience. It also enabled more Americans to take an interest in French cuisine after 1934 and thus paved the way for the more rapid increase in these numbers after 1961; even so, gourmet dining has remained largely an activity for upper- and upper-middle-class Americans.[15]

Despite its interest in gourmet dining, the American elite has not always been a custodian of the borrowed culture. Indeed, American connoisseurs of French cuisine often altered menus in ways that would have been unacceptable in France. While they profited from access to the repertoire of French wines and dishes, they sometimes incorporated into their dinners German, Italian, and traditional American dishes, promiscuously mixed with French dishes. As for matching wines with food, American gourmets often served German, Spanish, and American alongside French wines, and they frequently offered cocktails before dinner, even if the meal that followed was French. In effect, gourmet dining helped to reshape the culture of the American elite, but that group, in turn, modified French practices to serve its own preferences and customs.

Although a growing segment of Americans practiced a form of gourmet dining that borrowed heavily from the repertoire of French dishes, they were not always well informed about the dining culture of France. In particular, American food writers in recent years often discuss specific French recipes and cooking practices with little reference to Brillat-Savarin's insistence on gourmet dining as the key to achieving greater social conviviality among diners. And even as the adoption of French cuisine brought these diners closer to French ways, it opened a gap between them and Americans lower on the social scale, who had little interest in "upgrading" their diet to meet the standards of gourmets sometimes unclear about the benefits of such a change.[16]

In the course of my research, it has become clear that the history of gourmet dining in America is too large and complicated a subject to cover in a single volume. Accordingly, I have focused on two neglected institutions, gourmet dining societies and *Gourmet* magazine, while giving less attention to such important topics as the contribution of French restaurants in America, especially in the post–World War II era, and certain gourmet leaders, including James Beard and Craig Claiborne. Happily, readers will find ample treatment of these topics in other studies.

Furthermore, my emphasis on the sociocultural aspects of the history of gourmet dining, which link the movement to larger social and cultural trends, precludes considering the intricacies of gourmet cooking. Of course, the staging of a gourmet dinner would be impossible without this kitchen labor. As a consumer activity, gourmet dining depends on the work of skilled artisans to transform the raw materials for any particular recipe through a complicated process into finished products that please the palate. My emphasis, however, is primarily on the reception of the finished products in dining rooms and restaurants and the social implications of this activity. That being said, the primary justification for regarding gourmet dining as one type of luxury consumption is its reliance on the painstaking work of skilled artisans, a story that other authors have amply covered.

To illuminate the issues under consideration in this book, I have mixed a chronological with a topical approach. The first two chapters consider the ideological and material foundations of the gourmet movement—the development of a gourmet dining ethos over more than a century, from Brillat-Savarin to M. F. K. Fisher, and the challenge posed by nutritionists to this position, and then how the new or refashioned luxury lifestyle magazines, which shaped the values and lifestyles of a rising upper-middle class, reinforced that ethos. It of course depended on material resources available to the movement in large cities, including, among others, restaurants, fine-food shops, older dining societies, and wine dealerships.

The next two chapters examine the origins and development of a gourmet dining movement through the creation of international societies and their local branches, most of them founded by Frenchmen, which held regular dinners and disseminated their ideas and practices to the larger public. These chapters also document the selective recruitment practices of the dining societies, the ways in which they encouraged other Americans to take up gourmet dining, and their expansion after World War II.

Chapters 5, 6, and 7 deal with the establishment and impact of *Gourmet: The Magazine of Good Living*—the way the magazine selected its staff, identified and implemented its goals, and attempted to justify luxury dining in a period of relative austerity; its reliance on travel accounts, especially those of Samuel Chamberlain, to educate readers about European cuisines and cultures; and the fact that relatively few of the magazine's readers actually cooked from the recipes in the articles written by "*Gourmet* Chefs" Louis De Gouy and Louis Diat.

A final chapter examines the impact of the gourmet movement on Julia Child and her success in reshaping it primarily through the troubled but effective collaboration with her French counterpart, Simone Beck.

Chapter One

Food Fights in Twentieth-Century America

The Good Life versus the Healthy Life

W ith the advent of Prohibition in January 1920, the prospects for gourmet dining in America reached their nadir. By the terms of the Volstead Act, the manufacture and sale of alcohol, except for medical and religious purposes and the making of wine for home consumption, became illegal. Aside from its devastating effects on the beer, wine, and liquor industries, the law forced restaurants that made their profits largely on the sale of alcohol, including the renowned Sherry's and Delmonico's in New York, to close their doors. In their place came the speakeasies, where consumers bought illegal alcoholic beverages, and the cocktail party, featuring drinks made from illegal whiskey. In this environment, consumers often imbibed alcohol of poor quality that further diminished their already-modest interest in wine.

Prohibition wreaked greater havoc on existing gourmet practices because it coincided with the rise of the nutritionist ethos in America. Since 1900, food processors, nutritionists, and editors of women's magazines had made common cause in promoting a revolution in American eating habits. Adopting a supposedly scientific approach with great zeal, they downplayed the pleasures of the table in order to assure consumers' health through the manufacture of food products containing the requisite nutrients. In their view, food was a vehicle designed to deliver the vitamins, minerals, and calories that promoted good health. The new ethos, later dubbed "nutritionism," thus encouraged Americans to adopt a standardized diet based more on processed than fresh food.[1]

Advocates of this nutrionist approach to dining also promoted the use of processed foods to housewives on grounds of efficiency. Used in kitchens equipped with the new stoves and refrigerators, these foods would save housewives time and labor. In effect, nutritionism and the new appliances, both products of a second industrial revolution, appealed to American women by reducing the burden of preparing meals, while, at the same time, assuring the health of the family.

In this hostile, early twentieth-century environment, the relatively small party of gourmet advocates struggled to survive and make their voices heard.

They were, in fact, part of a growing, yet still small, revolt among some affluent Americans and intellectuals against modern industrial culture, including mass production and standardization, which were supposedly obliterating creativity and individuality. Applying their principles to culinary matters, these epicures rejected mass-produced (processed) foods in favor of fresh ingredients, meticulously prepared by a cook; their meals, in turn, would be occasions for experiencing a diversity of palate-pleasing flavors, as well as social interaction with their tablemates, which were the foundations of the good life.[2]

One sign of an emerging gourmet movement in America was the increasing publication of books and articles about food in various formats. The proliferation of restaurant reviews, food columns in newspapers and magazines, cookbooks, and essays on food signaled the opening of this new era in which food was becoming a topic of sufficient importance and interest to debate and discuss in print. To be sure, nutritionists writing in women's magazines accounted for much of this literature, but many books and articles were the product of a self-conscious community of gourmet proponents who linked the movement to its nineteenth-century roots. In the process, these gourmet advocates created a usable past for the movement that gave it a temporal and philosophical depth.

In fact, American gourmets were following in the footsteps of their European predecessors. At the heart of the gourmet enterprise, from its birth in the late eighteenth century, was an ongoing conversation, much of it in writing, about various facets of fine dining. In this discussion, French gastronomers took the lead. From published cookbooks, they considered a variety of recipes as options for the different courses of a dinner. To create a cohesive menu, they chose appropriate dishes, placing them in a proper order, and assigned wines for each course. On the dining side of the equation, food writers discussed proper table settings, room décor, and the service of the meal. In addition, there were questions about the number and kinds of guests who should be invited to dinner and the subjects they should talk about. At a more general level, food writers considered the appetite as a way of satisfying the senses as well as the role of gourmet dinners in creating social cohesion. The resulting written record helped to institutionalize gourmet dining in France while identifying for foreigners its essential components.

In recounting this story, I have traced the little-known role of twentieth-century American food writers in interpreting and updating the early nineteenth-century principles and practices of French cuisine in order to challenge the nutritionist ethos. I have also drawn on an abundant scholarly literature, supplemented by my own research into the distinctive approach to food of the women's magazines at the onset of World War II. Taken together, these materials provide evidence of an as-yet-unexplored debate between two different approaches to dining in America, which both sides conducted with a kind of missionary fervor. Updated to take account of current trends, the debate continues to influence the approach to foodways in the twenty-first century.

Food writers from the two camps differed substantially in their backgrounds, training, values, and the kind of audiences they wrote for. The modernist authors were almost all women, many of whom had studied in university home economics and nutrition programs and served as food writers for the leading women's magazines or consultants to food processors. They produced recipes and menus for millions of readers that would simplify the task of feeding their families, usually without the benefit of servants. The gourmet advocates, by contrast, were mostly males, well versed in the humanities and arts even when they had not attended universities; many had also traveled extensively in France and other parts of Europe. As independent writers, they pitched their publications to a relatively small and affluent audience interested in experiencing the joys of fine dining.

To compare and contrast their positions, I have chosen individuals who represented both camps in this dialogue. In the case of the gourmet proponents, Brillat-Savarin and M. F. K. Fisher were the preeminent food writers of the nineteenth and twentieth centuries, respectively, and thus among the most influential thinkers on the subject of gastronomy. The other gourmet advocates, George Saintsbury, André Simon, H. L. Mencken, Alfred Knopf, and Julian Street, were all key players in the renewal of gourmet dining and its promotion as a movement in the years following Prohibition. All were writers, except for Knopf, who published the work of five of these six kindred spirits.

The modernists presented their case most clearly in the women's magazines. Hence, rather than select individuals at the outset, I have chosen three representative women's magazines and then identified the food editor of each, as well as one or two of the most important writers in the food department. Here, I consider columns from *Good Housekeeping*, whose Institute every other women's magazine copied; the *Ladies' Home Journal*, which had the largest circulation among such magazines; and *Better Homes and Gardens*, a relatively new periodical founded in 1922 with a rapidly growing circulation. The articles, all from the year 1941, update the substantial secondary literature on the subject that covers the nutritionist ethos from its inception in the Victorian period up to the early 1930s. These articles also provide a useful contrast to *Gourmet*'s approach to fine dining.

Comparing and contrasting two such different forms of food writing poses some problems. The gastronomers dealt with such large questions as the link between dining and the good life, while the modernists' task was to present useful recipes and menus to readers. From a close reading of their articles, however, I have sought to discern the modernists' relative interest in taste, as opposed to nutrition and technology, and thus to infer from my findings their approach to food.

In presenting this contrast, I first treat the writings of Brillat-Savarin and his twentieth-century European disciples. I then turn to the rise of nutritionism in America, which implicitly challenged Brillat-Savarin's understanding of the relationship between dining and the good life. In conclusion, I consider how American advocates of gourmet dining reformulated Brillat-Savarin's ideas to question the claims of the dominant food establishment and present gourmet dining as a desirable alternative.

However, in identifying the underlying principles of the nutritionists and gastronomers, I am in no way suggesting that every American cook or diner fell into one camp or the other. In fact, many continued to prepare and consume traditional dishes they had learned from their families or cookbooks such as *The Joy of Cooking* that considered dining a source of pleasure as well as health. They took cooking seriously, employed a mix of fresh and processed ingredients, and balanced a concern for a nutritional diet with a desire to produce tasty meals. Even so, the debate over principles signaled the rise of a generation of gourmets who challenged the food establishment's effort to make their own approach to foodways the standard for all Americans.

European Gastronomical Authorities: Brillat-Savarin, Saintsbury, and Simon

In 1937, M. F. K. Fisher praised *The Physiology of Taste* (1826) as a study "without peer among books on eating . . . It is as near perfection as we yet know it." Ten years later Fisher's new translation of Brillat-Savarin's classic provided an important point of reference for gastronomers and the growing American audience for gourmet dining. Some members of this audience were already familiar with the 100th-anniversary translation of *The Physiology of Taste* published during Prohibition. In his introduction to that volume, Frank Crowninshield, the editor of *Vanity Fair*, who was raised in Paris, deplored the state of gastronomy in America.[3]

Born in Belley, just east of Lyon, in 1755, Brillat-Savarin was a member of the landed bourgeoisie and a devoted reader of Voltaire who became a lawyer and mayor of his hometown. In 1789, he was elected to the Third Estate; just five years later, after the Revolutionary Tribunal accused him of moderatism, he sought refuge in the United States for two years. Following his return to France, Brillat-Savarin settled in Paris, where he served as a member of the Cour de Cassation (the national appeals court) until his death in 1826. *The Physiology of Taste* grew out of his fascination with the Parisian restaurant scene and the commentary on it in Grimod de la Reynière's eight-volume restaurant guide, the *Almanach des gourmands* (1803–1813). Both men treated the pleasures of the table rather than the dazzling culinary techniques of Parisian chefs, and they regarded fine dining as an end in itself; however, Brillat-Savarin saw utopian possibilities in this activity that Grimod ignored. It could become, he believed, a means to create social bonds among the diners that would transform French society.[4]

In his book, Brillat-Savarin broke new ground by considering both the physiological roots of fine dining and its sociological consequences. Rather than write a cookbook, he treated the pleasures of the table, a subject that was of interest to everyone because all were "predestined" to enjoy the fruits of dining. To grasp the significance of fine dining, the author drew on medical insights he had acquired from doctor friends to explore the physiological facts of appetite and taste. In this respect, Brillat-Savarin, like the nutritionists, applied science to understanding the dining process. It is revealing, however, that his highest priority was to facilitate the quest for sensory pleasure rather than to improve the health of the diner, though the two goals were indirectly related to each other. He thus contributed to the creation of a sophisticated dining culture that sparked a search not only for excellent food and wine but also for a proper dining environment. This shared culinary culture, Brillat-Savarin believed, would inspire hosts to invite diverse dinner guests to enjoy animated conversation with each other in a salon-like environment.[5]

Brillat-Savarin considered gourmet dining as divinely inspired and a product of human nature, since every individual possessed the God-given senses of taste and smell, as well as an appetite. Based, as it was, on "our instinctive realization that by the very act we perform we are repairing our bodily losses" and on the social and aesthetic pleasures accompanying the act itself, he believed that the satisfaction of taste was among the few sources of pleasure in a life filled with pain.[6]

For the benefit of his readers, Brillat-Savarin recommended an intelligent and systematic approach to dining that he sometimes called gastronomy and at other times gourmandism. Gourmands, however, were not gluttons. The former displayed "an impassioned, considered and habitual preference for whatever pleases the taste" that was of no interest to gluttons who ate and drank too much.

True gourmandism required both the proper choice of menu items and an "exacting and knowing preparation" of them.[7]

In addition to producing pleasant physical sensations, gourmandism had a higher purpose, namely, to "spread that spirit of conviviality" among diverse individuals that "melts them into a whole, animates their conversation, and softens sharp corners of the conventional inequalities of position and breeding." Only the collaboration of an intelligent host and cooperative guests, however, could realize this goal. The former would have to limit the number of diners to twelve and select guests who represented varied professions and tastes. As for the guests, they would have to respect both the meal and their fellow diners; those who "gulp down in disgraceful indifference the most nobly prepared dishes" undermine the spirit of conviviality.[8]

The success of a dinner party also depended on the decorations, table setting, and music that established a proper environment in the dining room. According to Brillat-Savarin, "a sumptuous meal" should be eaten in a room decorated with "mirrors and paintings, sculptures and flowers, drenched with perfumes, enriched with lovely women, [and] filled with the strains of soft music." In this way, sound and sight—along with taste and smell—would serve gastronomy in awakening the senses. In such a setting, women provided part of the sensual décor rather than participating as equals in the festivities. Their presence no doubt contributed to Brillat-Savarin's expectation that the dining experience would generate a strong desire to procreate.[9]

Beyond the larger issues of gastronomy, Brillat-Savarin made a number of interesting observations about the dining experience. Based on its continuous cultivation from the time of Noah and Bacchus, he justified the serving of wine with meals. As for game, in the hands of a knowledgeable chef, it "is one of our favorite delicacies; it is a food at once healthy, warming, savorous, and stimulating to the taste, and is easily assimilated by anyone with a youthful digestive apparatus." More perplexing for modern readers was his claim that red meat was preferable to fish because it prepared workers for hard labor and would reduce the propensity of couples to propagate female descendants.[10]

Despite his effort to consider the dining event in universal terms, Brillat-Savarin occasionally revealed his French biases. In discussing *pot-au-feu*, he announced that "nowhere can be found soup as good as that of France." And he was convinced that the gastronomer, who chose from a wide variety of ingredients, would prefer French food and wine for their superior quality.[11]

Even though gastronomy was a science necessary to all men, Brillat-Savarin also recognized that a minority of educated and wealthy men would be its most devoted practitioners. "It is above all people of intelligence who hold gourmand-ism in high esteem; the rest are incapable of an operation which is made up of a series of appreciations and judgments." As for the rich, they were more in need of gastronomy because they were more likely to entertain than their less affluent compatriots. In addition, Brillat-Savarin identified professional associations and physical characteristics that encouraged gourmet practices. He argued that bank-ers, doctors, writers, and clergymen, as well as plump individuals, were most likely to join the ranks of gourmets.[12]

In effect, Brillat-Savarin turned food writing from its focus on preparing deli-cious dishes for an elegant dinner to codifying a dining culture that would be the centerpiece for achieving the good life. In that culture, he assigned to the host the responsibility of creating an environment conducive to the enjoyment of the dinner and choosing guests who were sufficiently diverse to enjoy convers-ing with each other. In turn, he enjoined the guests to demonstrate a true ap-preciation for the quality of the dinner and a respect for the intelligence of their fellow diners. However, he gave only occasional hints on how to select the ap-propriate dishes for a dinner and match them harmoniously with wines.

To instruct their readers on how to apply the general principles of gastronomy that Brillat-Savarin had elaborated to the selection of the specific dishes and wines to be paired with them was the task that both George Saintsbury and André Simon set for themselves. Saintsbury, the consummate wine amateur, discussed his ex-perience with a wide variety of wines and whiskeys. Simon, who was a wine dealer by profession, provided lists of wines and food items from which he chose the raw materials for recipes and menus. Both men also moved beyond the conventional dinner parties Brillat-Savarin proposed to consider new settings and institutions in which to cultivate the art of fine dining.

As Brillat-Savarin was the guru of gastronomers, Saintsbury became the "preeminent and citable master of *Wine*." Shortly after its publication in 1920, his *Notes on a Cellar Book* became a cult item among wine lovers on both sides of the Atlantic. Eleven years later, disciples, among them André Simon, founded the Saintsbury Club, dedicated to following their master in tasting good wines.[13]

Long before his celebrity as a wine lover, Saintsbury worked as a journalist and professor of literature at Edinburgh University, where he wrote several liter-ary biographies and multivolume histories of English and French literature. He was a man of his age, preferring broad subjects to the specialized studies of twentieth-century academics. But he is best remembered for *Notes on a Cellar Book*, written in his seventy-fifth year to celebrate the pleasures of wine at a moment when, for health reasons, his doctor had forbidden him to drink certain alcoholic beverages.[14]

To commemorate the centennial of Saintsbury's birth in 1943, André Simon dedicated *Vintagewise* to "the immortal memory of George Saintsbury." Despite the reverential language, *Vintagewise* was an extended commentary on Saintsbury's opinions of various wines, which reflected the mature judgment of a practiced wine taster recognized as such by the subject of his book. Indeed, Saintsbury regarded Simon's *Wine and Spirits* (1919) as "an excellent primer" and "a merry and wise book."[15]

Raised in a traditional French family in Paris, André Simon remained a devout Catholic and a patriot all his life. As a youth, he vacationed with the Symons family in Southampton, England, to improve his English and, in the process, met his future wife, Edith, who loved France and the French language as much as Simon loved England and English. Following their marriage and his service in the French army, Simon was sent to London by his employer, the Pommery and Greno champagne company. There he established his expertise in wine by writing for the *Wine Trade Review* and collaborating in the creation of the Wine Trade Club (1908), whose members tasted and discussed wines as preparation for selling them. In recognition of his success as a wine salesman, Pommery named Simon to head its London branch in 1911.[16]

Twenty-one years later, during a rapid decline in sales, Pommery removed Simon from that position and thus opened the way to his remarkable second career. Partnering with A. J. A. Symons, Simon created the Wine and Food Society (WFS) and its journal, *Wine and Food: A Gastronomical Quarterly*, which would serve, among other things, as an outlet for his writings. While it was initially a wine-only project, Symons advised that the inclusion of food would broaden interest in the society and the journal. Accordingly, the Society debuted with an Alsatian lunch at the Café Royal in London on November 14, 1933, followed a few months later by the appearance of the first issue of the journal. Reflecting on his career change ten years later, Simon remarked, "My boat, which sailed so pleasantly during some 35 years on Champagne, is now sailing not unpleasantly on the Black Sea of printer's ink."[17]

Both Simon and Saintsbury regarded alcohol, and especially wine, as the foundation of the good life, but they believed that the setting and manner of serving it enhanced the pleasure of consumption. Accordingly, Saintsbury remarked on the company he kept, the food he served with particular bottles of wine, and the choice of appropriate glasses. In the book's menu section, he advised serving Schabzieger cheese (a hard Swiss cheese flavored with powdered

Drawing of André Simon in his later years by Gavin Harrison from the book
jacket for Patrick Morrah, *André Simon* (London: Constable, 1987). Gavin Harrison.

clover), but only after grating and mixing it with butter to reduce the strong odor.
The cheese was to accompany a Chateau Léoville Barton, 1874.[18]

Saintsbury described his engagement with alcohol as a form of travel that
provided a continual adventure for the taste buds. He had "tried to be a (very
minor) Ulysses, steering ever from the known to the unknown" on his "voyages
to the Oracle of the Bottle." Closely linked to memorable encounters with family
and friends, this journey through alcohol engaged him both emotionally and
intellectually. Readers could find a model in his account for exploring a wide
variety of wines and whiskies, as well as purchasing and storing them.[19]

Saintsbury interspersed his pleasurable narrative of tasting and testing with
angry attacks on his enemies that remind us of the perilous setting in which he

wrote the book. In 1920, the brutality of World War I and the passage of Prohibition created a palpable sense of the fragility of civilized life. These developments were a call to action for Saintsbury, who responded with both his nostalgic account of the good life and a vigorous attack on its enemies.[20]

From beginning to end, Saintsbury excoriated temperance advocates. He proposed using jeroboams, emptied of their contents, to pelt "any Pussyfoot [Prohibitionist] who would make our dinner-tables dry places, and deprive our hearts of that which God sends to make them glad." Meanwhile, he sought to embarrass his religious opponents by citing the New Testament "advice of St. Paul and the practice of Christ." Beyond biblical passages, there were "cogent arguments to prove that Providence had the production of alcoholic liquors directly in its eye." How else could one explain the existence of cider apples, which were good for nothing except the making of cider? Thus, Prohibitionist teachings demonstrated both "thanklessness towards God and malice towards men," which invited divine retribution. "Providence . . . makes the punishment fit the crime (the thirst of the Pussyfoots in the Seventh Circle, *if they are allowed there,* will be ten times that of the drunkards)." "On those who would deprive us of it [alcohol]," he concluded, "let the curse of Nature rest." Despite his own health problems, Saintsbury also insisted that moderate consumption of alcohol was good for adults and assured readers that they could easily control the cost of it.[21]

Simon made his case for the good life in a more amiable fashion than Saintsbury when he published *The Art of Good Living* in 1929. In the tradition of Brillat-Savarin, Simon defended gastronomy as an activity designed to enhance daily life for everyone, rich or poor, who chose and prepared his or her own food and drink. And, like his mentor, Simon regarded gastronomy as incompatible with gluttony. To Brillat-Savarin's denunciation of gluttons, Simon added his own condemnation of nutritionists. The essential failing of both was their indifference to dining as a source of pleasure. Simon thus affirmed Brillat-Savarin's model of dining as a communal activity involving hosts and guests who could establish friendships through sharing a fine dinner and conversation at the table. As masters of "the wonderful harmony of the *grande cuisine,*" the French offered this art as their gift to the world.[22]

In promoting the pleasures of the table, which he regarded as an integral part of daily life, Simon urged gastronomers to use intelligence and moderation. As the standard for judging a fine dinner, they should consider the taste and smell of the food and the variety of the dishes, not the cost, size, or the richness of the ingredients. In considering the dining environment, they should also appreciate the harmony of "form and colour, sound and scent" that were the attributes of art and the "common heritage, the very core of what we are pleased to call Civilization." Simon was particularly attuned to the aesthetic and religious aspects of drinking wine in a communal setting.[23]

Individual preferences notwithstanding, Simon urged diners to consider certain realities in selecting dishes for any dinner. Like the nutritionist, the gourmet should anticipate the effects of food and drink on the dietary system; he must also be aware of seasonal changes so as to take advantage of mature wines and fresh vegetables and fruits. The same principle applied at restaurants. The savvy diner should choose the specialties of the chef and the featured wines of the restaurant over other options.[24]

Structuring a meal through courses was another way to make choices. According to Simon, a meal, like a book, should have an introduction, a story, and a "happy ending." In order to promote digestion, it should build from hors d'oeuvres and soup to the final courses, cheese and dessert, that were easy to digest. And to satisfy the law of simplicity, there should be only one peak. In addition, it would be wise to serve bland courses at the outset so that nothing would offend the "delicate" and "easily shocked" senses of taste and smell. Stronger flavors would come later in the meal. As for beverages, Simon sought to achieve a harmonious effect by pairing each dish with an appropriate wine. Through these choices, gastronomers would at once embrace the variety of nature in the dishes they chose and order that variety to achieve a harmony of tastes and colors.[25]

André Simon incorporated Saintsbury's reflections on his personal experiences with wine while developing a more systematic and practical approach to planning menus. His lists of ingredients and wines, along with his recipes and menus, opened a variety of options to readers who wanted to host a gourmet dinner. Simon's guidelines for creating a harmonious succession of courses and matching each one with appropriate wines were useful in assisting hosts to select particular dishes from the original voluminous lists. A few years later, through his experience with a variety of dining organizations, Simon showed how to apply Brillat-Savarin's principles not only to small dinner parties but also to larger occasions such as banquets.

The Nutritionist Approach to Dining

It is hardly surprising that *The Physiology of Taste* had a limited following in the United States. Many of its principal tenets ran counter to practices and beliefs in the New World. In a country where time was a precious commodity, the idea of lingering at the table to prolong a meal must have seemed a heresy. Further-more, since Americans were a mobile people, finding congenial dinner guests would have been more difficult than in France. The emphasis on wine as an es-sential element of the good life also created a gap between French and American practices. Finally, and most important, ideas about the proper relationship be-tween dining and health, which prevailed among French gastronomers from Brillat-Savarin to André Simon, seemed outdated to those who had mastered the new science of nutrition.

The nutritionist approach to food ignored Brillat-Savarin's focus on the ap-petite as the primary engine of dining and espoused instead the idea that Ameri-cans should eat what was good for them rather than what tasted good. The ori-gins of this revolutionary idea, as Laura Shapiro has shown, lay in the work of New England cooking school leaders Mary Lincoln, Fannie Farmer, and Ellen Richards, who created a domestic science movement that sought to "modernize" the preparation and consumption of food half a century after the death of Brillat-Savarin. That movement, in turn, triumphed in the early twentieth century, when nutritionists made common cause with food processors, appliance manufactur-ers, and food writers for the women's magazines. The new food establishment fervently embraced the idea of spreading their version of a scientific approach to dining, which shaped American foodways in the first half of the twentieth cen-tury and beyond.[26]

Often trained in some branch of home economics, such as nutrition, or in medicine or public health, the editors and writers in the food departments of the leading women's magazines shared a modern, utilitarian ethos. They firmly be-lieved that the secret to a healthy diet lay in the newly discovered constituents of food, including vitamins, minerals, and calories.

Collaboration between nutritionists and large food processors made sense to both parties, since the processors often added nutrients to their products that enabled the nutritionists to calculate their contribution to the diner's health. The large-scale operation of the processors also modeled for American women the proper time- and money-saving practices that they should follow in the kitchen. Accordingly, the magazines enthusiastically endorsed modern kitchen appli-ances of all kinds, as well as canned and packaged goods requiring little prepara-tion time.

It should be clear, however, that nutritionism did not bind its advocates to particular dishes or menus, but rather to viewing food as a vehicle for trans-porting vitamins, minerals, and calories to the body. The nutritionist approach, however, had severe consequences for those groups that consumed largely unprocessed food whose nutritional content was unknown. Indeed, a vigorous campaign against the dangers of unprocessed foods succeeded in converting many mainstream Americans and, over a longer period, many immigrants to a standardized diet comprised largely of processed food.[27]

As a by-product of promoting a nutritionist approach to food, many of the women's magazines developed their own laboratories, which tested, among other things, food items and recipes. *Good Housekeeping* led the way in 1900 with its Institute, *Better Homes and Gardens* followed with its Better Food and Equipment Department, and the *Ladies' Home Journal* created the New York workshop. Following the testing of recipes, food writers recommended particular ingredients and methods that the housewife could use in successfully preparing a dish with high nutritional value.[28]

Among the important exponents of this ethos was the head of the *Good Housekeeping* Institute, Katharine Fisher, who taught domestic science at McGill University and home economics at Teachers College, Columbia University, before joining the magazine in the late 1920s. Fisher was also coauthor of the fourth edition of the *Good Housekeeping Cook Book* (1931). Her collaborator, Dorothy Marsh, associate editor, was coauthor with Carol Brock of the *Good Housekeeping Party Book*. Byron MacFayden specialized in helping readers to recognize the kinds of dishes that men preferred to eat. The fact that Clementine Paddleford, a regular columnist for *Gourmet*, wrote occasional articles for *Good Housekeeping* suggests that the gourmet and scientific approaches were not always contradictory. Indeed, Paddleford's role at *Gourmet* was to inform readers of the availability of exotic foods, most of which were processed and available by mail order.[29]

Ann Batchelder, associate editor of *Ladies' Home Journal*, who was born and died in Windsor, Vermont, wrote *Ann Batchelder's Own Cook Book*. Unlike her colleagues, she insisted that cooking was an art, but her recipes, as we shall see, suggest otherwise. From Gladys Taber, a Wellesley graduate who lived on a Connecticut farm, the *Journal* received hearty recipes that rarely mentioned vitamins and calories. By contrast, Louella Shouer, also associate editor of the magazine, graduated in 1930 with a degree in institutional management, part of the Home Economics Division at Iowa State University. She was the author of *Quick and Easy Meals for Two*.[30]

The food editor of *Better Homes and Gardens*, Myrna Johnston, was author of the *Better Homes and Gardens Cook Book* (1965 and 1968 editions) and had served as a judge for the Pillsbury National Recipe contest. Her collaborators, Gladys Denny Shultz and Donald Cooley, wrote occasionally for the food section of the magazine as medical experts. The former covered child care from 1927 to 1945, including articles on the proper diet for children, while Cooley wrote on the link between food and health.[31]

The articles published in the three magazines in 1941 indicate the strong continuity between the approaches of nutritionists at the end of the Depression and their counterparts at the turn of the century. This continuity, in turn, suggests that the alliance of food processors, nutritionists, and women's magazines was alive and well. To varying degrees writers in all three magazines saw food in largely medical terms as a means to achieving good health. Accordingly, they devoted much ink to instructing readers on the basic elements of nutrition. The interest in this subject, already high in early 1941, peaked following the National Nutrition Conference for Defense in the late spring of that year, which gave a greater urgency to a subject already important to women's magazines.

The New Year's resolutions of each member of an imaginary family, presented by Katharine Fisher's *Good Housekeeping* Institute in the January 1941 issue, illustrated the assumption that food was considered a form of medicine. Mom: "Resolved that I'll serve meals with plenty of vim and vitamins . . ." Johnny: "resolved that I'll eat spinach" and "all my vegetables—so I'll be better at the bat."[32]

A series of articles in *Better Homes and Gardens* explained the secrets of vitamins and minerals. Donald Cooley asserted that minerals "jack you up and calm you down, build bones and biceps." Although scientists needed to learn more about where to find calcium, phosphorus, iron, and iodine, chemists had already discovered that it was possible to "count the units of the various vitamins" in a daily diet. To help readers achieve "balanced nutrition," *Better Homes and Gardens* published a chart listing the quantity of vitamins, proteins, and carbohydrates in different types of meat. The magazine also found confirmation of its approach in England, where scientists had restored iron and calcium to bread. Advertisers were equally fervent in touting the vitamin content of their products.[33]

It was also essential for Americans to understand the importance of actually consuming vitamins and minerals. Since "good food is cheaper than doctor's bills," parents, who were effectively dieticians, needed to be diplomats and schemers as well, "when it comes to plugging . . . family meals with health-hoisting minerals." Unfortunately, however, "families are funny about eating food just because it is good for you." It was therefore necessary for the housewife to prepare good-tasting meals to induce the family to eat right. When children were unwilling to eat healthy foods, the cook should "camouflage" the nutrients; desserts would serve as a vehicle "to slip in the daily quota of milk, fruit, eggs, etc. with their health-giving vitamins, minerals and other keeping fit aids." In effect, taste had become not the measure of good eating, but a means to that end. This was evident in a *Good Housekeeping* advertisement placed by the association of pork growers that ranked in order the reasons for eating pork as follows: protein and vitamin content, digestibility, palatability, and satiety.[34]

The relative indifference to flavor was also evident in the frequent preference for packaged goods over fresh ingredients, as well as the virtual absence of spices, herbs, garlic, and wine in most recipes; and even though the sale of wine had been legal for seven years, the magazines rarely recommended it as an appropriate beverage for dinner. Furthermore, few recipes were borrowed from other countries. The clearest exception to this rule was an article in *Better Homes and Gardens* presenting recipes for cooking South American dishes. It is significant, however, that the source of these recipes was Pearl Metzelthin's *World-Wide Cookbook*. As it happened, Metzelthin was a nutrionist who had adapted the recipes "a touch for our northern markets and less robust appetites."[35]

While nutritional balance was the highest priority, authors sometimes modified their approach to satisfy other demands. To accommodate men's need for a higher caloric intake than women, they increased the servings of meat on menus. "Give a Man Man's Food" rather than "sissy food," ordered Byron Mac-Fadyen. He insisted that men "like dishes they can sink their teeth into," including boiled beef with horseradish sauce, braised oxtails, and boiled tongue. For Clementine Paddleford, however, the right cheese might work as well as meat if it was "emphatic enough to thump manly appetites yet not too outspoken for the pleasure of the ladies," and, of course, it would have to provide "vitamins, minerals, and protein."[36]

The male appetite was not a constant, however; on hot days, men could enjoy light luncheons, especially if they were served in an enticing way. "Tempt folks' eyes—and appetites zoom like magic." All the same, writers recognized that a conscious effort to serve eye-catching food was in the woman's domain. "Feminine pretties" were "teasing and satisfying, but light on calories." Consistent with their promotion of modern ways, all three magazines used large color photographs to impress upon readers the impact of colorful food. Readers were also told to stuff crabmeat in hollowed-out oranges or attach candied orange daisies to baked ham without considering whether the flavor of the decoration was compatible with the original dish.[37]

The government effort to promote nutrition intensified the already-strong commitment of women's magazines to address the health issue. *Good Housekeeping* anticipated such intervention by urging its readers in January of 1941 to "make

America strong by making Americans stronger." Later *Ladies' Home Journal* ran a message from the U.S. surgeon general advising Americans to eat sufficient vitamins, minerals, and calories. In an article written after Pearl Harbor, the *Journal* pointed out that "your Uncle Sam aims to build a well-fed nation." The implications of this point were clear. Women were now "on-the-spot"; they would be responsible if their men suffered accidents because they were not well fed. The magazine also published a quiz on nutrition to acquaint readers with its significance.[38]

Meanwhile, *Good Housekeeping* praised the National Nutrition Conference for bringing together four home economists who were preparing the "greatest nutrition program in all history." To follow its recommendations, Katharine Fisher urged readers to "Keep Your Family Fit with Plenty of Vegetables." Meanwhile, the magazine provided space for Helen S. Mitchell, Director of Nutrition for the Civilian Defense Coordinator, Paul McNutt, to remind readers that "America Expects Every Cook to Do Her Duty" by providing family members with adequate nutrition. To that end, *Good Housekeeping* printed the National Nutritional Conference's daily diet yardstick, which recommended that every adult consume one meat serving, one egg, and several servings of fruit and vegetables, etc., every day.[39]

All three magazines urged the liberal use of canned and packaged goods, many of which were advertised in their pages. *Better Homes and Gardens'* monthly contest conferred a prize on readers who submitted the best recipes and rewarded them with a shipment of an ingredient advertised in the magazine and incorporated in the recipe. It is no wonder that one of the winning recipes featured canned vegetables or that recipes originating with staff writers included canned sweet potatoes and ham as well as a cheese soufflé featuring Nippy spreading cheese as the principal ingredient. In the July issue of the magazine, marshmallows were the main ingredient in both a chocolate marshmallow float and a chocolate walnut marlow.[40]

According to *Good Housekeeping*'s Dorothy Marsh, it was comforting to have a good supply of canned and packaged foods close at hand, from which housewives could make a series of lunches and dinners. Her colleagues, as well as staff writers on *Ladies' Home Journal*, advocated covering steak or veal with a can of creamed mushroom soup, topping fried canned shrimp with Roquefort cheese, or mixing one can of clam broth with one can of tomato soup to make tomato-clam consommé.[41]

In the minds of the home economists the emphasis on nutrition went hand in hand with the effort to economize time and money. Both required a scientific approach to food that was largely indifferent to the possible pleasure derived from eating. The convergence of these two approaches was evident in the claim that the consumption of sufficient vitamins and minerals would lower the doctor's bill for members of the family. Similarly, Clementine Paddleford recommended processed cheeses as among the best buys, because they contained a large supply of protein at a low price. Writers also considered more traditional ways to reduce food costs such as buying inexpensive cuts of meat or using leftovers.[42]

To save time, *Ladies' Home Journal* advocated that, when both spouses worked, they should join forces to prepare a meal from canned goods. Another possibility was to cook several meals from the same raw materials, such as ground beef, which they could make into meatloaf one night and meatballs the next. Equally advantageous was reliance on a series of menus that the spouses together could prepare in less than an hour.[43]

Despite the accent on efficiency and the apparent lack of interest in taste, a few writers proposed meals that required time to prepare and were designed to please the palate. For a March party, *Better Homes and Gardens* proposed lamb on a skewer, *Lyonnaise* potatoes, carrots, and a chocolate layer cake, while the home cook was to season meat for a spring barbecue with garlic, sage, and a marinade. "Folks with Food," a monthly article in *Good Housekeeping*, passed on recipes from celebrities, including roast duck with Bigerade sauce, made with a tablespoon of Madeira wine, and a cheese omelette, while Gladys Taber's monthly "Diary of Domesticity" in the *Ladies' Home Journal* featured such hearty, traditional dishes as "Goose for Christmas! Delicate and Golden Brown and Savory with Stuffing." However, the plum pudding contained no alcohol. After invoking the South's "old leisure" and "gentle manner of life," Ann Batchelder provided recipes for such substantial dishes as baked ham with chow-chow pickle, oyster and sweetbread pie, water cress and lettuce salad, lace cake (sponge), and pecan confections.[44]

The consensus on a nutritionist approach to food created common ground for the food processors and appliance manufacturers on the one side and women's magazines on the other. In addition, both sides advocated the efficient preparation of food that, in turn, required processing of the raw materials outside of the home and the use of kitchen aids and appliances to reduce cooking time in the home. A mutual dependence developed between the two sides. Through their laboratories, the magazines assessed the quality of kitchen appliances and processed food and recommended specific brands to readers. The manufacturers, in turn, chose magazines in which to advertise their products. In this relationship companies could influence the magazines' bottom line and vice versa.

Even more striking was the magazines' promotion of new kitchen technology without reference to brands. Grace McIlraith Ellis "doubly bless(ed) my automated kitchen helpers for helping get the kids off to school on time." In "The Ellises Meet the Blender—and All Hands Applaud," members of the family testified to its adaptability to their particular needs, while for Christine Cox "my broiler's my new cook . . . Don't miss the fun and satisfaction of making a friend

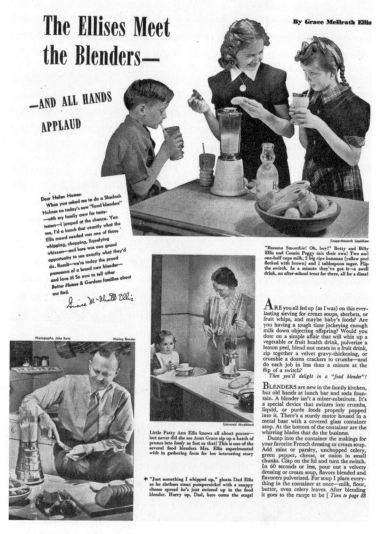

"The Ellises Meet the Blenders," *Better Homes and Gardens*, February 1941, p. 44. Used with permission from Meredith Corporation. All rights reserved.

of your broiler." It was as if the machines had become part of the family. During that same year, the magazines also urged readers to buy new toasters, coffee makers, waffle irons, refrigerators, and outdoor broilers.[45]

It should be clear from the foregoing that the reign of the food establishment was going strong on the eve of World War II. Women's magazines gave unrestrained support to the nutritionist ethos. Their focus—and presumably that of their readers—was on assuring that food enhanced the health of the American people, as measured by the consumption of calories, vitamins, and minerals. In such calculations, taste became secondary. Furthermore, as if Prohibition were still the law of the land, the menus and recipes in the magazines remained almost alcohol free, as did their advertising pages, while articles and advertisements promoted high-tech kitchens and processed foods as a way to feed the American family quickly and efficiently.

H. L. Mencken, Alfred Knopf, and Julian Street

While the women's magazines were the dominant force in shaping American attitudes toward food, there was a steady stream of publications urging a different approach to dining before and after the turn of the century. The best known and most representative of these works was George Ellwanger's *The Pleasures of the Table: An Account of Gastronomy from Ancient Days to Present Times* (1902). Ellwanger, who also wrote several books on gardening, insisted that Brillat-Savarin's "aphorisms must always occupy a place in epicurean literature." In addition to chapters on gastronomical history, Ellwanger evaluated contemporary American foodways in comparison to those of France, Italy, Germany, and Britain. Impressed by the abundance of fish, game, and produce, he believed that Americans could learn finesse from the French and develop an outstanding cuisine. Toward that end, he wrote chapters recommending the use of sauces, truffles, and salads to refine the American palate.[46]

The optimism of Ellwanger and colleagues, of course, reflected the still uncertain prospects of American foodways in the era before national Prohibition and the full triumph of the food establishment. Even so, Ellwanger's predecessor, Theodore Child, keenly sensed the threat of modern life to the pleasures of the table. "In these days of progress, science, gas-stoves, sophistication, and democracy, the gourmet's dream is to taste real meat cooked with real fire, and to drink wine made with real grapes." In the wake of Prohibition, a new generation of American epicures could find in the aspirations of Child and Ellwanger encouragement to fight the new regime. Meanwhile, they looked with sorrow and anger

on the diminished opportunities to enjoy the good life in both homes and restaurants. Indeed, some patrons of fine-dining establishments deserted them in
favor of the more reputable speakeasies where they could enjoy good meals with
fine wines.[47]

The opposition to Prohibition was an occasion not only to protest the ban on
alcoholic beverages but also to launch an attack against the food establishment.
Indeed, gastronomers regarded Prohibitionists and modernists as peas in the
same pod. Both had contributed to diminishing the pleasures of the table by
their indifference to the freshness and flavor of food products and the beverages
that might accompany them, and, in this sense, both were enemies of the good
life.

Among the first to view these two groups as a cabal working to deprive Americans of the pleasures of the table was the journalist H. L. Mencken, who in 1924
with George Jean Nathan launched the *American Mercury*. Mencken used his
new platform to invite submissions on food topics that would address what he
regarded as the deplorable culinary situation in America. Within a year, Jacques
Le Clercq, sounding much like his editor, alleged that "our cooking reflects our
mores; its formation is bound up with the characteristic philistinism of our
people. A nation capable of supporting the Fundamentalists, the American Legion, the Ku Klux Klan . . . and Billy Sunday is not likely to possess a tempera-
ment and a palate that rise higher." Mencken himself had already expressed his
regret that current writers on food topics were largely "female professors of what
is called domestic science . . . The meals they advocate are excellent for diabetics,
but fatal to epicures."[48]

Between 1925 and 1930, Mencken fleshed out his view of American cuisine
by regularly publishing both criticisms of the current culinary regime and ideas
for improving it. Among other things, he and the *American Mercury's* writers
blamed the Puritan ethos and mass production for turning the pleasures of life,
such as dining, into purely utilitarian functions. Prohibition was a particular
sore point, as Mencken pointed out. "I have enjoyed the caress of sound wine . . .
It has filled me with an immense satisfaction bordering on ecstasy." On other
occasions, Hendrik Van Loon attacked the excesses of science in "Food Fads and
Nutrition Nonsense." Writing about the decline of American bread, Van Loon
blamed mass production by giant trusts that gave priority to efficiency and hy-
giene for driving small bakers out of business and eradicating the source of
fresh bread for most Americans.[49]

But Mencken and the food writers he recruited also saw hope in the regional
and ethnic cuisines that, despite neglect, had survived. They pointed to the ex-

pertise of the Pennsylvania Dutch at producing excellent pastries, as well as the work of Jewish cooks, who turned out their distinctive *challah* and *luckshen*. Meanwhile, Mencken himself credited Maryland's black cooks for inventing such local dishes as Chicken Maryland, fried soft-shelled crabs, and panned oysters. And he gave a plug to the now-banned California wines that were, he thought, comparable to some of the better wines produced in Europe. As evidence that a simple peasant dish could bring pleasure to any household whether in France or the United States, the *American Mercury* also devoted a whole article to French *pot au feu*.[50]

It was not coincidental that Mencken's publisher, Alfred Knopf, who became the indispensable transatlantic link between the centers of gourmet dining in Europe and its practitioners in the New World, shared Mencken's views. In the midst of Prohibition, his firm had established a series on food and drink that made available to American readers some of the best books in English written on the subject, including André Simon's *The Art of Good Living* and G. B. Stern's *Bouquet* (1927), an autobiographical account of a wine-tasting vacation in France.[51]

Knopf's book list was an expression of his enthusiastic engagement with gastronomy. Buried in his papers is a cellar book, entitled "Lest We Forget," published by the Wine and Food Society with an introduction by André Simon, who reminded readers of Saintsbury's fervent belief that his expenditures on wine had been well worth the money. In various folders lie hundreds of wine labels with Knopf's notations on the time, place, and company in which he drank the wine and comments on its attributes. For the dinners Knopf gave at his home in Purchase, New York, gastronomers and literary types alike coveted an invitation. Guests, among them H. L. Mencken, knew in advance not to smoke during meals or to ask for cocktails; in return, Knopf served them the finest French wines from his cellar.[52]

At the time of its founding the Wine and Food Society of New York chose Knopf as a director, and during its first quarter of a century, he remained active as an officer and member of the organization. Despite his disdain for some of their rituals, he was also an early member of various other gourmet groups.[53]

As Prohibition neared its end in 1933, Knopf was on the lookout for American writers who could explain the arts of making and drinking wine. In that year, he published Phillip Wagner's *American Wines and How to Make Them*, a volume based on Wagner's experience producing wine on his Maryland property. In addition, as Knopf explained, "Right after Repeal, I had the pleasure of meeting Julian Street, an old-fashioned gentleman and man about town and a most knowledgeable authority on wine and food." From that meeting came the small volume entitled simply *Wines*, which "remains to this day the most charming of all introductions on the subject."[54]

Julian Street was more than a "man about town"; he had traveled widely in Europe, Japan, and America for thirty years and, through his travel writings, had established himself as a man of letters. In addition to his short volumes on the food and entertainment scene in Paris and New York, written before World War I, he had done more than any other American author between 1929 and 1933 to awaken readers to the declining standards of public dining and urge upon them a renewed interest in the pleasures of the table. His two 1931 articles published in the *Saturday Evening Post*, entitled "What's the Matter with Food?" conveyed the gourmet point of view to the large readership of that magazine. For a smaller audience, *Where Paris Dines* (1929), a well-received guide to over a hundred restaurants in that culinary center, had done the same thing. Meanwhile, in 1935, the French government awarded Street the Légion d'Honneur in recognition of his services to French culture. In enlisting Street to reacquaint Americans with the intricacies of wine and food, Knopf was banking on a seasoned writer who had extensive knowledge of the French culinary tradition.[55]

Despite their titles, Street devoted all three works to the advocacy of good living in the tradition of Brillat-Savarin and André Simon, whose ideas he incorporated into his food writings. In *Where Paris Dines*, Street explored the contributions of French restaurants to the pleasures of the table. In "What's the Matter with Food?" he examined France's overseas culinary empire in America from the opening of Delmonico's to the current scene in America's big cities, where French chefs still predominated in the best hotel and restaurant kitchens despite Prohibition. Even *Wines*, which focused primarily on beverages, portrayed them as a key element in supporting fine dining.

Street promoted the French tradition in dining as the only way to avert what he called "the disappearance of the gourmet" in America. Accordingly, he instructed readers to "remember that wine is a civilizing influence" much like literature, painting, and music. "Without wine the art of conversation languishes, and the art of dining dies." He reiterated that good food, wine, and good living were inseparable. "Food is the tune, wine the accompaniment." To make the most of food and beverages, however, would require the proper arrangement of the meal. In line with Simon's ideas, Street would orchestrate the various courses of the meal to assure that they mounted "in a gradual crescendo to [the] principal course, usually a roast or game, with which [the] finest wine is served." To illustrate this order, Street offered a series of menus, borrowed from gourmet friends, in which wines were carefully matched to the dishes they accompanied.[56]

Among obstacles to fulfilling the promise of good living, Street noted the standardizing of the American diet that made it impossible to enjoy seasonal specialties and to showcase the creative ideas of great chefs. Accordingly, Street urged his readers to acknowledge French superiority in the culinary realm and thus to disregard American culinary traditions. To truly enjoy their meals, diners should accept the idea that dinner was the "evening's entertainment." If they did so, the chef would have time to work his magic in the kitchen, and they could pay proper respects to the excellence of his creation.[57]

While all three of Street's works on the good life affirmed French culinary standards, each had a more specific audience in mind and somewhat different goals. Street aimed *Where Paris Dines* at well-to-do Americans who were, in ever larger numbers, traveling to Europe. Many tourists already knew the names of the most famous restaurants that Street's guide covered in two chapters, so he devoted the bulk of his book to smaller, less elegant restaurants as part of a strategy to encourage a more intimate and adventurous tourism. In the process, Americans could venture beyond the familiar, experience the "thrill of discovery," and learn about representative elements of French life. They would also be able to test the cooking of new chefs on their way up and experience provincial dishes then popular in Paris. While "sumptuous restaurants impart[ed] to the city a definite and widespread color," they did not reflect the solid virtues of the middle class.[58]

To get the most out of these restaurants, tourists should consult the head waiter a day in advance about what they would like to eat so that the chef could market accordingly and then plan to spend the whole evening at the restaurant. To illustrate the advantages of this approach, Street pointed out that at Auberge Jean, his favorite small restaurant, he took the chef's recommendations of cream soup, bouillabaisse, wild duck with oranges, and a bottle of Côtes du Rhône. "Whether partly through luck or because the man is a wonderful cook, this is the best meal I have had this season in any restaurant of less than the highest order." Of course, patrons could run into eccentric proprietors like Mme Genot, who dictated the menu and admitted only those whom she deemed worthy.

Street also urged tourists to integrate their dining and touring experiences by judiciously placing accounts of historical sites after descriptions of nearby restaurants. In this way, diners would find the Quatre Sergeants well located if they wished to visit the nearby Marais after their meal. There followed a brief description of tourist highlights around the Place des Vosges.[59]

"What's the Matter with Food," published as attacks on Prohibition were mounting, addressed a much larger readership on that controversial topic. Street designed the two articles to present the devastating effects of Prohibition on good living. In the first article, he prepared readers for this devastation by praising the restaurants of the Gilded Age, from Delmonico's in New York to Antoine's in New Orleans, as well as the new hotels of the 1900s, for bringing an authentic French cuisine to the tables of the New World. With the advent of Prohibition, however, "the art of noble dining . . . [was] assassinated" by "the majority that is satisfied merely with something to eat." As a result, the relatively small cadre of discerning diners now faced obstacles to enjoying gourmet meals. For one thing, French chefs hesitated to work in a country that accepted Prohibition, while those who wanted to eat well and enjoy wine with their meals had no choice but to dine in selected speakeasies. Only the repeal of Prohibition would change this bleak situation.[60]

Street wrote *Wines* in a triumphant vein as a vindication of his attacks on Prohibition. In 193 pages, he offered a history of wine and a tour of the principal wine-producing areas of the world, including the United States, as well as advice on the care and serving of wine. No doubt with designs on readers from the "Lost Generation," many of whom had traveled in France, Street opened with Hemingway's paean to wine as "one of the most civilized things in the world" that offered great pleasure to the senses. He regretted, however, that Americans typically justified consuming alcoholic beverages for reasons of health rather than pleasure. Even so, after the ordeal of Prohibition, the time was ripe for Americans to overcome their shameful excesses and enjoy the moderate consumption of wines modeled by the French.[61]

Julian Street explicitly endorsed André Simon's concept of the good life. He advised readers to take to heart Simon's commitment to the pleasures of the table as a model that would restore America's culinary life after the devastation wrought by Prohibition. Accordingly, Street advocated the careful orchestration of the dining experience that required attention to food and drink as well as the art of hospitality. Moreover, he joined Simon in viewing the dinner party as an institution that would nourish the fine art of conversation and, in turn, create new social bonds among diners.

M. F. K. Fisher

Responding to a 1943 query from Julian Street, Harold Price, the moving spirit of the San Francisco Wine and Food Society, reported his impressions of M. F. K. Fisher. He touted her new book, entitled *Gastronomic Me*, for its autobiographical sketches "with gastronomic overtones." As for *Serve It Forth*, her first book, it was, in Price's opinion, "the most distinguished book, stylistically and otherwise published in many a day on gastronomy."[62]

As for Fisher's personal qualities, Price, who was at that moment involved in an affair with her, made no effort to disguise his feelings: "She is like a Hellenic goddess—a combination of Venus and Pallas Athena—nothing less. She is 34 years old, and a widow . . . She lives in a wild savage landscape in the San Bernardino Mts, but was until recently a writer for Paramount Pictures . . ." Price noted Fisher's travels in Europe, her studies in Dijon, and her skillful managing of a small vineyard at Vevey, Switzerland, with her second husband, Dillwyn Parish. These experiences complemented her unusual personal assets. "She knows more about food—that is really *knows* than any woman I have ever met. She has a voice like the perfume of violets made audible, a strange mixture of child-like timbre and naiveté, but nevertheless capable on occasion of lusty Rabelaisianisms. She is quite tall, as beautiful as a dream and is very feminine, yet completely unlike anyone else."[63]

Price's laudatory profile of Fisher calls our attention to certain distinguishing features of her life and career. Much like George Saintsbury, M. F. K. Fisher developed a unique voice to express a strongly personal response to food experiences based in part on a keen sense of the way the dining context helped to shape them. Like Simon and Street, she and Saintsbury regarded the gastronomer as a connoisseur of food and wine; however, the two of them refused to limit the application of this expertise to formal dinner parties or banquets. With company or without, eating a snack or a full meal, at any time or place, the gastronomer could enjoy the pleasures of the table.

Fisher's genuine originality, however, has obscured the fact that the rising community of writers and activists interested in fine dining both supported and were influenced by her work; she had the good fortune to publish a first book in 1937, well after the end of Prohibition, by which time Simon, Street, and other food writers had created and cultivated an audience eager to read about gourmet dining. Fisher's pre-1950 publications, which expressed the core ideas in her approach to food, contributed significantly to the momentum of the gourmet societies and *Gourmet* in the early years. I will accordingly focus exclusively on these writings.

As her relationship with Price suggests, Fisher was greatly indebted to fellow gourmet activists. Aside from praising her work, Price offered Fisher the use of his "rare and often fantastic gastronomical library" to help in translating *The Physiology of Taste*. Phil Townsend Hanna, the moving spirit of the Los Angeles

M. F. K. Fisher in her later years. The photographer and date are unknown.
Kennedy Golden.

branch of the Wine and Food Society, who edited *Westways Magazine*, not only published Fisher's first article, "Pacific Village," in 1935 but, two years later, recommended *Serve It Forth*, this "new and delightful book," to his readers. Support of a different kind came from the Medical Friends of Wine, who honored her at a Bohemian Club dinner in 1944.[64]

Fisher also found sustenance in two new periodicals devoted to gastronomy. From the first issue of *Gourmet*, she cooked a recipe for creamed oysters, while publishing her first article for the magazine, "Three Swiss Inns," in September 1941. She was equally enamored of André Simon's *Wine and Food*. In a curious letter to the editor published in the winter of 1944, Fisher identified herself as "an unknown woman, but one who admires sincerely your staunch loyalty to the fine art of living." Even so, Simon and his readers must have wondered about the source of her report that American soldiers were dreaming of the wine they would drink after the war as they ate spam and dried eggs on the front lines.[65]

Compared to other gourmet proponents, Fisher was more conscious of the grand tradition of gastronomy and less literal in following its dictums. On the opening page of *Serve It Forth*, she noted that food writers either imitated Brillat-Savarin or produced mundane recipe books with long lists of ingredients and quantities. To find her own way, Fisher exploited the wisdom of Brillat-Savarin, while illustrating his ideas through a careful distillation of her own experiences and those of individuals and societies from the past. In her culinary travels, he was an abiding presence who comforted her in the midst of new experiences. She felt "immune, safe in a charmed gastronomical circle" with Lucullus, Brillat-Savarin, and Rabelais as she digested her first French restaurant meal in Dijon. Beyond his role as protector, Brillat-Savarin served Fisher as a guide to higher culinary standards. In considering a modern kitchen "with its efficiency, its lack of imagination," she supposed that he "would have belched at (it) gastronomically."[66]

Brillat-Savarin and other gourmet advocates bolstered Fisher's strenuous campaign to dethrone the scientific approach of the food establishment. This campaign was especially delicate because Fisher forcefully rejected the approach of women nutritionists, whose views were accepted by most middle-class housewives. Moreover, both nutritionists and housewives were sympathetic to elements of the Victorian code of conduct.

Nonetheless, Fisher proceeded with her campaign. Insisting that marginalizing the aesthetic and sensual elements of life had impoverished experience, she advocated the satisfaction of appetites whether at the table or in the bedroom. And, as a first step, Fisher insisted on recognizing that appetites and tastes were worth discussing even at the table. It should no longer be considered "vulgar and almost foreign" to "cry out with pleasure"—a gastronomic orgasm—after eating a delicious meringue.[67]

Changed attitudes, Fisher believed, would lead to better eating. Instead of the obsession with nutrients to service the body after the meal, diners would enjoy the taste of their food and the satisfaction of their appetites at the table. She deplored the idea of consuming various products like milk because they were "good for you." As for the reliance on processed foods such as mass-produced bread, "no machine-sliced, beige-colored sponge, for God's sake!" Packaged puddings she regarded as "doubtful triumphs of science over human hunger." Under the circumstances, she would prefer to go without dessert.[68]

Arguing against the prevailing American habit of preparing and eating meals quickly, Fisher insisted that to produce memorable meals "and serve them is one of the most satisfying of all civilized amenities." Accordingly, she objected to the nutritionists' increasing focus on time-saving methods of preparation that often resulted in tasteless dinners. While Fisher preferred to cook simple meals, she nonetheless sought to serve her guests something they had never before eaten. In this way, she would arouse their interest in the meal and, in the end, receive the cherished compliments for what she regarded as an artistic endeavor. Not surprisingly, she, like her admirers, looked to France as the model for great cuisine.[69]

Repeating Seneca's rhetorical question, "When shall we live, if not now?" Fisher argued that gratification of the senses should be an ongoing process. She would restore "sight" to the taste-blind with fresh produce, meats, and tasty menus. Roasted oysters, prepared with an "ungenteel gourmandise" and "as beautifully rounded as the Songs of Solomon," would please the palate, while "irreverent souls" remedied the "genteel methods" (leaving out onions) of cooking oyster bisque by adding cayenne pepper. To challenge the power of large producers and restore flavor to a favorite beverage, she advocated that Americans buy beer from "small honest breweries."[70]

Among the inhibitions that ruled the day, Fisher was particularly exercised by efforts to disguise the realities of preparing and eating foods. She denounced "home economics articles" (usually written by nutritionists) for "dress(ing) up" oyster stew while dismissing magazine campaigns to build efficient kitchens that were decorated to disguise their real functions as in "Let-Us-Keep-Our-Kitchens-Gay." As for disguising the origins of food served at the table, "One way to horrify at least eight out of ten Anglo-Saxons is to suggest their eating anything but the actual red fibrous meat of a beast." "Why is it worse . . . to see an animal's head cooked and prepared for our pleasure than a thigh or a tail or a rib?" As long as the animals had to be killed, there was no moral justification for preferring one body part to another. (Fisher admitted that her first glimpse of a *"tête de veau,"* half a head with one eye "closed in a savory wink" and a half tongue "lolling stiffly from the neat half-mouth," was a shocking sight.) Even if the diners were not going to eat the head, its presence on the table could serve an aesthetic purpose that would, in turn, stimulate the appetite. Remembering the pleasure she once took in seeing a whole pig served at the table, Fisher admonished a favorite cookbook writer for advocating that cooks should sever the head from the body in the kitchen.[71]

Great appetites, according to Fisher, were at the heart of great eating. She admired the way French gourmets ate with "gusto" and a "frank sensuous realization of food." In the United States, where "taste-blind" diners knew batting averages better than flavors, cooks would have to appeal to the sense of taste as well as to smell and sight. Moreover, Fisher would have to educate her readers by reporting on her own pleasurable experiences, such as a bouillabaisse feast when she abandoned decorum to satisfy her appetite. "We mopped and dunked at its (shellfish) juices and sucked a hundred creatures from their shells." On another occasion, she applauded a woman who ate with "sensuous slowness" and regretted that her taste buds did not reach "clear to the bottom of (her) stomach." Even many men, she believed, would find this frank acknowledgment of gastronomic pleasures unseemly.[72]

While older gourmet advocates had a clear vision of possible menus for gourmet meals, Fisher refused to invoke current recipes as the final word on good taste. Rather, she validated individual preferences based in part on the setting in which they consumed the food and drink. She gave short shrift, for example, to the debate over whether white wine or cocktails should accompany raw oysters. In the dispute over the authenticity of Manhattan or New England clam chowder, she grew irritated: "Who knows? Furthermore, who cares? You should eat according to your tastes." In short, "rigid rules and recipes" should not limit adventurous eating. Nor need diners think only of eating an entire meal in order to satisfy their appetites. Fisher often enjoyed the flavor of single items consumed away from the table between meals, such as, for example, rough pieces of chocolate that she devoured on an Alpine club hike in France after an exhausting day of hiking or a cold papaya served on a freighter on a hot Caribbean day. She recalled the "rush of cold pulp" from a tangerine that had been heating on a radiator and literally exploded in her mouth. In effect, she would exercise her appetite and taste outside the boundaries of formal dining with the right food in the right situation.[73]

Beyond appetite and taste, Fisher insisted that diners "eat with their minds" as well as their stomachs. Thinking about food, of course, was an activity embraced by nutritionists, but it was thinking of a different sort than Fisher's. She quoted La Rochefoucauld's dictum that "to eat is a necessity, but to eat intelligently is an art" to express her disdain for the nutritionists' exclusive interest in discovering the proper fuel to keep the body working, as if it were a furnace. "In Paris, the gourmets eat with quiet deliberation, rolling each mouthful slowly toward their gullets." In the tradition of Brillat-Savarin and Alexandre Dumas, "the fine art of eating" was "as much a matter of spirit as of body." Indeed, Fisher wrote at length about dining alone because it offered an opportunity to savor food more fully and to contemplate it. In these circumstances, as when "Lucullus dines with Lucullus," the diner is not really alone.[74]

While Fisher enjoyed dining alone, she also insisted on the pleasure of having good company at a good meal. In giving a dinner party, the motives of the host and the selection of guests were important considerations. "Sharing our meals should be a joyful and trustful act, rather than the cursory fulfillment of our social obligations." Guests at dinner parties should be carefully chosen for "their ability to eat—and drink!—with the right mixture of abandon and restraint." The ideal guest came equipped with an appetite to enjoy the meal, but would not abandon inhibitions altogether. Unrestrained appetites led to gluttony that dulled the mind and turned the guest into an uninteresting table companion.[75]

The number of guests was as important as their personalities. To create an intimate environment, the host should invite no more than ten to a dinner. Six was the perfect number, but only if they enjoyed eating, drinking, and conversation to make the evening a success. Also, they should come in the proper frame of mind so that long, leisurely conversation that Fisher regarded as a hallmark of civilization would accompany the meal. Only if the occasion thoroughly engaged mind and body, intellect and appetites could it be a success. "If Time, so fleeting, must like humans die, let it be filled with good food and good talk, and then embalmed in the perfumes of conviviality."[76]

In the process of reevaluating the place of food in the lives of her fellow Americans, Fisher insisted that its preparation and consumption should become not only an important subject of discussion but also a spiritual experience. She turned the so-called Victorian views upside down by attacking them for diminishing the fullness of life and its "natural realization" that required attention to food. Pretending otherwise was "a sinful waste of human thought and energy and deep delight." Rightly understood, the proper preparation of a good meal was a spiritual activity. Through the feel of its dough and its smell, the cook could experience the "sanctity of bread." "You can stand and look at them (the loaves), even the first time, with an almost mystical pride and feeling of self-pleasure." The mystery of the bread dough's rising and falling "will make you feel . . . newborn into a better world than this one often seems." As with preparation, so with dining, which was "a communion of more than our bodies when bread is broken and wine drunk." Fisher described a waitress in Burgundy pouring wine, who "turned her back to me like a priest taking Communion, and drank it down . . ." It was the same waitress who "wore the exalted look of a believer describing a miracle at Lourdes as she told me . . . how Monsieur Paul threw chopped chives into hot sweet butter . . ." The chef himself she described as a "hermit-priest of gastronomy."[77]

The only woman and the only member of the Lost Generation among the gastronomers treated here, Fisher, nonetheless, was a strong proponent of traditional foodways. Like her fellow gastronomers, she was dazzled by French cuisine and strove to transplant French ways to America and to expand the audience for fine dining in this country among the largely affluent men and women who read her books and articles. Fisher's clarion call to recognize the importance of satisfying appetites provided a model for women who wished to transcend the obsession with slim bodies and dieting fostered in the women's magazines. Her willingness to leave aside traditional recipes and menus and to experiment with new combinations of ingredients and dishes, as well as to bypass French formalities at the table, however, distinguished her perspective from that of other gastronomers. All the same, she urged her readers to be "missionaries bringing flavor and light to the taste-blind." Fisher was, in reality, talking about her own mission in life, which she fulfilled with great zest.[78]

Fisher and her fellow gourmet advocates set themselves a difficult task. In the face of Prohibition and the rising power of nutritionists, they promoted fine dining in the United States by introducing their American readers to a way of thinking about food that had developed in France since 1800. To counter the prevailing American approach, food writers carefully explained the principles of gourmet dining. From the outset, these gourmet advocates insisted that, in addition to providing essential sustenance for bodily health, dining should be an enjoyable experience delighting the senses and opening opportunities for conversations with fellow diners from different walks of life.

Although there was no way to change American notions about dining in a short span of time, the failure of Prohibition worked to the advantage of the missionaries of the good life by essentially casting doubt on current foodways. Indeed, after reflecting on the unexpected consequences of the "dry" era—especially the boost it gave to whiskey drinking—some Americans began to rethink their approach to food and even to consider a possible link between foodways and the idea of a good life. Gourmet advocates, in turn, recognizing the disillusionment with Prohibition among their readers, sharpened their rhetoric to denounce current drinking practices. George Saintsbury's spirited attack on Prohibition and his equally spirited defense of the pleasures of wine and other forms of alcoholic drink certainly galvanized readers to consider a new approach to alcohol. Alfred Knopf served the cause by bringing to the attention of readers the ideas of two like-minded proponents of gourmet dining devoted to Brillat-Savarin's ideas. Both André Simon and Julian Street advanced the campaign by clarifying for readers how the nineteenth-century tradition of fine dining had established a set of guidelines that would help to assure excellent meals and nurture closer relationships between the diners. Finally, M. F. K. Fisher reformulated

Brillat-Savarin's ideas to bring them in updated fashion to the same American audience. Following in his footsteps, Fisher insisted on the centrality of taste to the pursuit of good living, while recognizing that Americans might find an informal setting more conducive to enjoying that life.

As witnesses to the closing of many great restaurants and the decline in the quality of cooking across the nation, gourmet advocates were united in their commitment to challenge both Prohibition and the food establishment in order to promote gourmet dining. They were, however, as strongly opposed to the drinking excesses that arose in the wake of Prohibition as they were to Prohibition itself. In the face of the speakeasy culture and the pervasive cocktail, their promotion of moderate drinking was a kind of halfway house between Prohibition and jazz-age excesses. At the same time, advocates denounced the food establishment for its determined promotion of processed foods, quick preparation of meals, and the eat-to-live philosophy that seemed to be winning the day in America; in its place they proposed a new dining culture.

The gourmet advocates succeeded in reaching a relatively small, affluent audience, who shared their commitment to expanding the knowledge of and interest in gourmet dining. For these American readers, the proponents clarified French ideas and practices and, in the process, laid the groundwork for their adaptation to an American setting. New converts to gourmet dining soon joined earlier practitioners drawn largely from the American elite.

Chapter Two

Building a Foundation for Gourmet Dining in America

L ooking back at the prospects for gourmet dining even in the midst of Prohibi- tion, it is evident that gourmet advocates, though small in number, were not entirely bereft of resources. They exploited the ongoing conversation in print me- dia about the pleasures of the table that originated in France after 1800. They also frequented big-city restaurants or clubs where European-trained chefs were pre- paring French dishes. And they benefited from the network of markets and spe- cialty food shops that supplied the restaurants with the fish, game, farm products, and imported delicacies, such as foie gras and truffles, essential to preparing gour- met dishes. Following the repeal of Prohibition, those interested in fine dining could also count on a renewed supply of imported European wines, although the production of American wines was seriously compromised.

Less promising, however, were the prospects for gourmet dining in the Ameri- can home. While some affluent families regularly dined on gourmet fare, the great majority of Americans lacked the resources to do so. For one thing, most middle- class housewives no longer had servants or the requisite skills to prepare gourmet meals for their families. Moreover, instruction through apprenticeships, cook- books, and/or cooking classes designed to teach the essential cooking techniques was in short supply. Even if home cooks had been able to produce gourmet dishes, their families often lacked the knowledge to appreciate these dishes and to insist on high standards.

Even so, the record number of Americans who set sail for Europe in the 1920s dramatically improved the long-run prospects for gourmet dining. They followed in the wake of several thousand American writers and artists of the Lost Genera- tion, who settled in and around Paris and used their pens and brushes to spread the word about the good life in that city. The services of travel agencies and the economic prosperity of the 1920s facilitated the planning and execution of trans- atlantic voyages that in 1927 alone brought up to three hundred thousand Ameri- cans to Paris. There, they could drink with impunity and test the offerings in French restaurants, while appreciating the continent's historic monuments.[1]

This record-setting European invasion reflected changes in the American class structure. The 1920s witnessed the first signs of the emergence of an upper-middle class, whose members were usually college educated and pursuing lucrative professional careers. Their educational and occupational status prepared them to embrace the more sophisticated lifestyle displayed in the new or revamped luxury lifestyle magazines, which now incorporated food columns with frequent attention to French cuisine. These articles, in turn, reinforced the work of Brillat-Savarin and his disciples.

In addition to social class, gender roles shaped the ideas of these potential recruits to gourmet dining. Upper-middle-class women found it difficult to choose between the pleasures of the table and recipes from the women's magazines, many of them addressed to dieters, that inexperienced cooks could prepare quickly. Even so, class often trumped gender as a number of these women, persuaded by the gourmet ethos, joined male counterparts in the quest to satisfy their tastebuds.[2]

In the public realm, however, fine dining remained largely an upper-class male activity. Men populated the existing dining societies, based largely in men's clubs, and dominated the ranks of chefs, wine dealers, and restaurant and gourmet food shop owners. Women's participation, initially limited to occasional dinners in fine restaurants and reading accounts of gourmet dining in the lifestyle magazines, grew significantly as these periodicals turned to women to write their food columns.

A New Social Class and Its Periodicals

The key to the development of the gourmet movement in America was the rise of a new class, whose members sought to express individual taste preferences through the acquisition of stylish clothes, artistically decorated homes, and meals designed to entertain the palate. The upper-middle class came of age after World War II, but emerged gradually during the 1920s as men and women flocked to universities; the former sought higher education to take advantage of the increasing availability of managerial and professional positions, while their female classmates, a few of whom entered business or the professions, usually sought suitable marriages. By midcentury, the new class constituted 10 to 15 percent of the American workforce.[3]

The upper-middle-class lifestyle was affordable, largely because male graduates of universities earned a living sufficient to support a higher level of consumption. However, material factors, such as occupation and wealth, were less important in defining the new class than its commitment to the values of intelligence, cosmopolitanism, and self-actualization that the universities and the example of upper-class practices helped to foster. Accordingly, many members of the new class spent heavily on travel, cultural events, and decorative items to create a more elegant and adventurous lifestyle. Wives especially played an important role in shaping the new culture. While members of the upper-middle class thus helped to popularize a more expressive culture, they could not match the level of spending of their upper-class counterparts. Even so, their allegiance to the cause of gourmet dining created a critical mass that, in turn, brought the movement to the attention of a larger public.

New periodicals, including the *New Yorker,* as well as the renovated *House and Garden* and *Vogue,* not only publicized gourmet dining but serviced the new class by clarifying opportunities to enhance the status of its members and introduce them to a more sophisticated culture. To be sure, gourmet advocates effectively communicated the gospel of good living, but potential converts required more than a conviction in the value of the good life. They needed continuous advice on how to implement that life, which was effectively presented in regular food columns instructing readers on where to find fresh ingredients and how to cook and serve them with wine and less subtly in the myriad advertisements for alcoholic beverages. In a timely way, the new or revamped luxury lifestyle magazines served as midwives to the gourmet dining movement by dispensing instruction on more tasteful ways to live, while at the same time profiting from their growing subscriber base. They reflected and supported the worldly standards of the upper-middle class while keeping readers abreast of cultural developments in Europe, this paving the way for the founding of *Gourmet.*[4]

The man most responsible for this change was Condé Nast, whose publishing company owned *Vogue, Vanity Fair,* and *House and Garden,* printed the *New Yorker,* and, long after Nast's death, bought *Gourmet.* From the outset, Nast used his publications as a vehicle for coaching Americans in the ways of "high fashion" and "gracious living." During his previous tenure at *Colliers,* he sought without success to promote "exclusivity, affordable luxury and the highest quality." With his own magazine empire now in hand, he could devote himself to this end.[5]

Accordingly, he hired as the first editor of *Vanity Fair* Frank Crowninshield, who was raised in Paris and appreciated the good life. In the first issue of that magazine, the editor announced that "Americans are increasingly devoted to pleasure, to happiness, to dancing, to sport . . . to the delights of the country," a trend the magazine would support. So did *House and Garden* and *Vogue,* which

Nast made over to accomplish this same goal. The former would have as its new editor Richardson Wright, who loved gardens and gourmet dining. Meanwhile, the new *Vogue* would continue to promote high fashion, but would do so with erotic photos and sketches. Established in 1925, the *New Yorker* focused, like *Vanity Fair* and, to a lesser extent, *Vogue*, on presenting the New York cultural scene to readers in and out of the city.[6]

The Hearst Corporation reinforced this trend when it challenged Condé Nast by purchasing and revamping *House Beautiful* and *Town and Country* to compete with *House and Garden*. Meanwhile, on the fashion front, *Harper's Bazaar*, founded in the nineteenth century, addressed the same female audience as *Vogue*, while *Esquire* sought to persuade the relatively affluent man that attention to style was appropriate for men as well as women.[7]

The luxury lifestyle magazines propagated a hedonistic message in their articles that was reinforced by their advertisements. The eagerness among advertisers of luxury items to reach an affluent audience limited the circulation of the magazines and raised their prestige. Accordingly, they were advertisement-heavy and drew their advertisers disproportionately from the purveyors of luxury goods and services. In subscribing to these magazines, readers could prepare for a shopping spree by immersing themselves in the advertisements and articles devoted to achieving an elegant lifestyle. Products that were advertised ran the gamut from clothing and furniture to automobiles, travel, tobacco, and alcoholic beverages, although the proportions varied with the magazine's theme.[8]

The new magazines devoted themselves, in principle, to raising the level of fashion, home decorating, and travel, while leaving the matter of dining for several years to women's magazines. By the early 1930s, however, the advocates of upgrading clothing and house-decorating styles would seek to apply this idea to the dining scene as well. Existing magazine editors like Richardson Wright and Frank Crowninshield were well equipped to implement this change, while their counterparts at *Vogue*, *House Beautiful*, and the *New Yorker* were quick to follow suit, as if to insist that gourmet dining was now an essential counterpart to fashionable dress and well-decorated homes.[9]

The introduction of food columns in the luxury lifestyle magazines followed on the heels of the legalization of alcohol in 1934 and emphasized from the outset a gourmet, as opposed to a nutritionist, approach to dining. Editors accordingly recruited journalists with different training and background from those who wrote for women's magazines. Most had lived and traveled in Europe, especially France; all were focused on the taste of food rather than its chemistry; and they took for granted that wine was a central feature of the dining experience.

Sheila Hibbert, June Platt, Mary Grosvenor Ellsworth, Jeanne Owen, Mary Mabon, and M. F. K. Fisher thus crafted a new genre of food writing to encourage in their readers a new kind of dining experience. Ellsworth spoke for all of them when she wrote, "I can't and don't pretend to domestic science. My ambition is domestic art. If I can develop the cunning, the perception necessary to produce a perfectly balanced sauce, I shall never care about its calories, vitamins, or mineral content." Male writers like Frank Schoonmaker and Tom Marvel, whose articles and books informed readers about the wide range of available wines, joined their female colleagues in this enterprise.[10]

Vogue, which initially mentioned food only as an aside in articles about travel, first reviewed New York restaurants in a column entitled "Vogue Covers the Town" in its July 1, 1933, issue. "The Gourmet Guide," listing New York restaurants and smart clubs, became a regular feature in the December 15 issue of the same year. To keep its readers well informed on the suddenly relevant matter of consuming alcohol, the magazine also published Samuel Chamberlain's "Wines and Wherefores." There, readers could learn which wines to drink and how to drink them. More frequent articles on travel destinations with information about restaurants appeared as well.[11]

House and Garden and *House Beautiful* outdid *Vogue*. *House and Garden* first published a food column in the July 1932 issue. In November 1933, the magazine featured an article by June Platt, who became the regular food writer for the magazine, as well as Frank Schoonmaker's "Prepare Your Cellars for Repeal." Over the next nine years, Platt wrote an average of eight articles about food per year. In addition, editor Wright supplied a number of his own food and wine articles, as did his Wine and Food Society friends Crosby Gaige and Jeanne Owen.[12]

Even before its acquisition by Hearst, *House Beautiful* gave special attention to food beginning in 1934 with regular articles by Sheila Hibben. Three years later, Mary Grosvenor Ellsworth replaced Hibben and supplied the magazine for the next two years with a monthly article featuring recipes. During the war and early postwar years, M. F. K. Fisher succeeded Ellsworth.[13]

The annals of the *New Yorker* tell a similar tale. From 1925 to 1934, there were no articles about food or restaurants aside from occasional comments in "Talk of the Town" and "Tables for Two." In 1930, the latter noted facetiously that some speakeasies were beginning to serve outstanding meals. "If things continue to progress in this alarming way, we are going to have a nation of gourmets on our hands who never heard of drinking for the effect and not liking the taste." In the process "civilization is creeping into New York and meals are becoming more sacred."[14]

Editor Harold Ross confirmed this new interest in food on the part of the *New Yorker* in a letter inviting Julian Street to "do an occasional column for us" on restaurants beginning in September 1930. Street, however, balked. After insisting that the magazine pay him a salary and meal expenses, he undermined the proposal by announcing that, even in New York's ten best restaurants, it was impossible to eat a good meal so long as wine was unavailable. Street then proposed that he review the finest speakeasies, a plan that Ross rejected because it would put the *New Yorker* in the position of outing restaurant owners who broke the law.[15]

With the appearance of Sheila Hibben's April 21, 1934, column entitled "Markets and Menus," the *New Yorker* made food a regular feature of the magazine. Published eight or ten times a year through the 1930s, Hibben's columns continued until her death in 1964. As compared to food columns in other lifestyle magazines, Hibben focused more on locating fresh ingredients in various Manhattan neighborhoods than on providing recipes. Her first column proposed *chile rellenos* requiring fresh tarragon and cheese, while two weeks later she advised readers on how to find mussels to put in a *poulette* sauce (white sauce with lemon juice and parsley).[16]

The *New Yorker* also took note of the end of Prohibition by publishing in October of 1934 the first of a series of Frank Schoonmaker articles on "Wine and Liquor" designed to educate its readers for the new era. In 1937, the magazine began a "Restaurants" column, for which Hibben wrote the first two reviews before this task was assigned to various writers. One of them, GCS, was bold enough to recommend in his or her first column honeycomb tripe fricassee with oysters and onions.[17]

Luxury lifestyle magazines had no monopoly on the treatment of food and alcohol, as is already clear from H. L. Mencken's pioneering work in the *American Mercury*. When Scribner's sales fell dramatically in the 1930s, the publisher appealed to new subscribers by introducing lifestyle features, among them a monthly article by G. Selmer Fougner on "Wines, Spirits, and Good Living." Launched in September of 1937, it continued until the magazine folded after its May 1939 issue. More enduring was the response of the *Atlantic*, which introduced a series of food articles by M. F. K. Fisher beginning in 1937, followed over the next four years by André Simon's and Charles Codman's articles on wine. Codman was a wine buyer for S.S. Pierce.[18]

The opening of lifestyle and more traditional magazines to articles on food and drink was an important new development. It broadened the audience for this subject beyond the women's magazines and also brought to American readers a different point of view about food. In addition, it divided the profession of food journalism into two camps, although both featured women as the primary purveyors of recipes for the home.

Imported Wine, Wine Producers, and Food

A gourmet movement was unimaginable without the availability of good wine. In fact, there were already professional wine importers and dealers during Prohibition who were only too eager to satisfy the demand for their product. Some, in fact, had dealt illegally through speakeasies to bring wine of varying quality to such consumers. And following Prohibition, there were interested buyers as well, especially the owners of fine restaurants and the managers of men's clubs, who would advise their customers on the appropriate beverages to consume.

What follows is a brief account of the wine industry as it transitioned from the Prohibition era. It is important to note that, even though my interest is largely in wine sales, importers and distributors of alcohol handled both wine and whisky, while the large firms, often located in New York, sold their products in other American cities.

Prohibition jolted the wine production and distribution system of the country. In the case of distribution, there was a struggle to determine which dealers would be granted licenses to sell the relatively small quantities of wine and whisky that religious and medical institutions might need or that could be used for cooking purposes as permitted under the Volstead Act. In this way, the distributors would generate a small income to tide them over during the lean years.

More important was the question of how and how quickly the importation of wine and other alcoholic beverages would resume after repeal. In an October 1933 article on that subject, *Time* noted that "when the liquor trade ceases to agitate at the present tempo . . . most of the business will settle into the hands of more venerable importers who maintained their European connections through the dry years." The evidence would seem to support *Time*'s claim, with this qualification: a number of bootleggers also established good connections with wine producers in Europe and were able to compete with the older firms in the post-repeal period.[19]

Among the leading prewar dealers was Bellows and Company, based in New York, which was purchased by Frederick Wildman and colleagues in 1933. In that same year, Wildman reestablished ties with Bellows' former French partners during a European swing. At that point, Bellows was already a century-old company with excellent connections to many of the elite social clubs in large cities across the country that sought to replenish their inventories. Wildman, who was listed in the *Social Register*, was especially well placed to renew contacts with the company's former customers. He reported to Julian Street that "our New York and other club connections should be excellent. Most of the leading clubs of the entire country were clients of the old firm." Among them, he mentioned the University and Metropolitan in New York, the Pacific Union and Bohemian in San Francisco, and the Somerset and Harvard in Boston.[20]

Another large importer was Julius Wile and Sons, founded in New York in 1877, which resumed business on both coasts following repeal. The fact that the company was advertising both Benedictine and Cointreau for cooking purposes in 1932 is evidence of its continuing contacts with European suppliers during Prohibition. Moreover, the company sent Julius Wile, grandson of the founder, to Europe in 1936 to learn the wine business from old family connections.[21]

The largest distributors of alcohol in the years following Prohibition also had long histories. Subsidiaries of the National Distillers Products Corporation made their initial contacts with alcohol suppliers and customers well before Prohibition. In the late 1920s, National Distillers acquired seven distilleries, which, taken together, were storing half the whisky inventory in the United States; and in 1933 the company took over Alex D. Shaw, a wine-importing firm that maintained a substantial inventory during Prohibition. Thus, when Prohibition ended, National Distillers was prepared to supply whisky and wine to interested American consumers.[22]

Louis Rosenstiel, who "hung on through the bleak days of Prohibition," ran Schenley, National Distillers' chief competitor. As repeal approached, Rosenstiel renewed his contacts with wine and whisky dealers. Indeed, by 1933, Schenley controlled 20 percent of the whisky available in the United States. Using introductions arranged by friends, Rosenstiel went to Europe in 1932 and bought a supply of Burgundy, Bordeaux, Rhine wines, and Champagne to sell following repeal.[23]

Time was thus correct in claiming that older firms were able to take advantage of superior contacts and inventories of wine and whisky to secure dominance in the importing and distribution of alcohol following repeal. And, clearly, they were ready to do business even before repeal.

Prohibition had a damaging effect on wine production in the United States, even though the total production of grapes, 80 percent of which came from California, doubled during this period, as did the production of wine. However, quality diminished as growers concentrated on producing table and raisin grapes that could withstand the long shipments to customers east of the Mississippi, who converted the grapes into homemade wine. To make room for the new grapes, growers sacrificed varietals so that, by the end of Prohibition, there were "too many grapes of the wrong kind."[24]

To make matters worse, as repeal neared, many California winemakers salvaged these inferior grapes by making them into inferior wine. They did so even though they had to use aging processes that had never before been tested. The wineries did further damage by fermenting the wine at high temperatures and selling it before it was properly aged in order to increase income and cover expenses. Often growers shipped the wine in barrels that they had once used for pickles or molasses.[25]

Vineyard owners also exacerbated long-standing problems of the California wine industry. Whereas before Prohibition wineries produced more table than fortified wines, after repeal the production of fortified wines rose dramatically, thus favoring the growers from the Central Valley who produced the sweet grapes with a higher alcohol content used for making sherry, port, and muscatel. Meanwhile, interest in the finer table wines of the Sonoma and Napa valleys declined substantially.[26]

To correct these problems required years of work. Only gradually could California growers afford to uproot the raisin and table grape vines planted in the 1920s and reintroduce such varietals as cabernet sauvignon and pinot noir. Understandably, this slow process did not show significant results until the war years. Even so, there was some continuity in Napa Valley, where the four great wineries of the early twentieth century, Beaulieu, Inglenook, Berenger, and Larkmead, continued to produce the best wines.[27]

From this brief survey, it is fair to conclude that American wine drinkers profited from the relative ease with which the leading wine importers made available fine imported wines. Many restaurants, clubs, wine retailers, and their customers replenished their European wine stocks soon after repeal. However, the supply of drinkable California wines was severely affected by wine growers' destruction of varietal grapes and by the absence of an informed market. The preference for imported wines also reduced the demand for domestic wines.

Even as the food establishment was narrowing dining options by flooding the shelves of grocery stores with standardized, processed foods, the founders of the gourmet movement could count on the legendary bounty of North America to supply the raw materials for its dinners. For much of the nineteenth century, the proverbial table, groaning under the weight of platters laden with various meats, vegetables, and desserts, astonished European observers at hotels and inns across America. Even as late as the 1920s, Rudyard Kipling noted the remarkable quality, quantity, and variety of edibles produced in North America, but worried that Americans were wasting this "bounty." The remedy would be a *National Cookery Book for the U.S.A.* that would help Americans codify recipes for local and regional fare.[28]

No doubt, Kipling's cookbook would have enabled Americans to cook many of the dishes that Mark Twain hungered for in 1878. Nostalgic for the food of his country after a long European tour, he sent ahead a "bill of fare, which will go home in the steamer that precedes me and be hot when I arrive." On the list were seventy-six items, not including fresh fruits that were enumerated in a separate postscript. The list ran the gamut from meat, fish, vegetables, and baked goods to wild game. It featured specialties from every region of the country but was notable as well for its insistence on items specifically designated as American: coffee, butter, broiled chicken, toast, mince pie, and pastry. Particularly impressive was the range of game, shell fish, and fish dishes that Twain hoped to sample: wild turkey, woodcock, prairie hen, Missouri partridge, and coon to satisfy his taste for game; as for shell fish, he ordered oysters fried, stewed, on the half shell, roasted in shell, and in soup, as well as clam soup and cherrystone clams, soft-shell crabs, and San Francisco mussels. In the fish category, Twain specified perch, shad, brook trout, lake trout, and black bass, each identified by locale. The list of red meat, by contrast, consisted solely of porterhouse steak and roast beef. As for vegetables, there were boiled onions, pumpkins, asparagus, butter beans, hominy, and five different potato dishes. For breads and desserts, Twain preferred southern-style dishes: apple puffs, peach cobbler, hot hoe-cake, and hot light bread. He ordered all of these foods to be served in the American way, that is, without adornment by sauces except for butter and cream.[29]

As Americans migrated from farms to large cities, it became more difficult to access some of the foods that were once available to Twain and his contemporaries. Game and fish, then in close proximity to the farms where most Americans lived, now had to be shipped to cities; increasingly, meat from farm-raised animals including pigs, cattle, and chickens replaced them. And, with the mechanization of farm life, the increased production of wheat and corn brought about a larger consumption of these grains. In the process, the variety of available food products began to diminish, as some French chefs discovered. To remedy the scarcity of fresh greens for salads, for example, Louis Diat, chef at the Ritz-Carlton Hotel in New York, paid an acquaintance to grow them for the hotel kitchen.[30]

Even so, regional dishes and ingredients, often the product of America's ethnic diversity, remained a part of the American diet. French chefs in Louisiana, as well as cities such as New York and San Francisco where French immigrants settled in large numbers, wielded a disproportionate influence. The Pennsylvania Dutch were known for their sausage culture, excellent vegetable gardens featuring cabbages and potatoes, and a strong baking tradition. Among their most famous dishes were scrapple (pork scraps and corn meal) and pepper pot (a kind of tripe soup). In the Southwest, the influence was primarily Spanish. There corn, beans, and chili peppers were the principal ingredients of popular dishes such as beans and sausage mixed with chilis. Other favorites included tamales, *arroz con pollo*, and rice, beans, and chili peppers. The Spaniards also pioneered in barbecuing. Italian influence came only in the twentieth century when Americans outside of the Italian community adopted spaghetti with tomato sauce and pizza.[31]

The abundance and quality of American food provided an essential foundation for the gourmet movement. Members could count on a steady supply of various foodstuffs and thus turn their attention to the preparation of dishes that were based on lesser-used ingredients such as herbs and spices and/or methods for preparing and cooking those ingredients, including the use of stocks, sauces, and marinades.[32]

Home Cooks and Professional Chefs

In order to prepare gourmet meals in the home, housewives and their servants depended on recipe collections or cooking classes presenting gourmet recipes that were accessible to them. Sometimes, the family handed down those recipes. However, even though the first third of the twentieth century witnessed the publication of new cookbooks at a record pace, most of them did not fully suit the needs and interests of cooks who hoped to explore traditional American cuisine or ethnic cooking traditions, including French cuisine. Not until after 1934 did food articles in the luxury magazines partially fill this void, and it was somewhat later before their authors published these recipes in cookbooks.

The dominant trend in American cooking was the standardization of the diet based on the mass production of processed food and the modernization of kitchen appliances. Equally important was the reaction to mass immigration beginning in the late nineteenth century by cookbook writers, especially from the New England school, who attempted to create a uniform diet for all Americans. A product of this school, *The Fanny Farmer Cookbook*, published in 1896, sold over one and a half million copies in the next four decades. Reinforcing this trend was the strong inclination of American housewives to rely on cookbooks compiled by food processors such as General Mills and General Foods that supplied recipes to promote the purchase of their products. In these and other cookbooks, the infrequent recipes from foreign sources were mostly devoted to bland versions of Italian spaghetti and chop suey.[33]

Short of cookbooks, American housewives might have found other ways to learn foreign recipes. However, the increasing difficulty in hiring foreign cooks after the passage of the Immigration Restriction Act of 1924 limited these possibilities. To be sure, *The Settlement Cookbook* and a few others incorporated ethnic recipes that encouraged middle-class housewives to deviate from mainstream foodways. It would have been difficult, however, for housewives in the 1900s to use such recent French cookbooks as Charles Ranhofer's *The Epicurean* or the translated version of Escoffier's *Guide Culinaire*, designed primarily for the restaurant chef. Not only did they assume knowledge of cooking techniques beyond the skills of most upper-middle-class housewives, but their size was intimidating. Meanwhile, cooking schools that had served housewives of different classes in the nineteenth century were in decline. For example, there was no replacement for Pierre Blot's New York Cooking Academy of the late 1860s, which taught French cuisine to American housewives. Under these circumstances, French cooking was confined largely to the homes of the American elite, who could afford to hire professional chefs from France.[34]

Among the culinary assets of the United States in 1934 were the several thousand foreign chefs, many of whom were at or near the top of the cooking hierarchy in the country's leading hotels, clubs, and restaurants. They and their predecessors, trained by prestigious chefs, such as Escoffier, in some of the best European hotels and restaurants, first arrived on American shores in large numbers after the Civil War and were in great demand in the late nineteenth century, when America's nouveaux riches dined lavishly. Most were French chefs, who were essentially staffing the colonial outposts of the French culinary empire that extended from Europe to the New World.

In the years immediately before the rise of the gourmet dining movement, however, circumstances had changed. The 1924 Immigration Restriction Act imperiled the future of immigrant chefs by making those who were already in America literally a dying breed. In addition, the demand for elegant meals had declined substantially as a trend toward informal dining swept the country in the early twentieth century. With the implementation of Prohibition in 1920, gourmet dining suffered a more serious blow. Suddenly, restaurants were unable to match their dishes with appropriate wines. In this situation, gourmet diners preferred to dine at home, where some had laid in ample wine supplies, or to test some of the better speakeasies that had access to illegally imported wines. Then came the Depression, which diminished the resources of some Americans who had once frequented the best restaurants.[35]

In this perilous setting, immigrant chefs took steps to stabilize their situation. Already, they had established three organizations designed to provide health and death benefits for members. French chefs dominated the oldest of these groups, the Société Culinaire Philanthropique, founded in 1868, as they did the Vatel, while Italians were the largest group in the Chefs de Cuisine Association of America. In 1929, as the market fell, the three groups established the American Culinary Federation (ACF), an umbrella organization through which they could collaborate more effectively in achieving their common interests. Among other things, they created the *Culinary Review*, a monthly newsletter designed to advance the professional interests of the membership.[36]

The highest priority for members of the ACF was establishing the status of chefs in a country that did not regard cooking as a serious enterprise. Too often, the public confused chefs with kitchen helpers, who hoped to address their problems by unionizing. The new ACF promoted the idea of the chef as a member of a prestigious, middle-class, professional association, who, like lawyers and doctors, engaged in a demanding endeavor requiring both intelligence and training. The chief goal of the ACF was thus to raise the bar to entering the profession through additional training.

To accomplish this goal, the ACF created a gourmet dining society of its own (see chap. 3) in which chefs dined side by side with community leaders at restaurants staffed by well-known colleagues. They also devoted attention in the *Culinary Review* to educating future culinary professionals. Beginning in 1931, the president of the ACF, Charles Scotto, head chef at the Pierre Hotel in New York, promoted European-style apprenticeships, through which most of the immigrant chefs had received their training, as a solution to the problem.[37]

In the fall of 1935, Lucius Boomer, manager of the Waldorf Astoria, launched an apprenticeship program along the lines of the ACF proposal. Among other things, it included a strong dose of identity medicine supplied by the Waldorf's executive chef, Gabriel Lugot, who oversaw the program. He insisted that apprentices "be proud of the profession," understand their heritage from Escoffier and Brillat-Savarin, and record new recipes, as well as their reflections on the cooking process, in personal diaries.[38]

The ACF and hotel organizations also started a new training program in Culinary Arts at the Food Trades Vocational High School in New York in 1941. A four-year high school curriculum for students interested in becoming chefs, it was intended to be more rigorous than the existing courses in "Cafeteria and Catering" for home economics students. Graduates would learn French "for menu preparation" and emerge with a "complete knowledge of food preparation" through study of the Escoffier and Ranhofer cookbooks.[39]

Perhaps these groups would have established a European-style apprenticeship program in the United States, if World War II had not intervened; however, with the advent of the GI Bill, which subsidized tuition for higher education, the founders of a new postsecondary chef's school, the New Haven Restaurant Institute, appealed to GIs interested in cooking as a profession to enter their training program. A one-year curriculum at the outset, it soon expanded to two and then four years, gradually enrolled a few women, and eventually became the Culinary Institute of America with a campus in Hyde Park, New York, in 1972. At least part of the training was an apprenticeship. Once again, the Escoffier cookbook became the principal text.[40]

For the period under consideration here, it is clear that the most influential chefs in the most prestigious restaurants generally received their training as apprentices in Europe. Nonetheless, the immigrant chefs' interest in creating an American training program is evidence that they saw such a program as a way to increase respect for the cooking profession in the United States.

Restaurants, Wine Retailers, Specialty Food Shops, and Markets

To narrow the task of identifying gourmet restaurants and their food and wine purveyors in mid-1930s America, I have followed André Simon's lead in focusing on New York, Boston, Chicago, San Francisco, Los Angeles, and New Orleans, the cities where he located Wine and Food Society chapters. Based on information Simon gathered over thirty years as a wine dealer, he clearly believed that these six cities were best equipped to support a WFS chapter. In my survey of each city, I have identified restaurants that served authentic French dishes along with one or two featuring other ethnic cuisines, as well as suppliers of gourmet food and wine. It is also useful to note that stores catering to the carriage trade often stocked both food and wine, while several of them provided mail-order service to Americans living outside of these metropolitan areas.

In choosing their venues, gourmet dining societies preferred large hotel restaurants to their smaller counterparts, because they could more easily feed groups of fifty to three hundred diners. In addition, prestigious immigrant chefs, who could prepare the *haute cuisine* dinners anticipated by many dining society members, often headed the kitchens in these hotels. For that reason, hotel restaurants figure prominently in this survey. To provide as accurate an assessment of the restaurants as possible, I have relied on guidebooks, as well as magazine and newspaper reviews primarily from the 1930s.

It will become clear, as well, that the six cities were not equally endowed with gourmet resources. The presence of a significant expatriate, immigrant, and Franco-American population, along with well-traveled Americans, who enjoyed French cuisine in New York, New Orleans, and San Francisco explains the relative abundance of French restaurants in these cities.

Indeed, New York had been and remained the preeminent dining city in the United States. Its restaurants provided a greater diversity of ethnic cuisines, and more of them succeeded in meeting a high culinary standard than counterparts in other cities. Even a century earlier, New York established its preeminence with the founding of Delmonico's, generally recognized as the finest restaurant in the United States until its demise in 1923. One important turning point was the appointment of Louis Diat, an Escoffier disciple and creator of *crème vichyssoise*, to head the kitchen of the new Ritz-Carlton Hotel in 1910. Until his retirement in 1951, the Ritz maintained its reputation for excellence. Another important milestone was the opening of the Hotel Pierre in 1930, which featured Charles Scotto, also an Escoffier disciple, as head chef. Meanwhile, the Waldorf-Astoria, whose executive chef, Gabriel Lugot, served from 1932 to 1950, was also highly regarded. All three chefs were masters of classic French cuisine.[41]

But the vibrancy of the New York dining scene came as much from smaller restaurants as from the hotels. Most remarkable were two speakeasies that evolved in the 1920s into highly regarded restaurants: Jack and Charlie's "21" Club and the Colony. Their patrons were as enamored of the fine food they ate there as of the publicity they received in the New York press. Specialties of the Colony included *tournedos Mirabeau* (filet mignon with anchovy fillets, olives, and tarragon leaves) and chicken *diable* Colony (coated in mustard, bread crumbs, and melted butter). As for the "21" Club, it featured duck *à la press* and "21" club chicken hash.[42]

Among other fine French restaurants was the Café Chambord, whose onion soup and lobster in snail sauce were its most prized dishes. And, to illustrate the diversity of New York restaurants, there was Keen's English chophouse, offering beefsteak and kidney pudding and English mutton chop, as well as Luchow's, one of New York's oldest German restaurants, known for its sauerbraten, venison, goose, ragout, pig knuckles, and sauerkraut. For seafood, Billy the Oysterman was popular among New Yorkers.[43]

To serve these many fine restaurants and the homes of their patrons required superior sources of food, wine, and liquor. Among them were the Washington and Fulton Street markets, the former supplying meat and produce, the latter fish. Various New York department stores, including Macy's, which had sold wines and liquor since the nineteenth century, supplied a variety of gourmet products. On the food side, customers could purchase boneless sardines, York house assorted biscuits for cheese, and French filets of mackerel in ravigote sauce (veal *velouté* with white wine, vinegar, shallots, and herbs). As for other department stores, Gimbel's epicure shop and Wanamaker's pantry shelf stocked such delicacies as a smorgasbord in cans and aquavit to wash it down.[44]

In addition, small specialty shops, usually located in upper-crust neighborhoods, offered various options. Founded in 1912, Vendome Table Delights sold imported items as well as gourmet dishes to go. There customers could buy duck *à l'orange*, cold borscht, escargots, chicken livers wrapped in bacon, *petite marmite* (beef and chicken soup with cabbage balls and vegetables), and frozen *zabaglione*. The adjacent Vendome liquor store sold alcoholic beverages. As worthy rivals in the carriage trade, Charles and Co., which also sold by mail-order catalogue, stocked green turtle soup, water-ground cornmeal, herbs of various kinds, Bel Paese and Brie, *pâté de foie gras* and a variety of terrines, Italian olive oil, imported Bass Ale, and Beck's Pilsner. New Yorkers who were looking for fresh bakery goods could satisfy their needs at Duvernoy and Jean's.[45]

One of the major liquor retailers, Sherry Wine and Spirits, had its roots in the bootlegging activity of founder Jack Aaron, who, with his brother Sam, opened the store shortly after Prohibition. Their competitor and eventual partner, Morris Lehmann, improved his inventory by consulting Henry Hollis, the former Vermont senator and Prohibitionist whose expertise was French wines. After 1965, the store was renamed Sherry-Lehmann.[46]

Among the six cities considered here, New Orleans sported the most stable culinary scene. All of its best restaurants and specialty food shops had been in place for at least a generation before the gourmet movement emerged, and they continued to serve or sell fine food and wine over the next quarter of a century. Most of these restaurants were famous for their Creole cuisine, defined as French cuisine modified by local ingredients as well as Spanish and African influences. In New Orleans, Antoine's was considered the first among equals. Its proprietor, Roy Alciatore, had inherited the position from his father and grandfather, in time to celebrate the 1940 centennial with a new wine list. The restaurant was known for its oysters Rockefeller (with Worcestershire sauce, anchovy sauce, spinach, green onions, celery, parsley, lettuce, butter, bread crumbs, and absinthe), *pom-*

pano en papillote (oiled paper), and *café brulot* (with cognac, sugar, cloves, cinnamon, orange, and lemon peel).[47]

Antoine's two chief competitors in the 1930s were Arnaud's, established in 1918 by the "Count" Arnaud, who in real life was Léon Bertrand Arnaud Cazenave, and Galatoire's, opened by Jean Galatoire in 1905. Arnaud presided over his restaurant until 1948, when his daughter Germaine succeeded him, while Galatoire logged only eleven years before three nephews arrived from France to take over the business. The former was well known for its shrimp Arnaud, oysters Bienville, and watercress soup à la Germaine, while the latter's trout *Marguery* (cooked in white wine and fish stock thickened with eggs and butter) and oyster patties were customer favorites.[48]

Two other restaurants deserve mention. Although Broussard's was founded only in 1920, its proprietor, Joseph Broussard, began his career at Antoine's, from which he borrowed the *poulet en papillote* that Jules Alciatore invented; the restaurant was also known for its crab-meat Broussard. In addition to the predominantly French restaurants of New Orleans, there was Kolb's, established in 1899, which served such German dishes as sauerbraten, Wiener schnitzel, and pigs' knuckles, along with Creole specialties.[49]

By far the most reputable retail purveyor of gourmet food and wine in New Orleans was Solari's, which opened in 1868 and survived until 1965. It was a grocery store, charcuterie, patisserie, and wine and liquor store rolled into one. During much of the twentieth century, Omar Cheer ran the business and maintained an inventory of excellent wines. Among the items listed in the 1930 catalogue, which supplemented sales in the store, were such imported cheeses as Roquefort, port de salut, four kinds of Camembert, and English stilton; other delicacies included truffles, tripe, goose liver, shad roe, and herring. Clementine Paddleford, the food journalist, considered Solari's "one of America's finest grocery stores."[50]

The dining scene in San Francisco reflected the presence of the city's substantial Italian, French, and Chinese populations. In the 1930s and early 1940s the Palace Hotel hired in succession Philip Roemer, Albert Bohn, and Lucien Heyraud to head a kitchen that featured both French and American dishes. Heyraud, trained under Escoffier at the Savoy Hotel in London, was admired for his *coquille St. Jacques, filet de boeuf Grand Veneur* (beef fillet with venison sauce), and *petite marmite Henry IV*. Almost as popular as the Palace, the St. Francis Hotel could boast the cooking of Joseph Delon and Pierre Coste, who had been trained at the École Hotelière in Grenoble. Delon was known for such dishes as *canard rouennaise* (duck liver with a Bordelaise sauce) and *Rex sole bonne femme* (shallots, parsley, and mushrooms in white wine and fish stock). Meanwhile,

French chefs Victor Laborie and Adrien Jouan presided over the kitchen of the Cercle de l'Union, whose membership had broadened from the descendants of French-speaking immigrants to San Franciscans interested in French culture. Laborie was known for his *gigot roti Bretonne* (roast lamb with white beans).[51]

San Francisco was particularly well populated with small restaurants serving authentic French cuisine, many of which had an excellent survival record. Among them was Jack's, which opened before the great fire of 1906 and recovered quickly in the aftermath. Its intimate atmosphere and genial hosts, the Blanquie family, made the restaurant an attractive venue. Among other specialties, Jack's served *poulet sauté aux fonds d'artichauds* (sautéed chicken with artichoke hearts) and *filet de sole Marguery*. A few blocks from Jack's was the Blue Fox with Chef Fred Soulage presiding in the kitchen, where he prepared lamb sweetbreads *poulette* (white sauce with lemon and parsley) and frog legs. To provide an Italian finish to the meal, diners could order *zabaglione*. Among San Francisco's many excellent Italian restaurants, Vanessi's was highly regarded for its Italian risotto and chicken à la Vanessi, spicy lasagna, and veal cutlet Milanese (dipped in egg with breadcrumbs and parmesan cheese, then fried in butter).[52]

For meat and produce, restaurateurs could supply themselves at shops on Market Street, while those who sought gourmet food and drink found it at Goldberg-Bowen, a "famous purveyor of gustatory delights." In addition to alcoholic beverages, the store stocked cold cuts, cheese, and three-bean salads and, from its "all-time best sandwich shop," served egg salad, roast beef, and other fillings on fresh sourdough bread. As evidenced by an advertisement for Matthieu's Importers in Los Angeles, the store's reputation was statewide: "Mr. Mattieu's fifteen years experience . . . with Goldberg-Bowen of San Francisco is at your disposal."[53]

With a relatively small French population that translated into a scarcity of French restaurants, Chicago had a far less stable and reputable restaurant scene than either New Orleans or San Francisco. German eateries were, of course, more numerous, but few seem to have been both durable and appealing to gourmet diners. Intellectuals and writers frequented Schlogel's, a German-American restaurant, whose chef, Paul Weber, prepared Wiener schnitzel, hassenpfeffer, and stewed chicken à la Schlogel. Meanwhile, the Red Star Inn became a rough approximation of Luchow's in New York. It served hassenpfeffer along with a fine German lentil soup, to a clientele that included Prince Henry of Prussia. And for a rough parallel to Keen's in New York, Chicago could offer the clublike St. Hubert's Old English Grill, which admitted only men to the first floor and served beef, lamb, kidneys, and English mutton chops.[54]

Among the best French restaurants, and well known for its Creole dishes, was Teddy's l'Aiglon managed by Theodore Majerus. Its specialties included *moules marinières, poulet belle meunière* (in butter), and *pompano en papillote*, while the wine list drew praise from its Gold Coast clients. On the Near North Side was Julien's, Chicago's oldest French restaurant, which was prized for its "home-like atmosphere" as well as scallops, lettuce salads, and frog legs cooked by Ma Julien.[55]

Not until the Byfield brothers opened the Pump Room at the Ambassador East Hotel in the late 1930s was there a notable hotel restaurant. To be sure, the brothers had earlier run the College Inn at the Sherman Hotel, reputed for Chef Jean Gazabat's chicken shortcake, lobster Newburg, and creamed finnan haddie. Chicagoans regarded the College Inn as the "most interesting and unique restaurant" in Chicago—words that would also describe the Pump Room.[56]

As for gourmet food shops, markets, and wine dealers, the Fulton and South Water Street markets offered not only fresh produce but also meat and fish to retailers. Two venerable Chicago stores sold both food specialties and wines. Already in 1934, Hillman's had several stores in the Chicago area, while Stop and Shop was well located on Washington Avenue in the loop; later Hillman's bought out Stop and Shop, but neither store survived the twentieth century.[57]

The dining scene in Boston was relatively stable but offered fewer restaurant options than other large cities. Accordingly, Bostonians relied heavily on their hotels and clubs. Among the former was the Vendome and the Ritz-Carlton (opened in 1927). Both served French specialties, particularly the Ritz, where Charles Bonino presided in the kitchen and was acclaimed for *noisettes d'agneau favorite* (morsels of lamb garnished with truffles and foie gras, potatoes, and asparagus). Also well known for its French dishes was the Somerset Club, not to be confused with the hotel by the same name. Among smaller Boston restaurants Locke Ober, which first opened in the late nineteenth century, offered French cuisine as well as traditional American fare, although the main floor was off limits to women until the 1970s; owned by Locke Ober, Joseph's was also well known for the quality of its French menu.[58]

For fresh produce, meat, and fish, Boston restaurateurs made their purchases at Quincy market, while S.S. Pierce, the granddaddy of all purveyors of specialty foods and wines in the United States, was located nearby. Shopping at this store, which was founded in 1831, became a habit of the Boston upper class as Justice Oliver Wendell Holmes, Jr., explained: "I was brought up on S.S. Pierce groceries and I wouldn't dare change." From the outset Pierce stocked wines and spirits as well as such delicacies as terrapin stew and Singapore pineapple. After repeal, Charles and Russell Codman served as Pierce's wine buyers and kept up its inventory of imported wines; in addition, the store stocked Stilton cheese, smoked whale meat, fancy soups, Bombay duck, and rattlesnake meat. By 1930, the original store had added five suburban branches, which employed one thousand people, and attracted a more diverse clientele.[59]

Compared to the five other cities, the Los Angeles scene was clearly the most chaotic. Restaurants came and went, while their success rested as much on the personality of the owner and the glamour of Hollywood stars in attendance as on the quality of the menu. Epitomizing this genre were the restaurants of colorful entrepreneurs Billy Wilkerson, Dave Chasen, and Mike Romanoff. In 1933, Wilkerson launched the Vendome Café, which served French and Italian food, and then opened La Rue's, specializing in French food, in 1945. Dave Chasen's Southern Pit Barbecue, with six tables and fourteen counter stools, was such a hit that two years after its opening in 1936, Chasen replaced it with Chasen's, a full-scale restaurant serving American and Continental specialties, which remained a Hollywood legend until its recent demise. Equally legendary was Mike Romanoff's, which opened in 1941 and also mixed Continental with American dishes. Unfortunately, none of these restaurants were part of an infrastructure that could support gourmet dining in 1935, when the Los Angeles Wine and Food Society formed its chapter.[60]

Among restaurants whose fame rested more on their cooking than their glamour was Perino's, highly regarded for its French and Italian specialties from 1932, when it first opened, until the late twentieth century. Beginning in 1932, Angelenos enjoyed the smorgasbord at Bit of Sweden, where Chef Kenneth Hansen presided over the kitchen. After it closed, Hansen opened the Scandia in 1946, which also featured smorgasbord. He was selected by the Los Angeles Wine and Food Society in 1937, 1949, and again in 1954 to receive its Cordon Bleu, awarded annually to the chef who prepared the best meal for the Society during that year.[61]

More impressive was the number of fine wine and food shops in the Los Angeles area, such as Young's Market, founded in 1888 as a full-scale grocery store and bakery that sold fresh meat, prawns, Columbia River smelts, scallops, crab meat, green ripe olives, and Danish blue cheese. In addition, Young's had a catering and delivery service and a bakery and, on special occasions, offered cooking lessons to its customers. Indeed, in 1937, "Alphonse of La Touraine" taught customers how to make canapés and appetizers. Immediately following the Beer Act of 1933, the market stocked Bass Ale, Pilsner XXX, and Scotch Ale.[62]

Founded by J. S. Foto and Frank Vitale in 1923, the Bohemian Distributing Company was a wholesale outfit that specialized in fine food, wines, and liquor. After Prohibition, the company also brewed and promoted Acme beer, while maintaining a large inventory of fine wines and whisky.[63]

In 1934, Fred Beck, an advertising man, joined with other entrepreneurs to found the Farmer's Market, which provided a venue for farmers to sell their fresh produce. The market benefited from Beck's daily column in the *Los Angeles Times* promoting its wares; however, over time, shops and restaurants replaced many stands where farmers once sold their produce.[64]

Two other important venues for the carriage trade were Balzer's market and Jurgensen's Grocery. Founded by Albert Balzer in early 1923, the market supplied cheeses and high-quality canned goods to upscale Angelenos, but it could not compete with Jurgensen's. The latter, established in 1935 in Pasadena and expanded to other sections of Los Angeles, bought out Balzer's markets in 1959.[65]

Gourmet Dining Societies

The growth of large city clubs in the mid-nineteenth century that provided the business and professional elite with facilities for dining, reading, and entertaining friends also created a supportive environment for gourmet dining societies. After 1880, newly formed country clubs offered comparable facilities for upper-class recreation. The impact of these clubs—urban and country—on gourmet dining was substantial. Many hired European-trained chefs, created wine cellars, and built large dining rooms that eventually accommodated the entire membership of the new gourmet dining societies formed after repeal.[66]

In addition, there were a number of smaller clubs in each of these cities that appealed to individuals with special interests. The Odd Volume Club in Boston, the Zamarano in Los Angeles, and the Roxburghe in San Francisco brought together individuals who collected old books; those interested in the arts could join the Tavern Club in Chicago and its counterpart in Boston, while the Sunset Club in Los Angeles offered opportunities to discuss contemporary political issues. Meanwhile, San Franciscans interested in French culture and cuisine could join the Cercle de l'Union. These clubs either maintained dining facilities or found appropriate ones for their meetings.

Before and after the founding of elite city clubs, businessmen in large cities formed small dining societies to satisfy a need for socializing that led over time to improving the quality of their meals. Members of these dining societies—all males—almost always had overlapping memberships in the larger city clubs where they also held their dinners. Among the best known of these societies were WEDA (Wyckoff Economical Dining Association, named after its founder, Alexander Wyckoff) and the Zodiac Club, so named because the club identified each of the members with a zodiac sign. These clubs were founded in 1838 and 1868, respectively, in New York, while Bostonians, who in 1881 were planning a world's fair for the city, launched the Beacon Society. Even though the proposed fair never came to pass, the fare at the Algonquin Club, where the society met, was apparently more than palatable. The common features of these societies were a small membership (twelve in the New York clubs, ten in the Beacon Society) and monthly meetings for six months of the year. In addition, the societies rotated responsibilities for planning the meals among club members and collectively critiqued them at their completion.[67]

While Le Club des Arts Gastronomiques resembled its New York and Boston predecessors in many ways, the harsh realities of Prohibition left their mark on club practices. In the absence of alcoholic beverages in public venues, members met in each others' homes and shared the contents of their wine cellars. In so doing these Boston Brahmins intended to "preserve the culinary arts" and promote "standards of drinking compatible with the spirit of New England conservatism" that would also "glorify the aesthetic and hygienic properties of wines and liquors." Russell Sturgis Codman and Sohier Welch, a dedicated amateur gourmet, founded Le Club, which was limited to twelve members, all male. Among its contributions to the larger gourmet movement were the wine manuals written by two distinguished members, Charles Codman and Philip Dexter, an attorney. The brothers Codman and Dexter were sufficiently knowledgeable to educate their colleagues in gastronomic matters. In this sense, Le Club was a kind of bridge between the old dining societies and the new gourmet movement that featured a mingling of amateurs and professionals.[68]

Given the remarkable expertise of its members, it is not surprising that Le Club planned meals and selected members with great care. Among the stringent qualifications for membership were an interest in wine, the possession of a wine cellar, and a willingness to host a dinner once every two years. Applicants had to be unanimously approved by their fellow diners.

The dinners were ceremonial and ritualistic; members wore burgundy waistcoats with gilt buttons, "ornamented with a bunch of grapes in relief," and a tricolor ribbon. In addition, the club plates and the matching club banner with family crest were set at each diner's place, while members awarded medals to meritorious cooks and wives who promoted the club's activities. According to club rules, late arrival to dinners and smoking were forbidden. Following the

Table setting, Le Club des Arts Gastronmiques, Boston, Massachusetts, from the frontispiece of Russell S. Codman, Jr., *Vintage Dinners* (Boston: Anchor Linotype Printing Co., 1937). Laura Codman.

meal, it was customary to toast the cook and evaluate the wines. In adopting these practices, Le Club set a precedent for future gourmet societies.[69]

On the culinary side, Le Club des Arts Gastronomiques often deviated from standard French menus. Indeed, members sometimes incorporated American dishes into their meals and accompanied those dishes with wines from two or more European countries. As Russell Codman explained, serious French wine drinkers usually stocked their cellars with the best wines from their own part of France and/or from the rest of the country. By contrast, the Bostonians' wine and whisky stock was comprehensive, including selections from all over Europe, although Codman remarked that "Claret is my forte." After drinking great German and French wines as well as cognac, Armagnac, and rum from Sohier Welch's cellar, André Simon, visiting Boston to recruit members for a chapter of the Wine and Food Society, remarked, "It is highly improbable, but it is just possible, to imagine another more or less similar collection of fine wines being assembled again. What is absolutely beyond anything in the nature of a second edition is the sequence of spirits which followed."[70]

The Bostonians took pride in the American dishes they served, including meat, potatoes, and vegetables, sometimes unadorned by sauces. In such instances, it was the wines and cheese that added a European flavor as, for example, the "memorable meal" served on December 17, 1936, at Sohier Welch's home. He noted that "the altar upon which this gastronomical feast was offered was raised upon two main pillars, both as distinctly American as they were excellent, the oyster crabs and the mongrel goose." The latter was, in fact, prepared by his mother in a cream and Madeira sauce. There followed the European wines; Champagne was "an admirable wine to sing to those dainty little crabs a cheery lullaby." However, "the wine of the evening," five different Burgundies from the commune of Vosne-Romanée with vintages ranging from 1923 to 1934, honored the goose and the cheeses.[71]

Simon also gave high praise to Le Club cuisine after attending the November 17, 1937, dinner at Charles Codman's home. He enjoyed a special breed of guinea chick paired with a Volnay Clos des Ducs (1926). It was followed by a whole Brie—the first time he had ever seen such a thing in a private house—and two Burgundies. The meal ended with "the best of all caramel custards I have ever tasted." Despite the rule that women were not admitted to the dinners, the members made an exception for Theodora Codman, who was invited to receive their compliments.[72]

Le Club spawned a new dining society in 1936, while continuing its activities into the postwar era. Organized by Frederic Celler and Henry Lewis at the Locke Ober Café, where all dinners were held, the Cellar Club limited its membership to eighteen individuals, among them Felix Pereira and Frederic Celler, who also joined Le Club. Rejecting the "undue formality" and "ostentation" of Le Club, the founders of the Cellar Club limited expenses to $5.50 per person for dinner, wine, and service by planning simpler meals. One such dinner consisted of bouillon, soft-shell crabs, Locke-Ober steak and fries, and Roquefort cheese. The Cellar Club had its own wine cellar that was surely more modest than those of Le Club's members.[73]

Le Club des Arts Gastronomiques embodied perfectly the existing ideal of a gourmet dining society. It was small, composed of carefully selected members of the social elite, and insisted on high standards of dining. However, it deviated in one important respect, which was not intended to be a precedent. The location of all dinners shifted from clubs or restaurants to members' homes in order to assure an adequate supply of wine. Even so, the practices of Le Club and its predecessors provided a model for subsequent gourmet societies, all of which, however, had a much larger membership.

Despite Prohibition and the rise of nutritionism, the prospects for gourmet dining in 1934 were better than they had been in 1920. For one thing, the expanding cadre of upper-middle-class gourmet diners promised over time to create a critical mass of Americans who would be interested in joining the small and isolated upper-class practitioners of fine dining.

The vast majority of Americans, however, were moving in the opposite direction. The increasing standardization of the diet, accompanied by a focus on nutritionism, put a damper on the prospects for cultivating fine dining even of a more modest kind in the American home. While ethnic groups continued to prepare dishes from the home country, the Immigration Restriction Act slowed their growth and the infusion of culinary ideas from new immigrants. Meanwhile, advocates of Americanization pressured the immigrants to conform to mainstream foodways. In this way, the gap between gourmet diners and the rest of the country widened.

Those Americans who were interested in enjoying a French meal were thus more likely to dine in restaurants than at home. However, the effects of the Depression on the customer base were significant. Furthermore, for those individuals who hoped to find their French dinners in Paris, the cost of travel was a serious impediment. While chefs struggled to maintain their jobs as the restaurant business declined, the newly established American Culinary Federation enabled them to more effectively explain the special status of highly trained professional chefs and their role in creating the good life in America.

One important factor in the resurrection of gourmet dining after 1934 was the rapid recovery of wine importing, engineered by firms that laid careful plans during the last years of Prohibition. On the food side of the equation, large American cities could still rely on local markets and/or specialty food stores to supply stocks of fresh and imported ingredients. However, the trend toward processed foods reduced demand at these venues.

Balancing the strengths and weaknesses of the resources available for gourmet dining in the mid-1930s gives only a partial picture of the long-run prospects for incorporating French cuisine into the American diet. It is important to

complete this picture by considering the receptivity of the larger American population to the values that were inherent in the concept of gourmet dining. After
all, the success of the enterprise in France was clearly based on the compatibility
of the values of early French promoters of the new restaurants with those of a
significant segment of the French population. While only a minority could afford to eat regularly in fine restaurants, others could enjoy some of the new
dishes in a more modest way in their own homes. They could also take pride in
the fact that their country had become the great gastronomic center of the Western world.[74]

Bourgeois promoters of gourmet dining like Brillat-Savarin viewed it as a way
of transcending for a time the everyday task of making a living through hard work.
There was, of course, an element of necessity in all forms of dining. However, as
he argued, food and drink could not only satisfy bodily needs but also lift the spirit
and please the senses. By valuing the dining experience for its sensuality, beauty,
and leisurely flow, as well as its intellectual and social functions, gastronomers
endowed it with a significance far beyond the material function it also served.
Embracing leisure and beauty, they appealed not only to aristocrats, from whom
they borrowed these values, but also to the rising bourgeoisie that hoped to secure
a higher station in life. For a few hours each day or each week, bourgeois diners
could, in effect, behave as if they were aristocrats.[75]

While the aristocratic ethos was widely accepted in France, the prevailing
value system in America was, and remained, essentially middle class. Many Americans regarded sensuality, leisure, beauty, and intellect with suspicion. This tension between mainstream French and American culture, which was, in reality,
a tension between upper- and middle-class values, weakened the appeal of gourmet dining in America.

Indeed, the widespread acceptance of nutritionism and Prohibition reflected
Americans' preference for middle-class values. In responding to both of these issues, they considered dining as an activity that sustained and improved the health
of the diner through the consumption of the proper nutrients, but regarded with
indifference or fear its effect on thoughts, feelings, and social relations. Nutritionism was appealing precisely because it provided scientific evidence that diners were
fueling their bodies efficiently. In turn, time saved at the table and in the kitchen
would enable diners to do more and better work at the office or in the factory and
take better care of their families.

From this utilitarian perspective, Prohibition also made sense. Excessive
drinking that affected workers' health and their work ethic cost companies and
their customers dearly, while many mothers and children suffered from drunken

and abusive husbands and fathers. Strangely, however, there was never a full-scale test of the impact of a dry regime on workers and families in America. Indeed, through illegal speakeasies, bathtub gin, and the legal production of wine at home, the consumption of alcohol actually continued at a brisk pace. As a result, Americans emerged from the Depression with a taste for cocktails and an even weaker inclination toward the moderate consumption of wine with dinner so central to the gourmet ideal.

In short, while Americans possessed many of the material and intellectual resources to support a gourmet movement, the majority values in the mid-1930s were hostile to importing gourmet dining from France. That limited, but did not prevent, the movement from making headway. However, in order to widen their appeal, gourmet advocates would have to convert their fellow Americans to the appreciation of leisure and sensuality. Among other things, they would have to discard the old adage that "time is money" in favor of something like "time is pleasure." Only then would it be possible to extend the dinner hour to permit greater enjoyment of a meal and of the company of fellow diners.

Equally challenging was the idea of embracing sensual experiences rather than regarding them as a threat to virtuous behavior. Indeed, only if Americans agreed to this proposition would they be able to welcome the work of skilled artisans, who created tasty dinners and an environment including visual and auditory experiences in which to enjoy them. The success of gourmet dining thus rested on the possibility of converting Americans to values that seemed alien to many of them. In the absence of a major educational campaign, the gap between the growing population of gourmet diners, who were exposed to French cuisine through their travels and magazine reading, and their majority counterparts, whose resources and opportunities were more limited, was likely to widen.

~~~~~~

Chapter Three

Origins, Rituals, and Menus of Gourmet Dining Societies, 1934–1961

———

The gourmet movement in America was founded in 1934. French wine producers and dealers, eager to stimulate the demand for wine in the United States, supplied the catalyst for the movement. They drew on the resources of large American cities, including fine restaurants, French immigrant chefs, elite men's clubs, wine importers, and the interest of college-educated Americans, who were visiting Europe with great regularity and reading the luxury lifestyle magazines. In an age when Americans increasingly ate to live, the societies challenged the hegemony of nutritionists who promoted processed foods and valued vitamins and calories more than the taste of food and wine. They also sought to spread French cuisine beyond the American upper class where it was already a familiar feature.

Chronicles by members of these groups, archival records, proceedings in society journals, and press accounts illuminate both the societies' culinary activities and their social significance for members. Inasmuch as the dining societies were closely associated with urban men's clubs, they provide an opportunity to test the claims of Thorstein Veblen and his recent disciples on the role of these clubs in enhancing members' "cultural capital," as expressed through refined tastes. By taking as their mission the development of culinary connoisseurship, the dining societies, in fact, made a significant, yet specialized, contribution to increasing their members' cultural capital.

In these respects, gourmet dining societies seem to exemplify the conspicuous consumption of Thorstein Veblen's leisure class. According to Veblen and the recent scholarship on elite clubs, the members, men only, who already possessed far more than the necessities of life, enhanced their reputations by cultivating an aesthetic sense. As connoisseurs, they purchased fine clothing, food, and alcohol and developed refined manners so as to consume/display these items appropriately. Like the gourmet diners, the leisure class also joined groups featuring rituals and elaborate dress, which were all the more conspicuous during the depressions of the 1890s and 1930s. Meanwhile, both groups sought to spread their ways to nonmembers: the leisure class by establishing a standard that "coerced" classes below them who wished to be recognized as "reputable"; the diners by publicizing their activities in the press.[1]

Veblen and his recent followers are on solid ground in identifying a class of people who consumed luxury goods in the 1890s and/or the 1930s. However, their assessment of the motives of the leisure class and their gourmet dining successors is too narrow to explain the behavior of either group. Some gourmet diners did join societies to raise their social standing, but many were also interested in enjoying the pleasures of the table, often downplayed in America. And it would be a mistake to ignore the economic side of gourmet dining. Entrepreneurs profited from supplying wine and gourmet foods to their affluent customers, while gourmet diners, on occasion, sought to parlay connections with individuals of high social standing into profitable wine sales. Furthermore, Veblen's belief that an instinct of workmanship was the driving force behind human behavior was no more convincing than gourmet leaders' claim that satisfaction of the senses was the overriding motivation for their actions. In the absence of definitive evidence about instincts, the records show the mixed motives of members for joining gourmet societies. While some sought the pleasures of the table and others hoped to raise their social standing, many joined for both these and other reasons.

American gourmet dining societies arose at a time when French cuisine set the standard for all gourmet diners in the Western world. Indeed, Frenchmen pioneered such societies when they founded the Club des Cent (restricted to one hundred members) in 1914 to monitor the cuisine of France's hotels and restaurants. It is not surprising, then, that the heads of the first three international gourmet dining societies in America were Frenchmen and that these societies featured French cuisine.[2]

The rise of a new breed of dining societies was an important development in the country's history. By committing themselves to the spread of French culinary ways, members of the societies rejected as provincial and unwise the excessive focus of nutritionists on achieving a healthy diet through processed foods; at the same time, gourmets embraced repeal as an opportunity to enhance fine dishes with appropriate wines. In this way, the gourmet societies bridged the Atlantic and diminished the cultural distance in culinary matters between America and Europe.

To accomplish this goal, the societies sought to transform the attitudes of members and, through them, of the public. In bylaws and constitutions, they stipulated proper decorum at the table, often based on the conventions of upper-class Europeans, so that members would enjoy both the food and the company.

To fulfill their mission, gourmet groups reached out to knowledgeable wine and food professionals, some of whom joined the societies. The dinner and wine committees, which brought together amateurs and professionals, including chefs and wine experts, planned the menus and selected the wines. In the process, interested amateurs learned from professionals how to arrange courses and match each course with the right wine, while the professionals received recognition from elite members of their communities.

Origins of the Gourmet Movement

The death of the most renowned chef of the early twentieth century in 1935 did not go unnoticed in New York City. To honor Auguste Escoffier's memory, a new gourmet dining society, Les Amis d'Escoffier, was established in 1935, and two other societies gave commemorative dinners featuring his cookery. In spite of the Great Depression, gourmet dining societies were alive and well and becoming an important feature of the large-city landscape. As Henry Taft, brother of President William Howard Taft, remarked, "I see new clubs being formed on much the same model as our Society [the Wine and Food Society]. The idea has taken a hold not alone in this city [New York] but elsewhere." The vitality of these groups was evident in their growing membership and competition for attention from the media.[3]

Three major gourmet societies emerged in the 1930s. One of them, the London-based Wine and Food Society (WFS), created six new chapters in America. Les Amis d'Escoffier, comprised of hotel managers, restaurant owners, and international chefs who worked in the United States, as well as elite members of the community, also developed a network of branches in large American cities. The third group, La Confrérie des Chevaliers du Tastevin (the brotherhood of the Knights of the Wine Cup), which promoted Burgundy wines and culture, created its own branches after 1945. All three survived the unfavorable conditions during World War II to thrive in the postwar world.

The goals of the new societies had much in common. All three assumed that American gourmet societies, like their French counterparts, would plan and consume multicourse French meals, matched with appropriate wines for each course, to be served at periodic society dinners. In so doing, they exploited the repeal of Prohibition, but not without a sympathetic gesture toward Prohibitionists. Consistent with French practice, gourmet societies rejected alcoholic excess, especially the drinking of cocktails before dinner, in favor of moderate wine consumption. According to one proponent, gourmets were "high-minded, temperate advocates of *haute cuisine* as the highest expression of civilization and culture." However, all three societies struggled to achieve autonomy from wine dealers and producers upon whose largesse they depended in the early years.[4]

There were also significant differences between the three groups in their approach to culinary matters. The Escoffier and Tastevin societies dedicated themselves to the celebration of classical French cuisine as espoused by Escoffier that was reflected in the French wines they served. Meanwhile, branches of the Wine and Food Society deviated occasionally from the French cooking and wines that they also venerated to experiment with other national cuisines, including traditional American dishes, during their monthly dinners and wine tastings.

The groups' approaches to ceremonies and rituals were also distinctive. While the WFS kept its focus on culinary matters, the Escoffier Society made a great deal out of minor changes in costume and the dinner ritual. The Tastevin went much farther. From the outset, the Burgundy founders invented a tradition by appropriating rituals and costumes from various sources to enhance the effect of their large-scale dinners in an impressive château.

In the postwar era, the gourmet dining movement left a legacy of two distinctive models of excellence. The Tastevin embedded dining activities in ceremonies highlighting Burgundy's regional and historical character and, under its New York leaders, worked closely with the best French chefs in the city to orchestrate splendid dinners in the French classical tradition. That experience contrasted sharply with the more frequent, but informal, activity of the core group of the Wine and Food Society of San Francisco (WFSSF). They dined at each other's homes or in small restaurants and created their own menus, often prepared by members of the core group.[5]

The experimentation by members of the WFSSF was not a coincidence. More men were taking up cooking as a hobby that was distinguished from women's work in preparing everyday meals. As weekend cooks entertaining friends or family, the men barbecued meat or prepared ethnic dishes. Cookbook authors encouraged male cooks by praising their natural aptitude for cooking. Already in 1929 *Good Housekeeping* presented cooking lessons for male readers, while in the following year Charles Browne, future director of the WFSNY, aimed his *Gun Club Cookbook* at male gourmets. It was only a short step to the 1939 founding of the Society of Amateur Chefs of America.[6]

In treating the expansion of the three major societies, I have considered only the oldest chapters in each organization. My intention is to focus on the origins of the three societies and the important changes they set in motion, while avoiding the confusion and superficial treatment that would result from exploring the histories of several dozen different chapters.

Origins of the Gourmet Dining Societies

André Simon, assisted by his friend and collaborator A. J. A. Symons, founded the Wine and Food Society in London in 1933; within a year, it grew to over one thousand members. The idea of expanding the Society to the United States came from Simon's 1934 talks with French officials, who hoped to exploit his success in selling wine to Anglo-Saxons and his reputation as a gourmet expert. They agreed to send him to America even though Simon intended to promote wine in general, rather than French wines in particular, while launching new chapters of his Wine and Food Society. Accordingly, Simon and his wife Edith set sail for the United States in November of 1934.[7]

As the Simons arrived in Manhattan, there was a great deal of ferment surrounding the repeal of Prohibition. Three gourmet society projects were at various stages of gestation and might have provided competition for the Wine and Food Society. Simon, however, bested the competition by winning support for his project from Frederick Wildman, the president of Bellows and Company. The two men understood that joining forces would advance their objectives. A strong WFS chapter in New York would boost Wildman's wine sales, while his contacts with members of leading New York social clubs provided a pool of potential recruits for the WFS.[8]

Once Wildman was on board, another important player, Julian Street, endorsed the new WFS. He already respected Simon's expertise and believed that he was "not narrow-mindedly a Frenchman." And he was no doubt much taken with Simon's considerable charm. Beyond that, Street, as a director of Bellows and Company, had a strong interest in solidifying his friendship with Wildman. In short order, Street became the first member of the WFS of New York and gave a key dinner party to introduce Simon to Henry Taft, as well as Woodrow Wilson's close advisor, Colonel Edward M. House. Taft was soon named the first president of the New York chapter.[9]

Wildman also joined the WFS and used Bellows' resources to strengthen the fledgling organization. On November 6, 1935, as the WFSNY prepared for its first dinner, Wildman hosted a luncheon for several New York journalists. The laudatory accounts of that event, written by G. Selmer Fougner and Lucius Beebe, put the WFSNY on the social agenda of elite New Yorkers interested in fine dining. Clearly, Beebe's enthusiasm for the WFSNY soared as he drank the Chateau Ausone 1831 served with a grilled breast of baby chicken at Wildman's lunch. "So rare, so holy a vintage was approached by all with reverence . . . We had not expected a miracle, but we got one."[10]

Simon followed the same approach he had used in New York to launch five other American chapters of the WFS in the winter of 1934/35. During his cross-country swing, he visited Boston, Chicago, San Francisco, Los Angeles, and New Orleans. In each city, he identified food professionals like Wildman with reputations as wine connoisseurs, who then introduced him to potential recruits for a new chapter of the WFS. From these recruits, Simon found an individual to serve as honorary secretary for the new WFS branch and, with his help, organized a first dinner to meet and greet prospective members.[11]

In establishing these new branches, the role of men's clubs was significant. Already, Simon had recruited fellow members of the Saintsbury and Ye Sette of Odd Volumes clubs in founding the WFS of London. To recruit their counterparts in the United States, he and his American friends followed the same course. Charles Browne, mayor of Princeton, organized a recruitment dinner, attended by 125 people at the University Club in New York. In Boston, Simon chose leaders for the new WFS chapter from Le Club des Arts Gastronomiques. Following the advice of the French Consulate in San Francisco, he approached Le Cercle de l'Union. In Los Angeles, it was the eventual honorary secretary Phil T. Hanna who recruited heavily from two small men's clubs to which he belonged; eleven Zamoranos and six Sunsetters eventually joined the WFSLA.[12]

Only three months after the New York chapter's inaugural dinner, the Wine and Food Society encountered serious competition from the newly organized Les Amis d'Escoffier. Its founder, G. Selmer Fougner, author of the *New York Sun* daily column "Along the Wine Trail," had initially been well disposed to the WFS. However, Fougner's authoritative pronouncements on culinary matters, for which he was known as "the Baron," rubbed many, including Simon, the wrong way. (Fougner's friend and fellow correspondent Lucius Beebe called him "a gusty and inflammatory personage.") In a letter to Julian Street, Simon remarked, "Poor Fougner is to my mind a vain and somewhat greedy jay with a few peacock feathers stuck in his tail: his croaking is worse than his bite." Simon had accordingly passed over Fougner in choosing the leaders of the New York branch of the WFS.[13]

Fougner's response was to create a rival gourmet society that drew most of its members from the American Culinary Federation. It was entirely appropriate for the ACF to honor Auguste Escoffier, who had died in 1935, since two of its leading officers, Joseph Donon and Charles Scotto, along with other members, had been trained by Escoffier. In addition to honoring their mentor, the founders expected the new society to enhance the prestige of all chefs, increase their job opportunities, "stimulate popular interest in fine food and wine," and provide an occasion for chefs and restaurant executives to enjoy having someone else plan and prepare a fine dinner. In order to keep the costs at $6 per person, however, they served only two wines with each meal. Meanwhile, the *Culinary Review*, the monthly newsletter of the ACF, agreed to reprint Fougner's *Sun* columns that publicized society dinners.[14]

Unmistakable signs of a rivalry between the two societies developed in 1936. Simon chided the chefs for making "friendship" the highest priority of the group, rather than fine dining, and regretted that spending was limited to $6 per person for each meal. The total, he argued, would be inadequate to dine in an Epicurean fashion of "extravagant luxury." How could they afford "nightingales' tongues" at that price? Ignoring the fact that the new society was composed largely of professional food types, Simon asserted that people of means and taste should be willing to pay more for fine dinners.[15]

The rivalry continued when the WFS, deliberately appropriating its rival's name and turf, held an Escoffier dinner in the fall of 1936 at the Pierre Hotel, whose chef was Charles Scotto, president of the American Culinary Federation; Fougner, in turn, rebuked the WFS in a column entitled "Imitation Is the Sincerest Form of Flattery" and, without naming names, identified the WFS as "the so-called gourmet group" that was operating on "a somewhat commercial basis." Not to be outdone, the Escoffier Society held its own dinner at the Pierre just two months after the WFSNY event. This rivalry caught the attention of Julian Street, who remarked to WFSNY president Taft, "A few other societies such as ours can do no harm, in fact I think it is all for the good of the cause if they are properly and knowingly conducted. I think ours is the best certainly, and hope it will remain so." André Simon concurred. Asserting that "indifference" was more dangerous than opposition, he proposed that the WFS exploit the opposition just as a sailboat uses a headwind to move forward. Meanwhile, from 1937 to 1939, the leaders of the Escoffier Society, following the example of the WFS, established chapters in Chicago, St. Louis, Boston, Washington, D.C., St. Paul, and New Orleans, thus making the society a national organization like its rival.[16]

On March 27, 1940, a third international gourmet society, the Burgundy-based Confrérie des Chevaliers du Tastevin, launched its American history with a dinner at the St. Regis Hotel in New York. Among those inducted into the society were wine dealers Charles Codman and Frederick Wildman, both members of the WFS, as well as journalists G. Selmer Fougner and Lucius Beebe, already members of the Escoffier Society. Believing that the advent of more societies would strengthen the cause of gourmet dining, wine and food professionals did their part in making each of these societies a viable entity by joining two or more of them.[17]

The founders of the Burgundy-based Tastevin intended to raise the sagging sales of Burgundy wine by creating their new organization on November 16, 1934, a day after André Simon sailed to America to establish the WFS. Two men from Nuits St. Georges, Camille Rodier, author of several books on Burgundy wines and secretary general of the local tourist office, and Georges Faiveley, whose family owned Burgundy vineyards, promoted their product at home and abroad by linking it to regional history and culture. They held the Society dinners incorporating Burgundy dishes and wines in a medieval chateau.[18]

Recognizing the potential of the U.S. market, the Tastevin invited William C. Bullitt, the American Ambassador to France, to attend its spring 1937 dinner, where he was inducted into the society. The man responsible for bringing Bullitt to Nuits St. Georges was the Franco-Swiss entrepreneur Jules Bohy, owner of the Hotel Bohy-Lafayette in Paris, where many American veterans had stayed. Worried about the future of the Tastevin in the event of war and hoping to stimulate wine sales, Faiveley and Rodier authorized Bohy to establish a Tastevin organization in America. One week before the outbreak of World War II, Bohy embarked on the *Normandie* for a three-week stay that was extended to six years.[19]

Between June 1940 and Pearl Harbor, Bohy organized three New York dinners after his St. Regis debut, and one in New Orleans. Following the practices of most other gourmet leaders, he suspended further meetings of the Tastevin until the outcome of the war seemed clear. Despite the interruption of the war years, however, all three societies prepared to renew their dinners in the postwar period.[20]

Rules, Rituals, and Practices

There was a rough consensus among gourmet practitioners about how they ought to behave during society dinners. While each society, and sometimes chapters within societies, put its own stamp on practices and principles, several written documents codified these rules for members. The most definitive of these guides was "A Gourmet's Code of Modern Dining," written by J. George

Frederick, the founder of the New York Gourmet Society, and Roy Alciatore. In addition, the Escoffier Society prepared a constitution and bylaws, while Simon's recruitment brochure and the Los Angeles branch's short written document spell out WFS expectations for decorum. With exceptions noted, the following practices and principles were accepted by both national and local gourmet groups.[21]

The WFS and the Escoffier Society called for the improvement of "food, wine and the arts of the table" through the creation of dining societies. To reach this goal, both societies set high standards for their dinners and strongly emphasized the distinction between the gourmet, who pursued a cuisine of high quality, and the gourmand, who was solely interested in quantity. All three societies forbad the consumption of whisky and the practice of smoking before and during the meals, because they dulled the palate. In addition, the Tastevin and the Escoffier societies refused to serve water at the table so as to give proper homage to the French wines that were served. Inasmuch as the chef determined the flavor of each dish, salt, pepper, and condiments were also absent from the table.[22]

Of course, there were disagreements among practitioners about elements of this code. Despite the ban on whiskey, G. Selmer Fougner was proud of his three thousand cocktail recipes, many of which he presented in *Scribner's*, while Lucius Beebe defended the cocktail as "representative of the most civilized and urbane habits of American tosspots." Although he enjoyed wine, Beebe deplored the "postured sniffing of debatable vintage years" and sneered at André Simon for ordering "a bowl of flowers removed [from the table] because it obliterated the bouquet of the Chateau Latour '20."[23]

As important as the quality of the food was the environment for gourmet dining. To honor the food, and out of respect for fellow diners, the Escoffier bylaws stipulated that diners arrive on time or risk missing the courses already served. Once launched, meals were to proceed in a leisurely fashion so as to encourage social interactions. As the *Chicago Daily Tribune* explained in 1935, gourmet diners were seeking "slower, better meals" accompanied by lively conversation in a quiet atmosphere, uninterrupted by music, dancing, or speeches. To assure such an environment, the Escoffier Society, following in the footsteps of the Club des Cent and the British upper class, forbad conversations about politics, religion, and business affairs. The society also enjoined diners to remain silent as each new dish was served and banned speeches during and after meals. Despite this rule, Selmer Fougner delivered lectures on gastronomy during desserts that "lasted as long as there was a bottle of vintage cognac convenient to (his) hand." For a dinner-ending ceremony during which the chef was invited to receive the applause of diners and a critical review of his creations, the Tastevin and Escoffier societies made an exception.[24]

To pay homage to the excellence of the cuisine, there were strict rules about dress. WFS members dined in black tie and dinner jacket, while the Tastevin required at first a white tie to increase the level of formality. As for the Escoffier Society, members dressed in business suits, protected by bibs tucked into their collars.[25]

The gourmet societies rotated dinners from one prestigious club or hotel restaurant to another so long as they could accommodate the membership of a group that ranged from fifty to three hundred. The Escoffier Society gathered twice a year for their banquets, while the WFS chapters usually held one dinner a month except for the summer season. In addition to one official dinner per

Escoffier dinner at the Waldorf-Astoria, New York City, on the centennial of Auguste Escoffier's birth, from *Life*, December 23, 1946, p. 41. Copyright Allan Grant. Used with permission. All Rights Reserved.

year, Tastevin chapters could add other unofficial dinners and tastings, but the setting of these events was a far cry from those of the parent organization. For the picturesque cellar of the Château Clos de Vougeot, Americans substituted "dignified" spaces in leading hotels furnished with platforms on which to conduct the induction ceremonies. To experience a "chapitre" (official gathering), Americans could travel to Burgundy.[26]

The size of chapters varied. By 1936, the New York chapter of the WFS had five hundred members and an attendance, including members and guests, that reached 337 for a dinner at the Hotel Pierre in 1936 and 532 for a champagne tasting at the Ritz-Carlton in 1939. The opening tasting of the Boston branch at the Somerset Hotel in December 1936 attracted 150 members and guests, as did the "perfect dinner" at the Copley Plaza on March 15, 1937. With a limit of fifty members in Chicago and one hundred in San Francisco and Los Angeles, dinners were more intimate. In order not to turn away prospective members after the chapter reached one hundred, Los Angeles created a waiting list. While the Escoffier Society limited membership to one hundred in all but the Chicago chapter (fifty), each member could invite a guest to chapter dinners. After World War II, Tastevin branches ranged in size from twenty-five to more than a hundred members in New York City.[27]

In addition to their famous bibs, members of the Escoffier Society honored their patron in various ways. In the Sheraton Park dining room in Washington, "a silver fountain spilled water softly at one end of the room, while just behind the head of the table, Escoffier ruled the room—from his white-draped portrait." In Chicago, diners set a place at a table in the center of the room with a black-draped chair where waiters paused to offer each course for inspection before serving the guests. At the spring 1937 Escoffier dinner in New York, waiters unveiled a wax bas-relief of the great chef sculpted by his wife. Diners were suitably moved by the occasion.[28]

At least two branches of the Wine and Food Society, New York and San Francisco, paid special attention to the printing of menus. Most notable was the artistry of the San Francisco menu designers. As for New York, the eight-page menu for the inaugural dinner in November 1935 featured a cover illustration of chefs grilling wild game in medieval times. Inside was the customary list of courses and wines along with recipes for each of the dishes.[29]

Among the three societies, the Tastevin alone developed a hierarchical organization with appropriate titles for different ranks, as well as a much stronger emphasis on ceremony and ritual, especially in its initiation of new members. This was a short theatrical production with members as witnesses, while the officers and inductees performed on stage. The Tastevin banner provided the backdrop; props included a wine barrel, mallets, a root of the vine, and a large goblet. To the strains of Verdi's Triumphal March, officers in red and yellow robes marched to the stage, where the Tastevin's highest official waited. He, in turn, asked each initiate to come forward and strike the wine barrel three times with a wooden mallet; the inductee then swore to "lead a gastronomic life with irreproachable wine habits," to "empty the wine glass when filled and to fill it when emptied as prescribed by Notre bon Maître François Rabelais," and to "contribute with all your winy power to the active propagation of French wines in general and of those of Burgundy in particular." Initiates then drank from the cup of honor, which "contains the well being of the body and the happiness of the soul. This great wine, which gives us youth and lifts from our shoulders the weight of the years, which lightens the burden of cares and memories from our souls . . . Par Bacchus, par Noé père de la vigne (by Noah, father of the vine), par St. Vincent, patron des vignerons (by St. Vincent, patron of wine growers). Nous vous armons (elevate) chevaliers du Tastevin." The presiding officer then struck the candidates' shoulders three times with a root of the vine and embraced each of them, while bestowing the token of membership, the tastevin attached to a red and gold ribbon. Following this ritual, one of the new initiates delivered a short speech in behalf of the others. And then, as was customary at the Clos de Vougeot, diners performed the "Ban Bourguignon" (a Burgundian chant for happy occasions that includes hand-clapping and twisting of hands over the head and the singing of "la-la-la").[30]

Ceremonies did not always go as planned. At the December 1941 induction, Jules Bohy, wielding the vine root, tapped Lucius Beebe on the head rather than the shoulders, precipitating laughter from the audience. Beebe, in turn, misfired as he drank wine from the silver chalice and soiled his white shirt. Thus, an evening that began with "formal grandeur" ended, in Beebe's words, with "glad whoops and banshee screams."[31]

In the late 1940s, Tastevin rehearsal dinners were also occasions for examining new candidates. The examination, which required a knowledge of the seven-page Burgundy section of William Bird's *French Wines*, would not have dimmed the festivities. Candidates who knew the names of one red wine and one white wine from the Côte de Beaune and the Côte du Nuits and could tell which one they preferred and why were on course to pass the 1949 exam.[32]

Given the general agreement on principles and practices between the three major societies, rituals excepted, it is not surprising that journalists sometimes confused them. One reported that the WFS asked its members to tuck their napkins under their chins and forbad the discussion of politics, religion, and business, when, in fact, these were Escoffier Society rules.[33]

Wine Dealers and Producers

The three gourmet societies struggled in various ways to achieve their independence from the wine industry. Even the Escoffier Society, which banned wine dealers from membership to escape any hint of dependency, permitted them to attend society dinners as guests. Furthermore, although the Wine and Food Society never directly promoted wine, dealers and producers joined the various chapters at least in part to cultivate relationships with individual members and the organization that might result in future sales. From the outset, a practice developed in the WFS that was potentially compromising for both sides. Wine dealers and/ or producers supplied wines without charge to their fellow members for tastings and dinners. In the process, it became more difficult for members of the WFS to offer honest opinions about the quality of the wine and for the dealers to pretend that their relationship with the WFS was disinterested.[34]

For that reason, WFS chapters tried to control the damages by providing that dealers and producers were entitled to individual but not corporate membership and were not to serve on governing councils. To assure its independence, the WFSLA tracked the proportion of dealers to the total membership. According to Honorary Secretary Phil Hanna, only half a dozen of its one hundred members were "financially interested" in wine. Many among those who had no such interest made substantial donations of wine until, in 1939, the chapter created its own cellar. San Francisco soon followed suit.[35]

Nonetheless, the two California chapters tied themselves so closely to the state's wine industry that they risked becoming unofficial public relations agents for the producers. The link between chapters and producers was the Wine Institute, run by Leon Adams, which California growers had established; Adams and his close friend Maynard Amerine, an oenologist at the University of California, Davis, were both members of the WFSSF. Together with wine producers, they assured donations of California wine to many chapter dinners and wine tastings; in the process they succeeded in securing the unofficial support of some members of the WFSSF for their ongoing campaign to spread the consumption of California wines. As World War II approached, members of the San Francisco society organized tastings of California wines at the Golden Gate International Exposition and served as judges of competitions among the wine makers.[36]

Meanwhile, the WFSSF supported the efforts of eastern dealers to fill the vacuum that would follow the end of European wine imports during World War II with California wines. Among the most interested were Frank Schoonmaker and Julian Street, both of whom had written successful wine manuals at the time of repeal that devoted a chapter to California wines and were themselves involved in the promotion of wine sales. In 1938, Schoonmaker toured California, identified its best wines, and agreed to designate them "Frank Schoonmaker Selections," a step that promised great rewards for their producers. However, he exacted a price. Winemakers who labeled their wines with the names of European regions (e.g., Burgundy) would have to renounce this practice and identify them according to the region where they were produced and the predominant grape used in making the wine.[37]

The WFSSF immediately took note of the recognition of two Inglenook wines, a 1933 Napa cabernet and a 1933 Johannisberg Riesling, as "Frank Schoonmaker Selections." Harold Price, honorary secretary of the WFSSF, with support from Amerine and Adams, arranged a special WFS dinner that included the two wines selected by Schoonmaker and some nineteenth-century vintages. The dinner not only honored Inglenook but encouraged Frank Schoonmaker in his pioneering venture.[38]

Martin Ray's Paul Masson winery found its champion in Julian Street, who was advising Bellows and Company about palatable American wines. After tasting Ray's pinot noir, Street immediately telegraphed Ray: "your pinot noir 1936 tasted tonight is first American red wine I ever drank with entire pleasure." As Street explained to Harold Price, he now believed that California could produce "admirable, pure, unadulterated, uncooked, unfooled-with wines of excellent quality—wines that a critical person can truly enjoy." At Price's urging, the WFSSF recognized Ray's achievement with a special dinner featuring Masson cabernet sauvignon 1936 and the now famous Masson pinot noir 1936.[39]

The WFSSF promotion of California wines went further. In 1939, Adams and Amerine urged members of the WFSSF, who were doctors, to launch the Society for the Medical Friends of Wine. Modeled on the Médecins Amis du Vin, a French gourmet society, it was populated by doctors who advocated the moderate consumption of wine as a health measure; however, despite its French origins, the Society almost always served California wine. After each dinner, a speaker presented research on the effects of wine on the human body and related topics. In the near future, Adams and Amerine hoped to organize similar societies for engineers and lawyers in other cities, but they never implemented their plan.[40]

Since the New York chapter of the WFS drank mostly imported wines, members dealt more frequently with wine dealers than producers. Indeed, Jeanne Owen, French widow of an American businessman, cookbook author, and honorary secretary of the WFSNY, organized dealers to ante up "cash and kind" for tastings of "almost Oriental magnificence." Owen reminded officers of the society that only the generosity of the dealers, who provided all the wine for tastings and dinners, kept the treasury in the black. Even so, members of the WFSNY were confident that, with donations from a dozen or more dealers, no one of them could use the Society for commercial purposes. Still, in 1955, André Simon described the WFSNY as "a first-class highly successful sales promotion organization." Clearly, the chapter fell short of his expectations.[41]

The situation of the Tastevin was even more delicate, since the organization was designed to promote the consumption of Burgundy wines. Indeed, Gordon Brown, the treasurer of the New York Tastevin, asserted in 1945 that the group was both a "club for gentlemen who appreciate the value and enjoyment of wine" and a trade association indirectly advancing the interests of the wine trade. This dual identity, in turn, posed a potential conflict of interest, since Tastevin leaders, including Rodier, Faiveley, and Bohy, profited from the production and sale of Burgundy wine, as did many of the American officers who were engaged in the food and wine business. Brown, who enjoyed the "priceless . . . prestige" of the Tastevin, worried that the members might become "unwittingly involved in somebody's wine business."[42]

Among other things, Brown objected to the exclusive rights granted to Dreyfus, Ashby and Co. to import Burgundy wines especially designated as "Confrérie selections." He argued that Bohy should either open this trade to all American importers or obtain their endorsement of the monopoly. Without explanation, the French leaders of the Tastevin rejected Brown's proposal, thus leaving Dreyfus as the sole importer of these wines.[43]

In response to Brown's protest, Bohy claimed that since the 1930s the sale of Confrérie wines had been a prerogative of the society's governing body. He acknowledged that Faiveley and Rodier headed wine firms and that six members of the governing council served as blind tasters for the Confrérie selections. However, the Tastevin owned no vineyards and was not "run as a Business Firm but as an Association of connoisseurs and lovers of fine wines and good food." To be sure, the organization made a small profit on wine sales but used the money for society expenses.[44]

Nonetheless, Brown's concerns had some merit. Bohy was "the primary representative of several Burgundian wine organizations" and had worked with

Dreyfus, Ashby and Co. as a wine salesman since 1940. At a meeting of the society's governing body in 1949, Bohy admitted that he was importing 910 cases of wine per year, including the Confrérie selections he sold to various Tastevin leaders, and he insisted that such wines be served at Confrérie dinners. In addition, Bohy also marketed Tastevin wine glasses, with or without the society's insignia, to members and hotels.[45]

American leaders never decided whether the Confrérie's involvement in the wine trade was a conflict of interest. It seems clear, however, that the volume of trade was insufficient to worry most members of the society or wine importers who continued to collaborate with the Tastevin. Compared with the overall sales of Burgundy wines, which increased during the 1950s, Tastevin's share was a small one.[46]

The Dining Experience: Classical French Menus

No issue could be more important to a gourmet society than the selection of food and wine to serve at its dinners. The pioneers of the movement, among whom French expatriates played a large role, hoped to rescue dining in America from the clutches of the food establishment by modeling French cuisine for Americans. Even so, the three major societies and branches within those societies had different ideas about exactly what role French cuisine should play and to what extent there was a place for other cuisines at the societies' dinners. Two different approaches were represented. The Tastevin and the Escoffier societies, consistent with their mission, showcased *haute cuisine* at all their dinners and served only French wine, while branches of the WFS pursued a more eclectic approach. They featured French, mostly *haute, cuisine* for the majority of their dinners, but they also tried other national cuisines and wines. To illustrate these practices, I will provide some examples of representative meals for each of the three societies and discuss in greater detail several outstanding dinners. It would, unfortunately, take another book to present the menus of the numerous branches of all three gourmet societies.

In pursuing their goals, the three societies relied heavily on restaurants in large hotels with well-trained French chefs in the kitchen, who were capable of serving a gourmet dining group of from fifty to several hundred prominent men—and occasionally women. In so doing, they had much to gain or lose, since the societies evaluated the meals they prepared and publicized the results in local, and occasionally national, media.

French chefs in the United States, especially in large hotels, did not await the founding of the dining societies to offer French cuisine to patrons, many of whom were already accustomed to it. Indeed, their dinner menus often listed French dishes and wines alongside American options. Following the major headings on such hotel menus, a prospective diner was likely to find dishes that were regularly available in tourist restaurants in France, although no single restaurant offered all the choices listed below. Under soups, diners could choose from *petite marmite, onion au gratin*, and leek and potato. Among fish dishes, sole, roe, or trout prepared *à la meunière* (lightly floured, fried in butter, with lemon juice, *noisette* butter, and parsley), as well as mussels, sole, turbot, and trout, all prepared *à la Marguery* (cooked in white wine and fish stock thickened with egg and butter), were available. So were frog legs prepared *à la Provençal*, while veal kidney and chicken, as well as sole, were cooked *à la bonne femme* (with bacon, small onions, and potato balls). Restaurants served *Béarnaise* as a sauce for New York sirloin, tenderloin, and sole; diners could also choose clams, chicken livers, tripe, and sirloin in a Bordeaux sauce. Somewhat more exotic was sweetbreads *financière* (with chicken quenelles, cockscombs, truffles, mushrooms, Madeira, chicken consommé, and *sauce espagnol*). Typically, Brie and Camembert were listed under cheeses, while desserts ranged from *crêpes suzette, poire melba, meringue glacé*, and *oeufs à la neige* to assorted French pastry. Thus, well before the founding of dining societies, most French chefs were serving basic French dishes.[47]

Of course, these chefs could, if requested to do so, offer a variety of other French dishes to their more receptive and knowledgeable guests, including members of the dining societies. Even so, the latter's fare, in general, was not adventurous. Many society dinners featured the best cuts of beef, including tenderloin and filet mignon, as well as crowns or saddles of lamb; however, despite the prominence of red meat, more fowl than beef or lamb was served. Wild ducks and partridge, as well as domestic game birds, including guinea hen, Cornish game hen, and squab, were popular. Members dined on rabbit on several occasions, while venison, veal, pork, and organ meats appeared occasionally as main courses.[48]

Some gourmet diners regarded these menu choices as insufficiently imaginative. In a letter inviting members of the WFSSF to a 1940 Bordelais dinner at which lamb was served, the physician Marius Francoz urged the society to "get away from the proverbial food that one generally gets at a banquet and to omit chicken, steak, and roast beef." Judging from subsequent menus, the society ignored this advice, although lamb was frequently served.[49]

Among the three gourmet societies, Les Amis d'Escoffier followed their mentor's advice by simplifying the lavish meals of the late Victorian period to

"set an example that can be followed by the rank and file of American amateurs," whose stomachs and budgets would not withstand the consumption of
"whole boiled turtles, nests of plover's eggs, flocks of ortolans, etc." Accordingly,
they chose dishes from the repertoire of French *haute cuisine*, including one of
Escoffier's signature dishes at each event, as well as one of the specialties of the
host chef.[50]

From the founding of the society in 1935, G. Selmer Fougner was certain that
the Escoffier group was on the road "to become the high authority and final arbiter in all matters epicurean." In addition, he knew that the diners were quite
up to the task because they were "the best known chefs of America." The fullest
realization of Fougner's hopes for the society must have been the celebrated
fourth dinner of the Escoffier group at the Hotel Pierre in January 1937. According to the Baron, "rarely has the magic of fine cookery been demonstrated with
greater perfection than was done on that memorable night." It was, without
question, traditional French cuisine featuring one of Escoffier's favorite recipes,
the *Poularde Rose de Mai* (chicken breast served with a tomato mousse), accompanied by a *reserve du cardinal* 1928 (Burgundy). However, the presentation of
this dish on the trial run two days before the dinner caused a ruckus. One member of the Bonne Bouche (tasty mouthful) dinner committee, believing that the
molded chicken in the center of the platter was made of papier mâché, sum-
moned Chef Scotto from the kitchen to reprimand him for violating Escoffier's
rule that decorations must be edible. Scotto scornfully responded that the
chicken had been sculpted from tomato mousse.[51]

While the Escoffier Society received good marks from critics in the New York
press, the culinary performance of the more affluent Tastevin, which could afford to serve a greater variety of fine wines, was more noteworthy. Among various acclaimed dinners held by the Tastevin, Clementine Paddleford of the *Herald Tribune* singled out the May 1948 event as "one of the great dinners of the
year." From records in the society archives, it is possible to reconstruct the planning process from start to finish and thus to understand the ingredients, material and otherwise, that went into creating the dinner. Memos and menus clarify
the collaboration between Chef Louis Diat of the Ritz-Carlton and Gordon
Brown, treasurer of the New York Tastevin and chair of the dinner committee,
in achieving success.[52]

The first and most important decision for the committee was to choose
wines for the event. Accordingly, at its first meeting, Brown set a date for a wine
tasting, after which the committee discussed menu options and locations for
the dinner. Five members of the dinner committee, the presidents of Julius

Wile and Peter Greig importing firms, and three members of the French embassy attended a blind tasting at the offices of Julius Wile and Sons. To choose two Burgundy wines, one each from the regions of Beaune and Côte de Nuits, the tasters eliminated ten of the twelve wines, only to realize that they had selected two from Beaune; a second tasting was necessary to select a Côte de Nuits.[53]

At the second dinner committee meeting, convened two months before the event, members chose the Ritz-Carlton Hotel as the dinner site and clarified menu options. There followed negotiations with the hotel to determine the cost of the meal, including wines, and a date for a rehearsal dinner at least ten days ahead of the actual event to allow time for a second rehearsal dinner if needed. Brown reported to the hotel the number of diners who would attend the occasion and the Society's rules for decorum and service. He also arranged the seating, publicity, initiation ceremony, and menu printing.[54]

Using the selection of wines to guide the choice of dishes, the committee presented the resulting menu to Chef Diat in time for him to prepare the rehearsal dinner. On that occasion, committee members found the dishes tasty but sought replacements that were more seasonal, more suited to the wines, and more appropriate to the order of the dishes in the meal. According to Brown, the stuffed sole had too strong a flavor so that it broke the "upward trend of taste enjoyment" that was to culminate in the asparagus Hollandaise. To remedy this problem, the committee eliminated the fish stuffing in favor of a milder Bercy butter preparation (with shallots, beef marrow, and white wine, etc.). Because lamb and new potatoes were in season, the members replaced the saddle of veal with a baron of lamb that would be served with fresh peas. On the dessert front, Brown rejected "the more elaborate and rich *Savarin*" (a rum-flavored cake filled with cream and fruit) in favor of *glace vanille aux fraises parisiennes* (vanilla ice cream with Parisian strawberries) that were then in season. The strawberries would be soaked in Grand Marnier for twenty-four hours. Given these substantial revisions, Brown invited the committee to a second rehearsal to test the new dessert and the compatibility of the revamped fish and meat courses with the accompanying Corton Charlemagne 1937 (a white wine) and the Musigny Comte de Vogüe 1937 (red).[55]

The luncheon was a great success. Brown reported the committee's "enthusiasm" for the pairings of the wines with their respective fish and meat courses. However, he proposed another meeting to test two preparations of the strawberries—either with all or half of the berries soaked in Grand Marnier. As for the asparagus, Brown maintained that six stalks constituted a serving "small enough to leave one wishing there would be one more stalk, yet not so large as to spoil the effect of the next course."[56]

Once the menu was set, Brown sent out detailed instructions about service and decorum. He wanted to set the right tone by assuring a warm welcome to diners, as if they were arriving at a private home. To prevent smoking before the end of the dinner, he also urged members to introduce their guests to officers on the council who could deter the "absent-minded" from reaching for a cigarette.[57]

The proper serving of wine was also a high priority for Brown. Each guest should have as much Corton Charlemagne as he wanted, but waiters should guard against wasting the wine. As for the red wines, the Beaune Noirot Carrière 1937 and the Musigny should be opened an hour before the meal. Just ahead of the lamb course, waiters were to pour a single glass per guest from the bottle of Beaune placed in a basket to avoid disturbing the sediment; only after the guests had drunk the Beaune should the Musigny be poured. And, following each pouring, waiters were to right the bottles to prevent dripping and thus to leave the "impression that the wine is precious."[58]

In addition, Brown invited Chef Diat to join the diners after dessert and drink a glass of Musigny with them. After a toast from the members, Roy Alicatore would critique the meal and give Diat a chance to respond. Brown regarded this interchange as an opportunity for members to take a more active role in the proceedings, but he also wanted the commentator to offer a measured appraisal rather than the harsh review that Chef Lugot of the Waldorf received after the fall 1947 dinner. Following the exchange between Diat and Alciatore, members of the council would depart to don their robes for the ceremonial portion of the evening.[59]

While the planning documents suggest a highly organized and orderly event, Brown knew that, as the evening wore on, diners would reach various stages of inebriation. The singing would become increasingly festive, the oratory excessive. And he worried that once the officers drank with initiates other members would resent the council "taking advantage of their position to get an extra gulp of good wine." "Cat-calls and other disruption of the ceremonies from the balance of the conclave who at that juncture are full of everything including Cognac and Champagne" would ensue as they did at the St. Regis in December of 1948. A "voluntary communion to partake of the cup that was held in readiness for them" provoked unruly behavior on that occasion.[60]

Most members were happy to leave the planning of the New York dinners in the hands of Brown, but not Lucius Beebe. Writing "from the stomach," he complained that the Society supplied too little food and wine and too much ritual and oratory for the high cost of the dinners. In his view, each diner should be served two bottles of wine and two pounds of beef to assure that no one left the proceeding either "sober or hungry." In response, Brown reminded Beebe that the Tastevin was founded to promote the culture and wine of Burgundy, not simply to eat and drink. Moreover, diners would have to pay higher fees for more food and wine. All the same, Beebe made his point. At the next dinner, Brown instructed the manager of the Hotel Pierre to serve Beebe a "larger portion" of fish.[61]

The mercurial Beebe had apparently changed his mind two years later. He reported in *Gourmet* that the spring 1949 Tastevin dinner at the Pierre Hotel under the direction of Chef Manuel Orta was "a gustatory tour de force which is still reverently spoken of by those who attended it." The *Chateaubriand marchand de vin* (a butter sauce flavored with red wine and shallots) accompanied by a Clos de Vougeot 1937 was "the gustatory capstone of the evening" and caused Jules Bohy "to swoon presumably with rapture." By giving "equal billing" to food and wine, Americans had outdone their French progenitors who made wines the focus of their dinners. Having abandoned his appeal for more food and drink, Beebe acclaimed Escoffier for eliminating the "indiscriminate profusion" of French cuisine in the nineteenth century so that diners could enjoy "a few perfect and harmonious dishes."[62]

Serving a suckling pig, La Confrérie des Chevaliers du Tastevin dinner, Chateau Clos du Vougeot, France, from *La Confrérie des Chevaliers du Tastevin* (Paris: Éditions E.P.I.C., 1950), p. 81. La Confrérie des Chevaliers du Tastevin.

Every chapter of the Wine and Food Society engaged in culinary eclecticism, but none matched the WFSLA, which, within a month of its founding, promised that dinners would be "international in their scope, including menus and wines typical of France, Germany, Italy, Spain, Sweden, and the United States, etc." While the Los Angeles group fully implemented its program, the WFSSF embraced a more restrained version of eclecticism, which the Society exhibited during a California dinner at the Palace Hotel featuring Alameda County wines for a dinner mixing Italian and French dishes.[63]

Among the biggest differences between the California societies and other WFS groups was the members' involvement in cooking their own dinners and in weekend jaunts to California vineyards. Los Angeles held its first such dinner in 1936, followed a few months later by the San Francisco branch. These dinners promoted closer friendships between the members, while improving cooking skills. In 1939, the Los Angeles and San Francisco chapters joined forces for

WFSSF members prepare their own dinner, California Golf Club, Baden, California, April 15, 1941. The Wine and Food Society of San Francisco.

their members' dinner, prepared by chefs from both groups, at the Sonoma Inn as part of the vineyard tour. While amateur chefs were emerging on the East Coast at this time, none of them turned gourmet society events into an opportunity for a collective cooking enterprise.[64]

As World War II approached, however, the two societies began to go their separate ways. What drove them apart was the ignorance of the WFSLA members about French food and wines, based, in part, on the absence of established French restaurants in Los Angeles, whose chefs could instruct them. On one occasion, the chapter dropped plans to serve a Creole meal because the unnamed chef could not cook it. On another, John Shaw, who was responsible for organizing a Bordeaux dinner, proposed false labeling of one dish: "Any good, sound, and distinctive French dishes will do and we could attach a Bordelaise nomenclature to them." A decade later, the chapter served the following menu at the Lakeside country club: deviled crabs en Ramequins à la Northeast harbor, Maine; *vol au vent* (round puffed pastry, but no filling specified); a Caesar salad (recently invented in Mexico); a *Savoy surprise* (no ingredients identified); and gin and tonic (on the beverage list). It was an odd pairing of dishes and drinks. Five years later at the Beverly Hills Hotel, menu planners put the cheese course immediately after the hors d'oeuvres and followed artichoke hearts with guava jelly. No wonder wine expert Roy Brady, a member of the WFSLA, remarked that "preciosity and rejoicing ignorance reach their finest flower" in the American branches of the WFS. Some have an "uncontrollable impulse to scatter 'le' and 'la' through the menu in wild abandon," and to serve immature red wines. Brady was surely expressing the same frustration with the WFSLA approach to gourmet dining as the San Franciscans must have experienced fifteen years earlier.[65]

By contrast, the Wine and Food Society of San Francisco took great care in planning menus and evaluating wines. Wine experts educated other members in the etiquette of wine drinking and the standards for judging wines. To develop members' taste, the wine committee held blind tastings. Often, wines were evaluated by numerical ratings and/or written and verbal comments. However, even the most reputable wines sometimes disappointed expectations.[66]

After the war, joint visits to California vineyards with the Los Angeles chapter were less frequent; the society also downplayed promotional activities for the California wine industry and established its own wine cellar. Tastings of California wines continued, but they were outnumbered by those devoted to French, German, and Italian wines, the latter arranged through the appropriate consulates to educate both members and guests. At the same time, the WFSSF gave increasing attention to gastronomy in France by sponsoring vintage tours in 1949 and 1952 that established links with gourmets on the East Coast and in France, thus helping to nationalize and internationalize the gourmet movement. By the late 1950s, membership in the WFSSF had become "one of the most sought-after distinctions in the city."[67]

The Dining Experience: Heirs to Brillat-Savarin

Mastering the skills necessary to cook gourmet meals, a core group of the Wine and Food Society of San Francisco took turns preparing dinners for each other or eating together in local restaurants. This group of a dozen or so members of the WFSSF was pioneering a model of gourmet dining that stood in stark contrast to the approach of the New York Tastevin. At their small, unofficial dinners, the San Franciscans adopted Brillat-Savarin's vision of a dozen diners from diverse backgrounds gathering over a well-planned meal in a calm and attractive environment to experience the pleasures of the table and solidify friendships with each other. In the process, they prepared familiar dishes, experimented with new ones, and considered

Charles Pierre Mathé hosts selected members of the WFSSF at the Bohemian Club, November 5, 1940. The Wine and Food Society of San Francisco.

a variety of wine pairings with each dish. Joined by their appreciation of gourmet dining, the core group enlivened the official dinners of the WFSSF as well.[68]

Among the most active participants in this coterie was the honorary secretary of the WFSSF, attorney Harold Price, who kept a wine cellar at home and a library of culinary classics that he later lent to M. F. K. Fisher. Two dentists made different contributions to the group. George Selleck developed a national reputation as an amateur chef, while Raoul Blanquie, a good chef in his own right, was the son of the owner of Jack's, one of San Francisco's best French restaurants.

Paris-born Michel Weill, a charter member of the society and nephew of Raphael, founder of the White House Department Store in San Francisco, was an amateur gourmet only slightly less celebrated than his uncle. Other active members included James Howe, a journalist and gentleman farmer whose beat was Europe during and after World War I; Chaffee Hall, the founder of Hallcrest in 1941, a vineyard in the Santa Cruz Mountains that supplied wine to the Waldorf Astoria; Jeff F. Smith, a key figure in the evolution of the Cercle de l'Union; Robert Sproul, then president of the University of California; and attorney Farnham Griffiths, who served on the University's Board of Regents. In addition, Leon Adams, Maynard Amerine, and Salvatore Lucia, a wine researcher at the University of California, San Francisco, provided the society with significant expertise on wine.[69]

The success of this experiment in self-directed gourmet dining owed much to the culinary scene in San Francisco. As Julian Street noted, "the character of the people" of San Francisco created a hospitable site for gourmet dining that encouraged the proliferation of good restaurants staffed by fine chefs from whom chapter leaders learned much about French cuisine. The latter's competence was recognized by both Julian Street, who believed that the WFSSF was "doing the best of the lot [of WFS chapters]," and André Simon, who enthused that it "has gone from strength to strength."[70]

Following the practice of the two California societies, core members of the WFSSF featured a hands-on approach in a more intimate setting. Participants often contributed the ingredients for the dinner, toiled over the stove or the barbecue pit, and served the wines. Both James Howe and Chaffee Hall produced their own wine from grapes that they grew, and on occasion Howe brought to dinner pheasants that he raised. Meanwhile, George Selleck, Raoul Blanquie, and Maynard Amerine, all excellent cooks, often prepared dinners for six to ten friends. As for the traditional task of selecting and serving wines from their own cellars, Jeff Smith and Harold Price, among others, were happy to oblige.[71]

This hands-on approach and the growing esprit de corps in the society encouraged the transformation of dinner menus, especially those designed for small, informal occasions attended by a core group of the society. So did the presence in the city of several art presses, especially the Grabhorn, and the interest of George Holl in designing innovative menus. Holl, art director for West Coast Fox theaters and a society member, had received the Julian Medal as a student at the Art Institute in San Francisco, lived in Paris for several years after World War I, and designed 121 menus for the WFSSF. These menus and others enhanced the pleasures of taste and smell associated with fine dining by exploiting the shapes and colors of food, wine, and the pastoral landscape where they were produced along with table settings to appeal to the visual sense of diners. Depending on the occasion, artists transformed the menu into an accordion, a wine cask butt, or a map of France. Unfortunately, the names of the printers and designers who followed Holl are not known (see color gallery).[72]

An excellent example of this artistry was a menu inserted in the folds of an accordion, an instrument commonly used in Italian popular music. In addition to the list of courses for an Italian dinner, the menu presented two scenes drawn in Italian Renaissance style, one depicting the production of wine in a rural setting, the other a dinner in Florence with the Palacio Vecchio in the background.

The man most responsible for the coterie's energetic pursuit of the pleasures of the table was George Selleck. Both official postwar members' dinners and smaller affairs that he hosted and attended reflected his influence. As one member remarked, "a dinner at [the] Sellecks is the perennial promise of a gastronomic adventure." Often, however, Selleck shared the hosting responsibilities at friends' homes, as when they entertained Alexander Woollcott, *New Yorker* drama critic, member of the Algonquin Circle, and the lead actor in Hart and Kaufman's *The Man Who Came to Dinner* (1939). Serving as an invitation, the playbill announced that there would be no performance on March 31, 1940, because "the man who came to dinner is going out to dinner"—out indeed, to dine with members of the WFSSF at the home of James Howe. Apparently, Woollcott bristled when he heard that the festivities would continue until midnight and defiantly ordered his chauffer to pick him up at 10 p.m. To his surprise, the meal was so delicious and his hosts so gracious that he stayed well past midnight to regale them with stories of Gertrude Stein and Eleanor Roosevelt, while the chauffer waited in Howe's driveway. The dinner itself was presented as a theatrical performance, with the cast including viticulturist Amerine and counselor Price. As chef, Selleck prepared a *selle d'agneau au carré* (saddle and breast of lamb) with which sommelier Raoul Blanquie paired a Chateau La Mission Haut Brion 1923. A Chambertin Charmes 1929 accompanied the *fondue aux truffes de Franche Conté* (Franche Conté truffle fondue).[73]

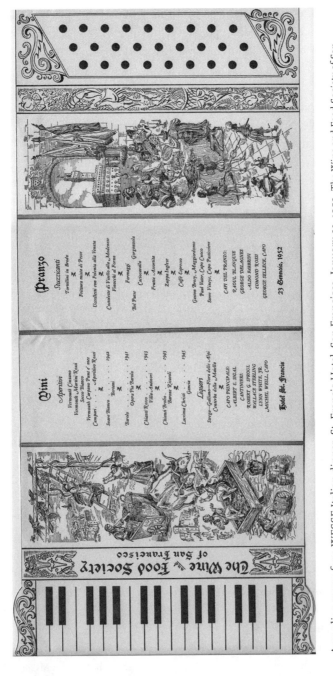

Accordion menu for a WFSSF Italian dinner, St. Francis Hotel, San Francisco, January 23, 1952. The Wine and Food Society of San Francisco. (For more WFSSF menus, see the color illustrations following page 128.)

In 1948, Selleck's friends honored him with a dinner at the Bohemian Club, for which they designed a booklet entitled *The Bent Elbow* in appreciation of "his unselfish service as a dispenser of happiness and good food." Aside from a blow-by-blow account of each item on the menu, the booklet satirized gourmet pretences. Attorney Farnham Griffiths' lament that gourmets only drink wine from labeled bottles and read menus written in French was illustrated by Ogden Nash's "The Strange Case of Mr. Palliser's Palate." Nash mocked a gentleman gourmet who infuriated his wife by discussing such elaborate dishes as *Huîtres en Robe de chambre* (oysters in a bathrobe). After she scornfully invited him to Hamburger Heaven, he found a recipe entitled "Croques Madame" in the cookbook and, following the instructions in the title, avenged himself.[74]

Even though the dinner was in his honor, Selleck prepared the hors d'oeuvres, while James Howe brought four pheasants for the soup from his own farm. For the main course, Chef Robert Hohman of the Bohemian Club served a *roti de sirloin, maître d'hôtel* (roast sirloin in savory butter with parsley and lemon juice) paired with a Richebourg 1937 Domaine de la Romanée Conti.[75]

A far different occasion was the dinner for Joseph Wechsberg, widely admired for his witty articles on fine dining in *Gourmet* and the *New Yorker*, which featured two Chateau Cheval Blanc Bordeaux and two Richebourg Burgundies that provided the "vinous interest" of the meal. Lulled by the wine, the diners "fell into a reminiscent mood" and recounted the experiences of their favorite dinners. For Wechsberg, it was a meal at Chef Fernand Point's Pyramide restaurant, while Jeff Smith praised the Selleck dinner in honor of Woollcott.[76]

Meanwhile, Harold Price brought Chateau Cheval Blanc to the attention of Le Club des Arts Gastronomiques after a trip to Boston in the winter of 1942; on that occasion he was a guest at two of their dinners that "surpassed anything I had ever sat down to in the quality and number of wines." Soon Price and wine dealer Russell Codman were corresponding about a possible wine tasting to compare 1920 vintages of Chateau Cheval Blanc and Chateau Latour. After Codman arranged the tasting for a Le Club dinner, he read Price's letter to the tasters to celebrate the transcontinental connection between oenophiles. Dinners at Le Club and the WFSSF also honored Price for his promotion of high standards in wine tasting.[77]

In pursuit of the same goal, the WFSSF collaborated with the French Consulate to plan a tour of French vineyards. Ten members of the WFS, including five from San Francisco, as well as cookbook writer James Beard and his future collaborator Alexander Watt, visited the major wine regions of France. The latter two wrote lively accounts of the trip. According to Beard, theirs was "the most comprehensive trip through France's vineyards ever planned for laymen." In twenty-two days, the group sampled over four hundred wines and was entertained officially on over thirty occasions. Even so, they returned to America happy and "with their digestive apparatuses working admirably."[78]

Thanks to connections with authorities in France, the group received VIP treatment from important figures in French wine circles. On one exceptional day, the travelers tasted great Medoc wines after an informal luncheon at the Jean Cruse chateau and before a "brilliant" dinner hosted by Philippe de Rothschild in the dining room overlooking his wine cellar. Two vintage Mouton-Rothschilds, the 1923 to accompany a *contrefilet de boeuf bouquetière* (beef tenderloin garnished with vegetables) and an 1881 with the cheese platter—"a *great* wine," which had held up well—were served.[79]

Only the "perfect meal" at La Pyramide surpassed the Rothschild feast. In "all his colossal grandeur," the 300-pound owner, Fernand Point, and his wife shepherded the tour group through the meal. They enjoyed a *volailles de Bresse en chaud-froid* (chicken breast covered with mayonnaise and capped with truffles) and drank a Chateau Grillet 1947 before the main course: *feuilletes de perdreaux Pyramide* (thin slices of partridges baked in pastry) accompanied by a 1947 Beaujolais. As one member remarked, "There are many symphonies performed every day that are not played to music."[80]

When their French hosts visited California the next year, the WFSSF performed symphonies in a California key. The small dinner for Jean Cruse featured a garnished beef sirloin accompanied by a Fountaingrove cabernet sauvignon 1936. For Philippe de Rothschild and his traveling companion, Princesse de Liechtenstein, proprietor of the Moselle estates of Kesselstatt, who were touring California wineries with Frank Schoonmaker, the WFSSF served a crown of lamb with a Georges de Latour cabernet sauvignon private reserve 1943, followed by other California wines.[81]

While wine often drove the Californians' selection of dishes, there was considerable interest in experimenting with new recipes to expand the horizons of Society members. On one occasion, George Selleck cooked recipes from *Gourmet* author Samuel Chamberlain's *Bouquet de France* (1952), which was also used by Farnham Griffiths as a tour guide. For the main course, Selleck prepared *canards sauvages à l'ancienne* (fricasseed wild duck with mushrooms and onions) accompanied by a Cheval Blanc 1934, one of four 1934 clarets served at dinner.[82]

More than any other gourmet group, the core members of the WFSSF experienced the joys of consuming and producing great French food. An informal apprenticeship in the WFSSF, where they learned much about French cuisine from San Francisco's French chefs, prepared them for this experience; they were, no doubt, encouraged to cook for themselves by the example of Merle Armitage, Crosby Gaige, and Charles Browne, cookbook writers and amateur chefs from both coasts. Even so, the San Franciscans were among the first American men to practice gourmet cooking as a hobby and thus to anticipate the more modest middle-class, suburban barbecuers of postwar America. At the same time, they developed an expertise in French wines that gave them entrée into very select wine circles in Boston and France, which they visited and hosted. But what is unique about this coterie from the WFSSF is the way their comradeship in the kitchen and at the table nurtured the kind of social interaction that Brillat-Savarin had envisioned. In Raoul Blanquie's words, the diners established "close and lasting friendships" that were based on a common appreciation "of the finer and civilized things of life." Symptomatic of this growing intimacy was the inclusion of wives at small dinners despite the fact that the parent WFSSF admitted women only on ladies' nights after 1943.[83]

In stark contrast, the New York Tastevin used medieval robes and appropriate props to convey a sense of a traditional environment as the setting for enjoying classical French cooking and the great wines of Burgundy. The Tastevin thus presents an interesting case of the appeal of ritual, hierarchy, and costumes to members and aspirants of the American upper class. It was, in reality, an invented tradition, borrowed from a variety of sources by the clever French founders of the Tastevin. Their American followers, in turn, accepted these practices because they enhanced the French culinary tradition that Americans hoped to acquire for their own purposes. Both the practices and the dining experience identified American members of the Tastevin as part of a long-standing elite descending from French gourmets to Thomas Jefferson, who distinguished themselves by their connoisseurship. At the same time, under Gordon Brown's tutelage, they came to demand and to enjoy the fine cuisine that great French cooks in New York hotel restaurants were capable of producing.

While these two culinary success stories are significant, the establishment of an institutional structure for the promotion of gourmet dining is also an important legacy of the gourmet movement. It was a particularly bold move for André Simon to found six branches of his WFS in major American cities in the midst of the Depression and to locate American leaders who could in turn organize and run local chapters. The idea of using the dinner committees to educate the members was not entirely original, but it was ingenious. For the first time, dining societies became more than pleasant gatherings of their members.

They were now charged with initiating these members into the ways of fine dining.

This achievement required the energy and conviction not only of André Simon but of his French counterparts Jules Bohy and Joseph Donon, as well as Americans like Julian Street, Frederick Wildman, Gordon Brown, Roy Alciatore, and G. Selmer Fougner. It is true, of course, that the founders had a material interest in the success of the movement, but their work was often a labor of love. The wine dealers, restaurateurs, chefs, and journalists identified above were themselves devoted to good living, the camaraderie of the men's clubs, and the possibility of profiting from this venture. As such, they contributed their time and energy to assure the success of the movement. Together they recruited new members, sought subsidies for wine to accompany their dinners, and extolled the pleasures of the table.

Chapter Four

Selectivity and Publicity in the Gourmet Dining Movement

The rise of Café Society in the 1930s highlighted the themes of selectivity and publicity that were central to the gourmet dining movement. Consisting of a few hundred fashionable entertainers, Hollywood stars, prominent writers and artists, as well as some heirs of older wealth, who gathered in New York's chic bars and restaurants, Café Society was defined above all by its obsession with media attention and luxury consumption. For journalist Lucius Beebe, who coined the term in his *New York Herald Tribune* column, "This New York," members of Café Society turned gourmet dining into a glamorous experience that enhanced its publicity value for journalists and readers alike.[1]

In a more nuanced way than Beebe's Café Society, gourmet societies sought to achieve their own version of selectivity and publicity, themes that were sometimes in tension with each other. The societies were unusual in developing dual processes of selection: one served to recruit amateurs, in part, by examining their social credentials, while the other accepted as members food and wine professionals primarily based on their expertise. These two elites had once done business with each other in restaurants, clubs, and wine shops where the professionals served the amateurs; in the dining societies, they would mingle on a more level playing field. To recruit the most knowledgeable food and wine experts as well as appropriate publicists, the societies tempered social exclusivity by including a smattering of Italians and Jews who would probably not have been invited to join their amateur colleagues in WASP social clubs. In a few cases, however, wine professionals were themselves members of the social elite. Even so, the two elites never fully merged. Inevitably, the professionals viewed the gourmet dining society, in part, as a business opportunity, while their amateur counterparts were more interested in protecting their privacy and social standing.[2]

Most gourmet societies initially excluded women altogether or invited them to participate infrequently. That situation contrasts strongly with the practices of parent organizations of the WFS and the Tastevin that admitted women to their proceedings and, in the case of the WFS, to the governing board during the 1930s. Two factors help to explain these differences. The Europeans were less affected than Americans by nineteenth-century, gender-separate frontier practices and the divisive effects of Prohibition, dieting, and the ethos of nutrition in the twentieth century. Far more than men, American women believed that rich and elegant food and wine would expand the waistline and jeopardize bodily health. In the process, there emerged a kind of war of the sexes on dining practices that began to diminish after repeal.

Significant economic and cultural barriers also limited the diversity of the societies. Especially during the Depression, few Americans could afford to pay for lavish dinners. An equally formidable barrier was the expectation that members would welcome French culinary ways, including what were for most Americans exotic dishes and wines.

To gauge the effects of exclusivity, I have examined the development of the societies over time. Although the paucity of membership lists makes this a difficult task, I have gleaned from other records the names, occupations, and social activities of many members and, wherever possible, checked their names in the *Social Register*. In addition, the scholarly literature on exclusive clubs has been helpful in assessing the significance of the members' activities.

Meanwhile, local newspapers and magazines with a national circulation provide ample evidence of the societies' efforts to publicize their activities. Both members and journalists were often ambivalent about this publicity. Members worried that it might threaten their privacy and require a significant expenditure of time and money, while journalists felt uncomfortable writing articles about fine dining in the midst of a depression and were confused about whether reports on gourmet dinners should be considered society news or an opportunity to write about an as yet unrecognized art form.

To fulfill their obligation to reach the larger public, gourmet leaders found ways to control the public image of gourmet dining so as to maximize its appeal to a cosmopolitan audience. They educated the press and, as food writers themselves, reported on society activities as insiders. Moreover, movement leaders discovered that a focus on the chef, amateur or professional, was an appealing way to present the drama and artistry of gourmet dining to interested readers. And, for those who were indifferent to the dining side of gourmet activity, the discussion of rituals and special dress was often of interest. As the subject of gourmet dining became more familiar to the public, department stores, guidebook authors, and restaurants invited well-known gourmet authorities to authenticate their products for potential consumers.

In the end, the dissemination activities of gourmet society publicists played a significant role in promoting the expansion of the three original gourmet dining societies and the creation of three new international societies in the postwar period. The publicity also energized and instructed the growing number of Americans who cooked gourmet meals at home and found or founded informal associations that enabled them to do so with friends and family. By the late 1950s, Americans were more likely to eat in ethnic restaurants and prepare dishes from the repertoire of European national cuisines. Wine drinking and cooking with wine were both clearly on the rise.[3]

Social Composition of the Gourmet Societies

Several examples reveal that the cost of dinners, which included wines, at official gourmet functions constrained membership in the three major societies. Consider that while the Palace Hotel in San Francisco charged $1.75 for its most expensive entrée in July 1941, the second and third dinners of the Wine and Food Society of Los Angeles, held in 1935, were priced at $3.75 and $5, respectively, for each member; the fact that André Simon regarded the $6 fee for the Escoffier Society's first dinner in 1936 as inadequate to meet gourmet standards suggests that most branches of the WFS were charging more for their meals. Indeed, the WFSSF billed its members $10 for the 1940 Dîner de Noël des Pape Clément. To a WPA (Works Progress Administration) worker making $10 a week during the New Deal, any of these prices were prohibitive.[4]

After the war, prices, as well as salaries, rose. While the Dames d'Escoffier paid $20 apiece for their first meal in 1959, that price was far below the $30 that the New York Tastevin charged its members in 1947. By 1958, the Tastevin priced its dinners in Washington, D.C., at $40. Only relatively affluent Americans could afford to pay for such meals.[5]

Each of the three gourmet societies was elitist in its own way, but only the Wine and Food Society leaders systematically articulated their views. The Escoffier Society drew 60 percent of its one hundred members from the American Culinary Federation, composed mainly of chefs from prestigious establishments in large cities. In New York, the chefs formed a natural alliance with restaurant owners from the Society of Restaurateurs who represented the superior eating establishments in the city. Interested individuals from these organizations applied to the executive committee of the ACF for membership in the society, but it is not clear whether there was an excess of applicants over places and, if so, on what basis the committee made its selections. Each member invited a guest in order to convert leaders in business, the arts, and journalism to the pleasures of the table.[6]

More exclusive were smaller dinners organized by G. Selmer Fougner, who claimed to belong to fourteen different gourmet groups, including the Lucullus Club, founded in 1939 and comprised of "old guard" members of the Society of Restaurateurs. Each Lucullus member was expected to plan and host a meal at his own restaurant. As Fougner pointed out, the members constituted a jury of peers who judged the quality of food and wine in a professional way. Among the restaurants that hosted this group were the Crillon, Luchow's, the Marguery, and the famed Colony.[7]

The recruitment process for the Tastevin varied from chapter to chapter. As Richard de Rochemont pointed out, the more exclusive groups in Philadelphia, Dallas, and Wilmington, Delaware, systematically recruited from the social elite. By contrast, food and wine professionals played a significant role in establishing the New York Tastevin after 1945, although some amateurs resisted their influence and sought to raise the society's social standing. De Rochemont concluded that "the spirit of the order is democratic without any nonsense about being proletarian" but admitted that the Tastevin invited "only those who really love wine and camaraderie and are willing to spend their money for both" to become members. In this instance, self-selection was a substitute for peer decisions.[8]

In the WFS, where amateurs dominated from the outset, the goals of the society were somewhat broader and less commercial; leaders, accordingly, gave more attention to social, rather than professional, status and prestige in their recruitment. Unfortunately, membership lists are not available for the five original chapters. For those members identified by name in various documents, the majority were not listed in the *Social Register.*[9]

André Simon acknowledged that, as an unremitting proponent of high culinary standards, he was an elitist, although he repudiated discrimination based on "money, dress, occupation or looks." In principle, the Wine and Food Society was open to anyone interested in the pleasures of the table; in Simon's view, the poor, as well as the rich, could and should enjoy eating well, although lack of time and energy limited the interest of the former. However, he also claimed that WFS members should be drawn from "the thinking few" who believed in the importance of enjoying fine dining.[10]

This principled stance partly guided Simon's views and actions, but he also regarded social prestige as an important ingredient in a successful WFS branch. In recruiting American members, Simon took advantage of connections with men's clubs, which later hosted many of the society's dinners. Based on these

connections, it would be more accurate to say that Simon recruited those "thinking few" who were socially well connected.

A case in point was the selection of the first head of the Chicago branch of the
WFS in December 1934. Simon regretted the choice of caterer Arnold Shircliffe
because, as a food professional, his social connections were limited. Simon preferred Suzette Dewey, who had sent him a copy of the wine manual she had
written on the eve of repeal. In Simon's view, Dewey "had every possible qualification to make an outstanding social and cultural success" of the WFS of Chicago. Indeed, Dewey would have been "another Theodora Codman," the honorary secretary of the WFS of Boston. These two women were socially well connected,
were possessed of great charm and intelligence, and had written knowledgeably
about French food and wine. Under Dewey's leadership the Chicago chapter
"would have brought together many . . . of the much traveled and highly cul-
tured men and women . . . around Chicago." Unfortunately, Dewey and her husband, Charles, were about to move to Washington, D.C., where he would serve
in the House of Representatives. In her absence, Shircliffe, who lacked the social
graces and cosmopolitan experience that would have engaged upper-class Chicagoans, became the leader. To be sure, Simon publicly praised Shircliffe for his
kindness and dedication to advancing the Society. However, as Simon feared,
food professionals dominated the membership during the 1930s and set what he
regarded as the wrong tone for the society.[11]

Leaders of the Los Angeles chapter shared Simon's preference for recruiting
a socially well-connected membership, while constantly denying this point. They
pretended to be indifferent about members' "social standing or financial rating,
although we do number in our organization the leading citizens of the community," including "two well-known Pacific Coast bank presidents, brokers, lawyers, writers, college professors, motion picture actors"; with their guests they
constituted a "cross-section of the first-rank citizens of Southern California."
Even so, Phil Hanna insisted that there was no "snobbishness in selecting our
members." Their interest in food and wine and their good table manners were
the sole criteria for selection.[12]

On later occasions social prestige was an even more important factor. Leaders
of the new Long Beach branch announced that eight of their members are "past
presidents of the Virginia Country Club of Long Beach, the premiere social organization of that city." In recruiting other members, they promised to "take very
special pains with all candidates to see that they are of the proper caliber." There
was a parallel to Long Beach in the Wilmington, Delaware, chapter of the Tastevin,
whose recruits were drawn heavily from the Wilmington Club.[13]

But it is also true that the Los Angeles chapter considered applicants' interests in wine and food as borne out in the following three questions that appeared on the application form: "Do you have wine served in your home regularly?" "Are you interested in broadening your knowledge of wine and food?" "Do you do any cooking as a personal pleasure and if so what are your specialties?" While the answers to the first two questions are not available, thirty-two respondents identified their cooking specialties, which almost perfectly reflect the prevailing view of what and how men should cook; most barbecued and grilled meat, prepared game, or cooked on camping trips. Three specialized in preparing crepes, while half a dozen cooked such sophisticated dishes as chicken stuffed with pâté de foie gras, lemon chicken raviolis, East Indian curry, kidney stew, and eggplant au gratin (Martinique style).[14]

Despite the effort to recruit members of the socioeconomic elite, there was some ethnic and class diversity in the gourmet societies from 1934 to 1961. Based on evidence from photographs and names, there were no black or Asian gourmet society members in this period. However, societies recruited Jewish wine dealers and food writers, along with Italian wine producers and chefs, to educate other society members in the subtleties of gourmet dining or to promote it to the larger public. Particularly notable was the number of Italian chefs, especially in Boston, on the rolls of the Escoffier Society. Italian wine producers appear with some frequency on the membership lists of the WFSLA and WFSSF. As for Jews, a number of wine dealers and publicists joined both the WFSNY and the New York Tastevin.[15]

The profile of the gourmet societies is clear. All three branches sought a combination of elites, professional and socioeconomic, although the proportions were different in each. A professional elite dominated the Escoffier Society, while in the WFS the socioeconomic elite was more prominent. At least at the outset, the Tastevin was somewhere in between. In effect, the necessity of recruiting experts in food and wine opened the doors of all societies to ethnic minorities in small numbers.

Local Autonomy, Gender Exclusivity, and Ethnic Exclusivity

Among credentials for membership, societies, with two exceptions, assumed gender to be of great importance. The Escoffier Society recruited from all-male organizations and remained an all-male society until November 1958. As for the Dames d'Escoffier, which debuted only in 1959, its members were all women.[16]

In 1937, Theodora Codman became the first American woman to be inducted into the Tastevin at a ceremony in Nuits St. Georges. It was not until 1950 that an American chapter meeting, attended by a number of other women, witnessed the induction of Madame René Fribourg following her nomination by Burgundy officials. By 1957, five women belonged to the New York Tastevin, where Jeanne Owen had become an officer, while the Washington branch had three female members. However, women guests and members attended only wine tastings and ladies' nights, although, in principle, they were entitled to be present at all induction ceremonies.[17]

The London chapter of the Wine and Food Society set the model for gender relations in the WFS by opening membership to women in 1933 and including one woman on the Board of Directors. The East Coast branches in the United States followed this model. Jeanne Owen, who was named to the New York Board of Directors in 1935, became the honorary secretary of the society in 1937 and promptly recruited other women volunteers for the Tasting Committee that served wine and snacks at society tastings. In 1936, Theodora Codman became the honorary secretary of the Boston chapter. A number of new branches of the WFS in California and Ohio admitted women to membership in the late 1950s.[18]

The Chicago, Los Angeles, and San Francisco branches of the WFS became male preserves, although, at the founding meeting, the Chicago Stewards passed a resolution opening the new society to "local epicures of both sexes." Apparently, this promise was not kept. It is interesting to note that the San Francisco and Chicago chapters, in 1943 and 1949, respectively, sought a middle ground by designating one of the annual dinners as a ladies' night. With the encouragement of their spouses, officers' wives in the WFS of Chicago organized a dinner in 1961 for men and women that would be conducted according to WFS rules. The idea was to groom the women to create their own independent gourmet society.[19]

It seems clear that in the first months after the founding of the WFSLA its leaders still entertained the possibility of women participating in the society's affairs. Following her conversation with Richard Day, Alma Whitaker understood that the members could invite anyone who enjoyed fine dining to join the society "no matter what his (or her) social standing." A March 1935 announcement to society members also promised "a special luncheon . . . for the ladies of the society who will have entire charge of the planning and service." By 1939, sentiments had changed; an all-male chapter appeared to be seeking a victory in the battle of the sexes:

> If a woman was young and beautiful more often than not she was finicky as to her diet; and that if she were elderly no amount of personal magnetism, no

conversational ability can compensate for the distracting influence she might exert. The ladies, God bless 'em!, have been hammering at the door of the citadel ever since, but there has been no relenting and it seems probable there never shall be. The officers of the Society feel that eating in the grand manner is one of the few pleasures and privileges left to mankind in a fast-growing matriarchy.

In 1945, Phil Hanna announced that "we have never had women in attendance at any of our functions."[20]

These attitudes were far from unique. In Washington, D.C., the Carlton maître d'hôtel, Alfred Mazzou, confessed that "a nice looking woman keeps your mind away from the good food," while C. C. Schiffeler of the Raleigh Hotel protested that "women always think of diet instead of the art of dining." Meanwhile, Baron Fougner announced authoritatively that "not even we could put food before women. Therefore we do not invite them." It is interesting to note that such French gastronomers as Brillat-Savarin and Curnonsky were bachelors who sometimes excluded women to avoid distraction from their culinary activities, although the former also advocated diversity at the table.[21]

In 1936, André Simon expressed his opposition to the Los Angeles chapter's all-male status and urged that its leaders at least consider helping interested women form their own chapter, which might be called "The Tappit [crested] Hens." The leaders of the chapter apparently ignored this advice.[22]

The issue lay dormant during the war. Then, a letter from Elizabeth Stocker, soliciting information about the practices of the chapter, brought a response from Secretary Hanna, who acknowledged that Los Angeles was the only WFS chapter to exclude women from membership and all dinners. "In this respect it is similar to many other rather smallish Los Angeles clubs." Two years later, Mrs. Neil McCarthy, whose husband was a legal advisor to Hollywood studios, proposed the creation of a WFS branch in Beverly Hills that would recruit both men and women who were engaged in the motion picture industry. Despite Simon's support for McCarthy, Hanna and Dwight Whiting rejected the proposal. Whiting informed Hanna that agreement to Simon's proposal would be "the first plank in a long series of moves to break down our own policy and admit women members"; however, he recommended Society support for a "Ladies group" that the WFSLA would carefully monitor. Privately, Whiting wrote Hanna: "I see no reason why we should allow ourselves to be pushed around by Mrs. McCarthy or any other charming members of the fair sex and that's that!"[23]

The WFSLA's resistance to a new chapter shook the normally unflappable André Simon. He reminded Hanna that the purpose of the WFS was "to bring together and to serve *all* who believe that a right understanding of wine and food is an essential part of personal contentment and health." He pointedly underlined the word "*all.*" "It was never intended that the Society should be run on the basis of a dining club for a few men to enjoy better meals and each others company." Differences in political views, social standing, and sex were irrelevant; the only requirement for membership was an interest in food and wine.[24]

As it turned out, however, gender was only one reason for opposing the new chapter. Whiting and Hanna were equally concerned about McCarthy's proposal to recruit new members from the motion picture industry. In a confidential letter to Simon, Hanna explained that the new branch would be undignified, fall into "evil ways," and thus damage the reputation of the WFS. Indeed, in 1935, when Hollywood supplied half the members of the WFSLA, they had "proposed fantastic schemes" and "hedonistic goings-on" such as "spraying exotic perfumes" at each course. This behavior was no aberration because "Hollywood is notorious for its extravagant excesses in the way of dinners and parties—uncouth and vulgar affairs attended mainly by those who come to be seen, to get their names and pictures in the papers, and who have no genuine or honest interest in wine and food or the amenities of polite social conduct." It was unfortunately necessary "to do business with these people, but we do not care to mingle with many of them socially." Of course, the civilized exceptions to the rule—"the cream"—were already among the dozen Hollywood members of the WFSLA.[25]

It is quite likely that the "civilized exceptions" were gentiles like Edward Arnold and Jean Hersholt. Many of the "uncouth and vulgar" were probably Jews. According to Phil Hanna, he and other members had refused to sanction the schemes of the Hollywood set, and most of them soon "deserted" the society; however, in order to belatedly achieve their ambition, this same Hollywood element was now behind the drive to establish a new chapter.[26]

Even twenty years later such anti-Semitism marred the deliberations of the WFS in Southern California. According to Roy Brady, a leading Los Angeles gourmet, efforts to form a Westwood branch of the Society ran into strong opposition from five individuals who "did not wish to belong to an organization" that included three Jewish wine merchants. These wine merchants, in turn, complained that their gentile counterparts were trying to steal customers from them. While the conflict temporarily delayed the establishment of the Westwood branch, one of the Jewish wine merchants eventually became the first head of that branch.[27]

The McCarthy proposal also threatened the Los Angeles chapter's sense of autonomy, since Mrs. McCarthy counseled with Crosby Gaige, a member of the gender-inclusive New York branch. Such outside intervention stiffened the resolve of Whiting and Hanna to resist Simon's position, which they strongly opposed anyway. Furthermore, they believed that their branch represented metropolitan Los Angeles, defined as the area within a 100-mile radius of the city's center. As even André Simon agreed, new branches required the approval of the original society. Simon urged Mrs. McCarthy to communicate with Hanna and Whiting and told the latter that the new branch could not come into existence without the "good feelings" of its predecessor. In fact, there is no record that Mrs. McCarthy ever contacted the officers of the WFSLA.[28]

In a concluding resolution, the Los Angeles chapter buried the gender issue that was central to their opposition to the new chapter. "Unless convincing information is presented to" the Los Angeles Board of Governors that a new chapter would promote the ideals of the WFS and conduct business "with dignity," the Board would oppose it. However, Chairman Whiting acknowledged that the Los Angeles branch was becoming "a gathering place for older gentlemen to wine and dine themselves" and thus was not fulfilling its responsibility to spread gastronomy to all who were interested. He proposed that the WFSLA become an umbrella organization for branches located in independent cities in metropolitan Los Angeles. Each of the new societies would recruit younger members and meet with them in smaller gatherings. With the acceptance of this plan, new all-male societies appeared throughout metropolitan Los Angeles in 1949.[29]

Even so, there was an undercurrent of support among members to include women in some Society activities, as evidenced by a proposal that women and music be allowed at WFS events "once in a while." Toward that end, Whiting presented a resolution to the Board of Governors endorsing "an occasional party at which ladies are permitted," believing, however, that the Board "will not care for it." A month later, a mock invitation expressed the predominant feeling of members on the subject: "It will be a pleasure to have you as a guest at the 'Wine and Food but No Women or Song Society.'"[30]

Apparently there was little change in members' attitudes over the next decade. In 1960, the *Los Angeles Times* reported that "one of the last strongholds of masculinity is the Wine and Food Society." Members defended their exclusivity on the grounds that the "weaker sex" is "more calorie conscious," "can't cope with the adventurous menus," and would likely arrive late to dinners. The female author of the article was, nonetheless, grateful that Society leaders Harold Janes and Hernando Courtright permitted her to sample dishes from the dinner.[31]

There is a clear parallel between the crisis over women's membership in the WFSLA and the efforts of the New York and Washington, D.C., chapters of the Tastevin to determine their own membership policies. In both cases, the local chapters sought to control the selection of their members in order to maintain intimate and exclusive men's clubs. Both local groups faced resistance from parent organizations in Europe. However, the Tastevin officials were better positioned than André Simon to resist their rebellious branches in America. They had appointed Jules Bohy to govern the American branches, although he was to report his decisions to an advisory council, composed largely of Americans. By contrast, the American branches of the WFS were autonomous from the outset.

Under the leadership of Gordon Brown, some members of the advisory council challenged the parent organization's practice of inducting American residents into the Tastevin without consultation. When the Burgundy council decided to increase revenues by expanding chapter size, the New Yorkers denied the council's right to determine either chapter size or the selection of its members. They also argued that the change would diminish the selectivity and prestige of the society and, by increasing the number of diners, the quality of its dinners. At the March 9, 1949, meeting, the advisory council voted to limit the American Tastevin to one hundred members, seventy-five in the New York branch with the balance in Washington, and to induct no more than three candidates at any given meeting. To enhance the society's prestige, members would select "influential and well-to-do guests" who "conform to our gastronomic ideals" and might become future members.[32]

The response from France was revealing. The Burgundians insisted that the American Tastevin "must not constitute a 'small chapel' nor a . . . closed gastronomique [*sic*] club," but should promote "the great wines of France in general and those of Burgundy in particular." Even in the selection of new members, the Americans must bow to the decisions of the parent organization. To rub salt in the wounds, the council then advised Americans to open their branch "to women at one dinner every year."[33]

Out of this conflict came a solution that satisfied both sides. From 1949 to 1950, the council in France raised the membership limit for American branches from one hundred to five hundred "in order to cover all expenses"; instead of increasing the size of existing chapters, however, the council decided to establish new chapters in St. Louis, Chicago, and Los Angeles. Although there is no record of the factors that led to this decision, it seems evident that the Burgundy council wished to conciliate American members who had the potential to remedy the organization's financial problems. In the end, Americans got their "small chapels," while the Tastevin assured itself of much-needed new revenue.[34]

Interactions with the Washington Tastevin, however, disabused the New Yorkers of their view that autonomy was always desirable. After the creation of the Washington chapter in 1946, Henry Howells, the president of U.S. Industries, Inc., who was also well connected in diplomatic circles, ran the organization for the next twenty-five years. He sought to induct into the society important political and diplomatic officials. In addition, Howells supplemented official Tastevin dinners with wine tastings and unofficial monthly dinners, much like those of the WFS. Despite the Tastevin's commitment to promote Burgundy wines, he authorized the serving of American wines at some of these functions.[35]

Conflict between the New York and Washington chapters arose over the character of the latter's inductees and the lack of decorum at meetings. According to Tastevin rules, Jules Bohy presided at all official Tastevin dinners in America, since only he could induct new members. Joined by Maurice Roux, a businessman and former officer in the French navy, Bohy attended the Washington dinner at the La Salle du Bois restaurant in January 1948. It was, by all accounts, a gastronomic success. Chef Joseph Karriou prepared a tender *poularde au foie gras de Strasbourg* (capon with foie gras from Strasbourg) accompanied by a Clos de Vougeot 1937, a Confrérie selection, and *cotelettes de chevreuil, sauce poivrade* (venison cutlets with a pepper sauce) served with a Beaune Grèves 1934 Vigne de l'Enfant Jésus. Not only did the *Washington Times Herald* critic extol the dinner, but she was also impressed with the "calm, contemplative, almost reverent" mood of the occasion.[36]

The New York officials thought otherwise. Writing to Bohy, Maurice Roux praised the dinner but criticized the selection and behavior of guests and members. Even when they violated the Tastevin's no-smoking rule, Howells intervened to stop the smoking only after prodding from Bohy. As for Senator Burton Wheeler, Roux commented that "his manners are as bad as his policies." Wheeler smoked cigars until he was reprimanded and then kept an unlit cigar in his mouth throughout the dinner. Worse still, he was an isolationist who opposed aid to France in 1940, but had no scruples about attending an event that celebrated French culture. To add insult to injury, Wheeler's son was among the evening's three initiates; the other two knew nothing about wine and treated the occasion as a joke. Roux concluded that the dinner "was 'sloppily' arranged," lacked "dignity and decorum," and was "unworthy of the standards we have established in New York, under your [Bohy's] leadership." Reflecting the feelings of the American council, Roux advised Bohy to educate the Washington chapter about Tastevin standards before it was too late.[37]

Bohy followed Roux's advice. He explained to Howells that the invitation to Wheeler was entirely inappropriate: "we can only have with us great friends of France." In the future, the American council would have to approve all new members and even guests who were politicians. He also reprimanded Howells for not enforcing the "no-smoking" rule during meals and invited him to attend the next meeting of the council in New York so that he could learn how to conduct a Tastevin dinner.[38]

Howells was unrepentant. In the fall of 1948, he defiantly announced that the chapter would initiate ten new members, including the Republican House whip, Leslie Arents, Senators J. William Fulbright and Homer Ferguson, and John L. Lewis, head of the United Mine Workers. Equally defiant was Howells' explanation for this decision: "they are all Americans . . . in the main their knowledge is just a gracious appreciation of wines and food. I am making myself personally responsible to see that these men are at least casually informed on the wines of Burgundy and will attempt to have them in qualifying condition by mid-January."[39]

Such reassurance was not reassuring to the New York officials, who insisted that, before induction, a written nomination detail the candidate's qualifications and that he pass an examination on Burgundy wine. In Bohy's absence, Gordon Brown responded to Howells and, despite his previous defense of local autonomy, insisted that the American Tastevin respect the wishes of the Burgundians. If the society expanded too quickly, it would resemble "certain other so-called 'gourmet' organizations in this country who have lost all prestige as such" (probably a reference to the new and less dignified WFS chapters).[40]

Even so, Howells attempted to satisfy some of the demands of the American council. He drew up bylaws for the Washington chapter, devised a membership application form, and read a copy of the New York chapter's examination for candidates. However, Howell's interest in the society's "ceremonials, costumes and rituals" alarmed Bohy, who pointed out that only officers could wear robes, while Bohy alone conducted initiations. Innovations in the ceremony "may run into 'fantaisie' [sic] and I feel sure that is not what you want." To understand Tastevin rituals, Bohy urged Howells to attend a ceremony at Chateau Clos de Vougeot.[41]

There was more trouble ahead. After reports of a March 19, 1950, tasting of California wines hosted by the Washington chapter, Bohy wrote Howells:

"Although your last exclusive tasting of American wines has weakened the effect of the Coca-Cola affair, you must proceed with caution and do nothing without my advice." He added, "I have just received from Washington an anonymous note accompanied by a clipping from a newspaper which reads: 'Dear Mr. Bohy: When are you going to sponsor Coca-Cola? March 20 (no signature).'" Unfortunately, Tastevin archives offer no clues about the nature of the Coca-Cola affair.[42]

Howells understood Bohy's letter to be an implicit attack on the serving of California wines and justified the tasting as "a first step to the use of Burgundy wine." As for the anonymous letter, Bohy should disregard it since the author was not courageous enough to reveal his name. Howells also tried to reassure Bohy that Washington would only consider "dignified" candidates for membership.[43]

The archival record does not reveal whether Howells and the Washington chapter emerged from the doghouse after 1951. However, a 1956 inventory of the chapter's wine cellar featured prominently red Bordeaux, sauternes, and Rhine wines amidst the Burgundies. Tastevin officials would not have been pleased with this selection.[44]

While the New York–Burgundy and New York–Washington conflicts both raised the question of autonomy, the content of these tensions clarifies Gordon Brown's decision to prize decorum over autonomy. He initially insisted on autonomy as the best way to create a small, prestigious chapter adhering to decorum and serving fine food and wine, much as Phil Hanna and Dwight Whiting had done in resisting André Simon. Howells, by contrast, was eager to expand membership to well-known politicians who did not share the ideals of the society and to start them out on California wines. Thus, as the New Yorkers came to realize, autonomy was a double-edged sword. Breaches in decorum in Washington could, in fact, tarnish the reputation of all members and chapters of the Tastevin. Under the circumstances, Brown preferred disciplining the Washington chapter even if this diminished its autonomy.

In selecting members from the few Americans interested in and able to afford French cuisine, the expectation that applicants would show an interest in food and wine augmented the criteria typically used by men's clubs. Except for the WFS chapters in New York and Boston, women did not achieve full membership in any dining societies until the 1950s. A few Jews and Italians were valued for their expertise on culinary matters and the media, but there is no evidence that the societies considered blacks and Asians for membership in this era. Despite their small numbers, however, gourmet societies had a disproportionate impact on public opinion.

Spreading the Word: Learning to Control the Message

As journalists and authors in their own right, key leaders of the gourmet movement were well positioned to shape the image of the new gourmet societies. André Simon and G. Selmer Fougner, who headed two of the three international societies, were professional writers who had already promoted fine dining in periodicals and books. They were ably assisted by WFSNY president Richardson Wright, who edited *House and Garden*, and chairman Crosby Gaige, who, after retiring from a career as a Broadway producer, wrote articles on food for Wright's magazine and a column for *Country Life*. In addition, Phil Townsend Hanna, honorary secretary of the WFSLA, edited *Westways*, the AAA magazine for California. As for the Tastevin, its professional advocates included Major Edward Bowes, the CBS talent show host, Charles Codman, and Lucius Beebe. In addition, Fougner and Beebe wrote daily and weekly columns, respectively, in the New York City press; while Beebe's columns were also syndicated in seven big-city newspapers, Fougner wrote monthly articles for *Scribner's* in the late 1930s.[45]

Even so, much of the coverage of the movement came from professional journalists, who were not members of gourmet societies. Until 1941, newspapers routinely assigned the coverage of gourmet dinners to society-page reporters who were accustomed to writing about the activities of the upper class. Their strong inclination was to stress the elitist character of the movement or the excesses of gourmet dinners rather than their culinary character. While often unflattering, these images may well have drawn readers who followed the activities of the rich and famous. Moreover, since early reports on the society appeared during the depths of the Depression, when many Americans went hungry, writers often portrayed diners as self-indulgent and indifferent to the suffering of others.

Among the earliest of these accounts was the *New York Evening Journal's* write-up of the first WFSNY dinner at the Savoy Plaza, entitled "Wine Society Holds Fete (Reporter Holds Head)," which was ostensibly filed from "Indigestion Ward, Bellevue Hospital." The reporter doubted the diners' motives. "Out of a sense of duty to their fellow man, they banded together slightly less than a year ago and, purely in the interests of mankind, they held a series of experiments." As for the menu, "*le Coeur de pintadon lardé roti sur canapé*, looked, tasted, and was, in fact, a guinea hen." In effect, the writer convicted his subjects of pretension and hypocrisy. Not surprisingly, Julian Street objected to the author's tone in a note he scribbled on the article: "Example of boob who thinks good taste funny—to be so treated."[46]

Even more compromising was the handling of the WFS inaugural wine tasting on the front page of the *Boston Evening Transcript*. The reporter noted that "the membership of the Wine and Food Society bristles with Codmans, Coolidges . . . Gardners . . . and other such names society editors reverence." The tasting thus attracted "Boston debutantes and matrons . . . the majority [of whom] have inherited naturally good palates," in contrast to "other citizens" who would prefer to "guzzle raw spirits."[47]

The *Boston Evening American* account of the same tasting, entitled "Wine Sippers in Action, Tough (?) Job for Reporters," also highlighted the social prom-

First dinner of the WFSNY, from the *New York Evening Journal*, November 15, 1935, p. 12. Negative no. 82684d, Collection of The New-York Historical Society.

inence of the tasters. Accompanying the article was a series of captioned photographs that displayed prominent Bostonians eating hors d'oeuvres and drinking wine.[48]

Lucius Beebe contrasted the response of New York and Boston gourmets to this publicity. Surrounded by reporters and photographers, New Yorkers enjoyed their lavish meals and tastings. In Boston, by contrast, President William Aldrich, who had been photographed by the *Boston Evening American* with an olive in his mouth, resigned. After that, Bostonians gathered "in almost clandestine secrecy . . . Reporters are kept rigidly at bay and a photographer on the premises would cause far more terror and consternation than a bomb tossed through the window." Indeed, one woman asked, "Isn't it too bad there are no photographers here . . . so that we could refuse to let them take any pictures?"[49]

These early portrayals of the society, emphasizing its exclusivity and excesses, no doubt chastened many members of the WFS. To avoid reinforcing that image, Maynard Amerine and Harold Price of the WFSSF decided not to collaborate with *Life* for a story that was to be entitled *"Life* Goes to a Wine Party." The article would have publicized the WFSSF and California vineyards, consistent with Society goals, but the two men also imagined reactions to a proposed photograph of a place setting with six or eight wine glasses. Based on that image, readers might perceive all gourmet diners as "a bunch of soaks and gourmands."[50]

On occasion, gourmet leaders turned the tables and criticized what they believed to be aggressive behavior on the part of journalists. During a 1941 Tastevin dinner at the Hotel Pierre in New York, journalists urged Jules Bohy to hold the induction ceremony before the dinner so that they could get their story without waiting. Claiming that the dinner would be spoiled by any delay, Bohy denied the request and proclaimed that the press "had never seen such a breach of the prescribed rights of journalists." He then circulated the story in various publications and boasted that his firm stand against the journalists increased Americans' respect for the Tastevin.[51]

On other occasions, however, Bohy was all too eager to curry favor with the media in order to publicize Tastevin activities. Indeed, after he discovered that Edward Bowes was a wine connoisseur, he arranged a radio induction ceremony on April 11, 1940, so that Bowes' CBS national audience of twenty-five million listeners would hear the ceremony along with 1,500 spectators who witnessed it in the Columbia Broadcasting System Theatre. For both audiences, Bowes "exalted the benefits of the fine wines of Burgundy."[52]

Over time, reporters increasingly understood the wisdom of identifying gourmet leaders who could provide accurate information on society activities.

Announcing that "it takes the nice decision of a gourmet to plan the dinner for New Year's day," the *New York Times* called on Richardson Wright and Crosby Gaige for menu recommendations. Wright proposed roast goose for the main course while admonishing diners to eat slowly and enjoy the occasion; Gaige, in turn, recommended a roast Long Island duckling.[53]

Equally important was the discovery by both gourmet leaders and journalists that the gourmet chef, amateur or professional, was a promising angle for drawing the attention of readers to gourmet activities, while at the same time revealing certain unique qualities of the gourmet experience. The presence of men in the kitchen was novel enough; beyond that, readers had a certain fascination with the chef's outfit, as well as the equipment and artistry required for cooking. Flattering comparisons of the imaginative chef to the plodding housewife exaggerated the gulf between the two and portrayed gourmet dining as a masculine enterprise. As Jane Nickerson remarked, "Home dinners can never duplicate the luxuries of the Chevaliers du Tastevin."[54]

A turning point in media coverage was a spring 1937 article in the *New Yorker* that treated the Escoffier dinner at the Pierre Hotel. Coming less than three years after the launching of the gourmet movement, it provided an admiring and intelligent account of a society dinner in a magazine whose audience was likely to resonate positively to the story. Author Jack Alexander put himself in the shoes of Chef Scotto as the latter presided nervously over the serving of a multicourse dinner to so many authoritative peers; Alexander noted the difficulty of preparing *Le potage Rossolnick* (a chicken soup), with its many ingredients. Among the society's rituals, he appreciated the arrival of the evening's main course on carts pushed by chefs wearing their *toques blanches* and the diners sporting napkins tucked into their collars ("*serviettes au cou*").[55]

The greatest champion of the professional chef was G. Selmer Fougner, who lauded renowned chefs in "Along the Wine Trail," his newspaper column, and published menus and recipes from their finest dinners. Hotel managers and chefs must have been eager to host an Escoffier dinner because they were sure to receive generous praise. After a dinner at the Park Lane Hotel, Fougner touted previous chefs of Escoffier dinners: "Lugot of the Waldorf, Diat of the Ritz-Carlton, Schunk of the St. Regis . . . Martin of the Lafayette." Based on their performance, all of them were the equal of Escoffier, who was regarded as the top chef of his generation.[56]

West Coast journalists and readers alike were fascinated by the combination of social prominence and expertise in kitchen techniques possessed by WFS amateur chefs in Los Angeles and San Francisco. On several occasions, the *Los*

Angeles Times published photographs of chefs toiling over the stove as they prepared the society's dinner. It was intriguing to see these men "decked out fit to kill in white kitchen accoutrement" and using such complicated equipment as duck presses. As a "sight to be remembered," the *Times* described "Dwight Whiting circling the tables at a WFS dinner, flint gun in hand. He was fumigating the *rhum au baba* . . . [sic]." Meanwhile, journalist Douglas Downie, who appreciated the competence of the amateur chefs, could not resist taunting the WFSLA for its all-male membership policy. "Around you, ladies, are male cooks whose culinary artistry is so delectable that even the most beautiful of you aren't welcome at their dinners."[57]

As a model of culinary activity, Phil Hanna, editor of *Westways*, singled out a dinner cooked entirely from California ingredients by members of the WFSLA, "fine gourmets all." Hanna had already created a new column, entitled "Fine Food in California," through which he advocated "pure gastronomy—the tradition of Carême, Escoffier, and Francatelli." In creating a great cuisine, he argued, readers would be well advised to trust in the ingenuity of the chef rather than the "scientific gibberish" of vitamins and calories."[58]

Book-length works by gourmet leaders also disseminated a favorable image of amateur gourmet activity. Book designer Merle Armitage, a member of the WFSLA, aimed his *Fit for a King* at "those who do not employ chefs or cooks." Praising the gourmet movement for making America a major center of international cuisine, he insisted that, contrary to popular stereotypes of the "decadent" and "sensuous" gourmet, WFS members possessed "cultivated palates and exacting tastes." In addition, they not only recognized the primacy of France in culinary matters but also valued regional American cuisine.[59]

Commercial Collaboration

While the advocacy of gourmet dining by movement leaders was not overtly commercial, other organizations and individuals were eager to use these spokesmen to promote the sale of products, especially wine, and the patronage of gourmet restaurants. In return for monetary rewards and/or public recognition, gourmet experts agreed to help businesses and authors generate larger sales for their products and services.

Among the authors was Duncan Hines, who invited Julian Street to write a short chapter on wine for a new edition of his path-breaking guide for automobile tourists, *Adventures in Good Eating*. The decision to publish the article suggested that Hines believed that his readers' increasing interest in wine and their recognition of Street's name would improve sales of the guide. The broader recognition it would bring Street, as well as the stipends Hines paid, drew the former to this collaboration. In addition, the guide endorsed Street's earlier books on gourmet dining and called him the "greatest present American author on wines and gastronomy."[60]

It is at first surprising that Hines, who was supposedly indifferent to "European gustatory standards" and so obsessed with cleanliness that he advised readers to inspect the kitchens of restaurants where they planned to eat, should have collaborated with Street. In fact, Hines became a *Gourmet* subscriber in 1942 and an advocate for using fresh local produce. Of necessity, he recommended nondescript restaurants in small towns, but his choices for New York, such as Jack and Charlie's and Lüchow's, coincided with those of more worldly guides.[61]

Like Duncan Hines, Macy's advertisers established credentials with customers by linking their merchandise to the gourmet movement. A campaign to sell Burgundy wines that ran off and on from 1937 to 1959 featured the "Cosmopolitan Travels of Macy's Famous Taster," whose name, William Titon, the store only revealed to the public in his later years. Ads reminded readers that "Macy's Famous Taster" was one of the first American members of the Tastevin, "a 300-year-old Order of great Burgundy-tasting prestige." Membership, "the highest honor to which a gourmet may aspire," entitled Titon in 1941 to attend one of the first Tastevin dinners in America, where he dined on *"Paupiettes de Sole Mariées au Homard* (rolled fillets of sole garnished with lobster) and the unforgettable magnum of Musigny 1911," drunk from the ritual silver cup. Macy's Taster thus assured readers that, since Tastevin members knew their Burgundies, wines with the Tastevin label, sold at Macy's, were of uniformly high quality.[62]

Experts from gourmet dining societies employed a somewhat different tactic to promote various events and causes in the public realm that would call attention to gourmet dining. Among them were the Golden Gate International Exposition and the New York World's Fair, both of which opened in 1939. The willingness of officials at the two events to approve this promotional work further testifies to the increasing public confidence in gourmet experts.

The role of these experts was particularly important because of the mixed message the Fairs were sending. Large food processors exhibited packaged foods that were supposedly nutritious, delicious, and so easy to prepare that they would liberate women from kitchen drudgery. Given the size and prominence of these exhibits, visitors to the Fairs were at least as likely to encounter the processors' message as they were to discover the twenty-two international restaurants at the New York Fair and half a dozen at the San Francisco Exposition.[63]

Leaders of the gourmet movement informed their own followers and the public of this unparalleled opportunity to experience gourmet dining. André Simon not only alerted readers of *Wine and Food* to dining possibilities at the Fair but also provided a short introduction to *Food at the Fair: A Gastronomical Tour of the World* (1939), the guidebook that Crosby Gaige had written. A separate welcome from the WFSNY urged readers to take advantage of the "opportunity for the study of the gastronomic history and culture of [America's] neighbors overseas." It is interesting to note that the coverage of the international restaurants preceded that devoted to American eateries in the guidebook.[64]

Among international restaurants at the New York Fair, the French Pavillon, the favorite of many food writers and connoisseurs, garnered the most coverage in the press. Awed by the Bordeaux wine dinner served there, Fougner called it "the most outstanding event which has taken place in the United States since repeal." The seven Bordeaux wines each accompanied an excellent dish as, for example, the Pauillac from the Haut-Médoc region of Bordeaux that was paired with a lamb and tarragon dish. The good press was no doubt partly responsible for the reopening of the Pavillon in Manhattan after the Fair.[65]

One of the surprising aspects of the Golden Gate International Exposition was the presence of a Wine Temple where members of the WFSSF served wine for tastings and juried the state wine competition. To be sure, Leon Adams, head of the Wine Institute, regretted that the Temple was located in the Agricultural building, but *Vogue Magazine*, perhaps more realistic, rejoiced to hear that a temple had at last been "built to wine." Meanwhile, fairgoers had access to half a dozen international restaurants.[66]

In the year following the opening of the world's fairs, Antoine's celebrated its one hundredth anniversary in New Orleans. For gourmet enthusiasts across the country that restaurant had come to symbolize the possibilities of French-style cuisine in America. Original dishes, such as oysters Rockefeller, *pommes soufflés*, and *pampano en papillote*, confirmed its long record of culinary excellence. Indeed, in 1936, *Restaurant Magazine* rated Antoine's as the best restaurant in the country.[67]

As the 1940 centennial of the restaurant approached, Roy Alciatore, the third generation of the family to manage Antoine's, decided to revamp the wine list. In so doing, he created an opportunity for a wine dealer to improve wine sales and his company's image through an association with a prestigious restaurant. As a director of Bellows, Julian Street was hopeful that Alciatore would choose his firm for the task; instead, Frank Schoonmaker reworked the list to feature wines imported by his firm that were, even in Street's opinion, excellent selections. For failing to compete seriously for this project, Street berated Frederick Wildman.[68]

With the new wine list in place, Alciatore consulted various gourmet proponents about other ways to celebrate the centennial. He decisively rejected a proposal to run a gourmet train to New Orleans before agreeing to write a centennial "history" with Street's help, which appeared as a promotional pamphlet bearing endorsements from Franklin Roosevelt, Herbert Hoover, Street, and H. L. Mencken.[69]

Cover, "Antoine's Wine List, 1840–1940," New Orleans. Artist unknown.
Rick Blount, Antoine's.

While Street lost out to Schoonmaker at Antoine's, Gaston Lauryssen, general manager of the Hotel St. Regis in New York, commissioned Street to improve his hotel's wine list. Before publishing the list, Street organized both a tasting and a dinner to celebrate and publicize it. When the project was completed, André Simon endorsed Street's list in *Wine and Food* as "the finest of all the hotel wine lists" with "an admirable selection" of clarets and red Burgundies and one of the few that was "free from 'duds' " or poor vintages. In Simon's opinion, hoteliers who used the list as a model on which to build a cellar would "never regret it."[70]

War and Postwar Dissemination Activities

Consistent with the emphasis on winning the war, most gourmet proponents scaled down their activities and avoided publishing menus that might appear extravagant from a wartime perspective. In keeping with these constraints, the December 16, 1944, *Saturday Evening Post* article on George Selleck, while demonstrating the continuing appeal of the amateur chef to the reading public, emphasized Selleck's ability to turn out great meals with simple ingredients.[71]

Selleck came to the attention of the *Saturday Evening Post* through Alexander Woollcott, who reported on the May 1940 dinner Selleck had cooked for him in San Francisco. The ensuing article identified Selleck as a member of the WFS, while picturing him in a chef's *toque* and coat presiding over a barbecue of lamb and chicken. There were, however, no pictures of wine glasses or bottles. Indeed, the article portrayed wine as a cooking agent and Selleck as a war hero who turned "garbage" (edibles usually thrown away) into delicious dinners.[72]

Perhaps inspired by monthly musings on gourmet dining in Phil Hanna's newsletter, *Bohemian Life* (1939), or the recent launching of *Gourmet* (1941), Julian Street proposed to Bellows "a magazine for gourmets and lovers of wines and spirits" that the company would circulate gratis to its customers. To sustain "the civilized tradition of good eating and good bottles through this period of anxiety and difficult living," *Table Topics* featured short articles on famous restaurants abroad, the lives of celebrated gourmets, and the status of French vineyards in wartime. Interspersed through the narrative were recipes for related dishes and drinks and advertisements of Bellows' products. With an initial circulation of ten thousand, the pamphlet appeared as an anonymous publication.[73]

In the prosperous postwar era, gourmet activists for the first time could disseminate their message of elegant dining without apology. In this cause, the Tastevin reached a sizable public through the appeal of its rituals and costumes, which was already evident in 1937. Opening with a large photograph of robed leaders conducting an induction in the Tastevin's Burgundy cellar, Charles Codman regaled *Town and Country* readers with the charms of the society's induction ceremony.[74]

Following the war, Tastevin leaders worked hard to shape the image of their activities in the media. To assure publicity for their New York dinners, they invited journalists from the *Herald Tribune*, the *World-Telegram*, and the *Times* to their December 1947 dinner. The result was "good publicity" in all three papers and a bonus in the form of Jane Nickerson's illustrated *New York Times Magazine* article identifying the Tastevin as "an aristocracy of the palate" that caused even a celebrity chef like Louis Diat to be "touchy" about preparing a society dinner.[75]

The press was even more responsive to the December 1948 Tastevin dinner on the St. Regis roof. Gordon Brown wrote that "the publicity in the Herald Tribune and the New Yorker has brought many comments to me. In fact, I feel I could offer a readership check to the New Yorker, which must be very widely read. The Confrérie have a lot of intrigued and envious fans." Indeed, the *New Yorker* identified the Tastevin as "a group of knowing and specialized wine bibbers" and Brown as "a scholarly man" who refused Frank Paget's (manager of the Hotel Pierre) request for water to rinse his mouth in order to uphold the rule that only wine could be imbibed at Tastevin dinners. Hoping that he could "get the confrérie into the 'New Yorker' again and under more favorable comment and more imbued with reverence for Burgundy wines," Brown arranged to have *New Yorker* writer Geoffrey Hellman "sit between Dick de Rochemont and me." No such article appeared. So, after considering the $30 charge for hosting each journalist at a dinner, Brown decided that the cost was not worth the favorable publicity.[76]

All the same, the Tastevin had other, more ambitious schemes afoot. In December 1948, Richard de Rochemont, a Tastevin member and producer for the *March of Time*, shot and recorded a dinner at the St. Regis Hotel. De Rochemont arranged for the Voice of America to narrate the initiation ceremony while it was filmed for the *March of Time*. Designed to impress Frenchmen with the impact of the Tastevin in America, the script identified General George Patton, Ambassador William Bullitt, and Admiral H. K. Hewitt as past or present members. It then described the dignified setting, explained the Tastevin symbols, and portrayed the drama of the initiation. A well-placed microphone enabled the French audience to hear the ceremony and the rousing performance of the Ban Bourguignon.[77]

The postwar years were notable as well for the continued public interest in chefs. *Life Magazine* celebrated Escoffier and his disciples in the Escoffier Society in a one-page 1946 photo essay showing diners aligned on both sides of long banquet tables with their *"serviettes au cou."* In the brief account incorporating a menu of a six-course dinner accompanied by five wines, *Life* explained Chef Escoffier's central place in gastronomy (see illustration, chap. 3).[78]

Having featured George Selleck during the war, the *Saturday Evening Post* celebrated the work of the WFSSF's preferred professional chef, Lucien Heyraud of the Palace Hotel. The 1955 article recounted Heyraud's imaginative treatment of a pig for the society's Christmas dinner, while paying tribute to André Simon's leadership of the WFS and the "great gourmets" of the WFSSF.[79]

The postwar celebration of Selleck's talents continued with Clementine Paddleford's article in "This Week" (June 19, 1949) that lauded his barbecuing prowess. Others portrayed amateur chefs as either "rugged individualists" or "prosaic businessmen," whose adventures began before they entered the kitchen. As a case in point, Idwal Jones, amateur chef and gourmet author, recounted how friends planned to cook a brace of swans for the WFSLA members' dinner until they spotted young goats in a field that were soon captured, roasted, and sauced.[80]

Once launched, the idea of amateur gourmet chefs became quite conventional in the Los Angeles area, so that leaders of the Pasadena chapter of the WFS felt obliged to identify their members as "tasters, not basters." Meanwhile, the Beverly Hills chapter strayed further by flying Maxim's chefs from Paris to prepare a dinner at $300 per person. The group had already attracted attention for entertaining ex-President Truman aboard the *S.S. President Cleveland* just days after he left the White House.[81]

Reminiscent of the prewar *Fit for a King*, Crosby Gaige's *Dining with My Friends* sought to glamorize gourmet cooking by collecting recipes for dishes comprising a whole menu from 102 contributors, among them gourmet leaders Simon and Jeanne Owen, along with Arthur Eisenhower, brother of the president, and historian Samuel Eliot Morison. These menus of "voiceless amateurs," cooking in their homes, provided models for "creative people" in the reading audience. Alongside traditional French fare, there were several meals that must have shocked Gaige himself. As an example, Mrs. Walter Eddy, married to a biochemist at Columbia University, featured a tomato juice cocktail with Steero beef bouillon cubes and a bean pot beef stew with canned peas. No alcohol was served.[82]

As in the prewar years, advertisers used the prestige of gourmet dining societies to promote products and practices. A Macy's ad again trumpeted the expertise of "Macy's Wine Taster" and portrayed robed officers standing in vineyards and offering "a toast (in Burgundy, of course)" from their tastevins. Macy's assured readers that "the wonderful and precious are not for just the few . . . but for everybody."[83]

In the case of Antoine's, gourmet leaders promoted their own societies by associating them with the restaurant. That was one reason for Jules Bohy to hold the tenth-anniversary dinner of the New Orleans branch at Antoine's. Certainly,

Macy's advertisement for Burgundy wines from the *New York Times*, Dec. 8, 1959, p. 7. Macy's.

no other venue better illustrated the pleasures of the table, as Lucius Beebe proclaimed in his 1953 *Holiday* article, "The Miracle of Antoine's." He touted the restaurant's original dishes and praised its wine cellar as one of the four best in the country.[84]

No doubt the fame of Antoine's figured in Francis Parkinson Keyes' decision to use the restaurant in several of her key scenes, while featuring Alciatore as one of the lesser characters, in the murder mystery *Dinner at Antoine's* (1948). Jules Bohy was quick to recognize that the novel would be "a fine publicity" for the restaurant.[85]

In the postwar period, the *Los Angeles Times* reverted to prewar form by reporting news of gourmet dining on the society pages. Perhaps the paper justified this practice because one of two annual Tastevin dinners between 1957 and 1961 was an "exclusive" ladies' night. Articles and photos depicted the elegance of the women's dresses and the white-tie attire of their escorts, while four of the seven articles made no mention of food and wine.[86]

Focusing more on the famous rather than the glamorous, the *Washington Post* reported that, with its "upper crust gastronomically speaking," Washington was becoming a "tasty city." The paper had in mind such Tastevin diners as Senators Fulbright and Goldwater and their spouses, as well as French ambassadors Couve de Mouville and Hervé Alphand. Accounts of this sort did little to justify fine dining for the larger public but were perhaps less harmful in the late 1950s than in the 1930s, when the gourmet movement was trying to get a foothold in America.[87]

At the outset, no one knew whether culinary activities would be of interest to the media. Until 1934, food writing consisted largely of recipe columns in newspapers and the women's magazines. With the rise of gourmet dining societies, however, a more reflective approach to the subject developed, but before it took hold, writers exploited their audiences' fascination with the upper crust and their elaborate dinners. Based on such articles, readers could well believe that only *haute cuisine*, served with great ceremony in an elegant setting for a social elite, was truly gourmet dining. The coverage improved when food and wine professionals instructed food writers in the subtleties of fine dining and used knowledgeable in-house spokespersons to address the public.

The Growth of Gourmet Activity in America

The practices of selectivity and publicity apparently worked well for gourmet societies as indicated by their expansion over time. Off to a slow start in 1934, society activities diminished during World War II, but the rising cosmopolitan ethos in America created a more supportive climate in the postwar era. At the same time, war production brought about an economic revival that enabled more professionals and managers to enjoy luxury consumption of all kinds. By war's end, these groups were engaging more fully with Europe, whose cultural traditions seemed increasingly relevant to their lives.

Even so, the gourmet movement in the early postwar era was small. In a *New Yorker* column Angelica Gibbs found five hundred members in various chapters of the Wine and Food Society, some forty-five individuals in the new Confrérie des Chevaliers du Tastevin, and two hundred members in George Frederick's Gourmet Society in New York. Gibbs should have included, as well, the roughly seven hundred members of Les Amis d'Escoffier and fifty Medical Friends of Wine in San Francisco, for a total of about 1,500 individuals.[88]

Shortly before the end of the war, Phil Hanna, honorary secretary of the WF-SLA, forecast the future of gourmet dining with surprising accuracy. He claimed that "we shall witness the birth and growth of many dining clubs, plain and elegant. The trend was strongly in this direction before the war. All over the land chapters of the Wine and Food Society were flourishing." Moreover, "from Presque isle, Maine, to Point Loma, California, men's and women's social clubs" increasingly emphasized "the character and quality" of their dining. Thus, the future was bright for many gourmet dining groups.[89]

Among the original chapters of the WFS, none achieved the heights of the core group of the WFSSF. However, five of them survived, while the inactive New Orleans branch was briefly revived. From 1945 to 1959, the WFS grew to forty-four chapters, seven in greater Los Angeles, three in the Bay area, another in Honolulu, as well as chapters in Washington, D.C., Kansas City, Baltimore, Cleveland, and Phoenix. A number of the new chapters accepted women as members. All told, the American membership of the WFS increased from about five hundred to two thousand.[90]

The rapid expansion of the WFS suggests that it was receptive to bringing in outsiders whether properly credentialed or not. Virginia Stanton's experience, as reported in a 1959 *House Beautiful* article, gives credence to that impression. Stanton "got the whim whams" when she was asked to cook a dinner for thirty-five members of the Monterey WFS, but she conquered her fear by working with vintners and WFS veterans to create a menu and prepare a rehearsal dinner. Based on her success, Stanton urged interested outsiders to create their own chapters by applying to the WFS.[91]

Menu cover designed by the Grabhorn Press, San Francisco's most renowned art printer, for the November 12, 1941, WFSSF dinner at the Bohemian Club. From such crystal wine glasses, enhanced here by the play of light, diners would later sip an Amontillado Manuel Misa sherry and a 1926 Corton Clos du Roi Burgundy. The Wine and Food Society of San Francisco.

GALA FÊTE CHAMPÊTRE

AU VIGNOBLE DE
PAUL MASSON
à Saratoga , Californie
Mercredi le 17 Juillet, 1940

Le menu

Les ÉCREVISSES à la SARATOGAINE
Champagne Brut, Paul Masson 1936

Le JUS de BOEUF GRILLÉ
"VIEUX COSTAUD"

Le GRAND PLAT de GRILLADES ASSORTIES
AUX FLEURS de ZUCCHINI
Pinot Chardonnay, Paul Masson 1936

Le PREMIER QUARTIER d'AGNEAU GRILLE
MARINE AUX HERBES EXOTIQUES
MAIS INDIEN de l'AMÉRIQUE du NORD
Pinot Noir, Paul Masson 1936

Le FROMAGE
PORT SALUT de MAYENNE

Les FRUITS RAFRAICHIS

Le CAFÉ NOIR

COGNAC
Prunier Hostellerie

Le Chef : Dr. George Selleck
Le Sommelier : M. Harold Price
Le Grand Maître : Dr. Raoul Blanquie
Le Menu : M. George Holl

FÊTE CHAMPÊTRE SOUS LE PATRONAGE DE M. Martin Ray

Menu for the July 17, 1940, dinner at the Paul Masson Vineyard in Saratoga, California, to honor core members of the WFSSF for promoting Masson wines. By printing the menu on the butt of a wine cask decorated in grape vines, the designer cleverly linked the meal to its vineyard setting. The Wine and Food Society of San Francisco.

A 1946 collage of WFSSF menus / menu covers designed by George Holl and assembled by friends to commemorate his death. Three menus (*top center, bottom center, bottom right*) feature medieval script and floral patterns popularized by the arts and crafts movement. In a more contemporary style, Holl portrayed fellow member and chef George Selleck as an angel (*top right*). The Wine and Food Society of San Francisco.

BON VOYAGE
RAOUL

CERCLE de L'UNION
—SAN FRANCISCO—

offered by
Wine & Food Society Board of Directors

May 12, 1949

Menu cover for the May 12, 1949, dinner celebrating the voyage of Raoul Blanquie, the first chairman of the WFSSF. Inside, the dinner menu borders both sides of a map of France, decorated with images of regional foods, thus identifying Blanquie's destination and anticipating his gastronomic adventures. The Wine and Food Society of San Francisco.

Menu for the September 9, 1950, dinner honoring Georges Deslagnes, a physician and WFSSF member, and his wife, Alphonsine; bright images of fruits spilling from a basket suggest that this occasion will be a feast that is spirited, intimate, and informal. The Wine and Food Society of San Francisco.

Menu cover for the January 20, 1958, WFSSF dinner at Romanoff's incorporating food, wine, and elements of a table setting into a Cubist design. While WFSSF members selected the menu items, Romanoff's Los Angeles and/or San Francisco restaurants probably used the cover for other occasions. The Wine and Food Society of San Francisco.

The Inaugural *Gourmet* Cover, January 1941, drawn by Henry Stahlhut, boldly announces the magazine's intention to challenge the food establishment by treating dining as festive and sensual, while revealing the provenance of the food. Contributor/Gourmet, © Condé Nast Publications.

The afterglow of Franco-American wartime collaboration provides a perfect occasion for Lanson to present the taste of its Champagne as an experience shared by New Yorkers and Parisians. *Gourmet*, October 1946, p. 43. The Schlesinger Library, Radcliffe Institute, Harvard University. Champagne Lanson.

Despite the loss of Selmer Fougner, who, according to Lucius Beebe, died in gourmet style "filled with foie gras and truffles and leaking Romanée Conti at every joint," Escoffier chapters increased in number from seven to nineteen and the membership to more than a thousand; however, it is only possible to document local chapter activities for New York, Boston, Washington, and Chicago. Meanwhile, Joseph Donon turned the New York Escoffier dinners into fundraisers for the Escoffier museum and foundation by expanding the guest list to include wealthy New Yorkers who would contribute to the cause and pay for more sumptuous meals like those of the Tastevin.[92]

Of particular note was a 1959 movement among the wives of Boston's most distinguished chefs, who sought to experience fine dining for themselves. As Mrs. Richard Clark remarked, "for years I tied my husband's bow tie, fastened his cuff links and kissed him good by, then spent hours listening to him talk about what he ate and drank. At last it's my turn." Les Dames des Amis d'Escoffier, as they called themselves, wanted an annual dinner, and with the support of Boston's most prestigious chef, Charles Banino of the Ritz-Carlton, who helped to found Boston's Escoffier Society in 1937, they got what they asked for. Having assured the public that these women were "gourmets in their own right," Banino worked with them to design menus that were the culinary equivalents of the regular Escoffier dinners. Indeed, the inaugural event featured the same two Banino's specialties that he had cooked at the 1937 inaugural Escoffier dinner: *noisettes d'agneau clamart* (kernels of lamb with fresh peas) accompanied by a Chateau Haut Brion 1953 and *pigeonneau désossé en casserole Bordighera* (boned squab in a saucepan à la Bordighera) served with a Chateau Corton Grancey 1953. During the dinner, traditional rules against smoking, drinking cocktails, and talking about business affairs applied to the women as to their husbands. Records of these dinners continue to 1979.[93]

Following in the footsteps of the Wine and Food Society, leaders of the American Tastevin founded more chapters of the Burgundy parent organization between 1950 and 1961. Among them were Wilmington, Delaware, Los Angeles, Chicago, Philadelphia, Texas (Dallas was its actual home), San Francisco, Miami, and Memphis; in the process, the number of American members rose from forty-five to about six hundred.[94]

Aside from the expansion of existing societies, several new gourmet groups arose after 1945. The most opulent and least ritualistic of all gourmet societies, the Lucullus Circle, was founded in 1950 and named after a Roman general noted for his love of lavish dining; the group held five dinners a year in New York hotels and restaurants, required black-tie dress, and limited membership to fifty men. Several of its members, including the department store mogul Stanley Marcus, came from outside of New York. A French immigrant, Claudius C. Philippe, who, as food and wine manager of the Waldorf, helped prepare Escoffier dinners in the 1930s, founded the society, screened applicants, and arranged the dinners. The Circle's trademark was the pairing of two wines with every course so that each diner could compare them. During the meal, members critiqued the food and wine pairings but broached no controversial subjects. Until the brandy appeared, they also refrained from smoking.[95]

The creation of the Commandérie de Bordeaux in 1957 as a counterpart to the Tastevin illustrates the way older gourmet societies spawned newer ones. Representatives of the Bordeaux region and American wine dealers sought to create an organization like the Tastevin on American soil to promote Bordeaux wines. Standing in the way were various organizations representing subregions of Bordeaux. By 1958, the approval of a single organization representing the whole Bordeaux area paved the way for the first meeting of an American Commandérie at the Brussels restaurant in New York. H. Gregory Thomas, the president of Chanel perfume company in America and an officer of the New York Tastevin, headed the group. At six feet eight inches tall, Thomas was a Charles de Gaulle look-alike, as well as French educated and the only American elected to the prestigious Club des Cents.[96]

Some Tastevin members found a comfortable home in the hierarchical and ritualistic Commandérie. A number of them also joined the Chaîne des Rotisseurs, whose members wore a ribbon and chain around their necks. Founded in 1248 as a medieval guild of roasting chefs, it was dedicated to the maintenance of high standards in the preparation of food. In 1950, Curnonsky, the elected "Prince of Gastronomers" in France, revived the society to bring together chefs, restaurateurs, hotel men, and amateur gourmets in the manner of the Escoffier Society. After its debut in 1960, the society, under the leadership of Paul Spitzler, a meat and poultry supplier, established branches in the United States.[97]

More illustrative of the gourmet fever gripping elements of the American upper-middle class were the informal groups that sprang up across the country. Several announced their existence in the "Sugar and Spice" columns of *Gourmet*, while acknowledging the recipes from the magazine as the source of their gourmet menus. Even before the end of the war, *Gourmet's* editors assured readers that many such societies already existed and, given the "ingenuity" of interested people "who like good food" and "good company," they were certain that more would materialize.[98]

After the war, letters to the editor reported the creation of such societies more frequently. In Chicago, ten men formed the Streeterville and Sanitary Canal Gourmet and Study Society to hold monthly dinners at each others' houses. From the Presidio in Moneterey Colonel D. W. Hickey, Jr., wrote to praise the very active Women's Club cooking class that periodically served ethnic meals. The most recent menu featured Arabic, Korean, Chinese, and Hungarian dishes, among others. Meanwhile, Mrs. Rachel Wilmat of Nashville, who studied at the Cordon Bleu, founded a gourmet club with seventy-five women who met four times a year. All of the members were students in her cooking school.[99]

Among groups that acknowledged *Gourmet's* role in their activities was "Les Amis d'AliBab" (referring to the French author of *Gastronomie Pratique* [Paris: Ernest Flammarion, 1906]). Writing from a New York hospital, Francis Paul Salvatore announced that he and his physician colleagues had established this group and were using both the *Gourmet Cookbook* and Chamberlain's *Bouquet de France* to prepare meals for each other. Similarly, Mrs. Joseph Tucker of Clayton, Missouri, reported that she and her husband had formed a gourmet group of four couples that used recipes from the magazine. So did the self-professed "distinguished Dallas celebrants," who formed "Gourmets Ltd.," for which they gave credit to *Gourmet*. Meanwhile, members of the Gourmet Club in Arcadia, California, were required to subscribe to *Gourmet* magazine.[100]

By all tangible measures, the movement to expand gourmet dining in America had achieved its objective. The Depression, World War II, and the cold war notwithstanding, three international societies, featuring the sometimes awkward combination of selectivity and publicity, took root in the United States. With the return of prosperity and the rise of internationalism, the movement spread from organizations created by food and wine professionals to grassroots groups often energized by *Gourmet* magazine. Friends and neighbors were learning to cook gourmet recipes and were gathering to enjoy the fruits of their labors accompanied by a bottle of wine. The opening of new gourmet restaurants in big cities across the country also contributed to this expansion.

In important respects, however, appearances are deceiving. While it is true that the population of gourmet diners was expanding, it is doubtful that this expansion achieved the goal set by the movement's founders. After all, André Simon and Julian Street believed that gourmet dining should challenge the nutritionists' goal of turning meals into occasions exclusively devoted to ingesting the proper nutrients. Instead, they urged Americans to value dining as an opportunity to exercise the senses in order to experience the flavors and textures of their

food, while enjoying leisurely conversations with tablemates. And both men insisted that even a simple, well-prepared peasant dish should be considered a gourmet dinner. Indeed, Street's guide to Parisian restaurants deliberately emphasized the smaller, simpler restaurants featuring family cooking and urged readers
to savor the dining experience as an entire evening's entertainment.

For Street and Simon, moreover, gourmet dining was an everyday practice
rather than an occasional extravagant meal. The gourmet, after all, was a connoisseur of food and wine, skilled in recognizing good flavors and textures; this knowledge he or she used to structure any and all meals so that each dish harmonized
with the others and with the accompanying wines. According to the occasion, a
connoisseur might prefer a single-course meal or a complex dinner, a dish with a
rich cream or a light wine sauce. And for the beverage, gourmet diners could
choose among several vintage Burgundies or one regional wine, depending on the
fare. However, finding a strategy for educating the members of a dining society,
most of whom had had little opportunity to experience French cuisine, was not a
simple matter.

To accomplish their ambitious plan to change the American dining culture,
Street and Simon looked to the creation of dining societies. From the outset, the
principal activity of these societies was the staging of elegant dinners a few times
a year in hotel restaurants to familiarize Americans with *haute cuisine*. However,
the equation of gourmet dining with lavish meals for special occasions was a poor
way to challenge the dominant nutritionist approach. Priced beyond the means
of the average American and relying on men's clubs to recruit members and host
dinners, this approach isolated the activities of the gourmet societies from the
lives of middle-class Americans. Furthermore, planning *haute cuisine* menus left
little time for modeling more modest dinners that would have introduced middle-
class Americans to French home cooking.

Moreover, members' close links with men's clubs and their primary engagement with planning rarified dinners focused attention on the increased status
conferred by belonging to a gourmet society. The appeal of membership thus
rested in some measure on the promise of advancing up the social ladder by
joining an exclusive club. To be sure, the dining societies succeeded in publicizing their activities and attracting new members to their organizations, but they
lost sight of their larger objective, which was to challenge the nutritionist model
of dining.

Nevertheless, the mixed motives of founders and followers alike cast doubt on
Thorstein Veblen's claim that conspicuous consumption alone explains the behavior of gourmet diners. In fact, his claim tells us more about Veblen's obsession

with the instinct of workmanship and his refusal to acknowledge the value of the aesthetic dimension of life than it does about the complex motivations behind the activities of gourmet diners. The movement, in reality, incorporated a variety of personalities and constituencies with differing motivations, including the California gourmets, who happily produced, as well as consumed, gourmet food. Their practice suggests a strain of do-it-yourself activism that many Americans of different social classes embraced. Like Veblen, they valued workmanship—or was it "conspicuous production"?—and found in gourmet dining a new way to work and consume at a single occasion.

Chapter Five

Beating the Nazis with Truffles and Tripe

The Early Years of *Gourmet: The Magazine of Good Living*

In his path-breaking study, *The Lonely Crowd* (1950), David Riesman noted that "tossed salads and garlic, elaborate sauces, dishes en casserole, *Gourmet* magazine, wine and liqueurs, spread west from New York and east from San Francisco." He rightly saw this development as part of a dramatic shift in sensibility: Americans were dropping their Puritanical reluctance to talk about and enjoy food; "many people are and many more feel that they must be gourmets." In the new era, as Riesman pointed out, great opportunities were available for personalizing meals and experiencing the sensual joys of eating and talking about food as a result, in part, of the founding of *Gourmet*.[1]

The magazine both promoted and benefited from urban Americans' improved access to and rising interest in gourmet products. After the war, the proliferation of ethnic restaurants in large cities and the greater ease of travel to Europe made gourmet dining more accessible. That was particularly true of New York, which already offered a variety of opportunities to enjoy fine cuisine. Among new restaurants, the most notable was Henri Soulé's Pavillon, usually proclaimed the finest French restaurant in America. Attesting to its excellence was the fact that several chefs, who first worked in the Pavillon kitchen, founded their own restaurants in Manhattan in the 1950s, including La Caravelle and La Côte Basque. Upscale tourists, as well as New Yorkers, enjoyed these new French restaurants along with their older ethnic counterparts. As Tom Marvel remarked in his *Gourmet* restaurant column, "You can roam the world via the restaurants of New York."[2]

Improvements in transatlantic travel made it easier for Americans to enjoy European dining in Europe as well. Following the postwar recovery, the substantial decline in steamship and air fares contributed to a twofold increase in the number of Americans traveling to Europe between 1950 and 1956. With the rise of jet service in 1958 and the availability of special excursion rates, travelers could afford to visit Europe for shorter periods of time and more frequently. In 1960 alone, almost eight hundred thousand American tourists crossed the

Atlantic, most of them by airplane. Furthermore, France remained a popular destination for the majority of these travelers.[3]

A third development that facilitated the spread of gourmet dining was the greater accessibility of specialty food products. By the early 1950s, Spice Island sales were booming, while imports of European beers rose dramatically. For many years, Americans had shopped for these items in specialty food shops and department stores. However, the growing market convinced General Foods to produce a new line of fifty-three "gourmet foods" in 1958, sold not only in small shops but also in supermarkets. Among these foods were canned lobster Newburg, *baba au rhum*, and cointreau marmalade. Of course, the availability of these items was no guarantee that they would meet gourmet standards of freshness and/or proper preparation.[4]

To reach this promised land of the 1950s, however, *Gourmet* first had to survive the leaner war years. As the first issue of the magazine came off the press in 1941, the upper-middle-class audience, to which it was directed, was reading the luxury lifestyle magazines for advice on clothing fashions and home decorating. In the realm of food, the dominant voice on culinary matters remained the women's magazines. However, the new food columns in the *New Yorker* and *House and Garden*, with their focus on the pleasures of the table, anticipated the rise of *Gourmet*, which, after 1941, became the first and only magazine devoted primarily to fine dining. Not until 1956 with the appearance of *Bon Appetit* was there a competitor in the field. *Gourmet's* tardy arrival suggests how much more difficult it was for Americans to overcome inhibitions to the momentary enjoyment of subtle flavors than it was to appreciate the more durable decoration of clothing and homes.[5]

Like the gourmet dining societies, *Gourmet* adopted an antimodern ethos celebrating traditional foodways, especially French cuisine, in order to challenge the practices and beliefs of nutritionists, the large corporate food processors, and the women's magazines. To the founders of *Gourmet*, who saw dining as an opportunity to exercise the taste buds with a variety of interesting flavors and to enjoy the experience in the company of family and friends, such an "eat-to-live" approach made little sense. Much as home decorators and fashion designers rejected mass-produced merchandise in favor of handcrafted dresses, ceramics, and jewelry, often designed in France, *Gourmet* praised French chefs who used fresh ingredients to cook hearty meals offering a greater variety and intensity of flavors and textures than processed foods.

To establish itself as a luxury lifestyle magazine, *Gourmet* built on the success of the gourmet dining societies, whose members were potential subscribers and whose activities the staff frequently reported in the magazine. (André Simon told Julian Street that he received *Gourmet* "regularly" and "like[d] it very much.") Often *Gourmet* deferred to leaders of the dining societies as authorities on the food, wine, and protocol for gourmet dining. Equally important, the pioneering quarterly journal of the Wine and Food Society served as a model for the *Gourmet* staff. To be sure, *Wine and Food* circulated almost exclusively among members of the Society. Even so, its editor and authors were interested in the taste rather than the nutritional value of food and wine; and, in exploring a variety of national and regional cuisines, they used the travel narrative as a format for presenting information about the distinctive dishes they encountered. *Gourmet* was to follow suit. Like *Wine and Food*, and despite the much more frequent appearance of recipes, *Gourmet* was primarily concerned with expanding readers' culinary horizons.[6]

There, the similarities end. Unlike gourmet dining societies, which were run by Frenchmen, *Gourmet* was published by an American, Earle MacAusland, who, along with his staff, admired French and other ethnic cuisines and hoped to introduce his readers to them. Moreover, MacAusland sought to establish a mass circulation magazine rather than an exclusive dining society. For this reason, *Gourmet* had to maximize advertising income and make allowances for its readers' preferences in food and drink. In the process, the magazine reshaped gourmet dining to accommodate Americans' liking for the cocktail and to insist on the value of traditional American dishes.

To broaden its audience, *Gourmet* also used a variety of formats that would appeal to different readers. As one reader argued, the new publication should bring about a "culinary reunion" for gourmet society members, food and wine professionals, food writers, veteran and would-be travelers, and amateur gourmets. Particularly important was the growing legion of American travelers, who could no longer visit Europe and especially France, but cherished memories of their previous trips; following in the footsteps of the *New Yorker*, *Gourmet* also addressed Americans interested in enjoying New York's cultural activities.[7]

Furthermore, *Gourmet* dramatically altered the gender base of the gourmet movement. While most dining societies excluded women, the magazine assumed that dietary issues were too important to be left to the devices of either sex. Accordingly, *Gourmet* published articles by both male and female authors addressed to members of both sexes. In the process, the audience for gourmet activities grew rapidly, as reflected in the rising number of subscriptions to *Gourmet* and a 1958 *New Yorker* cartoon, depicting a sign posted on the magazine's office door that read "out to lunch, back at 5." Bursting with pride at this attention from a magazine "we esteem," *Gourmet* reprinted the cartoon. Most gratifying, however, was the cartoonist's assumption that *New Yorker* readers were familiar with *Gourmet*.[8]

Even so, many believed that *Gourmet*'s publisher, Earle MacAusland, selected the wrong time to launch his magazine. As the first issue appeared in January 1941, the United States was emerging from the worst depression in its history and was edging toward war. Resources, previously devoted to consumerism and combating the Depression, were increasingly used to prepare the nation for the military struggle that followed the attack on Pearl Harbor ten months later. It was no time to be advocating foie gras and caviar for dinner.[9]

Despite the constraints imposed by the coming war, *Gourmet* authors discovered aspects of the wartime environment that they could turn to their advantage. Staff and audience were part of the growing community of well-traveled Americans, many of whom appreciated fine dining. The rising tide of internationalism created an opportunity to educate more Americans about culinary traditions in other countries, so long as *Gourmet* did not denigrate traditional American cooking. Moreover, the staff understood that the defense of the American way of life as a war aim could as easily include elegant dining as more conventional consumer items.

In fact, the war environment encouraged a crusading approach in which editors, writers, and readers took the high ground. In their view, gourmet dining was one of the central elements of Western civilization for which America was fighting. Properly understood, the everyday act of eating to live could become an uplifting art that ennobled the lives of cooks and diners alike. By launching *Gourmet* as the war in Europe was expanding, the founders, as they saw it, could provide a refuge for chefs, who were the practitioners of a great art form they could no longer practice in Europe.

The advent of rationing intensified the magazine's sense of purpose. Editors insisted that, unlike other Americans, gourmet diners could eat well without diminishing the food resources necessary to fight the war. By advocating a diet based on nonrationed foods, they positioned the magazine squarely in the patriot camp. Meanwhile, *Gourmet*'s promotion of traditional American dishes, as well as the fostering of French cuisine, struck a chord with readers who condemned the Nazi war on the United States and the occupation of France. In these ways, the magazine shrewdly made use of issues arising from the war to build a case for gourmet dining in America.

Selecting a Staff, Generating a Vision

As MacAusland well understood, much was at stake in the hiring of staff members and the selection of the first *Gourmet* authors. At a time when nutritionists and the women's magazines dominated discussions about food, the staff of the magazine would be responsible for forcefully advocating the principles of gourmet dining to a larger and more diverse audience. To accomplish this task, MacAusland deliberately selected authors who could present gourmet activities in an appealing and sometimes dramatic light. Only those who had traveled widely, eaten well, and could write effectively about their experiences need apply. For articles presenting instructions in cooking, MacAusland sought food professionals who explained basic cooking methods clearly, while reviewers of New York restaurants and cultural events would have to be connoisseurs of food and wine and knowledgeable about the current restaurant scene. From the outset, MacAusland sought editorial assistance from women and published articles from several female authors. Moreover, a husband-and-wife team, Samuel and Narcissa Chamberlain, fashioned *Gourmet's* most popular travel narratives.

Before launching the magazine, MacAusland's knowledge of gourmet dining was limited, although he had experienced the business side of the publishing industry. The son of a Scottish immigrant silversmith, he grew up in Boston and attended MIT for a year. After dropping out, MacAusland sold advertising to various magazines in New York until he became the publisher of the *National Parent-Teacher Magazine* in 1935. There, and at Butterick Publishing Company, he worked with periodicals that published recipes for their readers.[10]

By MacAusland's own account, the idea for the founding of *Gourmet* came to him while he was paging through images of luxury food items and fine French and German wines in an S.S. Pierce catalogue. He already had a taste for expensive French food, as well as British suits, which spurred his interest in approaching fine dining as an art form, much as *Vogue* was accustomed to doing in presenting women's fashions to its readers. As an admirer of the *New Yorker*, MacAusland also sought to turn its sophisticated style to the appreciation and promotion of gourmet dining.[11]

To recruit a staff that could produce the magazine he envisioned, MacAusland contacted Lucious Beebe and others familiar with fine dining in New York. Based on these consultations, he selected Pearl V. Metzelthin to be the first editor of *Gourmet*. As the wife of a German diplomat, she had lived in China for several years, traveled widely in other countries, and had recently published

A World Wide Cook Book. Moreover, Metzelthin was a nutritionist who advised airlines in the interwar period on how to improve their food service and would thus be able to represent nutritionists' concerns in a magazine that was generally unsympathetic to that position. Within three years, however, Metzelthin left *Gourmet*. From 1943 until 1961 and beyond, MacAusland maintained the titles of publisher and editor, although the masthead listed various associate, executive, senior, and managing editors.[12]

More durable and more effective in the early days of the magazine was Louis P. De Gouy, who MacAusland chose to be the first of two "*Gourmet* Chefs." De Gouy and his successor Louis Diat provided thorough coverage of traditional French cooking during the magazine's first two decades. Before taking his position with *Gourmet*, De Gouy had a distinguished career as a chef, much of it in the United States, and had published several cookbooks (see chap. 7 for De Gouy's biography). For the magazine, he would write two articles every month, each of which supplied a variety of recipes for a particular course in the meal. Most, but not all, of the recipes were for French dishes.[13]

Both Ralph Reinhold (treasurer, 1941 to 1950) and Gladys Guggenheim Straus (vice-president, 1941 to 1948) were officers of *Gourmet* and served shorter stints as associate editors. Reinhold, a successful publisher who founded *American Artist* and managed *Architectural Forum* for six years, probably knew MacAusland through their respective publishing ventures. Given his interest in magazines with an artistic bent, Reinhold's involvement with *Gourmet* was an appropriate venture for him.[14]

It is likely that Reinhold suggested Straus to MacAusland as a possible collaborator in founding the new magazine. She had a long-time interest in food, but from a nutritionist perspective, and was then serving as nutrition commissioner for metropolitan New York; the nutritionist approach notwithstanding, she published two collections of her favorite recipes, many drawn from *Gourmet* itself; even so, she regarded garlic as an antisocial ingredient and so omitted it from all but her Provençal recipes. It is interesting to note that Straus moved into the associate editor's role in September of 1943 just as Pearl Metzelthin exited the magazine; one nutritionist replaced another. Perhaps MacAusland accepted this deviation from the magazine's approach because of Straus' financial support for *Gourmet*.[15]

The founders' strategy for recruiting a large subscriber base was to use a variety of formats to convince potential readers that food and drink were pleasurable to read about, as well as to consume. Virtually every issue contained several travel articles exploring the wide range of dining options from which subscribers could choose. Among the most notable travelogues were Samuel Chamberlain's explorations of France, Italy, and England; Ruth Harkness' series on Mexico; Lillian Langseth-Christensen's *Viennese Memoir*; and Robert Tristram Coffin's evocations of life on a Maine saltwater farm. Other series, more focused on dining experiences per se, examined great gourmets of the past and their favorite dishes ("Gourmet Lives") and fine dinners that had been served over the centuries ("Memorable Meals").[16]

In a surprising number of these travel narratives, food played a secondary role to the adventures of their main characters. The contributions of both Coffin (seventy-five articles from 1943 to 1955) and Stephen Longstreet (ninety-three articles from 1942 to 1957) were cases in point. Take, for example, Coffin's accounts of life on a Maine farm in the nineteenth century when the family did most of the work by hand. The cultivation, gathering, and cooking of the food was an adventure worth recounting, but only one of several. By contrast, Longstreet's various series depicted the around-the-world adventures of members of the Longstreet family, most of them in comfortable hotels. While capturing local color and the eccentric behavior of the family, Longstreet paused briefly to describe exotic meals that the family ate. Most likely, the regular appearance of articles by these two authors reflected their storytelling prowess and the editors' uncertainty about readers' appetite for a magazine fully devoted to food.[17]

By featuring recipes from largely French and European or traditional American regional sources, often prepared with and accompanied by wine, *Gourmet* offered a variety of cooking options that were not available in the women's magazines. In addition to recipes in the monthly articles of the *"Gourmet* Chef," *Gourmet* published others without bylines in "The Last Touch," a monthly feature often devoted to sauces, and "The Soup Kettle," which appeared occasionally. Some authors included recipes in their articles for illustrative purposes. Among these options, the *Gourmet* chef's recipes came closer to meeting the needs of readers than those presented in other articles (see chap. 7).[18]

In its monthly columns, *Gourmet* also provided extensive information on New York restaurants ("Spécialités de la Maison," "Let's Eat Out"), food, and cultural events in the city ("Along the Boulevard"), as well as sources of specialty foods such as olives, dried fruit, clams, and smoked pheasant from New York and elsewhere ("Food Flashes," "Gourmet's Garden of Eating"). At first glance, these columns appeared to favor New York readers, but, as letters in "Sugar and Spice" attested, visitors to New York were grateful for information on the best restaurants, shops, and events to frequent. By addressing this audience, *Gour-*

met was following in the footsteps of the *New Yorker* and *Vanity Fair*, which clearly thrived on disseminating news of the New York arts and entertainment scene to readers from every section of the country.

There was room in *Gourmet* for readers' opinions as well. From the first issue, "Sugar and Spice" published their views about articles, recipes, and the magazine in general. Perhaps because so many of the letters solicited new recipes from the editors, *Gourmet* introduced a column entitled "You Asked for It" in October 1944 that consisted of readers' requests for recipes and, in response, the particular version of the recipe selected by the editors.

From the outset, the magazine appealed to the eye as well as the intellect. Especially popular were the evocative color illustrations on *Gourmet's* covers, at least for the first fifteen years when Henry Stahlhut was drawing them. Appropriately enough, these covers depicted an appetizing dish or meal featured in that month's issue. Black-and-white sketches by Stahlhut, Samuel Chamberlain, and others provided images of the cooking process or the geographical setting for culinary specialties. In *New Yorker* fashion, the magazine also featured several cartoons in each issue.[19]

This systematic effort on *Gourmet's* part to appeal to a variety of readers, some of whom had relatively little interest in food, was apparently successful. Letters to "Sugar and Spice" reveal that readers discovered in *Gourmet* articles therapy for the pain, boredom, and indignities of everyday life among other things. A businessman from Billings, Montana, for example, read *Gourmet* as an antidote to the business journals he pored over at his work. By contrast, a Kingston, Ontario, man reported that after reading several *Gourmet* articles to his hospitalized wife, she ate everything on her lunch tray. As for a female subscriber from Oak Park, Illinois, whenever she felt "the least bit blue," she read *Gourmet* and found herself "floating into the sky and the blues are gone."[20]

Other readers valued the literary and artistic quality of the magazine; Julian Wright Williams found *Gourmet* articles as "interesting" as those in the *New Yorker*, while Willard Hougland, who read Balzac at age ten, believed that the magazine "is about the only fit reading I've found." Equally appealing to some readers were the illustrations, especially the cover. Arthur Dahlmann, a Fort Wayne resident, arranged the covers of *Gourmet* as a mural on the wall behind his stove. By contrast, it was the November 1947 cover that particularly appealed to Mrs. S. Burford Crossman of Huntington, Long Island, who copied the drawings of peasants, guns, and vegetables on to her cutter sleigh for decoration. Meanwhile, Mrs. I. W. Williams set her table monthly to harmonize with each successive magazine cover.[21]

Of course, these readers and many others subscribed to the magazine for more conventional purposes. Many valued the information on travel and cuisine that assisted them in deciding where to go, what to eat, and where to stay when they got there. Others were pleased to use the recipes and menus to help in preparing interesting dishes that were previously unfamiliar to them. Many readers, however, simply enjoyed reading the recipes.

On the occasion of its first issue, *Gourmet* printed a manifesto signed by the publisher, editor, and chef that defined the gourmet as someone dedicated to "food perfection," but also more broadly to "good living, as [the magazine's] subtitle suggested." According to the manifesto, members of the gourmet community included those who brought intelligence, art, and imagination to the preparation of food regardless of social class or country. "A thrifty French housewife," as well as Americans who exhibited a "thirst of discovery" and made good use of the country's great abundance, were equally welcome. This version of gourmet dining was not inconsistent with the Bible's endorsement of good living, "Take thine ease, eat, drink, and be merry." In any event, "the hurly-burly of our modern daily existence," much more than organized religion, was the great obstacle to establishing the practice of gourmet dining. Accordingly, the signers of the manifesto called for a retreat from this madness in order to enjoy "the pursuit of happiness" of earlier times.[22]

The statement of purpose managed to convey that the gourmet as a perfectionist merited an exalted status, although, in principle, anyone might become one. It acknowledged obliquely the primacy of France in the gourmet order, but insisted as well on the legitimacy of traditional American cooking. As Anne Mendelson has argued, *Gourmet* promoted a version of gourmet dining blending "American—especially New England—culinary patriotism and a reverent coverage of all things French." Furthermore, readers could rest assured, based on the explicit endorsement of the Bible, that fine dining was also a Godly activity.[23]

In denouncing the fast pace of modern life, *Gourmet* joined forces with the intelligentsia of the interwar period to lament the triumph of prosperity at the expense of the good life. In the magazine's view, the scientific ethos responsible for this prosperity was an inadequate replacement for the traditions of an earlier period. Consistent with the general criticism of mass production, the *Gourmet* staff decried the indifference of the food processors and nutritionists alike to the selection of high-quality ingredients and the serving of tasty meals. Instead, the magazine celebrated the French housewife and America's traditional dishes as models for restoring "sensuous pleasure" to the dining experience and giving it a joyful dimension. These older ways of preparing food and accounts of elegant dinners in the past would guide readers to a revival of gastronomy.[24]

Gourmet displayed the perfect symbol for the traditional ethos on the cover of its first issue: a boar's head sporting a tusk replete with an apple in its mouth (see color gallery). There were holly sprigs between the ears and, for good measure, a glass of red wine off to the side. In choosing the boar's head, often paraded at medieval Christmas feasts as a prelude to the serving of a suckling pig, the magazine's editors boldly expressed their intention to value gastronomic traditions as a way of reviving the pleasures of the table in America. The arresting cover also suggested the decorative possibilities of the boar's head and, in contrast to the food processors, confronted the diners with the fact that a life had been dispatched to sustain their pleasure. Here was an image perfectly designed to represent *Gourmet*'s antimodern approach to food, implicitly rejecting the scientific ethos of nutritionists and food processors. And, to clinch that point, *Gourmet*'s boar was a traditional artist's portrait, drawn by Henry Stahlhut, rather than a color photograph of the kind used by women's magazines to represent food. Meanwhile, editor Pearl Metzelthin assured readers who served this dish that guests would acknowledge their "status as . . . gastronomical fashion leader[s]."[25]

In some of its early articles *Gourmet* reinforced this traditional ethos by contrasting the results of nutritionist and traditional approaches in the selection and preparation of food products. One such contrast exploited the wartime setting to link nutritionists, French producers of foie gras, and Nazis. "Our agricultural science is taking good care of quantity food production, and chemical science is improving nutritional efficiency. But that isn't all there is to food. By pumping a chemically balanced porridge down his neck through a rubber hose, a gander can be well nourished, and do a perfect goose-step!" Other critics delivered the same message less graphically. One argued that "surely we have been endowed with the sensation of taste for some purpose. Eating should mean roasts, sauces, puddings, pies—not calories, vitamins, minerals." Another critic, affronted by the nutritionists' insistence on eating "yards and yards of spinach" à la Popeye, asserted that living to 108 on a diet of spinach would be a curse.[26]

Since very few countries had modernized as quickly and thoroughly as the United States, *Gourmet*'s many travel narratives offered opportunities for the magazine to feature its traditional approach to fine dining. Consistent with its promise to be a "magazine of good living," travel narratives explored the connection between food, drink, and the mores of particular regions or countries. They identified the principal ingredients and cooking techniques that were used in

different geographical areas, while considering how the ingredients were produced and transformed in the cooking process. To conclude, the narratives recounted diners' response to the flavors and textures of the meal and the setting
in which it was served. Through these accounts, writers and readers traveled the
globe, past and present, including certain regions of the United States. In the
process, they enjoyed vicarious travel, especially during the war years when
actual travel was restricted, and also acquired some knowledge of traditional
ways.[27]

American travel narratives featured areas of the country with a long history
and distinctive culinary traditions, including not only New England but also the
South. Robert P. Tristam Coffin described life on a traditional Maine saltwater
farm, where members of the family gathered, grew, or hunted the ingredients
for their meals before drying, canning, or smoking many of them. One of the
memorable occasions was "Christmas on Paradise," the island where the farm
was situated. Highlights of the Christmas dinner included an hors d'oeuvre of
lobster tomally, followed by a stuffed goose for the main course, and a dessert of
squash pie. Meanwhile, Kennebec turkeys (red herring) were hanging in the
attic and maple syrup candy was boiling on the stove. It is not clear how *Gourmet*
expected the New York apartment dweller to respond to this passing way of life.[28]

"Dixie Serves the Dinner" transported readers for the Thanksgiving holiday
to a prerevolutionary plantation house in the Deep South where guests enjoyed
Southern hospitality, especially from the "beaming Negroes" who "love their
'white folks.'" An illustration of a fawning black servant reinforced the verbal
stereotype. At the plantation house the dinner menu featured turtle soup, wild
turkey with chestnuts and stuffing, wild rice, and, for dessert, plum pudding or
frozen eggnog. However, the article acknowledged that poor whites and blacks,
who also followed regional traditions, did not fare as well as folks in the "big
house." The former ate possum and black-eyed peas, the latter fresh pork and
sweet potatoes.[29]

For advocates of traditional cuisine, New Orleans was a particularly seductive American city, where readers could experience a version of French cuisine
adapted to the special ingredients of the region. At the approach of Mardi Gras
in 1941, *Gourmet* dispatched Louis De Gouy, who already had worked as a chef
in the city, to report on the local cuisine. He observed that the city was "steeped
in tradition [and] peopled by warm blooded, joy-loving, romantic Latins." In
large measure because of its culinary specialties, New Orleans' French Quarter was also "mysterious, exotic, [and] pungent." After reviewing the great restaurants of the city and the 1941 menu of the Tastevin at Antoine's, De Gouy

recommended such dishes as oysters à la Rockefeller and *pompano en papillote*, along with creole soup, gumbo filé, and New Orleans pralines.[30]

Promoting the idea of a great American culinary tradition freed *Gourmet* to approach French cuisine as the first among equals without offending American pride. Accordingly, the magazine chose as its lead article for the first two issues "Burgundy at a Snail's Pace," which presented a leisurely journey through that region to whet the appetites of potential subscribers. By introducing readers to a relatively modest culinary experience rather than to the exalted *haute cuisine* restaurants of Paris, *Gourmet* demonstrated sensitivity to the kind of fine dining appropriate during an international crisis.[31]

The author of the Burgundy articles, Samuel Chamberlain, who had lived in France for more than ten years, launched his journey by dining at *Aux Trois Faisons* (At the Three Pheasants), a Dijon restaurant, where he enjoyed the signature dish, *suprême de brochet Dijonnaise* ("sublimated pickerel"). In his view, the quality of the cuisine was a reflection of the slower pace of life in that region. After all, it took time to produce good food and wine, to prepare them properly in the kitchen and the wine cellar, and to do them justice at the table. Chamberlain warned Americans to consider this last point carefully. "Instead of violating your wine like a brute, assure yourself of its possession by the most soft and adroit caresses." Although the author rented a car, he traveled only a mile and a half per day so as to enjoy the local scene. There, he discovered and sketched the architectural splendors of a bygone era and the humane dimensions of village life.[32]

As they launched the magazine during the war period, *Gourmet* authors carefully balanced the focus of their travel narratives. It was essential, of course, to acknowledge France's primacy in culinary matters, but not to dwell on lavish dinners. Moreover, as patriotic sentiments soared during the war, it was equally important to recognize the promising foundations for gourmet dining that earlier generations of Americans had laid. The *Gourmet* staff was clearly attentive to maintaining this delicate balance. At the same time, the magazine's appreciative treatment of traditional foodways merged seamlessly with an acceptance of the status quo in gender and racial matters.

Financial Considerations

In 1941, MacAusland struggled to secure sufficient funds to launch the new magazine. Apparently, he borrowed money from his father and two brothers. It is also likely that Ralph Reinhold and Gladys Guggenheim Straus invested in the magazine. Aside from these sources, the publisher was dependent on subscriptions and advertising revenues, which came primarily from whisky dealers. In encouraging these advertisements, *Gourmet* rejected decisively the approach to food and drink in women's magazines and, to a lesser extent, in gourmet dining societies. In fact, MacAusland was complying with the practices of most well-traveled Americans, who were happy to drink wine at meals but had no intention of giving up their cocktails.[33]

To further solidify its financial situation, *Gourmet*, on occasion, collected articles or recipes that had originally appeared in the magazine for publication. This prospect first materialized in 1943 when Samuel Chamberlain published his *Gourmet* articles on "Clementine in the Kitchen" as a book with Hastings House in cooperation with *Gourmet*. By 1950, with the appearance of *The Gourmet Cookbook*, Volume 1, the magazine had emerged as a full-blown publisher that handled both printing and distribution for in-house books. Considering the six-figure sales of the two volumes of *The Gourmet Cookbook*, this publishing venture must have been a lucrative enterprise.[34]

Three other relatively short-term ventures offered services to subscribers based on *Gourmet's* expertise in travel and fine dining. In 1946, the magazine challenged Duncan Hines' *Adventures in Good Eating* by publishing *Gourmet's Guide to Good Eating in the United States and Canada*. With recommended restaurants classified by cities within states, *Gourmet* borrowed Hines' organizing scheme, while basing the selection of restaurants on the recommendation of *Gourmet* subscribers who lived nearby rather than professional reviewers. For recommending a restaurant MacAusland set the following guideline: it should "serve the best food of its kind in that vicinity" and be "clean (but doesn't put cleanliness above goodliness)." He added that the proponent should feel comfortable meeting another gourmet within the restaurant. Clearly, MacAusland intended his stipulation about cleanliness to distance *Gourmet's Guide* from Hines' obsession on this subject. Unlike other *Gourmet* publications, the guide was sold in bookstores as well as through the magazine.[35]

Gourmet also created a travel service and a guest club. The magazine launched the former in August of 1953 to promote cruises to Europe and elsewhere and escorted tours sponsored by American Express and Thomas Cook to various parts of Europe. In 1956 and 1957, wine expert Tom Marvel, who was then writing the "Specialités de la Maison" column for the magazine, led one-month wine tours to Europe arranged by the travel service. He remarked that "we're very first class as to travel and hotel accommodations; we're invited to wine cellars and wine tastings."[36]

Sponsored by MacAusland himself with funding from the Franklin National Bank of Long Island, *Gourmet* Guest Club came into existence in 1954. Members received a restaurant directory listing 530 participating restaurants in all parts of the country, where they could use their gourmet guest cards to charge meals. The restaurants supposedly met gourmet standards. Even so, the fact that the magazine terminated all three ventures in 1957 suggests that none of them did much to improve the bottom line.[37]

Advertising, along with subscriptions, remained the principal revenue generator for the magazine, while, at the same time, threatening to compromise *Gourmet*'s commitment to the highest standards in recommending food, wines, and restaurants to its readers. Given the magazine's financial constraints, however, MacAusland had no choice but to accept advertisements from these sources even when their products were not necessarily of the highest quality.

By publishing equal numbers of articles on wine and cocktails, *Gourmet* succeeded in creating a hospitable environment for the advertisers of both kinds of beverages. Moreover, despite the prominence of whisky advertisements—by far the biggest source of advertising revenue for the magazine—the American wine industry and *Gourmet* benefited greatly from wine ads placed in the magazine, as well as *Gourmet*'s efforts to educate readers in the subtleties of wine drinking. Carl Bundschu, manager of Inglenook and director of the Wine Institute, noted the "generous support" that the California wine industry was giving to *Gourmet*. No doubt he was referring to the full-page monthly ads from the California Wine Advisory Board that began in the first issue of the magazine. As for *Gourmet* articles promoting wine consumption, Bundschu added, "I hope they [California wine producers] appreciate the wonderful education work you are doing." In this instance, the wine industry and the magazine shared common goals, although the tight relationship probably curbed *Gourmet*'s freedom to critique California wines.[38]

Aside from soliciting ads for alcoholic beverages, the magazine sought to attract advertisers for other gourmet products. The resulting relationship between the two parties was similar to that established by women's magazines with its advertisers and by the dining societies with wine dealers who donated wine. Inevitably, doubts arose as to whether *Gourmet*'s dependence on advertisers compromised its status as the arbiter of good taste in fine dining, particularly when it compared the products of large, mainstream corporations with those of smaller firms. A case in point was *Gourmet*'s failure to name a good flour for readers to use in the many bread recipes it published; a scorching letter denounced *Gourmet*'s silence on the subject, which "can only be interpreted as a supine terror of the advertising strength of Pillsbury *et al.*"[39]

In reply, the magazine pointed out that Pillsbury was not one of its advertisers, but insisted on maintaining "editorial impartiality" by at first refusing to indicate a preference for any brand; later, *Gourmet* revealed the names of three flours that "taste like grain" and advised the letter writer and other readers to lobby the big millers to improve their product. This response raised more questions than it answered. If impartiality was the goal, why did the magazine suddenly identify three acceptable flours? Regarding *Gourmet's* refusal to confront even a big flour company that did not advertise in the magazine, it seems likely that MacAusland wanted to offer a friendly environment to large, mainstream corporations and, thus, to encourage lucrative advertisements from all of them.[40]

On other occasions, *Gourmet* clearly struggled to establish a proper stance toward its advertisers. For example, the magazine instituted a policy to list in "Let's Eat Out" only restaurants outside the New York area that were advertisers; inevitably, however, many of the city restaurants listed in the column were also advertisers. It was thus not clear whether the latter were selected for the quality of their fare or their contribution to advertising revenues. Equally problematic was the choice of restaurants for review in "Specialités de la Maison," many of which also placed ads in the magazine. In one case, an advertisement for Henri's actually quoted the *Gourmet* reviewer's claim that the restaurant was "a New York institution without which the town seems unimaginable." In this instance, Henri's used *Gourmet's* review to promote its restaurant, while implicitly acknowledging the magazine's expertise in judging restaurants.[41]

A similar *quid pro quo* was evident in the Meiers Wine Cellar's full-page ads offering readers a free *Gourmet* magazine booklet with recipes that used their wines. The title on the booklet's cover, as pictured in the ad, used *Gourmet's* script. In effect, the magazine endorsed Meiers wines, while Meiers acknowledged *Gourmet's* stamp of approval as authoritative—roughly equivalent to the Good Housekeeping seal.[42]

Even stranger was *Gourmet's* cozy arrangement with Frank Schoonmaker to publish his four-page *News from the Vineyards* promoting Almaden wines in two or three issues per year from 1956 through 1959. While, at first, the typeface and separate pagination distinguished the newsletter from other *Gourmet* articles, the typeface was changed in the March 1957 issue to resemble that of the other magazine articles, while pages were numbered consecutively with previous and succeeding articles. Moreover, the authors of the *News from the Vineyards*, Schoonmaker and James Beard, wrote articles for both publications. It was as if *Gourmet* had outsourced four pages of its issue to gourmet experts who were promoting Almaden products with only "advertisement," written in small letters at the bottom of the pages to indicate that the articles in this section were not selected by *Gourmet*.[43]

Two other cases illustrate *Gourmet*'s entanglement with advertisers. One involved a *Gourmet* editor's contribution "to the setting and service" of an international Christmas dinner arranged by the J. Walter Thompson advertising agency for the U.S. Brewer's Foundation at the Ambassador Hotel. One explanation for this strange entanglement is that *Gourmet* sought to reward Reinhold beer for purchasing a full-page color ad in virtually every issue since January of 1941. A somewhat different case was the appearance on the magazine's May 1955 cover of a pear and avocado salad taken from the menu of the Colony Restaurant. The dish was perfectly appropriate for a spring cover, but the magazine was not accustomed to providing free advertising in such a visible space. Whether *Gourmet* was beholden to the Colony or simply found this dish particularly apt for the season is unclear. In any event, these cases indicate that *Gourmet* worked hard to create a hospitable environment for advertisers, sometimes at the cost of its objectivity. Unfortunately, in the absence of the magazine's financial records, there is no way to know whether these compromises were necessary.[44]

How *Gourmet* Fought World War II

As the first issue of *Gourmet* went to press in early 1941, the American public was increasingly attentive to the close link between American security and the future of Europe. The military situation was bleak. Japanese forces were in control of much of China, while the Nazis occupied most of Western Europe and appeared to be on the verge of defeating Great Britain. Isolationists continued to resist President Roosevelt's efforts to engage the United States on the side of the Allies, although public opinion was shifting in favor of the Allies. Among the president's staunchest associates in this fight was Henry Luce, editor of *Life* and *Time*, who published his "American Century" just days after the appearance of *Gourmet*'s first issue. There, Luce argued that the United States, as the dominant world power, must play a critical role in the international realm by joining the fight against Hitler to wage a campaign on behalf of culture. As the "intellectual, scientific, and artistic capital of the world," America would become the "sanctuary" for "the great principles of Western civilization," which had also guided the nation's development. As Luce well knew, eminent European intellectuals and artists including the novelist Thomas Mann and the painter Max Beckmann were already living in the United States.[45]

Even a cursory glance at "Sugar and Spice" confirms that *Gourmet*'s readers were firmly located in the Allied camp. They took Luce's language to heart and urged the broadening of America's role as a sanctuary for European culture to include the arts of the table. *Gourmet*, as they perceived it, was not an instrument of decadence, but the herald of a new era in American history. The "finest artists of the kitchen, along with home-coming expatriates and frustrated world travelers, who were used to the best and demanded it," would find a refuge in the United States. Already, European restaurateurs from the World's Fair were relocating to Manhattan. In the process, America was becoming a culinary, as it already was a scientific and artistic, capital. It would be, in the words of *Gourmet* readers, the "capital of the culinary world" or "the new gourmetland." And New York City would become a "cosmopolis which contains the world." Meanwhile, with the "eclipse of Paris as a gourmet center," *Gourmet* magazine would become a clearing house for information about fine dining in the unoccupied Western world.[46]

Gourmet's biggest hurdle was to overcome the idea expressed by some of its readers and no doubt harbored by many Americans that, in the midst of a national emergency, fine dining was morally incompatible with the war effort. In the April 1941 issue, a reader raised this issue in dramatic fashion. Calling attention to *Gourmet*'s "Meal of the Month," a series featuring the favorite menus of New York's leading chefs, she asked rhetorically: "While Rome burns, would you have the palate catered to in the western hemisphere? The menu . . . was most revolting. Could anyone dare to attempt such orgies at a time like this? Imagine what a British soldier might feel on reading this!"[47]

Wasting no time, publisher Earle MacAusland seized the occasion to respond to this attack in the very same issue; assuring readers that they need not apologize for promoting gourmet dining, he viewed the purchase of fine food, cars, clothes, and music as a desirable stimulus for the economy; eight months later Lucius Beebe, always eager to promote fine dining, reminded readers that the WFS in London continued to publish *Wine and Food* despite the Nazi bombing campaign; he added, "if the British still can think in terms of reasonable gastronomy, there's no valid reason we shouldn't as well."[48]

During this moment of crisis, *Gourmet* readers mustered a more fervent and principled defense of gourmet dining than either MacAusland or Beebe. One insisted that "the art of eating can be preserved only by practicing . . . It is not the least of the individual liberties worth cultivating and fighting to hold in a world threatened with regimentation." Another proclaimed, "*Gourmet* is a delight in every home of culture. I feel deeply that gracious living should spread

Gourmet's "Meal of the Month," March 1941, p. 28. Presented by Executive Chef, Paul Moreau, Hotel St. Regis, New York City: border drawing by Henry Stahlhut. The Schlesinger Library, Radcliffe Institute, Harvard University. Contributor/ Gourmet, © Condé Nast Publications.

through America at a time like this, making homes more desirable—something to be protected—even worth fighting for." In defining the purpose of the war as the defense of gracious living, readers were building on the argument of wartime advertisers who pitched refrigerators and Revere ware, a less rarified form of consumerism, as a way of life "worth fighting for." Even so, nine months later *Gourmet* discontinued its "Meal of the Month" column.[49]

It seems clear from readers' dialogues with the editors in "Sugar and Spice" that both were relieved—and perhaps a little guilty—to have found a justification for living well in the midst of a brutal war that caused much suffering. The magazine was making America "better, healthier and more humane" according to one reader. Another insisted that *Gourmet* was "wonderful! If some of us have not the courage and the persistence to hang on to our culture and our way of life, what will become of us?" *Gourmet*, in turn, was grateful for readers' support: "Thanks. You make us feel like benefactors of mankind. We admit we are, of course." And later: "we are helping to maintain what is genuinely a part of the culture of any people—the art of good and gracious living."[50]

While continuing to publish travelogues and other regular columns, the magazine followed closely the government's effort to promote effective use of the country's resources. When the Roosevelt administration introduced a program of food rationing in 1942, *Gourmet* offered an emphatic endorsement. The editors boldly asserted that "we should all become gourmets in this time of emergency"; and, in case readers hadn't gotten the point, the editors claimed that their traditional approach to dining was "a patriotic contribution to our war effort and the men and women in the service."[51]

Gourmet's editors joined government officials in advocating a proper diet to enhance the fighting capacity of the nation, although their conception of this diet differed significantly from the government's. In the September 1942 issue, editor Pearl Metzelthin remarked that it was "more important than ever to safeguard health and build for greater endurance and vitality." To fulfill this goal in gourmet fashion would mean preparing "health-giving foods pleasing to the palate." Readers echoed this theme. Mrs. S. A. Persley of New Haven asserted that *Gourmet*'s project of improving American cooking would enable soldiers to eat better, which, in turn, would strengthen army morale.[52]

The advent of rationing in 1943 would seem to have complicated *Gourmet*'s task by limiting the availability of beef, pork, sugar, coffee, butter, and canned goods, which had an important place in the magazine's recipes, not to mention the American diet. The editors of *Gourmet*, however, saw rationing as an opportunity to improve the American diet rather than as a deprivation. Scorning the popular trend toward ration recipes, *Gourmet* offered a bolder and more patriotic solution: cook with unrationed items based on a "sincere appreciation of nature's bounteous food supply," including many food items that Americans had previously ignored. In MacAusland's words, "get rid of canned goods, buy *Gourmet*"; he meant, as well, to dispense altogether with other rationed items in favor of organ meats, chicken, fish, or snapping turtle that were not rationed. According to both MacAusland and Metzelthin, the French peasant, skilled in making delicious meals from modest ingredients, could serve as an excellent example. Gates Hebard captured in verse the essence of the *Gourmet* plan:

> Nuts to the red stamps [for meat and butter],
> Pooh to the blue [for processed foods].
> If your ration book's empty, what's that to you?
> Use ingenuity plus—shout Hurray!
> The wonderful recipes found in *Gourmet*!

To buttress its position, the magazine quoted Lucius Beebe, who wrote in his *New York Herald Tribune* column that "*Gourmet* in many ways is a better solution to the rationing problems than anything that has come out of Washington."[53]

The editors' proposals resonated with staff and readers. Writing to "Sugar and Spice," Whiting Hollister proposed making soup and stews out of snapping turtles, while Clementine Paddleford, editor of the magazine's "Food Flashes" column, wanted to replace beef with turtle. Louis De Gouy described his solution to the rationing problem as "Turning Out the Innards." His column, accordingly, included recipes for dishes using hearts and tripe. Two months later, De Gouy bolstered his case for using innards by reminding readers of the heroic frugality of Abigail Adams during the Revolutionary War. On that occasion, he also recommended recipes for ox tongue escarlatte and calf's head vinaigrette. Meanwhile, Mrs. R. E. Clark argued that "the use of spices and wines for cooking, plus a large quantity of imagination" could improve the quality of various dishes, while in his *Gourmet* article Byron W. Dalrymple went farther. Now that the spice trade was cut off, Americans should grow their own.[54]

The idea of avoiding rationed items altogether made good sense, in principle, but was subject to interesting and, indeed, embarrassing twists and turns. Hammacher Schlemmer advertised two hundred items "Still Available—and all un-rationed! Rare delicacies and nourishing mainstays . . . caviar, shad roe, hearts of palm . . . green turtle soup, pâté, smoked frogs legs." In this instance, patriotism came at a price. Moreover, some rationed items were essential to gourmet cooking as it was defined by the magazine. Take butter, for example.

An article in the March 1943 issue noted that the use of compounded butters always improved hors d'oeuvres. For this reason, *Gourmet*'s recipes called for the use of butter, while gesturing without conviction to the reality of rationing. "If the scarcity of butter continues, it is possible to use some of the substitutes on the market." The message was clear: substitute chicken for beef, but avoid margarine at all cost.[55]

Not all readers were prepared to comply with *Gourmet*'s approach to wartime dining. William B. Van Houten urged the magazine to "rush to print with a series of good *Gourmet* 'ration recipes'" to make effective use of rationed ingredients. On the grounds that ration recipes were unnecessary as long as there was an abundant supply of unrationed ingredients available, the magazine decisively rejected his advice. Editors were even less receptive to Alda F. Haskel, who sent a recipe for steak. Referring to its cost in ration points, *Gourmet* observed that steaks are "out of this world."[56]

The magazine also touted its solution to the servant problem as a useful contribution to prosecuting the war. Editors noted that "maids and cooks have gone elsewhere for the time being." As they departed to offices and factories, the magazine would fill the vacuum. *Gourmet* invited even inexperienced housewives who aspired to go beyond processed foods and serve attractive, tasty fare to cook from the magazine's recipes. There is no way of knowing how many housewives followed *Gourmet*'s advice.[57]

Aside from advocating the use of unrationed items, *Gourmet* viewed French provincial cuisine as the prototype for gourmet dining, while promoting American food and wine in the absence of imports from Europe. This campaign, in turn, became an opportunity to link gourmet dining more closely with American life, since its most important component, wine, was now primarily an American rather than an imported product.[58]

Convincing testimony on this point came from Frank Schoonmaker and Tom Marvel, who published *American Wines* within months of *Gourmet*'s founding. The two authors reminded readers of Lief Erikson's characterization of America as Vineland and insisted that nothing had changed since those days. "More species of grapevines grow here than grow in all other parts of the world combined." In this way, they suggested, "Nature seems to have planned the United States to be a nation of wine drinkers." Eight months later, in the February 1942 issue, the magazine published the first in a series of eight articles by Samuel Chamberlain entitled "Best Cellars," which evaluated the quality of American wines and encouraged readers to consider their exploration "an adventure." In this way, increasingly, Americans could pursue patriotism and pleasure simultaneously.[59]

The first article in the "Best Cellars" series appeared just two months after Pearl Harbor. Almost immediately, advertisers took up the challenge of convincing Americans to "cherish wine from their own soil." An "All-American Thanksgiving," according to Frank Schoonmaker, would incorporate wine and food from the New World. "The turkey is a bird of America . . . The potato is a plant of America . . . The vine is the grape vine of America . . . It is suggested, nay urged, that American wine grace your Thanksgiving table of American food." Along with Schoonmaker, the California Wine Advisory Board sent monthly advertisements that mixed gourmet and patriotic themes. One, for example, insisted that "wine has a way with the foods of wartime," including kidneys, calves brains, and baked fish; all could be prepared in wine, and none of them appeared on the list of rationed items. Another Advisory Board advertisement depicted a couple seated at a piano poised to raise their glasses of wine, while a small insert alerted readers to their patriotic duty: "For Victory: Buy United States War Bonds and Stamps."[60]

In "Wine for the President," *Gourmet* offered a slightly different spin on the wine and patriotism theme. For this occasion, the magazine portrayed the founding fathers as wine drinkers to establish this practice as an American tradition. Opening with an image of George Washington toasting the flag with a glass of wine, the article identified Thomas Jefferson as the "outstanding wine connoisseur among presidents," while Franklin and Hamilton were labeled "bonvivants." Two years later, *Gourmet* celebrated Jefferson again as "beloved of all American gourmets for his pioneering in early American gastronomy and his attempts to establish a wine industry in this country." In fact, Jefferson preferred the taste of French to American-made wines and believed that the wine industry degraded its workers. Nonetheless, he was an excellent example of an American who not only valued wine but made a place for it at his table, and recalling his activities served to legitimate them for *Gourmet* readers.[61]

As the war progressed, *Gourmet* enjoyed the luxury of presenting support for French cuisine as a patriotic act. In this respect as well, Jefferson established a precedent. It was possible to be a great American and a Francophile at the same time, since France and America were once again joined in fighting for freedom. One could, for example, celebrate the presence in New York of "Madame Romaine's match box shop . . . a bit of Lyon quite untouched by the war." There, "all the culinary genius of the French is manifest in her omelette artistry."[62]

Sometimes, *Gourmet* acknowledged that the continued use of French products might, over time, create new patterns in American foodways. That was particularly the case during the war when certain products were "naturalized" in

Wine has a way with the foods of Wartime

The wine growers of California invite you to share some cheerful secrets of good eating. These secrets start with simple foods. A knowing recipe, a bit of wine at the right point in your cooking — and you come out with dishes great chefs could boast about. Dishes you'll enjoy most with glasses of good table wine

Kidneys en Brochette, with Red Wine:
To serve 4, cut in cubes 2 veal or 5 lamb kidneys, soak in salted water ½ hour. Drain and arrange on skewers, alternating kidney cubes with squares of bacon. Marinate 30 min. in this sauce: ½ cup red table wine, ¼ cup salad oil, salt, pepper, cayenne, mustard, grated onion. Remove from sauce, broil very slowly 15 min., basting with the remaining sauce. Serve very hot. Enjoy with this treat one of our fine California red table wines, a Burgundy or Claret. Or a good red wine bearing the name of the grape variety from which it was made, like Pinot Noir, Cabernet or Zinfandel

Baked Fish Vin Blanc: For 4 or 5 persons, salt and pepper 1½ lbs. fish fillets or thin slices. Poach 10 minutes in 1 cup California Rhine Wine and ½ cup bouillon with a bay leaf and 1 tbsp. each of chopped celery, parsley and onion. Remove fish to shallow baking dish and arrange with halves of 3 small tomatoes. Boil down liquid one half, add 2 tbsps. cream, season, and strain over fish. Bake in hot oven (450°) 10 minutes, or until lightly browned. With this tempting dish, serve a California white table wine of the Rhine Wine type, or one labeled with the name of the grape variety from which the wine was made

Breaded Calves Brains au Sauterne:
For 4 persons, parboil 2 pairs calves brains or 4 pairs lamb brains in usual way. Place under weight to flatten into patties. When cool, season, egg-and-crumb, and brown in oil. Prepare this "Sauce Delectable": Saute 5 minutes in oil a little chopped garlic, onion and parsley, a cup of chopped mushrooms, and a pinch each of marjoram and thyme. Blend in 1 tbsp. flour, stir in a cup of Sauterne. Add salt and pepper and bring to a simmer. Serve the patties very hot on crisp toast, the hot sauce in a separate bowl. Bring to table, well chilled, one of the delicate California Sauternes; or one of the fine varietals, such as a Sauvignon Blanc or a Semillon

For a big booklet of other interesting, point-saving recipes—write to the Wine Advisory Board, 85 Second Street, San Francisco, California.

"Wine Has a Way with the Foods of Wartime": California Wine Advisory Board Advertisement from *Gourmet*, October 1943, inside back cover. The Schlesinger Library, Radcliffe Institute, Harvard University. Provided by the Wine Appreciation Guild, South San Francisco, CA 94080, successor to the Wine Advisory Board.

Wine for the President

"Wine for the President," *Gourmet*, October 1942, p. 6: drawing of George
Washington by Henry Stahlhut. The Schlesinger Library, Radcliffe Institute,
Harvard University. Contributor/Gourmet, © Condé Nast Publications.

America, thus contributing to a convergence of practices on both sides of the
Atlantic, at least among elites. In New York City, for example, which had a history
of French restaurants dating back to Delmonico's, the magazine observed that
Roger Chauveron, chef of the Chambord, had "his own bit of France on Third
Avenue!" In effect, more Americans were now comfortable in accommodating
French institutions, products, and practices on American soil. This receptivity, in
turn, encouraged French firms like Lanson, whose Champagne ad depicted a

bottle linking Paris and New York, to celebrate the common drinking habits of Parisians and New Yorkers (see color gallery).[63]

But the most extensive exercise in naturalizing French ways in the United States was the twenty-episode serial entitled "Clementine in the Kitchen," which was so popular that its author, Samuel Chamberlain, collected the episodes in a book by the same title. According to a full-page ad in the March 1944 issue of *Gourmet*, twenty thousand copies of *Clementine in the Kitchen* had been sold in three months, thus making it "one of the best-sellers in the non-fiction field."

The story of the Beck family's repatriation from France was a semifictional account containing important elements of the Chamberlain family's experience, although the author created Clementine from a composite of two French cooks who had served the family on separate occasions. The book incorporated recipes and menus with a nostalgic picture of French and American life, of which food was an integral part. Appropriately, Chamberlain named the story's narrator Phineas Beck, which, when shortened to "*fin bec*," translates from French as "gourmet."[64]

Staunch expatriates, the Becks lived in France until the Munich Pact, when they returned to the United States. As part of their baggage, they brought with them Clementine, their Burgundian cook, who came equipped with recipes for twenty-five classic French dinners. Chamberlain was at pains to clarify that all of the recipes were for simple dishes eaten routinely in "countless conventional French homes." In no way would they embarrass American gourmets who sought to avoid extravagance during the war years. As Chamberlain explained, "we had no huge dinners."[65]

Adjusting to American life was not an easy thing for the Becks or Clementine, who were accustomed to shopping for fresh produce in the charming market of Senlis, where vendors, whom they knew and trusted, greeted them. And, of course, they were devoted to Burgundy wine and the truffles, so central to regional recipes. Indeed, the truffle became "a symbol of departed splendors, of a standard of civilized living which may never return." The Chamberlains took some consolation in the thought that "regardless of the turmoil in this world, the pigs are still sniffing at the roots of oak trees in Perigord!"[66]

Nonetheless, the Becks readjusted to American life, while enjoying Clementine's surprised reaction to novelties such as grocery carts in American supermarkets. Despite their expatriate life, family members were football fans with an appetite for corn, hot dogs, and beer, all of which they introduced to Clementine. Their America, however, was not destitute of the materials Clementine needed to concoct her classic French dinners. She found fish and vegetables, as well as French cuts of meat, at the Faneuil Hall market in Boston. And because French wines were scarce, the Becks planned a trip to sample California wines. Meanwhile, Clementine was already making a fine boeuf bourguignon with California wine. Happily, there was a "Latin food shop" nearby, run by an Italian-American whose inventory included Wisconsin provolone, Chicago salami, olive oil, and *tête de veau*. With these ingredients, Clementine proved that "*La cuisine française* could be transplanted—but not so thoroughly had not Clementine been transplanted too." Just as important, the neighbors were soon clamoring for invitations to sample Clementine's cooking at the Becks' table. The lesson was clear: Americans could learn to appreciate classic French cooking.[67]

As the story unfolded, it became evident that people, as well as food, could be naturalized. Clementine soon fell in love with a French-Canadian housepainter who worshipped Jimmy Foxx, the star of the Boston Red Sox. Their marriage clearly symbolized the new relationship between France and America. It was now possible for French people to retain their culture, live comfortably in America, and selectively enjoy the American way of life. Indeed, among Clementine's favorite recipes were ones for Smithfield ham, Southern batter bread, and apple pan dowdy. But, from *Gourmet*'s perspective, the most important shift portrayed in this story was the receptivity—even enthusiasm—of Americans for authentic French dishes made of ingredients available in America. The belief that appreciating French cuisine was one way for ambitious Americans to establish their credentials as members of the upper class no doubt augmented this enthusiasm, as Nathalie Jordi has argued. Regardless, Chamberlain believed he was witnessing a real change in the dining preferences of some Americans.[68]

The success of Clementine was immediately apparent to the *Gourmet* staff and no doubt encouraged the use of a similar formula with a different cast of characters. This time, the cook was a Russian immigrant living with a Los Angeles family in the 1920s. Episodes in the story ran from January through September of 1945, coinciding with the height of Soviet-American collaboration, and ended just as tensions between the two countries were growing.

Like Clementine, Katish was eager to master the American way of life, even to the point of learning to drive an old Ford. At the same time she initiated her hosts to the joys of such traditional Russian dishes as borscht, pirogues, and fish pies. Of particular note was the Russian celebration of Easter with painted eggs, pashka, and baba. It was this traditional Russian culture that *Gourmet* endorsed while remaining silent on the Soviet political system. Still, the magazine applauded the Russian soldiers for their collaboration in defeating the Nazis. The January 1946 *Gourmet* cover clarified this point by depicting a carafe of vodka and a bowl of caviar to "toast . . . the mighty czars of la Russie" as well as the "valiant Russian warriors of Moscow, of Leningrad, of Stalingrad." Note the use of "Russian warriors," not Soviets. In addition, "Old Russian embroidery" provided a background for the carafe, on which were engraved Czar Alexander I's initials. After the appearance of the Katish articles, they were published in book form and endorsed by M. F. K. Fisher as "a delight."[69]

As for German cuisine and dining practices, *Gourmet* wrote little about them, other than to condemn the effect of the Nazi campaign on French cuisine. News from Burgundy in "Clementine in the Kitchen" indicated that the "sales Boches" (dirty Germans) now occupied the Becks' former house and had destroyed their favorite restaurant. The Becks could only imagine the "expression of quiet scorn which he (Léon, owner of the restaurant) reserves for the Nazi occupation troops . . . [and] the sulphurous adjectives he is applying" to French collaborators. "We think too of his love for good food."[70]

Otherwise, the magazine's writers were silent about German cooking, although they occasionally praised particular German dishes or drinks without linking them to Nazi Germany. Take hasenfeffer, for example. According to *Gourmet*, it was not really a German dish, but had been created by French chef Urbain Dubois while cooking for Kaiser Wilhelm II. As for bock beer, citizens of Einhorn made it, but there was no mention of the city's location. On one occasion, *Gourmet* referred readers to two recipes from a German cookbook that was clearly published long before the war. And, as we have seen, it was possible to "naturalize" European foodways in America even, in one case, where the product was originally made in Germany. A Nuremberg refugee, after settling in New York City, turned to manufacturing what he called "American Lebkuchen" (Christmas cookies). According to *Gourmet*, "Lebkuchen has transferred its allegiance from Europe to America. This year it has become a naturalized citizen of the food world."[71]

On one occasion, Isaac Marcosson attacked Hitler's dietary practices as a likely cause of the war without in any way identifying them with the foodways of Germany. "If Hitler . . . would forsake his daily diet of glorified sawdust, and polish off a thick, juicy steak washed down by a bottle of red Burgundy, his outlook would be normal instead of pathological. The way to peace via security may be via the stomach."[72]

The Clementine and Katish series, as well as the treatment of German cuisine, illustrate the skillful strategy that *Gourmet* adopted to navigate the rough waters of the war years. In an adverse climate, editors and writers discovered values that supported gourmet dining. They rightly understood that the forces of internationalism were growing stronger under the leadership of Roosevelt and Luce. They also realized that "the defense of the American way of life" as a war aim was sufficiently broad to shelter the promotion of luxury dining. Furthermore, their program of avoiding rationed foods could qualify, in most instances, as genuinely patriotic. And, for a magazine that was eager to promote French cooking, a war to restore the independence of France from its Nazi occupiers was heaven-sent. It was far better to appropriate the dishes of an ally, whose values Americans shared, than to eat from the table of the enemy.

However, the practice of borrowing could have been an embarrassment if *Gourmet* had portrayed it as evidence of the country's incompetence in culinary ways. Instead, the magazine stressed that the United States, like France and other European countries, had a rich culinary heritage. There was no danger, then, in advocating some attention to French cooking; the new gourmet dining would evolve from America's strong culinary heritage enhanced by contributions from other traditions. *Gourmet* thus embraced the cultural nationalism of the Depression and war periods while, at the same time, tempering it with a strong dose of internationalism. In a similar fashion, the magazine endorsed wine drinking in the French manner, while also accepting cocktails as a legitimate form of alcoholic consumption. This more eclectic approach to gourmet dining proved to be more palatable and less expensive to American gourmets than the dining societies' efforts to embrace *haute cuisine*.

Gourmet also exploited a variety of formats, including travelogues, restaurant reviews, and collections of recipes, in order to swell its circulation. All were designed to open readers' eyes and stomachs to dishes and menus consumed in the past or in other countries that broadened the dining options available to readers. Such options were all the more appealing because their authors usually embedded them in stories that were skillfully written and augmented by the magazine's colorful covers, cartoons, and evocative sketches. For women, who were largely excluded from gourmet dining societies, the numerous articles containing recipes signaled that *Gourmet* was addressing their cooking needs, while insisting on higher standards than the women's magazines.

Having weathered the war years, *Gourmet*'s staff could anticipate the future with great confidence. It had taken, as Lucius Beebe remarked, "a stout heart and a sound stomach" to create a magazine about good living just as the Depression ended and the country was about to enter the war. Through a sensitive formulation of the idea of gourmet dining and careful attention to how it might advance the war effort, the magazine's staff enhanced both its own reputation and that of fine dining. Circulation during the magazine's first five years had risen to thirty thousand despite the war. With the return of peace, prosperity, and renewed consumer spending, the editors, for the first time, could promote the cause of fine dining without embarrassment or restraint. Recognizing that fact, *Gourmet* moved its offices in 1945 to a luxurious twenty-two-room suite in the Plaza Hotel Penthouse overlooking Central Park. In the postwar environment, Beebe predicted, "such de luxe gestures as Gourmet [*sic*] are sure to be chips—not potato either."[73]

Chapter Six

Gourmet's *Gastronomic Tours*

Samuel Chamberlain and His *Bouquets*

In *Bobos in Paradise*, David Brooks portrays the lifestyles of the bourgeois Bohemians, who, among other defining characteristics, plan their own vacations rather than opting for organized tours. As they travel, the Bobos deliberately slow the pace in order to develop close relationships with indigenous people and to understand their cultures. They give a high priority to experiencing the local cuisine and searching for the "gemlike little basilica far off the normal tourist paths." By demonstrating their independence from organized tourism, the Bobos also establish a claim to higher status in the social order.[1]

As it turns out, travelers and travel writers over the last two centuries have anticipated the Bobos by advertising their "off-the-beaten-path" itineraries as superior to the tours that guided travelers to the same old monuments in the same old places. Indeed, half a century before Brooks discovered the Bobos, Samuel Chamberlain, in his travel guides to France, Italy, and England, not only stigmatized package tours for middle-class Americans but designed an "off-the-beaten-track" travel experience that enabled his largely upper-middle-class travelers to establish their superiority to the mere tourist. Brooks' "travel snobs" now follow in their footsteps.[2]

But Chamberlain's guidebooks offered more to travelers than opportunities to rise in the social order. In considering other guidebooks and tours that were available to American tourists in Europe after World War II, it becomes clear that Chamberlain's books filled a special niche. As Christopher Endy has shown, the most important alternatives included the increasingly popular package tour, comfortable tourism along the beaten path as prescribed by *Fielding's Travel Guide to Europe*, or the so-called spontaneous, unstructured travel advocated by Arthur Frommer in *Europe on 5 Dollars a Day*. While Chamberlain was also a strong proponent of the unstructured journey, he never courted budget travelers and never mentioned the price of meals or auto rental, no doubt to suggest that money was no object to his readers. Instead, he advocated an automobile tour for the family emphasizing gastronomy and architecture in the provinces. In so doing, Chamberlain was on a personal mission to educate and excite his readers about two subjects that had enriched his own life.[3]

Consistent with his own and *Gourmet's* priorities, Chamberlain, with the assistance of his wife Narcissa, introduced travelers to the pleasures of fine dining in France, Italy, and Britain. The guidebooks recommended charming inns and epicurean restaurants where travelers could find authentic regional cuisine and provided recipes for some of the most popular dishes, while his photographs and drawings gave readers a better sense of the beauty and structural complexity of old churches, villages, and houses. Chamberlain embedded these architectural and culinary experiences in relatively unstructured automobile tours, which he and his wife had first experienced with their own children. The guidebooks thus provided a comprehensive view of the good life in elegant prose and appealing illustrations and invited readers to experience this life in their travels.

To suit the family's needs, travelers could customize itineraries from a variety of options presented in the guidebooks. Such a freewheeling strategy put the traveler, rather than the travel agency, both literally and metaphorically in the driver's seat. Of course, those who followed Chamberlain's recommendations to the letter would, ironically, have chosen a package tour in all but name. Furthermore, it was not clear whether travelers would be able to connect with the local population, as Chamberlain intended. After all, the car could become an isolation chamber or a link to the locals depending on passengers' inclinations and language skills.[4]

Despite Chamberlain's success as a travel writer, he never developed a systematic approach to evaluating restaurants. Well versed in French cuisine, he often adopted the vague standards of regional cuisine proponents, who often preferred small family restaurants based on ambiance more than the quality of their food. His relative unfamiliarity with Italian and British cuisine was also evident in the less authoritative treatment he gave to the foodways of those countries.

All the same, *Gourmet* editor Earle MacAusland made a timely decision to send Chamberlain to research his guidebooks in Europe in the 1950s as airlines were introducing jet travel on transatlantic routes and fares were dropping. However, the eagerness of *Gourmet* readers to set off for Europe was also a tribute to the appeal of Chamberlain's writing and illustrations. More than any other *Gourmet* author, not only did he contribute to the dramatic increase in American travel to Europe, but he and his publisher were also partly responsible for redirecting that traffic. To exploit his popularity after the success of *Bouquet de France*, MacAusland sent him to Italy and Britain, thus marking an important shift in the magazine's orientation. For the first time, *Gourmet* seriously considered the cultural and culinary claims of countries other than France and the United States.

The Author and His Audience

Well before launching *Gourmet* in 1941, Earle MacAusland knew that he had found his man. On the recommendation of a mutual friend, MacAusland sought out Chamberlain at MIT, where he taught graphic arts. And even though he quickly rejected MacAusland's offer to edit the new magazine, Chamberlain had a compelling idea for a story about the adventures of Clementine, the Burgundian cook, in adapting to American life. As MacAusland recognized, the story promised to appeal to the kind of readers *Gourmet* was seeking.[5]

Because he understood his readers' assumptions and aspirations, Chamberlain was well equipped to play the role of guide. He and his early readers had a common experience, shaped by generational, class, and geographical factors. Many were raised in small towns at the turn of the century when regional differences were diminishing and traditional values declining. Most gravitated toward cities as they came of age around 1920. Sons and daughters of well-educated, old-stock Americans who were predominantly professionals and businessmen, they sought to balance work with pleasure by embracing the consumer ethos and pursuing a pleasurable life in which travel and an elegant lifestyle figured prominently. And their children, in turn, who came of age after the Second World War, embraced consumerism with even more enthusiasm and resources than their parents. They too found in Chamberlain a compatible guide.

Chamberlain's familiarity with France and French culture, traditionally a marker of upper-class status, enabled him to instruct his readers in finding the good life through travel and an appreciation of traditional culture, including especially gastronomy and architecture. Traveling with him, they crossed mountains and provincial boundaries; in experiencing a new lifestyle, they also crossed the barriers between the middle and upper-middle class. Their new savoir faire would help to stamp them as members of that class.[6]

Born in 1895 to a family with New England roots, Chamberlain grew up in Aberdeen, Washington, where his father practiced medicine. To attend the University of Washington and MIT, he moved first to Seattle and then to Boston, following the path of other urban migrants to larger cities. Like many future Paris exiles, he interrupted his studies at MIT to join the American Field Service, which supplied ambulance drivers to evacuate wounded French soldiers from the battlefields. For his bravery during the Second Battle of the Marne, the French government awarded him the Croix de Guerre.[7]

Despite his daily brushes with death, Chamberlain enjoyed his first experience abroad. Among other memorable adventures, he and fellow ambulance corps drivers were pressed into service as pickers to preserve the grape crop in Champagne from a frost. During down times in the fields and on the front, he painted watercolors of local scenes; his photograph of the unit chef, M. Lebec, whose *poule au pot* (chicken stew), *navarin* (mutton stew with turnips), and *boeuf à la mode* (braised beef with vegetables) he enjoyed, was prophetic of his future career as artist and gastronomer.[8]

During the interwar period, Chamberlain exploited various opportunities to study, travel, and work in Europe. He launched a career as a commercial etcher, which enabled him to fund a summer trip to France in 1922. With fellowships from the American Field Service and the Guggenheim Foundation and sales of his etchings, Chamberlain and his wife extended their stay in France for most of the next decade. He apprenticed with professional artists to hone his skills in lithography and etching, while building a portfolio of sketches from Normandy, Brittany, and the Midi that would accompany his later articles in *Gourmet*. He even used an automobile to visit the provinces and thus laid the groundwork for the new approach to travel that he would advocate after the war.[9]

Chamberlain, however, was an expatriate with a difference. Unlike literary innovators Ernest Hemingway and F. Scott Fitzgerald or artistic pioneers Man Ray and Alexander Calder, his traveling companion in Normandy in the 1920s, Chamberlain had little interest in challenging artistic conventions or the genteel tradition. Instead, he embraced the preindustrial landscape and traditional culture of Europe and New England as the subjects of his black-and-white drawings and photographs. They, in turn, gave eloquent testimony to the charms of traditional life on both sides of the Atlantic, a message conveyed in picture books and guidebooks to well-educated American travelers, who developed an affinity for aesthetically pleasing buildings and vistas.[10]

In 1930, the Chamberlains with their two young daughters purchased a house in Senlis, near Paris, where they lived until 1934. During those years, as he later explained, "the noble art of gastronomy was creeping in, and the graphic arts were beginning to serve as accomplices to the epicurean theme." In the process, Chamberlain collected some 1,200 cookbooks and other gastronomical tomes. More important, he schooled himself in the diverse specialties and techniques of French cuisine by observing French cooks at work in their kitchens. Knowledge of gastronomy would strengthen his already firm grasp of traditional culture in France and would make Chamberlain's advice on travel and the good life more persuasive to readers.[11]

Like other exiles, the Chamberlains experienced financial problems during the Depression and returned to the United States. Following their arrival in 1934, the family made a relatively smooth transition to life in historic Marblehead near Boston, while Chamberlain himself embarked on a new career. He taught etching at MIT, learned photography, and published a series of illustrated volumes mostly documenting traditional New England life.[12]

In 1941, Chamberlain volunteered for a position as an Air Force intelligence officer and was soon assigned to the European sector. After a stint in Egypt, he joined the Italian campaign in the Naples area, where he found time to explore the hinterlands of Apulia by jeep, while recording his experience in sketches. During a brief stay in Britain in 1945 as a member of the U.S. Strategic Bombing Survey, Chamberlain dodged bombs, produced a report for the Survey, and sketched and photographed Cambridge and Oxford. For his war service, the American government awarded him the Legion of Merit, while France bestowed the Légion d'Honneur on him.[13]

After the war, Chamberlain resumed his work as an illustrator of America's colonial heritage until MacAusland approached him, this time to do a series of illustrated articles on France for *Gourmet*. He eagerly accepted this "traveling fellowship." When the first of these articles appeared to much fanfare in the March 1949 *Gourmet*, a little more than six years had passed since the publication of the concluding chapter of "Clementine in the Kitchen." No doubt the gap would have been shorter, but from 1945 to 1947 many roads, hotels, and restaurants were inaccessible to travelers in France.[14]

As was true of "Clementine," the three *Bouquets* owed their impact to Chamberlain's ability to express for readers their common experience as relatively affluent, educated, and well-traveled Americans in the first half of the twentieth century. After living through the isolationism of pre–World War II America, they served in the military or lived through one or both wars; many then traveled to Europe for pleasure. In the process, they came to appreciate the values that Americans and Europeans shared and to regard the Atlantic Alliance as a political expression of these shared values.

Chamberlain and his readers were particularly invested in French culture. Many resonated to his quotation of Jefferson in the introduction to *Bouquet de France*: "Everyone has two countries—his own and France." In Chamberlain's case—and for many of his readers—this was more than a cliché. France appealed to them because of the quality of its art and gastronomy, but also because they were striving to assimilate those elements of French culture that were already customary for upper-class Americans. Accordingly, readers valued Chamberlain's praise for American contributions to the restoration of the Cathedral of Rheims after World War I and to the liberation of southern France during the 1944 American landing at St. Raphael, and most shared the pride that he expressed in the mingling of American with other NATO soldiers on the streets of Fountainbleau in 1950.[15]

On a more mundane level, Chamberlain's readers must have understood his satisfaction in discovering that a Frenchman had built his Marblehead home and the ensuing decision he and his wife made to decorate it with "simple French furniture which is mingled harmoniously with a number of American and English pieces." Here was an appropriate metaphor for the convergence of European and American culture that *Gourmet* readers could happily endorse.[16]

Over the next quarter of a century, Chamberlain engaged in a love fest with his audience. He shared his enthusiasm for traditional European life in a respectful and innovative fashion and offered a concrete plan for *Gourmet* readers to explore that life for themselves. And he did so while rarely mentioning the unstable governments and frequent displays of anti-Americanism in France and Italy that might have discouraged travel in those countries. (Chamberlain noted slyly that at a refreshment stand on the roof of the Milan Cathedral "it is possible to slake one's thirst with capitalistic, non-Communist Coca Cola.")[17]

Readers found his judgments about restaurants, hotels, and cultural monuments entertaining and informative. Those who had been to Europe came away from his books with a sense of having revisited places they loved. Some regarded him as not only a guide but a personal friend. While there were few comments about his photographs and sketches in *Gourmet*'s letters-to-the-editor column, they must have contributed greatly to the popularity of his books. More remarkably, his food writing captured the imagination of his readers. He knew how to dramatize fine dining for a reading public that, for the most part, considered their meals as part of a daily routine. In Chamberlain's books, dining became, instead, an important event in the leisurely exploration of old towns and villages in remote areas of France, Italy, and Britain. In a letter to *Gourmet*, Walter Myers noted, "It requires genius to take such commonplaces as food and drink and give them the glamour of romance, spiced every now and then with a glittering touch of the literary."[18]

The close relationship Chamberlain established with readers owed much to his apparent high regard for the audience, as well as his modesty, wit, and wisdom. Chamberlain addressed his readers as "civilized friend(s)" who are "endowed with aesthetic sensibilities, educated taste buds and a normal *joie de vivre* (and that without any apple-polishing is my idea of a *Gourmet* reader)." He later remarked that his greatest reward in writing the travel guides were the reports about "many American tourists carrying these books with them on their trips abroad."[19]

Chamberlain expressed his sense of intimacy with readers by sharing his experiences in the first person "we" (he and his wife) and addressing them in the second person. "If you stay a day or more in the Evesham area, we have some delightful little side trips to suggest . . . If you poke around the churchyard long enough . . ." And he surely gained the trust of readers by refusing to flaunt his expertise. Even in discussing architecture and gastronomy, subjects he knew well, Chamberlain never hesitated to direct readers to sources providing more information than he was able to include in his book. In the introduction to *Italian Bouquet*, he thanked readers for suggesting other sources. In the introduction to *British Bouquet*, he identified three more comprehensive guidebooks.[20]

The response of readers to his articles and books confirms Chamberlain's success in connecting with them. Within a few months of *Gourmet*'s founding, "Clementine in the Kitchen" was already a favorite of the magazine's readers. Equally enthusiastic was the response to the various chapters of his three travel books, although I leave aside readers' opinions of the *Beauty of Britain*, the book version of which appeared in 1963.

Aside from the affectionate, somewhat nostalgic picture of small-town life in Senlis, France, and Marblehead, Massachusetts, it was the adventures of the exuberant and opinionated Clementine herself that appealed to readers. One called the whole series "a rare treat." Another announced that he had fallen in love with her. But it was the nostalgia theme that was most prominent, suggesting that readers who had already been to France but were unable to return after the outbreak of war found the Clementine articles a useful and entertaining substitute for travel.[21]

Readers' reception of *Bouquet de France* was as positive as the response to the Clementine series. The keynote in virtually all responses was a sense of familiarity and even intimacy between author and readers. Wesley King, who attended Chamberlain's lectures on etching at MIT, remarked, "I feel that your Sam Chamberlain series is really great. I would like to take the whole series to France this summer." Robert Gile spoke of *Bouquet* as "my Bible" during a recent drive through France, while adding that it was "one of the most delightful books I have read in some time." Parker Perry also called it "our bible. Michelin can star them, but Samuel's the guide for us." The MacKenzie family regarded Chamberlain as "such a man-after-our-own-hearts that we speak of him as 'Sam.'" Seven years later, Mary Webster remarked, "Many of our compatriots can't wait to see 'Les Dancing girls' of Paris, but this family studies its *Bouquet de France* and hits the provinces."[22]

Reactions to *Italian Bouquet* were similar. Even as chapters appeared in *Gourmet*, readers were eager to the see the full book. Michael Kahler was "enthralled" with the chapter on Tuscany. "I can only recommend it as a bible to other hotel students and apprentice gastronomes like myself." He was certain that the complete version would be "the most exciting (to the palate, that is) book of all times." Reviewing the published volume, Charlotte Turgeon, cookbook writer and subscriber to *Gourmet*, considered Chamberlain not only an "artist with pen, pencil, and camera, but an artist with words." Reading the book was "almost as good as a second trip" to Italy. "You can almost smell and taste the good Italian food he talks about." Turgeon even ventured to predict that in the aftermath of its publication "a flood of tourists, hopefully epicurean, each carrying this distinctive book, bound in white and gold," would descend on Italy. Chamberlain might have shuddered at the thought.[23]

MacAusland and his staff were fully aware of Chamberlain's value to the *Gourmet* enterprise and made every effort to showcase his articles so that readers would notice them. In *Gourmet*'s first issue, for example, the lead article was Chamberlain's "Burgundy at a Snail's Pace," which occupied five consecutive pages, while incorporating his sketches of historical buildings with the text. When the first chapter of "Bouquet de France" appeared, the editors paired it with an article by Curnonsky, France's most famous gastronomer, entitled "Discourse on French Cuisine," suggesting that Chamberlain was a culinary authority in the same league with his French counterpart.[24]

Once readers had made their voices heard, *Gourmet* editors sought to exploit the public enthusiasm for him. After *Gourmet*'s Travel Service was created in 1953, MacAusland wrote that the "many *Gourmet* readers" who had not yet profited from Chamberlain's "epicurean tour of the French provinces" would be able to do so with the assistance of the Travelways Service. For similar reasons, *Gourmet*'s advertisers exploited Chamberlain's name to promote visits to France. In the May 1950 issue, the French National Railroad reminded readers that its trains served the Basque country, which was the subject of that month's Chamberlain article. Of course, readers who opted for these services would be relinquishing some of their autonomy.[25]

When *Bouquet de France* appeared in book form during the Christmas season of 1952, *Gourmet* stimulated reader interest by running two-page advertisements with a strong pitch from MacAusland. Blurbs described "Bouquet" as "a strictly non-political, strictly appetizing and entertaining trip from the cobblestone streets of Normandy to aperitif time at Maxim's. If your heart belongs to la belle France, you will want to own—and give . . . *Bouquet de France*." In this way, *Gourmet* deftly reassured readers, who had no stomach for the current political scene in France, that Chamberlain would show them beautiful sites and delicious meals instead. The sale of more than a hundred thousand copies in the first two years after publication would suggest that readers were pleased with Chamberlain's focus.[26]

After *Italian Bouquet* appeared, *Gourmet's* strategy was to build sales by reminding readers of their enchantment with Chamberlain's previous *Bouquet*. According to one advertisement, Chamberlain's "new book" was a "picturebook, guidebook, [and] cookbook" rolled into one, which would serve both the adventurous and "the armchair traveler." The Christmas advertisement offered readers a package deal: "Four Books of Christmas for holiday giving," the two Chamberlain books and the two volumes of the *Gourmet Cookbook*. The ads continued the next year. To encourage sales, the May 1959 issue used a medical metaphor: "Diagnosis: spring fever. Rx: Chamberlain's Bouquets" (alongside the text was a picture of an office worker dreaming at his desk).[27]

Off the Beaten Path

Samuel Chamberlain created a new kind of guidebook to take advantage of his own skills, while serving the needs of *Gourmet* readers. As Chamberlain announced in the introduction to *Bouquet de France*, he approached France "with camera, sketchpads and tastebuds." The product was a guidebook, cookbook, and coffee-table book all rolled into one and aimed at the "food-conscious American." Like the traditional guidebook, Chamberlain's volumes provided readers with hotel and restaurant options while suggesting cultural sites worth visiting. It was, in this sense, a combination of the green (sites worth visiting) and red (restaurants and hotels) Michelin guides. In addition, each of his three travel books presented recipes in a supplementary "treasury" at the end of the book, while two of them interspersed more recipes in each chapter. And the lavish illustrations qualified all three volumes as coffee-table books.[28]

Conventional and distinctive at the same time, Chamberlain's philosophy of travel sought to draw readers off the beaten path so they would engage more deeply with the local people and culture and spend less time at better-known tourist sites. This theme echoed many travel writers of the past two centuries.

However, few had provided detailed accounts of provincial restaurants in almost every region of France, Italy, and Great Britain. In order to take advantage of less traveled routes without amenities and to allow for last-minute changes in the itinerary, Chamberlain also advocated travel by car and a reliance on the picnic for the midday meal.[29]

Chamberlain borrowed some of his ideas about travel from Maurice-Edmond Sailland, the French epicure, who, as a joke, dubbed himself Curnonsky (literally "why not sky?") to exploit the cult of Russian culture in early twentieth-century France. During the 1920s, Curnonsky and his companion Marcel Rouff wrote twenty-eight volumes on *La France Gastronomique*, which evaluated restaurants in every region of the country. These books were the product of a series of automobile trips to the French provinces and expressed the authors' enthusiasm for linking fine dining and touring by automobile. In addition to reports on French restaurants and inns, they also incorporated regional recipes. As a result of these publications, Curnonsky was voted *"prince élu des gastronomes"* (the elected Prince of Gastronomers), although he preferred the less pretentious and more accurate *"Sa rondeur"* or "His plumpness."[30]

In educating his American audience about French life and cuisine, Chamberlain borrowed heavily from Curnonsky, whom he had met in Paris in the 1920s, and also recommended the *Guide Michelin* for France and Italy. Like *Sa rondeur*, Chamberlain believed that the automobile would enable readers to explore small restaurants, towns, hotels, and monuments in out-of-the-way places; it would also transport the six-hundred-page guidebooks Chamberlain was writing. However, he put his own stamp on these books by marrying information about food, wine, and restaurants with a presentation of the visual charms of provincial towns. His illustrations documented aspects of everyday life from street scenes to local markets to five-hundred-year-old houses, and they served as a model for amateur artists, who Chamberlain urged to follow in his footsteps by sketching, painting, and shooting their way through Europe.[31]

At the heart of this enterprise was Chamberlain's commitment to travel rather than tourism. His goal was to assist readers in understanding the beauty of everyday life and the artistry displayed in the construction of modest buildings, squares, and public monuments. Experiencing the food and viewing the layout of small towns were two ways to learn about a regional culture. And these activities would encourage travelers to take charge of their journeys and proceed at a leisurely pace. All the same, Chamberlain was careful not to ask too much of his readers. In both Italy and France, he told them where to find locals who spoke English. And, in case they yearned for their compatriots, Chamberlain suggested various bars and restaurants where the food was "perfectly good" and the traveler could hear "the sweet music of American speech."[32]

Chamberlain denounced packaged tours that increasingly took Americans quickly through the capital cities of several different countries in a few weeks. To avoid competing with the hordes of tourists who were visiting cultural monuments, he advised his readers to bypass the capital cities altogether. Such counsel reinforced the inclination of the "displaced Anglo-Saxon," who "yearns to get off the beaten highway, away from his compatriots, and to explore untrodden paths." To fulfill their dreams, Chamberlain urged readers to take charge of their itinerary and customize their travels. In so doing, they could interact more fully with the local people, especially those who were not involved in the tourist industry, and experience more directly the local way of life.[33]

From March 1949, when Chamberlain published his first travel article on France, until September 1963, when the last chapter of the "Beauty of Britain" series appeared, he expressed his rising irritation with tourism. In *Bouquet de France*, Chamberlain mildly objected to visiting ski resorts at Chambéry and Chamonix that were "names straight from your travel folder." Hotels in those towns featured "cushioned comfort" and, as its counterpart, standardized " 'international' cooking" to please the palates of skiers from Europe and America. Similarly, restaurateurs on the Mediterranean coast, who believed that all Anglo-Saxons "recoil from a whisper of garlic or the gentlest zephyr of saffron," replaced their "vibrant, colorful, aromatic" dishes with the "cautious, conventional, international cuisine of the resort hotel."[34]

The situation was more worrisome in Britain in 1960. "Swarms of trippers" gathered at Beaulieu Abbey, which Lord Montagu had turned into a car museum. At Blenheim Palace, Chamberlain warned his readers to be prepared for "shuffling, gaping throngs" if they toured in the summer. As for the Lake District, travelers would find "coaches from the Midland manufacturing towns, bearing plump ladies in flowering dresses." At least they were gone by evening. Just across the Scottish border north of Carlisle, readers should avoid the "turnstile tourist trap" that featured "teashops, souvenir stands, tartan emporia and a rather seedy chap with bagpipes." According to Chamberlain, the shepherding of large groups through sites selected by a travel agency left them in a state of passivity.[35]

Abandoning the package tour, travelers would put themselves initially in Chamberlain's hands. With their cars, they would visit places that were normally inaccessible, thus enhancing their sense of adventure. Increasing options, however, would require making choices. By focusing readers on the epicurean theme and emphasizing the pleasures of visiting more modest cultural monuments, Chamberlain helped travelers to narrow these options. Where gastronomy was strong, readers could skimp on monuments and enjoy the restaurants. In less epicurean territory, they could spend more time visiting churches and museums.[36]

So as not to diminish the freedom that travelers gained by rejecting packaged tours, Chamberlain discussed whether and in what form they needed guides above and beyond his own books. Visiting the temples at Paestum, Italy, he was delighted that "there are no guides to pester you here." In Oxford, he strongly recommended that his readers avoid tours organized by travel agencies. Instead of being whisked through the major sites at the University, travelers could take their own leisurely stroll, while using *British Bouquet* supplemented by Alden's *Oxford Guide* as sources of information. Human and print guides were acceptable so long as they were not imposed by outsiders and fit the traveler's needs.[37]

The epicurean orientation often shaped the itineraries that Chamberlain recommended. His proposed "mild adventures" were usually quests for culinary experiences off the beaten path. Rather than launch his readers in Paris, he sent them immediately to one of France's lesser-known regions. Located in eastern France, La Bresse was the home of the country's greatest gourmet, Brillat-Savarin. There, with gastronomy as a guide, mild adventurers could forget about architectural monuments after visiting the Eglise de Brou in Bourg-en-Bresse. Instead, they would search out "villages rather than large towns," "meet smiling country chefs rather than headwaiters in tuxedos," and "sleep in quiet, clean rooms with running water rather than in a suite with a *salle de bain* (bathroom)."[38]

Beyond "mild adventures," it was possible to "get entirely off the beaten track" and have "the refreshing sensation of being a pioneer" in a Marches hill town like Ascoli Piceno, with its "completely undiscovered air." There one could enjoy a "picturesque food market" and a sixth-century baptistery. Farther south, Apulia was "for the more adventuresome, for those who like to go to the very end of the road, to discover what lies really far off the beaten track." In this case, it was the *trulli* (houses with conical roofs) in Alberobello that merited his fulsome introduction.[39]

Whether the destination was a monument, a town square, a hotel, or a restaurant, Chamberlain recommended the small, the simple, and the remote. In visiting such places, travelers would come to understand the daily life of the country and feast on authentic dishes and wines in the company of locals. In *Italian Bouquet*, Chamberlain noted his preference for the Italian Riveria as compared to its French counterpart because it has "a straight-forward simplicity that actually comes as somewhat of a relief." There were fewer fancy shops selling jewelry and perfume than on the French side of the border and more "undiscovered" monuments like the "deserted little chapel" on a "narrow dirt road" in L'Aquila. There, Chamberlain admired the details of the rose window and the "flawless doorway" that stood out against the church's "sun-baked façade." In the absence of tourists, he believed, travelers would be able to experience more fully the beauty of the architecture and the setting.[40]

As with monuments, Chamberlain recommended small towns and inns. He was, for example, quite taken with the thatched roofs and charming pubs of Clovelly in Devon. As for the "idyllic village" of Bibury in the Cotsworlds, photographers and painters would enjoy its seventeenth-century almshouses bordering "the sleepy river Coln." In Devizes, Chamberlain urged his readers to try out the Bear Hotel, located on a charming market square that was especially busy on market day, when "talkative farmers and cattle dealers, each with his pipe and pint," filled the public rooms. The excellent Sunday breakfast was another draw for travelers and locals.[41]

In his digest of Paris restaurants, provided reluctantly for those travelers who rejected his advice to avoid the capital, the names of some of the best-known and most expensive establishments headed the list, but Chamberlain deliberately ended with Chez Josephine "because it represents something quite priceless in the French tradition." Its intimacy and honest cuisine were representative of the typical French household, as well as the family restaurant. "The bouquet of France" came from "Josephine's quail roasting in the oven and her *boeuf bourguignon* gurgling gently on the back of the cook stove."[42]

One of the most notable institutions in Italy was the *trattoria*, often located on an obscure side street in the oldest part of the city and featuring a lively ambiance and a loyal, local clientele. Chamberlain carefully distinguished the *ristorante*, with its typewritten menu and leisurely waiters wearing white coats, from the trattoria, where waiters rushed about in shirt sleeves and supplied diners with handwritten menus; even if there were fewer dishes to select from, trattoria food was often better and the prices lower. More importantly, the diners rubbed elbows with each other. At the Dodici Aposoli in Verona, "gay with murals and uncontrived atmosphere," the presence of "robust, conversational businessmen" gave assurance that the food was tasty. As for the *Trattoria Rina* in Genoa, "Rina Augusto and his smiling family will offer you a chance to know warm-hearted Italian people for a fleeting hour or so—an unforgettable experience."[43]

When prospects were dim for finding a good restaurant, Chamberlain recommended that travelers buy picnic items after breakfast and stop for a roadside lunch. One of the advantages of this plan was that the traveler could forage for lunch in the market where there were opportunities to bargain with the shop-keepers and enjoy the sight of colorful food. Among the options in Italy were bread, *bel paese* cheese, a slice of *mortadella*, and a bottle of Chianti; in Britain, the traveler could buy Yorkshire ham, pork pies, cheeses, crackers, and a bottle of stout; in Nice, why not try a pizza as an appetizer to a *salade niçoise*, which would be both colorful and savory?[44]

To thoroughly enjoy these provincial adventures, Chamberlain advised read-ers to use cars and local inns to slow down their pace and enjoy the journey. As he explained, it was relaxing to drive through English villages on a summer day. Whenever an opportunity arose for a pleasant detour, such as visiting Stilton to investigate the origins of the cheese, it was easy enough to turn off the main road. A charming country inn could also be relaxing. At the Hôtel de Paris et de la Poste in Sens, "a coquettish little bar and a sheltered terrace for aperitif time" created the peaceful ambiance that "makes the relay post an unclouded joy." So did the sight and sound of Bressan fowl cooking on a spit that also anticipated the joys of the table.[45]

For a "week's total tranquility," Chamberlain recommended Orta San Giulio, a small village on Lake Orta in the Piedmont. It was an excellent place to catch up on correspondence or stroll the piazza with the townsfolk in the evening. The traveler could watch young boys waltzing in the piazza and, to end the evening, purchase a *caffè espresso* and a liqueur. "Does this sort of thing appeal to you?"[46]

Chamberlain also celebrated Orta San Giulio for the many opportunities it offered to artists. The "radiant little town" would be an excellent subject for the "water colorist," while the town hall would be "irresistible to the passing pencil sketcher," as Chamberlain himself demonstrated with his own pencil sketch of the intricate detail of the façade. The traveler could, thus, pass a few hours or a day in an activity he had chosen and learn more about the subject of his artwork.[47]

Indeed, Orta San Giulio was only one among many sites that Chamberlain recommended to amateur artists who were equipped with a pen, a brush, or a camera. In describing these sites, he often identified specific subjects to depict and gave instructions on the proper perspective and light conditions to show them well. In this way, the illustrations in his guidebook became models for travelers who wanted to create, as well as view, art and encouraged a more active engagement with the people and places they were visiting. Moreover, good art required painstaking work and was therefore conducive to slowing down the pace of travel and enabling travelers to reflect on what they were seeing.

The town hall—Orta

"The Town Hall—Orta": pencil sketch by Samuel Chamberlain from *Italian Bouquet: An Epicurean Tour of Italy* (New York: Gourmet, 1958), p. 57. The Schlesinger Library, Radcliffe Institute, Harvard University. Contributor/Gourmet, © Condé Nast Publications.

Chamberlain was familiar with the European tradition of painting and sketching important cultural sites and often placed his own work in the perspective of those who went before him. In that way, he hoped to educate his readers on changing approaches to depicting these sites. Take Lower Burgundy. It was "filled with a succession of beautiful towns which read like the pages from an artist's sketchbook." In Auxerre, Chamberlain photographed the clock tower, while noting that it was "precisely the sort of subject that many nineteenth-century artists chose for their colored lithographs." In his photograph, the clock tower provided the backdrop for a market day. An etching of the same scene showed market stalls and mingling buyers somewhat overwhelmed by the city buildings looming behind them.[48]

Befitting his preference for the charm of old villages where history was alive in the surviving architecture, Chamberlain identified "picturesque" buildings and "vistas opening up in many directions" in Thaxted (Essex), which he regarded as a "painter's town." By photographing the timbered Guildhall to highlight its over-hanging upper stories as well as the interesting vistas past the Guildhall to the church, Chamberlain demonstrated the artistic possibilities of the town. He re-marked that "this is one of the favorite sketch subjects for itinerant watercolorists, who are almost always at hand during the summer season." Just in case the artist should run out of subjects, Chamberlain's backup was the local church with its 181-foot spire, the "picture-book almshouses" nearby, and a windmill with its arms fallen off. "Why not bring your lunch and your sketchbook and enjoy this charm-ing corner of Essex?"[49]

On the Italian Riviera "pencil sketchers and water-colorists" could choose from a variety of fishing villages east of Nervi. After considering its "animation and color," Chamberlain declared Camogli "one of the most sketchable villages in Europe." In addition to the harbor, artists would find its fishing boats, the rococo church, and the steep white facades of the houses that fronted the harbor interesting subjects to capture in their work.[50]

But Chamberlain was also interested in documenting the encroachment of modern life in traditional settings. Among various examples of this development was a scene in Guildford where he photographed the local bishop blessing an array of new cars and trucks lining the sides of the streets beneath the Guildhall with its overhanging balcony and domed clock. "We have photographed it for you," he remarked, in order to encourage fellow cameramen to consider the juxtaposition of modern ways with traditional settings as subjects for their own work.[51]

Chamberlain's Gastronomy

Despite his success in devising an approach to travel that satisfied the needs of his readers, Chamberlain had difficulty in evaluating restaurants. Of course, he knew French cuisine well and accepted without hesitation French assumptions about the elements of fine dining. However, when he reviewed restaurants, he experienced the problems that plagued other French advocates of regional cuisine. Like Curnonsky and Rouff, Chamberlain searched for the distinctive dishes characteristic of each province. Like them, he expected to find such dishes in small restaurants that were essentially extensions of the home. They were family enterprises, featuring an intimate ambiance and a cook who was often the wife of the proprietor. Drawn to the restaurants by their location and ambiance, critics and customers alike sometimes weighted these factors more heavily than the food itself. Moreover, judging the quality of the food became problematic when tourist organizations in Paris initiated a program to identify regional dishes and modify them to suit the tastes of outsiders (Parisians and foreign tourists). In addition, skillful provincial chefs sometimes created new dishes without advertising them as such. Their French customers, in turn, often assumed that they were eating traditional, regional fare.[52]

Once outside of France, Chamberlain was on even shakier ground. He revealed his unfamiliarity with Italian and British cuisine and sought ways to compensate for his ignorance. One strategy was to approach these cuisines from the perspective of a Frenchman. This Gallocentric view, however, did little to educate his readers about the distinctiveness of these two culinary traditions.

In his guidebooks, Chamberlain advocated the French idea, shared to a lesser extent by other ethnic groups, that food plays a central role in creating a joyous life. Feasting in the remote Provençal village of Les Baux at l'Oustau de Baumanière, one of France's great restaurants, Chamberlain thought of its closest counterpart in the United States. What came to mind were the resort hotels in the Rocky Mountains. However, "the comparison stops when you taste Monsieur Thuilier's cooking!" By contrasting French and American practices, Chamberlain hoped to increase his readers' awareness of the special culinary opportunities available to them in France and other parts of Europe.[53]

What particularly heightened the enjoyment of dining in France was the festive atmosphere that surrounded a fine dinner. French chefs and diners alike celebrated in conversation and literature the satisfaction of the senses they were about to experience. As he roasted a pig at the Hôtel de l'Abbaye in Talloires, Chef Tiffenat proclaimed that "this dish should be anticipated like the first rendezvous of love and should be golden as a young gypsy." In somewhat different fashion, Chef Roger Thiry of the Relais de Corny in Lorraine gently mocked the more elaborate dinner he prepared and the diners who ate it. Midway through a menu in verse with commentary on each of the courses, Thiry remarked tongue in cheek that his guests drank "a little Bordeaux juice" to absolve them of their "gourmand sins."[54]

In his restaurant reviews, Chamberlain always noted the name and special-ties of the cook or chef, who was the key to creating a fine meal, whether from the repertoire of *haute cuisine* or *cuisine régionale*. In the latter case, Chamberlain expected the cook to prepare simple, straightforward dishes characteristic of the region. By contrast, a great chef should be able to "prepare . . . a wealth of intri-cate dishes" to satisfy his guests. As an example of the latter, Chamberlain sin-gled out Fernand Point at La Pyramide. Even though Point had no menu or wine list, diners were certain that whatever he served would be delicious and that his wine cellar contained virtually all of the most reputable French wines.[55]

In Chamberlain's view, however, it was the regional diversity of French cui-sine that made it truly great. To illustrate this concept, he imagined a culinary relief map of France on which mountains represented the areas of gastronomi-cal excellence. Paris and Lyon, both actually located near sea level, would be the two grand peaks. Chamberlain then represented Burgundy, Normandy, and Dau-phiny as "imposing plateaus," while noting "other mountain ranges of culinary splendor" in Alsace, the Pyrenees, Perigord, and the Riviera. To support his claim for Alsace, Chamberlain noted that it "is truffled with good restaurants as picturesque as they are palatable." By contrast, the center and north would ap-pear on the map as flat areas lacking in any notable cuisine. Auvergne, for ex-ample, had only a few passable restaurants.

Extending the concept of a culinary relief map to England made little sense in view of the virtual absence of regional specialties; however, Chamberlain had high praise for the two culinary capitals of Italy, Lombardy and Bologna, which he regarded as the rough equivalents of Paris and Lyon.[56]

Despite this exercise in geography, the idea of regional cuisine was much more complicated than Chamberlain acknowledged. To be sure, the conviction that smaller, remoter restaurants, which served local specialties, deserved notice like their more famous Parisian counterparts was valid, but only up to a point. The provincial eateries' easier access to fresh ingredients from the surrounding countryside and the greater variety of flavors, including zesty dishes from Provence and Languedoc, were assets that justified this attention. However, the contrast between Paris and the provinces raised two questions Chamberlain never ad-dressed. Was each of the regions, including Paris, truly distinctive, and should restaurants featuring regional cuisine be judged by different standards than Pa-risian restaurants serving *haute cuisine*?[57]

On several occasions, Chamberlain recognized that the distinction between Paris and the provinces, a central assumption in *Bouquet de France*, was no longer so clear. Provincial migration to Paris and the rapid shipment of fresh produce to the capital encouraged the rise of provincial restaurants representing virtually all regional cuisines in Paris. It was now possible to make a regional tour of France without leaving the capital. With this in mind, Chamberlain himself recommended that readers who could not visit Perigord eat at the Rotiserie Perigourdine to taste the "splendors of its cooking." Moreover, he acknowledged that *haute cuisine* was not confined to Paris. In Les Baux, he spoke in hushed tones of "*la grande cuisine française*" that Chef Thuilier prepared. Although Thuilier served some regional dishes, most of the cooking was "on a loftier plane."[58]

Even in the provinces, there was clear evidence that provincial distinctiveness had broken down. At Le Chapon Fin, regarded by many as the finest restaurant in Bordeaux, Chamberlain, to his surprise, discovered an excellent selection of Burgundy vintages on the wine list. In addition, Narcissa Chamberlain noted that the recipe for *canard à l'orange* was placed in the Pyrenées section, because it was submitted by M. Fouquet, whose restaurant was located in that region. However, Fouquet had learned to cook the dish in Normandy, where he was born. She also explained that *piperade*, a Basque egg dish, had recently become popular in Paris.[59]

Chamberlain's persistent advocacy of small regional restaurants made the quality of the cuisine a secondary consideration. Like Curnonsky and Rouff, he was so caught up in the discovery of diamonds in the rough and intent on enjoying their informality that he gave insufficient attention to the quality of the food they served. As for the standards that should be applied to dishes classified as *haute cuisine* versus those that belonged properly to *cuisine régionale*, Chamberlain said nothing, nor did he address the role of Paris-based organizations in shaping the cuisine of various provinces.[60]

It is also difficult to discern Chamberlain's own evaluation of restaurants because he relied heavily on French culinary authorities, many of whom were members of prestigious gourmet societies. In one case, he substituted an account of society rituals for commentary on the quality of their dinners. Approaching the Clos du Vougeot, the home base of the Tastevin, he remarked, "In this 'Acropolis of Burgundy,' the Confrérie des Chevaliers du Tastevin, a most active group of bon vivants and wine men, have established their order." At their "Rabelaisian banquets, held in the ancient cellar," they "don ceremonial robes, and join in food, wine, and song: '*C'est la chanson du vigneron, Au glou, glou, glou, glou du flacon*'" ("It's the song of the wine grower, the gurgle, gurgle, gurgle, gurgle of the bottle").[61]

After meeting Georges Legendre, long-time chef of the society, who was charged with preparing their quarterly feasts in Nuits St. Georges, Chamberlain identified four of his special dishes that were "beyond reproach," although there was no evidence that he had tasted the finished product; he then segued quickly to the claims of one "dignified member of the Tastevin tribe" that the wine of the Côte de Nuits is a curative (*"Un verre de Nuits prépare la votre"*). The claim was based on Louis XIV's belief that his illness in 1680 had been cured by drinking a Côte de Nuits wine. In the absence of Chamberlain's commentary, it is worth noting that Julia Child, who was initiated into the Tastevin at the Clos de Vougeot in 1953, thought that the dinner was undistinguished.[62]

In both England and France, Chamberlain regarded a restaurant proprietor or chef's membership in a prestigious gastronomic society as an index of the culinary quality of the establishment. There was some justification in relying on such authorities, but too often Chamberlain presented their views in place of his own dining experience at the restaurant. Indeed, aside from a brief list of the restaurant specialties and occasional comments about the freshness of the ingredients, Chamberlain largely confined his own assessment to the restaurant's ambiance.

The examples of Chamberlain's deference to authorities with links to gastronomic societies are numerous. On André Simon's word, he included the Connaught Hotel in the list of the top fifteen London restaurants. In addition, he considered it a good sign that the Hotel Central in Luneville had "received [the] unrestrained applause of a group of Wine and Food Society pilgrims" from England. He also reported that Raymond Thuilier, chef of L'Oustau de Baumanière, and Monsieur Chapuis, the chef at the Hotel du Grand Cerf at Senlis, as well as Edwin M. Adams of the Golden Lion in Stirling, were members of the Tastevin, while proprietor George Fuller at the Vineyard in Colerne was both a Chevalier and a "dedicated member of the Wine and Food Society." These affiliations, in Chamberlain's mind, seemed to guarantee a good meal.[63]

Reports from the Club des Cents, whose members frequented restaurants all over France in order to select two of them for annual awards based on the excellence of their cooking, also influenced Chamberlain. He praised Chef Raveau's Hotel de l'Esperance in Pouilly-sur-Loire because the Club des Cents, that "most exacting and erudite of gastronomic clubs," awarded Raveau a diploma. And he noted that Chef Barattero had posthumously received a Diploma of Honor from the Club for the excellence of his cooking. As for Barattero's worthy wife, Maxim's in Paris had invited her to cook the Hotel du Midi's regional dishes, which her husband had made famous.[64]

Chamberlain's strong commitment to French culinary practices was also evident in his guidebooks on Italy and Britain. Recognizing the low esteem in which British cooking was held, he initially agreed to take on the project only because publisher Earle MacAusland, who was of Scottish descent and greatly admired the British Isles, asked him to do so. Chamberlain, accordingly, entitled the series of articles he wrote for *Gourmet* "The Beauty of Britain," suggesting a focus on cultural and natural sites rather than cuisine. And his wife provided no recipes in the text of the articles or the book.[65]

So, why was there "A Treasury of British Recipes" at the end of *British Bouquet?* According to Chamberlain, the actual experience of British cooking turned out to be more positive than he anticipated, so he and Narcissa assembled it after the articles appeared in *Gourmet*. Evidently there were fewer "treasures" in Britain than in France or Italy, given that the supplement ran to thirty-three pages, about half the length of its Italian and French counterparts. Moreover, the Chamberlains failed to solicit the favorite recipes of chefs whose restaurants they had frequented, as they did for the French and Italian treasuries. Instead, the recipes selected for the Treasury came from a search through British cookbooks and consultations with Elizabeth David, the prominent cookbook writer.

Nonetheless, "A Treasury of British Recipes" was testimony to Chamberlain's increasing appreciation of British cooking. From the outset he praised Anglo-Saxon breakfasts. He also discovered excellent food at some country places as, for example, the White Hart Hotel in Lincoln, where he developed "a sudden rapture for fine English cooking" after feasting on roast *contrefilet* (tenderloin) of beef and boiled potatoes.[66]

Still, Chamberlain had clear reservations about the British culinary scene, reflecting the widespread belief that British cuisine was inferior to its French counterpart. In his opinion, menus throughout the British Isles had a sameness "that soon becomes wearisome," in large part because there were so few regional specialties in country hotels; instead, the same fried filet of plaice greeted the traveler on menus in every part of the country. And the quality of cooking varied widely. Some counties, like Windsor, were essentially culinary wastelands. Chamberlain warned his readers that "dedicated gourmets will not be particularly happy here, but it isn't quite fair to expect Windsor Castle and Lucullus too." Although he rarely gave low marks to individual restaurants, he noted that the roast chicken at the White Hart in Lewes "had been in the oven more than once." As for beverages, the poor handling of the wine in a number of restaurants disappointed Chamberlain.[67]

In his insistence on measuring the improvement in British cuisine by the growing number of French restaurants in Britain, Chamberlain revealed his Gallocentric bias. He noted that interest in French cooking had wavered at times, but he believed that its influence in London had been in the ascendancy since World War II. Of course, London did not "glitter as brilliantly as the great luminary in Paris but it gets brighter all the time."[68]

It is not surprising, then, that Chamberlain's list of thirty-one exemplary London restaurants in *British Bouquet* included eleven serving primarily French food and exactly the same number featuring British cooking. Among the other nine restaurants, four were Italian, one was Greek, and four had no clear ethnic identity. And, as goes London, so goes the larger metropolitan area. Chamberlain was particularly enthusiastic about the Hinds Head in Bray-on-Thames, an English inn with Gallic flourishes and a favorite haunt of the Wine and Food Society. As for the Bell Inn at Aston Clinton, which offered French and Italian dishes, "discriminating London Gourmets" who found it within easy driving distance were among its loyal patrons.[69]

In the case of the Gravetye Manor in East Grinstead, it was Londoners who transmitted the French influence to the periphery in the first place. After the Gore Hotel in London took over the Gravetye, its director, Peter Herbert, arranged the brilliant French menu, including *crêpe de fruits de mer* (seafood crepe) and *escalope de veau* (scalloped veal), and transformed its wine cellar and kitchen.[70]

In evaluating Italian cooking, Chamberlain kept in mind his own and his audience's relative ignorance of the subject. Indeed, the fact that there were almost three times as many recipes in the text of *Bouquet de France* as in *Italian Bouquet* suggests that the two Chamberlains were learning more about Italian cuisine before selecting appropriate recipes for their readers. As Samuel admitted, the "sublime pesto," served on the Italian Riviera and described in detail to his neophyte audience "as a gustatory experience not to be forgotten," was new to him as well. So were other Italian dishes, such as the "plump, wine-red octopus," which he did not recommend because it was "an acquired taste."[71]

Given his readers' ignorance of Italian cooking, Chamberlain remedied some basic misconceptions. He warned that the Italian restaurants they frequented in America, most of which were owned by Neapolitans and served pizza, minestrone, and spaghetti, in no way represented the astonishing variety of Italian cooking. And for those who were put off by the strong garlic flavor in the food served in Italian-American restaurants, he noted that Italian chefs in Italy were far more subtle in their use of it.[72]

The Chamberlains also used "A Treasury of Italian Recipes" to remedy readers' ignorance of Italian cuisine. They were, in fact, optimistic that this recipe collection would have a bigger impact than its French counterpart and even become "a worthy rival . . . to the Italian cookbooks in English that already exist."

Accordingly, they abandoned the organization of recipes by region that they had used in the French treasury in favor of a basic cookbook approach that ran from first course to last.[73]

In the body of *Italian Bouquet*, however, Chamberlain applied the regional approach to Italian cooking, while at the same time proclaiming that the uniform character of the Italian people, who were "gay, musical, creative, and openly friendly," shaped the cooking. As such, it followed that the Italians would enjoy spicy, aromatic food much like their neighbors in southern France. Indeed, Chamberlain had already reported in *Bouquet de France* that the Provençal specialties of *bouillabaisse*, *brandade*, and Chateauneuf-du-Pape were a product of the regional *"joie de vivre"* based in the climate, while the character of Languedoc's inhabitants, "gay, Gallic and gregarious," shaped its aromatic cooking. By insisting on the common ethnic character and diet in southern France and all of Italy, Chamberlain, in effect, obliterated the French-Italian border in favor of a different geography. No doubt, this identification of character with diet helped Chamberlain explain the roots of a cuisine with which he was not so familiar, but it was in conflict with the regional organizing principle of his books.[74]

Another aid in evaluating Italian cuisine was to gauge the response of French patrons to the dishes they were eating in Italian restaurants. Noting, for example, that Frenchmen occupied a third of the tables at the Ristorante Aldo in Milan, Chamberlain remarked that "few Parisian restaurants could have made them look more contented." Even granting that these Frenchmen enjoyed their meals and that they were possessed of fine palates, it was strange that Chamberlain used them as expert witnesses on the subject of Italian cuisine. Moreover, he was surely skating on thin ice in looking more favorably on the Dodici Apostoli in Verona because the proprietor spoke French or because several "robust, conversational businessmen" in that restaurant attacked their "ample fare and full-blooded Valpolicella with gusto."[75]

There were also problematic features in the treasuries attached to each of the guidebooks that were primarily the work of Narcissa Chamberlain. Of course, she had to cope with the problem of ingredients that were unavailable to American cooks; on these grounds, she had no choice but to omit certain representative recipes altogether, while revising others. She scrapped, for example, such Bordeaux specialties as *cèpes* (a type of mushroom) *à la bordelaise* and lamprey (an eel-like fish); the Auvergnac recipe for *potée*, because few housewives could obtain a whole pig's head; and the Nivernais recipes based on truffles, foie gras, and crayfish, because the ingredients would be difficult to obtain in America. More serious was the decision not to offer a recipe for the famous Norman specialty, *tripes à la mode de Caen.* Apparently, Narcissa doubted that Americans would eat organ meats, even though she had already included various recipes for kidney and liver.[76]

By contrast, there were fewer problems with absent ingredients in the Italian and British Treasuries, perhaps because the Chamberlains had a less exhaustive knowledge of those cuisines. Even so, they offered no Italian recipes for squid in order to avoid "a slight shock to the eye." Also, the haggis recipes in the British Treasury came with a warning that the sheep's stomach, essential to making it, would be difficult to order at an American butcher shop.[77]

In other recipes included in the French and Italian Treasuries, the Chamberlains advised substituting ingredients, even though some of these changes altered the taste of the dishes. In the French Treasury, for example, they recommended that readers who wished to serve snails use the "excellent" imported, canned variety. As for the Italian recipes, they considered "our [America's] good southern shrimp" an acceptable substitute for *scampi*, while baked ham could replace *prosciutto* and canned anchovies pinch-hit for the fresh variety. Particularly surprising was the Chamberlains' casual suggestion that any good-quality cooking oil was an acceptable substitute for olive oil.[78]

Chamberlain's travel books invited Americans interested in gourmet dining to pursue this interest in an "off-the-beaten-track" trip rather than a package tour. Distinctive in their formats compared to other guidebooks, Chamberlain's photos and sketches confirmed the visual appeal of Europe. As guidebooks, cookbooks, and coffee-table items, they could be used for a variety of purposes. Many armchair travelers found them entertaining and informative; even if they never set foot in Europe or ate a gourmet meal, they acquired from the texts a better sense of regional foodways, geography, and culture in the three countries he treated. Other readers were eager to follow Chamberlain's prescriptions for traveling in Europe. His proposed automobile tour, which maximized the traveler's flexibility, appealed to the independent spirit of some Americans without exceeding their capacity to navigate the roads and inns that Chamberlain documented in his guidebooks. Still others cooked from the recipes, translated by Narcissa.

One unanticipated result of Chamberlain's popularity was a shift away from the original emphasis in *Gourmet* on French and American cuisine. As it turned out, *Bouquet de France* exhausted the market for a guidebook emphasizing French cuisine. In order to exploit Chamberlain's appeal to readers, the magazine's editors sent him to Italy and later Britain. In the process, *Gourmet* gave a level of recognition to the cultures and cuisines of those two countries that it previously accorded only to France and America.[79]

It is also important to note that Chamberlain contributed to a subtle shift away from the male dominance of the gourmet movement in America. Of course, he authored the three guidebooks, but his wife's name appeared below his on the title pages of all three *Bouquets* as a translator of the recipes. No doubt, she was also heavily involved in planning their trips as family vacations to include their two daughters. In this way, the Chamberlains provided a genuinely new model for gourmet activity. At the same time, Chamberlain's preference for skipping capital cities with their elegant restaurants presided over by professional male chefs was part of a strategy to favor the small family restaurants in the provinces that often featured the cooking of a woman.

The striking similarities in the off-the-beaten-track strategy adopted by Chamberlain, his many predecessors, and David Brooks' bourgeois Bohemians suggest that using travel to bolster social status was a common practice. Both Chamberlain's readers and the Bobos achieved this goal by planning their own vacations—with assistance from guidebooks—slowing the pace of travel, and seeking close relationships with indigenous people, their cultures, and food-ways. Of course, with the advance of modernization, travelers had to work harder to find unbeaten paths. After all, in 1950, Americans experienced a sense of ad-venture in traveling through Europe by automobile. For Brooks' Bobos, by con-trast, only the frontiers of Africa and Latin America were sufficiently exotic to provide that same experience.[80]

While travel off the beaten track likely propelled travelers up the social ladder, it is unclear whether Chamberlain's readers or Brooks's Bobos met local people as they proposed to do, despite language barriers and the potential isolation of automobile travel. Letters to the editors in "Sugar and Spice" said nothing about such local encounters. Their silence suggests that such encounters were rare or nonexistent or that the letter writers had reasons for not reporting them.

Curiously, neither the Bobos nor Chamberlain, who sought escape from the developed world, acknowledged their dependence on the products of the indus-trial revolution. Chamberlain, for example, steered readers away from the manu-facturing belt in England and complained bitterly about noises from motor scooters in Italy, both of which made life uglier and more frenetic. However, it is obvious that transatlantic steamers and airplanes, good roads, and automo-biles provided the foundation of their own and the Bobos' travel schemes. Per-haps the romance of seeking an escape from the modern world blinded travelers to their real dependence on modern technology.

Given the popularity of his writings among *Gourmet* readers from the first issue through the 1960s, Chamberlain should be recognized for the important role he played in advancing the cause of gourmet dining. Both the sales of the guidebooks and the rapid expansion of subscriptions to the magazine give some measure of his influence. And it is quite likely that Chamberlain's readers, persuaded by his high opinion of gourmet dining societies, may have been partly responsible for swelling their ranks.

Chapter Seven

From Readers to Cooks?

The Influence of *Gourmet*/Gourmet Recipes

G*ourmet* magazine was the only periodical to regularly disseminate gourmet (usually French) recipes to the American public before 1956. With a circulation that rose from 30,000 in 1945 to about 173,000 readers by 1961, the magazine made these recipes available to a large and growing public. In addition, *Gourmet* republished many of the same recipes in the two-volume Gourmet *Cookbook* (1950, 1957), which sold three hundred thousand copies by July of 1960; some of these recipes also appeared in Gourmet's *Cookbook of Fish and Game*, Volume 1 (1947), and Gourmet's *Basic French Cook Book* (1961). Furthermore, Samuel Chamberlain's *Clementine in the Kitchen* (1943) and his *Bouquet de France* (1952) incorporated recipes originally published in the magazine. Taken together, these books comprised a significant contribution to the growing shelf of gourmet cookbooks and reinforced the impact of the recipes originally published in the magazine.[1]

Like other types of recipe collections, publications presenting gourmet recipes enabled some readers to cook new dishes, but they also served a variety of other functions. As scholars have shown in considering various types of recipe collections, the messages implicit in the recipes or explicit in introductions and commentaries are often as important as the recipes themselves. My own research establishes that gourmet cookbooks and articles, never before studied in this way, featured such messages but, for the most part, failed to convert readers into cooks. Inferences from letters to the editor, the recipes that appeared in the magazine and elsewhere, and the cooking skills of *Gourmet*'s readers confirm this failure.

Gourmet cookbooks and articles played an important role in portraying French cuisine and culture as keys to good living, while clarifying the gender and class cohorts of the audience the recipes addressed. The authors, effectively ambassadors for French culture, often cast their writings in the form of travel essays highlighting French artistry of all kinds from the construction of beautiful cathedrals to the preparation and enjoyment of excellent meals. In this way, the texts addressed primarily the aspirations of the growing upper-middle class, which sought to improve its social standing through gourmet dining, rather than the small population of French immigrants and their descendents in America, who wished to maintain their cultural and culinary heritage. As such, the audience for French cookbooks was different from that of earlier ethnic cookbooks.

Gourmet recipes were often gender coded. The magazine deliberately hired a professional chef rather than a home cook to present the principal lessons in French cooking. In so doing, *Gourmet* could associate itself and its readers with the grand tradition of French cuisine as embodied in a chef who had studied with Escoffier. Of course, the chef, always a man, could orient his cooking lessons in various ways. In tapping Louis De Gouy, known for his fish and game recipes, to be the first *Gourmet* chef, *Gourmet* signaled a clear gender orientation. De Gouy, after all, believed that a hunting or fishing trip was a necessary prelude to cooking the game that had been harvested. For these adventures, women need not apply. It is clear from the selection of De Gouy that *Gourmet* intended to appeal at the outset to potential male cooks.

As it turned out, however, American men went off to war, and women became the principal readers of the magazine. For those who aspired to cook, De Gouy's macho rhetoric became an obstacle to using the recipes. It is not surprising, then, that after De Gouy's death, *Gourmet* switched gears and pitched its recipes to women. The individuals charged with implementing this new approach were Louis Diat, the second *Gourmet* chef, and his American collaborator, Helen Ridley, who presented basic recipes from the viewpoint of Diat's mother, a small-town French housewife. In this venture, the collaborators addressed the cooking lessons in a clear and nonthreatening manner to the inexperienced American housewife.

From the outset, there were two significant obstacles for readers who might have considered cooking from the recipes in *Gourmet*: their lack of kitchen experience and the inadequacies of the recipes. Subscribers to *Gourmet* were, in general, deficient in the cooking skills required for this relatively complicated task. Their inexperience, in turn, was a function of parallel developments in the American food industry and the home. Until World War I and the passage of the Immigration Restriction Act of 1924 reduced the influx of immigrants and opened jobs in factories and offices to their predecessors, most well-to-do families had servants to cook their meals. At the same time, the revolution in food production made available boxed, canned, and packaged goods that required little preparation and were identifiable by their brand names. These new products not only were easy to cook but were also hailed by advertisers and home economists as more nutritious, cleaner, and safer than bulk foods. Meanwhile, redesigned kitchens, outfitted with the latest appliances, further simplified meal preparation. In effect, this revolution enabled inexperienced housewives, who had lost their servants, to prepare family meals, even when they were ignorant of basic cooking processes. It disabled them, however, from cooking dishes that required a knowledge of traditional kitchen techniques.[2]

The second obstacle to cooking *Gourmet* recipes was the absence of sufficient instructions on how to find and prepare the ingredients for a given dish. Often recipes listed ingredients without specifying where to find the most obscure items, the exact size and weight of each ingredient, and the appropriate size and type of poultry or cut of meat. Moreover, few cookbook writers explained in terms a novice cook could understand how to sauté, make a crust for a quiche, or properly combine the ingredients for mayonnaise.[3]

Of course, American cooks were not all in the same boat when it came to considering whether or not to prepare a gourmet recipe. In large cities on either coast, as opposed to urban and farm areas in the Midwest, would-be gourmet cooks had greater access to retail stores that stocked fine wines and specialty ingredients required for certain recipes. By contrast, the survival of traditional cooking skills may have been greater in rural areas.

Curiously, the rise of gourmet dining societies may also have inhibited progress toward home cooking of gourmet meals. The all-male membership of most of these societies implied that gourmet dining was for men only. Furthermore, the societies often created their menus from *haute cuisine* recipes rather than those of *cuisine bourgeoise*, which was more accessible to home cooks. Moreover, some journalists, who apparently equated gourmet dining and *haute cuisine*, believed that it was too complex for home cooks. Jane Nickerson, the *New York Times* food editor, remarked that "home dinners can never duplicate the luxuries of the Chevaliers du Tastevin."[4]

To evaluate the influence of recipes in *Gourmet*, I draw on "Sugar and Spice," the magazine's letters-to-the-editor column, where readers often reacted to the magazine's recipes. (A rigorous sampling of early readers would be impossible to obtain at this point.) Even though the evidence is anecdotal, the letters provide insight into readers' thoughts about cooking *Gourmet* recipes. After considering these responses, I briefly examine the quality of the recipes in gourmet cookbooks published between 1940 and 1961 by houses other than *Gourmet* to see how well they served inexperienced cooks. My main focus, however, will be articles by the *Gourmet* chefs, at least one of which appeared in every issue of the magazine from the founding to 1960. Through these articles the chefs intended to provide a comprehensive approach to French cuisine, including recipes for the various courses of dinners served during all seasons and holidays. I evaluate these recipes to see how well they met the needs of the magazine's readers. Of course, recipes appeared in other *Gourmet* articles, but largely to enable readers to imagine the flavor of the dishes rather than cook them.

Readers as Potential Cooks

While *Gourmet* published about half a dozen letters to the editor every month, only one on average actually commented on a recipe from the magazine that the writer had cooked. Most correspondents either sent one of their favorite recipes or asked for one from the magazine. While a number of subscribers reported reading the recipes, there is little evidence that they or *Gourmet*'s staff actually cooked them.

Letters from *Gourmet* readers who cooked from the magazine's recipes frequently asked where they could find gourmet ingredients that were scarce in their locale. Mrs. Jacqueline Swank, for example, wrote from Towanda, Pennsylvania, to report that there were no truffles or "even shallots" available in her area. She applauded the magazine for rejecting "lazy ways of cooking" and providing "a perfect escape from an ungentle, harried world." *Gourmet*, in turn, supplied her with mail-order addresses so that she could satisfy her quest for exotic ingredients.[5]

Other cooks expressed an appreciation for the quality of the recipes they prepared and were grateful to *Gourmet* for the opportunity to improve their cooking skills. In this vein, Mrs. H. Stanley Paschal reported that immediately after reading the latest issue of the magazine, she went straight to the stove to try out a few of the most promising recipes, while Miss Josephine Jenkins congratulated *Gourmet* on restoring pride in cooking and announced her plans for preparing a big meal including such dishes as *kreplach* in chicken broth, Welsh rarebit, and pecan pie, all from *Gourmet* recipes. Mrs. Meil Foster Cramer credited *Gourmet* for her improved cooking, which, according to friends, was now "inspired." There were also half a dozen reports of informal gourmet societies that used the magazine as a source of recipes.[6]

A more surprising and more persistent theme in "Sugar and Spice" was the confession of subscribers that they preferred reading to cooking the magazine's recipes. Publisher Earle MacAusland, who from the outset identified *Gourmet* as a lifestyle rather than a cooking magazine, was happy to endorse this practice. Consistent with this conception, he explained in the introduction to *The Gour-*

met Cookbook that "there are gourmets who never stirred a sauce, but who love the lore of gastronomy . . . Their belief is that a recipe never yet made a good cook, but that a gourmet's recipe certainly makes good reading." No doubt, MacAusland hoped to encourage both readers and cooks to subscribe to the magazine and buy *Gourmet* cookbooks, and he probably suspected that the cooks were in the minority among the magazine's readers.[7]

With such encouragement from the publisher, it is no wonder that readers often admitted their preference for reading over cooking the recipes. Mr. Albert Hawkins reported that he read cookbooks for pleasure much like others read detective stories. Among cookbooks, he particularly enjoyed perusing "*Gourmet* Magazine and *The Gourmet Cookbook*." Mr. J. C. Scharf, who would have cooked from the magazine's recipes if they had been helpful, remarked, "I esteem *Gourmet* for its literary quality, not for its recipes."[8]

J. Russell Scott enjoyed reading the recipes even when he didn't savor the fruits of them. As for Charles Fay, he found *Gourmet* a "fun magazine" because he could "read and dream over each and every special and fancy recipe, discuss it with my friends, and never have to make it." Mrs. Marie P. Randolph spoke for herself and her husband: "first we enjoy reading, then we enjoy eating." She said nothing, however, about whether they enjoyed the cooking that must have preceded the eating.[9]

"Because just reading it tastes so good," Mary Montgomery asked *Gourmet* to renew her subscription. That line pleased Father Pat, a *Gourmet* subscriber and Jesuit from Detroit, who enjoyed the magazine menus occasionally, but mainly "it tastes so good just reading it." Even though she said nothing about cooking, Mrs. Pearson Conlyn took *Gourmet* more seriously. Conlyn read the articles on "cookery in foreign and domestic places" as "travelogues." Each was "unique and different." Even Mrs. Meil Cramer, who credited *Gourmet* with improving her cooking, gave greater emphasis to the literary quality of the magazine, which provided "delectable reading material."[10]

Mrs. Lou E. Peck admitted that she was usually interested in magazines that gave advice on dieting. However, she lay down with a copy of *Gourmet*, took an aspirin to allay her hunger pangs, and read herself to sleep with the magazine. Mrs. Peck's fulfillment came in the form of a dream of *vol-au-vent* and whirling soup. She regarded the experience as a "rigorous test of character and will power" and experienced the joy of vicarious eating without weight gain or laboring over a hot stove.[11]

Such anecdotal evidence is significant, but not conclusive. It is confirmed, however, by the complication of household obligations in the postwar period, the absence of helpful gourmet recipes, and the emphasis on traditional gender roles. The decline of domestic help, especially cooks, in upper-middle-class homes after 1941 forced housewives to make difficult choices. House cleaning, laundry chores, and child care limited the time available for the preparation of daily meals. When it came time to cook, the inexperience of most housewives in kitchen fundamentals such as slicing, sautéing, and roasting complicated the effort. Under the circumstances, following complicated gourmet recipes was a daunting task. So, many novice cooks must have found the articles in women's magazines with recipes and menus featuring processed goods and requiring relatively little intervention from the cook quite tempting. Best-selling cookbooks such as *The Good Housekeeeping Cook Book* (1942) and *Joy of Cooking* (1936) enabled inexperienced cooks to proceed with somewhat more complicated dishes by offering clear and detailed instructions for virtually every step in the cooking process. Until they were more comfortable with kitchen routines, however, these housewives must have been grateful for the shortcuts in the former and the clear explanations in the latter.[12]

Writers of gourmet recipes, who were essentially competing with the women's magazines for the attention of these upper-middle-class readers, thus faced a difficult challenge. Their task was to convince the inexperienced housewife to spend more time in the kitchen preparing complex recipes, usually with fresh ingredients, rather than relying on recipes in the women's magazines. Only a patient instructor who understood the limited cooking skills of many housewives could teach them to master the kitchen fundamentals that were necessary to prepare gourmet recipes. Occasional testimony suggests that the recipe writers were oblivious to the needs of such readers. Mrs. Peter Oszarski, for example, asked plaintively, "Will you please explain in detail how to lard roasts, etc., what a larding needle is, and where it can be purchased?"[13]

Mrs. Oszarski's comments focus attention on the important question of how effectively various gourmet cookbooks and articles met the needs of their audience. To respond to this question, I checked the recipes of the *Gourmet* chefs, to see whether they contained information on the following points:

1. Appropriate cooking equipment from pots, pans, and knives to modern kitchen aids for preparing each step in the recipe.
2. Ingredients required for the recipe and, if unavailable at the local supermarket, instructions on where to find them or appropriate substitutes for exotic ingredients.

3. Steps leading up to cooking, including how to clean and cut up ingredients, truss fowl, cream ingredients, and separate eggs.

4. Cooking processes such as sautéing, broiling, and deep-fat frying and specification of the proper equipment to use in these processes.

5. Quantitative information such as the weight and/or volume of each ingredient, oven temperatures and times, and the number of servings each recipe would make.

6. Warnings about problems that might arise in following the instructions and advice on how to rectify these problems.

7. Intangibles: author's awareness of the mind-set and skill level of the audience; the author's conviction, clearly expressed to readers, that the instructions would enable them to cook the recipes; an authoritative but friendly tone.

Gourmet's Rivals: Gourmet Cookbooks Published by Other Houses

In order to appreciate the impact of *Gourmet* on home cooking, I evaluate the relative contributions of both *Gourmet* authors and those who wrote gourmet cookbooks for other publishers. For the purposes of this study, a gourmet cookbook must be focused primarily on presenting French recipes, since the public and food professionals were less likely to consider other ethnic cooking and traditional American dishes as "gourmet." As *Time* magazine insisted, "French cuisine is the central grand tradition for the growing multitude of home gourmet cooks." For this reason, I do not consider cookbooks that incorporated a number of French recipes—most notably Craig Claiborne's *New York Times Cook Book* (1961)—but put greater emphasis on multiethnic and/or American recipes. Of course, only those cookbooks that appeared in English or were translated into English would have had any significant influence on the American public.[14]

Among those books were a number of encyclopedic works devoted to a comprehensive coverage of French cuisine, some translated and some written originally in English, whose authors were Frenchmen. There were also several travel narratives that used recipes to help illustrate the food adventures of their authors. Close to that genre, but somewhat more oriented toward cooking, were the four cookbooks of Elizabeth David, while three reputable French authors directed their small volumes to the housewife, American or French. In addition, three celebrity chefs, who reached a large audience through their writings, as well as televised cooking classes, and service to the cooking profession, each produced an important volume.

Heading the list of encyclopedic works was the latest edition of Escoffier's *Guide Culinaire* (1938), which was in print throughout this period in an English translation as *The Escoffier Cook Book: A Guide to the Fine Art of Cookery* (New York: Crown Publishers, 1951 [1941]). Its strength was a series of clear explanations of virtually every basic technique and process useful to the practitioner of French cooking. However, Escoffier wrote it primarily for the expert in *haute cuisine* as opposed to the housewife or spouse. And, at 923 pages and with almost 3,000 recipes in the 1951 printing, its size and scope would have been daunting to most novice cooks. Inexperienced cooks would have had the same difficulties in using Henri Pellaprat's *Modern Culinary Art* (New York: French and European Publications, 1951), which weighed in at 738 pages and 3,500 recipes; André Simon's 827-page *A Concise Encyclopedia of Gastronomy* (London: Collins, 1952), with its 2,500 recipes; or the first English translation (1941) of the 1938 edition of Prosper Montagné's *Larousse Gastronomique* (1,101 pages and 8,500 recipes).[15]

Among the most effective narratives with recipes to illustrate dining experiences were Samuel and Narcissa Chamberlain's *Clementine in the Kitchen* and *Bouquet de France*. The *Alice B. Toklas Cook Book* (New York: Harper and Brothers, 1954) adopted the same strategy with equally good results. While these books were popular and probably served to pique an interest in French cooking, Toklas, like the Chamberlains, addressed her recipes more to the reader than to the cook. She wrote skimpy instructions and rarely warned readers of problems they were likely to encounter in preparing her recipes.[16]

Elizabeth David, the English writer and gourmet, launched her career with the classic *Mediterranean Food* (London: John Lehmann, 1950). Over the next ten years, she also published *French Country Cooking* (London: John Lehmann, 1951), *Summer Cooking* (London: Museum Press, 1955), and *French Provincial Cooking* (London: Michael Joseph, 1960). David's approach to food was unique. She highlighted the cultural environment in which the dishes were created and often incorporated the reactions of artists, writers, and travelers who consumed the dishes for which she supplied recipes. The latter were sketchy: a list of ingredients and instructions for combining them with little information about techniques. They would have sufficed for accomplished cooks, but not for novices.[17]

Interested American cooks could have learned a great deal from two popular French cookbooks translated into English by Charlotte Turgeon and a third one written for Americans by André Simon. The former were modest cookbooks with a few hundred basic recipes for housewives rather than chefs and thus emphasizing everyday dishes; both authors briefly explained important processes and techniques, while Turgeon adapted their recipes to American ways. Even so, reviewers agreed that while both *Tante Marie's French Kitchen* (New York: Oxford University Press, 1949) and *Good Food from France* (New York: M. Barrows, 1951) by Henri Pellaprat addressed the needs of the inexperienced French housewife, they were not sufficiently comprehensive and exact to meet those of the novice cook in the United States. As for *André Simon's French Cook Book* (Boston: Little, Brown, 1938), revised and updated by Crosby Gaige in 1948, its organization by full-scale menus rather than single dishes made it less appropriate for the beginning cook.[18]

Few Americans knew anything about *What's Cooking in France* (New York: Ives Washburn, 1952), a shortened version (sixty-three pages) of a larger manuscript by Louisette Bertholle and Simone Beck, Julia Child's future collaborators. Helmut Ripperger rewrote the recipes, which Charlotte Turgeon judged to be "few but excellent." Others disagreed, as will become evident. In any case, the publisher failed to promote the book.[19]

Among the cookbook authors who influenced a larger number of gourmets were Dione Lucas, James Beard, and Joseph Donon. "La doyenne of fine cuisine," Lucas was a British immigrant to New York and a graduate of the Cordon Bleu in Paris with permission to offer the school's diploma to her own students who had passed the Cordon Bleu examination. After opening a school and restaurant in London in 1934, she left for America in 1940 and within two years had established the Cordon Bleu Restaurant and School in New York. The *New Yorker* called it the "Athens" of cooking schools, which, along with gourmet dining societies, was spreading gourmet practices. An accomplished teacher, Lucas was also renowned for her dexterity as an omelette maker.[20]

To launch one of the first television cooking shows in 1948, Lucas drew on her expertise in teaching and cooking, as well as her "brisk British accent"; set in the Cordon Bleu Restaurant, the show was entitled "To the Queen's Taste" and reached an estimated 63,000 New Yorkers, as well as audiences in Philadelphia, Boston, and Providence. Over the next ten years the thirty-minute weekly show migrated from WCBS to WJZ and WPIX.

Shortly before launching the TV show, Lucas published *The Cordon Bleu Cookbook* and established herself as a leading authority on French cooking. In the introduction, she promised to teach readers to prepare French recipes adapted to the needs of the American housewife. However, in contrast to her cooking school, where she showed each student "how to prepare a dish, how to stir, how to roll out pastry and line a flan ring," Lucas offered no instructions in the fundamentals of cooking and expected readers to use the recipes "without outside help." Moreover, by her own account, the recipes relied more heavily on the cook's imagination than on the exact measurement of ingredients. This approach clearly frustrated inexperienced housewives. In addition, the absence of chapters on sauces and salads diminished the value of the cookbook.[21]

In the early postwar period, James Beard and Dione Lucas were rivals, along with heads of the gourmet dining societies, for leadership of the nascent gourmet movement. Beard was completing his TV show as Lucas launched hers, and he later followed in Lucas' footsteps by opening what became a highly regarded cooking school in 1956. Both published cookbooks, although Beard was far more prolific. Even so, Beard's cookbooks usually incorporated few French recipes as, for example, the *Fireside Book of Cooking*. Only in his collaborative project with Alexander Watt, entitled *Paris Cuisine*, did he focus primarily on French cooking.[22]

Beard and Watt met in 1949, when both men joined the Wine and Food Society tour of French vineyards. The friendship they developed led in 1950 to "field work" for a book project during Beard's seven-month Paris sabbatical. Already an expert on the Paris restaurant scene, Watt steered Beard to his favorite bistros and restaurants, from which they collected and tested sixty recipes. Beard then rewrote the recipes to make them accessible to an American audience.[23]

Despite the recipes, the book was, as Charlotte Turgeon pointed out, "a gastronomical guide book, not only of Paris but indirectly of provincial and colonial France." Rather than present the recipes by food category—meat, fish, desserts, etc.—Beard and Watt attached them to descriptions of the restaurants where they had dined. In this way, recipes for meat dishes were placed alongside others for fish, vegetables, and desserts, so that future cooks would have to consult the index to find options for various courses. More problematic was the absence of cooking instructions for complex processes. Take, for example, the recipe for *le Lièvre à la Royale* (regal hare) from the Rotisserie Perigourdine. The authors expected the reader to find a hare, "kill and dress" it herself, and "save the blood and mix it with a little vinegar so it will coagulate." This was a tall order for the novice—or perhaps any—American housewife![24]

With help from his editors, Joseph Donon improved on the work of Lucas, Beard, and Watt. While Lucas was "la doyenne of fine cuisine," Craig Claiborne dubbed Donon the "dean" of his profession. Following retirement as a private chef to the Vanderbilt heir, Mrs. Hamilton McK. Twombly, and while still heading the Escoffier Society, Donon published *The Classic French Cuisine* in 1959 to favorable reviews in the *New York Times*. Claiborne called it "an excellent book on French cuisine for home use," which was "adapted to the small kitchen." Charlotte Turgeon agreed. Because Donon rendered French practices "readily understandable" to Americans, she concluded that "this is a book for will-be gourmets." Donon's clarity, in turn, owed much to his editors, Narcissa Chamberlain and Ruth Bakalar.[25]

For both simple and complex dishes, Donon applied "precepts of *la haute cuisine française*" to home cooking. To help with this task, he provided instruction on how to distinguish between fresh and old fish, what kinds of chickens should be selected for particular recipes, and how to recognize tender, young artichokes and prepare them for cooking. Shrewdly, Donon gave a nod to nutritionists by urging American cooks to prepare irresistibly delicious dishes that happened to be nutritious and then match them with appropriate wines. He also recommended the use of electric blenders and frying kettles.[26]

In sum, American cooks could choose from a variety of gourmet cookbooks written by experts, most of whom had no link to *Gourmet* magazine. However, only Donon's manual, among them, met the needs of the novice cook. Even so, it never achieved a large circulation, in part because Alfred Knopf became frustrated with the lengthy editorial process and apparently wrote off the book even before it went to press. Equally important, Donon's book capped the career of an elderly immigrant chef, who had neither the interest nor the energy to promote his *magnum opus*.[27]

It is interesting to note that in January of 1958, just three months after Louis Diat's death, Earle MacAusland asked Donon if he would be interested in writing for *Gourmet* magazine. The timing of the letter indicates that MacAusland hoped to make Donon the third *Gourmet* chef. For his part, Donon considered writing an article or two, but thought better of it. And *Gourmet*, perhaps despairing to find a French chef with Donon's qualifications, eliminated the *Gourmet* chef altogether.[28]

Gourmet's First *Gourmet* Chef: Louis De Gouy

Louis De Gouy, the first "*Gourmet* chef," served in this capacity for seven years. Because he would be the primary source of recipes for readers who hoped to cook gourmet dishes from *Gourmet* articles, the selection was important to the magazine and its subscribers. And it was not by accident that *Gourmet* hired for this position a chef who was, of course, a man and a French national, rather than a home cook. After all, a chef would have a full grasp of the recipes, cooking techniques, and menu options in the French culinary repertoire. Selecting him was, thus, *Gourmet's* way of recognizing the prestige of *haute cuisine* and the importance of offering readers the opportunity to learn it from an expert. In this way, as well, *Gourmet* further distinguished the recipes De Gouy was publishing from those in the women's magazines.

De Gouy's versatility was also an asset to the magazine. Aside from his knowledge of French cooking, he had considerable experience preparing American dishes and was familiar as well with Central and Eastern European cooking. How he developed an expertise in sandwiches and soda fountain drinks, which became the subjects of two early cookbooks, remains a mystery.[29]

In some ways, the appointment of De Gouy worked out well. Certainly, his articles broadened readers' horizons by presenting recipes of varying national origins linked to the history and culture of various regions and nations. And he made a sincere effort to speak with an "American" voice that many readers surely appreciated. However, *Gourmet's* choice of De Gouy was probably based on the mistaken assumption that his principal audience would be American men, who were increasingly interested in challenging kitchen activities. No doubt, such an audience would have resonated to the masculine themes of his anecdotes. It was just the contrary, however, with the predominantly female audience that actually read his articles. Moreover, De Gouy's frequent failure to provide much-needed instruction in cooking fundamentals, as well as his habit of listing ingredients that were difficult to find, frustrated readers, as did his practice of suggesting that the cook needed special knowledge or intuition to prepare a recipe.

During De Gouy's seven-year tenure at *Gourmet*, he wrote two regular articles in each issue, one of which, "*Gastronomie sans argent*: To Tease Your Palate and Please Your Purse," was the magazine's nod to hard times. As the title suggested, readers could prepare these recipes from inexpensive ingredients, including leftovers. The *Gourmet* chef also wrote a monthly piece, often with a seasonal theme, on such topics as spring vegetables, fall game dishes, etc. As time passed, however, the distinction between these two formats eroded, perhaps because *Gourmet* attracted relatively affluent readers who had little concern about cutting their food budgets.

De Gouy brought to his task an unusual background. He served under his father, Jean De Gouy, while the latter was Esquire de cuisine for Emperor Franz Joseph of Austria and later chef for the Belgian royal family. Following this apprenticeship, De Gouy found a new mentor in Escoffier, a friend of his father's; he then worked at a number of prestigious European hotels, including the Hotel de Paris in France and the Carlton in England, before taking a position with the Waldorf Astoria in New York in 1911. De Gouy soon developed a reputation for excellence as a chef among wealthy Long Islanders for whom he catered parties and organized clambakes. He also served as "chef-steward" on the Astor yacht and, during its around-the-world cruise, on the J. P. Morgan yacht, *Wild Duck*. In 1917, he became the head chef of the fifth army corps of the American Expeditionary Forces.[30]

In the years after the war, the restless De Gouy sought new opportunities within the food profession. Sometime before 1931, he intended to establish a cooking school and restaurant, but there is no evidence that he proceeded with this plan. In 1936, he published the first of seventeen cookbooks, which addressed a teenage audience, while the next year he made his mark with a two-volume set entitled *The Derrydale Game and Fish Book*. These unusual volumes, destined for a small circulation, appealed to sportsmen of the leisure class, who could turn over their catch to chefs like De Gouy with European training; for its comprehensive coverage of the subject and "the feeling of life" it conveyed, M. F. K. Fisher introduced the 1950 edition as one of "the near great" cookbooks of all times.[31]

Both Fisher and the future publisher of *Gourmet* must have resonated to De Gouy's reflections on the current status of wild boar. "In our somewhat softened civilization the once powerful cult of the lovers of rich, high meat and game has faded into obscurity. In the present day of hurry and bustle, there is little serious attention given to the sober study of pleasures of the table." To enhance the flavor of game, De Gouy offered a variety of sauces, including *bourgeoise*, Spanish, *Parisienne*, with *fines herbes*, or baked with mushrooms to use on fish and game. His associates at the magazine obviously valued the fish volume, which they reprinted under the *Gourmet* label in 1947 just before he died.[32]

Given his interests, it is not surprising that De Gouy was also an enthusiastic defender of the gourmet ethos. He considered the founding of *Gourmet* to be one of many signs that Americans were clamoring for the "renewal of good cheer through good food and beverages appetizingly prepared." And he gave eloquent testimony to the gourmet's fascination with taste as an advocate of poached eggs Elysée Palace, which "make your tongue turn a somersault of delight." For him, cooking and dining were great adventures in the creation and appreciation of savory dishes.[33]

To implement his vision of gourmet dining, De Gouy emphasized exotic food, including game, fish, and Creole food that would open Americans to a new realm of experience. His strong interest in Creole cooking arose from firsthand experience during a stay in New Orleans in the winter of 1941. In the following year, De Gouy offered a recipe for Creole Bouillabaisse, but his most complete review of this cuisine came four years later, when he published recipes for a Gumbo filé with crabs, roast stuffed opossum Creole, and a Creole Cajun pecan tart, among other dishes.[34]

For his first article in the first issue of *Gourmet*, De Gouy presented the recipe for pheasant à la mode d'Alcantara (from his Derrydale cookbook), which had been discovered in 1806 during Napoleon's peninsular campaign; it had history as well as flavor to recommend it. He noted that "the game tradition of America is as old as the country itself" and reminded readers that historically they were much closer than Europeans to an era when hunting was necessary for survival. He clearly hoped that his recipes, ready at hand from his Derrydale books, would help to revive hunting and fishing for pleasure if not for survival. Five years later, he drew on the same source to present *Gourmet* readers with recipes for pheasant Demidoff and pheasant Titania. Other De Gouy fish and game articles in *Gourmet*, some of which had appeared in the Derrydale volumes, included the New England clambake (in one paragraph!), rabbit, venison, quail, lobster, crayfish, shad roe, scallops, eel, and fluke.[35]

It seems likely that *Gourmet*'s editors, who must have thought that the hunting angle would appeal to male readers, strongly endorsed De Gouy's approach. Indeed, in the October 1941 issue (p. 35), which featured a wild duck on the cover, the magazine printed an advertisement claiming that "shooting's only half the fun"; the other half is "cooking and eating what you've bagged . . . *Gourmet* is a man's magazine on food that men enjoy. No vitamins, no calories. Just good food, yes, and good drinks." And, to establish its authoritative character, *Gourmet* is the "only magazine with a professional chef," a true expert on fish and game.

The words of the advertisement perfectly expressed De Gouy's idea that the pleasure in tasting game was inseparably linked to the excitement of the hunt. Indeed, he wrote his debut article on pheasants from the perspective of the "happy hunter." Three years later, a large illustration of a hunter carrying a huge rifle hovered over the printed words that detailed the challenge of shooting rabbits. It was a perspective that may have appealed to the minority of *Gourmet* readers who were male and/or hunters rather than the majority audience, which was female.[36]

Even when De Gouy was not relishing the prospect of dining on venison or crayfish, he unconsciously associated sophisticated dining activities with men. Take his account of male officials carrying a dish of fresh mushrooms on toast

gastronomic possibilities are delicious. They are easy to raise and easy to keep, requiring hardly much more than a warm, dry shelter, a middling ration of grain, hay, and green vegetables, and a good recipe, to turn to *hasenpfeffer*.

The mere sight or suggestion of rabbit brings to the *au courant* the mouth-watering aroma of *hasenpfeffer*, the German spiced hare created, strangely enough, by a French chef, Urbain Dubois, when he was *esquire de cuisine* for the late and haughty Kaiser Wilhelm II. It may give you a severe twist to know that in Europe the sauce for *hasenpfeffer* was usually made without blood because fresh blood was hard to obtain. The sauce owed its scrumptious flavor to spices and wine, as in this recipe:

Hasenpfeffer. Wash 1 large dressed hare or rabbit (or 2 small ones), and cut into serving pieces. Allow the pieces to stand for 24 to 48 hours in a cool place, well covered with the following marinade: 2 cups vinegar, 1 cup water, 1 cup Claret (or 2 cups vinegar and 2 cups Claret, depending on the strength of the vinegar), 2 large onions, sliced, 1 tablespoon salt, 1 teaspoon black pepper, 1 teaspoon mustard seed (optional), 1 teaspoon crushed juniper berries, 8 whole cloves, and 6 bay leaves. Turn the pieces of meat every 12 hours; and when the marinating period is over, wipe them dry, dredge them lightly in a little flour, and sauté them in ¼ cup fat until they are well browned on all sides. Then drain off the fat. Strain the marinade, dilute it with ½ cup hot water, adding 1 tablespoon sugar (optional), and pour it over the meat. Bring the whole to a boil; cover the pot tightly, and simmer for about 40 minutes, or until the meat is tender. Salt and pepper to taste. Arrange the meat on a hot platter, and pour with a little flour if necessary. There should be an ample quantity of gravy. *Hasenpfeffer* is always served with potato dumplings, such as the following:

Potato Dumplings. Dip 8 slices bread in water, and squeeze the excess moisture from them. Mix the bread in a bowl with 1 medium-sized onion, grated, a pinch of minced parsley, and salt and pepper to taste. Grate 4 large raw potatoes, and add them to the bread mixture, together with 2 well-beaten eggs. Form the mixture into balls the size of a large walnut, roll them gently in flour, and cook them in boiling water or meat stock in a covered pot for 15 minutes. Drain, and serve very hot.

The gypsies knew a good thing when they saw it. How many tales of romantic England are set about the poacher!—every gypsy was suspected of having a rabbit at the bottom of that savory pot of his from which such delicious but unlawful odors *(Continued on page 42)*

Duncan Coburn

Illustration by Duncan Coburn from "Rabbits is Rabbits," *Gourmet*, January 1944, pp. 18–19. The Schlesinger Library, Radcliffe Institute, Harvard University. Contributor/Gourmet, © Condé Nast Publications.

from the kitchen to an unidentified French king. While appreciating the complex preparation of this dish, De Gouy observed that a stove is "no place for weaklings or dreamers." Women who read this article might be excused for thinking that De Gouy had them in mind.[37]

It was somewhat more difficult to masculinize leek soup, that everyday dish enjoyed by most Frenchmen. However, by naming among its greatest exponents Nero, King Arthur, and those Welshmen who wore the vegetable in their helmets while fighting the forces of the King of Northumbria, De Gouy succeeded in doing so. In this way, leeks became the Welsh national emblem. And even though Mary, Queen of Scots, was usually credited for the recipe De Gouy was presenting—braised leeks and custard sauce in the Scottish manner—he insisted that "each grateful gourmet give thanks to the anonymous cooks that added their bit."[38]

As for leftover pork, De Gouy introduced this dish by recounting a duel between a French dramatist, Sainte Foix, and a member of the king's guard over whether a slice of roast pork and bread served at the Procope restaurant in Paris was an appetizing meal, as Saint Foix proclaimed. When King Louis XV got word of the duel, he commanded the two men to return to the Procope, order a suckling pig, and charge it to the king.[39]

Of course, there were a few subjects that even De Gouy found difficult to masculinize, such as ice cream served on a summer's day. Writing in a nostalgic vein, he depicted a mother dishing large helpings to her brood of children; the accompanying illustration featured family members and their dog sprawled on the lawn.[40]

De Gouy's masculine rhetoric was no way to lure novice female cooks into the gourmet cooking fold. Equally ill-advised was his mixed message to readers about whether cooks were born or made. On the one hand, he praised Chef François Pierre for clarifying the correct way to make a soufflé: "crisp on the outside and soft in the center," because it "should dispel for all time the mysterious haze that surrounds the making of such a successful soufflé." In this instance, De Gouy exemplified the successful teacher, who was determined to demystify the cooking process for the benefit of his readers. However, what he gave he soon took away by claiming that "the pheasant is a mystery of which the key is revealed only to the initiated." The "bon gourmet" alone had a nose for determining the aroma that signaled the readiness of the pheasant for cooking. With such a warning, even the most intrepid neophyte cooks would have avoided this recipe.[41]

Readers were no doubt equally frustrated by the absence of adequate instructions for preparing some of De Gouy's exotic recipes. For starters, how many novice housewives in American cities would have been able to find a possum, rabbits, or a whole pig's head? Furthermore, once the game was in the kitchen, would they be able to prepare these animals for cooking? In the case of the possum, De Gouy's instructions called for removing the entrails, head, and tail of the animal, while in another recipe the cook was supposed to pluck, clean, sew, and truss a pheasant, after which she would remove the breastbone "(as you would of a small broiler) without damaging the bird." However, he provided no explanations for executing these tasks.[42]

De Gouy was no more helpful in his March 1942 Lenten article. There he provided recipes for an omelette, a soufflé, and a clam pie, thus requiring novice cooks to learn three new processes he had never explained. To be sure, his account of Madame Poularde creating her famous omelette restaurant at St. Michel was charming and also reminded readers of their own travels in Normandy. However, in the instructions for cooking *Omelette Mascotte* (with artichokes in a white wine sauce), De Gouy advised readers "to prepare the omelet as you ordinarily do." As for making a *roux* for scallops *à la Poulette* (in a white sauce flavored with lemon and parsley), the recipe called for adding "one tablespoon of a thick *roux* made from butter and flour." (For the *roux* to be used in gumbo filé, De Gouy mentioned no ingredients at all.)[43]

A problem of a different kind arose in connection with instructions for making the *Omelette Mascotte*. De Gouy referred readers to the recipe for Béchamel sauce, an ingredient in the omelette recipe, published in his November 1941 *Gourmet* article (p. 48). Four months later, for a cheese and tomato soufflé, he again referred them to the Béchamel recipe. Such a strategy might have been practical for a magazine with an established readership, but in the first two years of *Gourmet*'s existence, new subscribers were the rule rather than the exception. The fact that there were no reader complaints suggests that few were interested in preparing the soufflé and the rest had other recipes for Bechamel.[44]

Perhaps De Gouy's contribution as *Gourmet* chef would have been more significant if, like his successor, he had been able to focus his efforts on one rather than two articles in each issue of the magazine. As it was, however, *Gourmet*, no doubt with De Gouy's concurrence, decided to provide complementary approaches to gourmet dining. *"Gastronomie sans argent"* encouraged readers to believe that economical recipes, often based on leftovers, were a legitimate part of gourmet dining. Those who preferred recipes based on fresh or costly ingredients could usually find them in the topical article each month. Unfortunately, De Gouy was careless in categorizing his recipes. Simple, inexpensive recipes sometimes found their way into the topical articles and vice versa. No doubt, the distinction between the two formats came to seem outmoded once the war revived prosperity and *Gourmet* established its appeal to affluent Americans.

The division between economy and more elegant dishes emerged clearly on a few occasions. In one instance, the topical article prescribed ham recipes, while recipes for ham leftovers appeared in *"Gastronomie sans argent."* In another issue, De Gouy adopted the same approach to lamb dishes. On most occasions, however, the two articles were unrelated to each other. All the same, recipes in *"Gastronomie sans argent"* offered interesting options. Chipped beef creamed with biscuits and meatloaf with mushrooms, for example, could satisfy traditional American tastes, while duck aspic *bourgeois* was a French makeover with a more cosmopolitan audience in mind.[45]

However, De Gouy sometimes blurred the distinction between the two formats when he treated the same food item in *"Gastronomie sans argent"* and topical articles. Even though he twice featured meat pies in *"Gastronomie sans argent,"* the elegant setting for the 1860 New York City dinner in honor of the Prince of Wales, at which the prince was served steak and kidney pie, apparently justified the placement of meat pie recipes in a topical article as well. On another occasion, De Gouy served up recipes for American pancakes alongside those for blini and crêpes in a topical article, while considering only American-style pancakes in the *"Gastronomie sans argent"* article. Two articles on smorgasbord, despite the different formats, were very similar in content.[46]

Louis De Gouy was an adventurer in life and in food. Without question, the themes of the articles and the recipes, especially those for fresh fish and game, transported the *Gourmet* audience well beyond the repertoire of dishes offered in women's magazines. And De Gouy's sprightly style helped to familiarize *Gourmet* readers with a wide range of approaches to cooking and dining and thus helped them to appreciate French and European culture. Most of his recipes, however, were not suitable for inexperienced cooks. No wonder Charlotte Turgeon found *The* Gourmet *Cookbook*, Volume 1, which reproduced many of De Gouy's recipes, "not a book for daily use in everyone's kitchen." It was, she concluded, "a practical reference library for endless good meals." Nor were the recipes well suited for women, who must have tuned out De Gouy's macho message whenever they encountered it. Still, he deserves credit for advancing the gourmet cause by modeling for readers the imaginative and adventurous chef who believed that the preparation and consumption of food was an essential part of the good life.[47]

Gourmet's Second *Gourmet* Chef: Louis Diat

In early 1948, Louis Diat succeeded Louis De Gouy to become the second and last *Gourmet* chef. Over the next fourteen years, his recipes, which appeared in 133 articles, had a far greater impact on *Gourmet* readers than those of his predecessor. With the assistance of Helen E. Ridley, he made every effort to teach cooking fundamentals to his readers by identifying the ingredients, giving explicit instructions about how to find, prepare, and cook them, while warning about pitfalls that might arise in the process.

Recognizing that many of his readers knew little about this subject, Diat scrupulously explained the significance of various French dishes to the religious calendar of the Church, regional traditions, and seasonal festivities. He was also able to establish more continuity in his articles from month to month than his predecessor by writing several series based on such themes as "Tricks of My Trade" and "Menu Classique." During his tenure, and with the return of peace and prosperity, the magazine gradually phased out *"Gastronomie sans argent."*

Chosen at age twenty-five to become the first head chef of the New York Ritz Hotel, Louis Diat was present at the hotel's 1910 opening, one of the seminal events in the early years of the American century. Already, the Ritz had gained a reputation as the last word in elegance. Guest rooms were comfortable and well appointed, while in the kitchens, professional chefs prepared dishes from the repertoire of international cuisine. In effect, the opening of the new hotel, the first Ritz-Carlton in America, was an acknowledgement that Americans were capable of appreciating European elegance.

Despite his age, Diat was already a veteran chef who had apprenticed at fourteen in a well-known patisserie shop, the Maison Calondre in Moulins, and served as soup chef at the Hotel Bristol, among other Paris hotels, and as saucier at the Paris Ritz. From there he moved to the London Ritz, where he labored for four more years as saucier under the watchful eye of Escoffier. In the tradition of Ritz chefs, Diat not only was a master of classical French cooking but added to his repertoire dishes often requested by his Anglo-Saxon patrons. He could prepare such American specialties as clam chowder, chicken pie, and lobster Newburg; indeed, he wrote proudly that an American diner taught him how to make clam chowder. From his days in England, Diat knew how to prepare steak and kidney pie. His flexibility endeared him to patrons, who remained

Sketch of Louis Diat by Henry Stahlhut from *Gourmet*, February 1952, p. 18.
The Schlesinger Library, Radcliffe Institute, Harvard University. Contributor/Gourmet,
© Condé Nast Publications.

his supporters during a forty-one-year tenure at the Ritz. By applying for citizen-
ship shortly after his arrival in the United States, Diat also expressed his commitment to the American way of life.[48]

Three decades after the opening of the Ritz, just as the first issue of *Gourmet*
was going to press, Diat made his publishing debut with *Cooking à la Ritz* (1941).
In view of the American entry into World War II several months later, his timing
was poor. However, within six months of the end of the war, *Louis Diat's Home
Cookbook: French Cooking for Americans: La Cuisine de Ma Mère* (1946) appeared.
By then the eager editors of *Gourmet*, no doubt dubious about De Gouy's value
to the magazine, had already published the two introductory chapters and the

conclusion. Impressed by the fact that Diat addressed his cookbook to American housewives who knew little or nothing about French cooking, they must have had him in mind as a successor to De Gouy.[49]

From March 1948 until his death in October 1957, Diat wrote an article in almost every issue of *Gourmet*. In addition, there was enough material left in his notebooks for Helen Ridley to supply the magazine with numerous articles during the next four years. Diat also collected and revised articles from the magazine to publish his short book on sauces in 1951, while, a decade later, Ridley pulled together those and other recipes from *Gourmet* to produce a comprehensive cookbook under the magazine's imprint entitled Gourmet's *Basic French Cookbook*.

The effectiveness of the articles and books owes much to the remarkable collaboration between Ridley and Diat. Ridley earned a B.S. in home economics at Columbia University and taught home economics and adult evening classes on homemaking in the New York City school system for seven years, as well as organic chemistry at Hunter College; she also wrote several articles on nutritional topics for *Hygeia* and *Better Homes and Gardens*. In view of her experience, the J. Walter Thompson advertising agency hired her in 1940 to publicize some of their food accounts, while, on the side, Ridley worked with Diat and at least one other author as a ghostwriter.[50]

In order to serve Diat well, Helen Ridley sought to learn the gourmet approach to dining and downplay her earlier training as a nutritionist. Between 1941 and 1961, she accomplished this task, as is evident in the gradual transformation in her perspective. Ridley's own publications indicate this shift. In 1950, she wrote an article for *Good Housekeeping* on how to cook game—a far cry from her first article in the same magazine in 1938 entitled "The ABC of Keeping Cool" in summer.

The transformation was also evident in Ridley's work for Diat. In 1941, she arranged the recipes for *Cooking à la Ritz*, although it is not clear who translated the manuscript. For *Louis Diat's Home Cook Book*, Diat asked Ridley to translate and rewrite his recipes so as to make them accessible to the American housewife. To do this effectively, Ridley had to deepen her understanding of French cooking. As Diat's apprentice, she not only watched the cooking process at the Ritz but took lessons from him in her home. They also worked together at his desk so that she would understand "the lore of French cuisine," an important step in producing an effective English translation of the recipes. Accordingly, while the book was dedicated to his mother, Diat acknowledged "my sincerest appreciation to Helen Ridley, who in translating my thoughts, has accurately conveyed the significance of this book."[51]

Ridley's contribution to Diat's third book, *Sauces French and Famous*, must have been significant, because he invited her to write a brief foreword. Three years later, Diat orchestrated Ridley's first trip to France, where she met his brother, Lucien, chef at the Plaza-Athenée in Paris, and traveled to the Bourbonnais to dine with the Diats' sister on potato pie, which Ridley herself had learned to make from one of Louis Diat's recipes. As it turned out, he was traveling to the same places at the same time as Ridley. Following Diat's death, his widow gave Ridley access to the chef's notebooks, which enabled her to collect and edit the recipes for Gourmet's *Basic French Cookbook*. Later Ridley assumed the role of author for *The Ritz-Carlton Cook Book and Guide to Home Entertaining* (1968) with the assistance of Charles Banino, chef of the Boston Ritz.[52]

One of the hallmarks of Diat's approach was to introduce each article with an account of his own experience with the cooking processes and recipes he was explaining to readers. He first tested this approach with a brief personal note in the introduction to *Cooking à la Ritz* and then expanded it in his later books and articles. In creating this informal identity, Diat, most likely in conjunction with Ridley, sought to convince readers of the authenticity of the recipes and their accessibility to inexperienced cooks.

To accomplish these sometimes conflicting goals, Diat walked a narrow line. He must have realized that the title of his first book, *Cooking à la Ritz*, had been off-putting to many novice cooks. In order to convey his message more clearly, he entitled the second book *Louis Diat's Home Cook Book*. In it, he adopted the posture he would maintain in the articles and books he wrote for *Gourmet*. To reassure housewives, he shed his Ritz-Carlton chef's hat and presented himself as the eager disciple of his "smiling, friendly mother" dressed in "her white blouse and black skirt" in the modest kitchen of their Bourbonnais home. It was a sunny room, with a shiny stone floor and a big black stove. There she "guided the early years" and "inspired the later ones." She loved fine food and turned her children "into little gourmets" by teaching them how to "taste with discrimination" and how to cook. Her memory accordingly inspired Diat in all his kitchen work. As he told his readers, "I like to roast chicken the way my mother did."[53]

An important lesson of his childhood, which he applied in writing many of his *Gourmet* articles, was that gourmet dining did not require the expensive cuts of meat and rich sauces that were commonly served at the Ritz; rather, the true glory of French cooking lay in the basic dishes prepared by French provincial cooks. Together with Ridley, Diat therefore deemphasized *haute cuisine* recipes requiring excessive kitchen work and expense in favor of tasty dishes for everyday meals. To reassure his largely novice, feminine audience, Diat identified himself with his mother's kitchen and the simple dishes she cooked for her family. Through his cookbooks and articles, Diat's readers, in effect, would become apprentices to his modest, small-town French mother, whose cooking instructions enabled her eight-year-old son to make an excellent leek and potato soup.[54]

Diat empowered readers by insisting that clear instructions were far more important than genetic makeup in the development of a good cook. As an illustration of this principle, he aimed his instructions at the inexperienced housewife rather than the professional chef in order to teach her how to make French sauces. And he rejoiced that learning to make these sauces in the quiet of the home kitchen would be much easier than working in the pressured environment of a restaurant kitchen. Indeed, he recalled preparing a venison marinade at a New Year's Eve party for American friends. When the hostess followed suit the next day, her husband judged the new marinade to be better than Diat's, "which only goes to show you how quickly a housewife can master the tricks of my trade—if she really wants to." Given this approach, it was quite natural for Diat to question Brillat-Savarin's dictum that cooks could learn their métier, while roasters were born to theirs. With good instruction and sufficient practice, he claimed, anyone could learn to roast.[55]

At every turn, Diat strove to minimize American assumptions about the mystery of French cuisine and to suggest ways of avoiding potential problems. He continually emphasized the accessibility of recipes, even for French dishes that Americans regarded as exotic, like sauces and soufflés. The former offered "no more problems than cooking most other foods" and would likely yield more pleasure. As for dessert sauces, they were no more difficult to make than those for entrées so long as the cook learned the basic sauces from which specialized sauces could be prepared with only slight variations in the ingredients.[56]

Before presenting advice on how to make soufflés, Diat reassured housewives that these recipes were not part of the *haute cuisine* repertoire, nor did they require expensive ingredients. In fact, his readers could prepare entrée soufflés from four eggs, Béchamel sauce (butter, flour, milk), and a purée made of leftovers. And so long as the hostess made sure that her guests were occupied with drinks and hors d'oeuvres, she could make a first-course soufflé in the kitchen and call the guests to table just as she removed it from the oven. Diat advised, however, that dessert soufflés, which required monitoring during the meal, would be difficult to serve at dinner parties.[57]

Where problems were likely to occur, Diat also put housewives on notice in advance. In the case of mayonnaise, for example, the mixture could separate and become a "curdled mass instead of emulsion," when the cook added oil to the egg yolks. No doubt, Diat deliberately recounted his own experience of such a disaster, which occurred in front of his mother, to reassure his audience that such mistakes could happen to anyone, even one of the world's renowned chefs. Accordingly, his readers need not be discouraged by their own mistakes.[58]

Consistent with the approach of French home cooks like his mother, Diat advocated the adoption of a peasant mentality in his American readers. So that no food would go to waste, they should use leftovers for hors d'oeuvres and entrées. For the latter, Diat proposed eating meat leftovers with a sauce or grinding the meat to make a hash; cooks could also prepare a delicious, inexpensive meal from organ meats. The savings from these cost-cutting measures would then pay for more butter and cream, the staples of French cooking. In this way, his readers could eat well without dining "in the sophisticated elegance of the Ritz or Maxim's on caviar and *dinde truffé*" (truffled turkey).[59]

All the same, too much emphasis on the simplicity and femininity of Diat's background would have been counterproductive, since *Gourmet* readers expected their cooking instruction to come from an expert. To meet this expectation, Diat reminded his readers of the training he had received at prestigious hotel restaurants and the demanding clientele that he had satisfied over the years. Already as a young man at the Maison Calondre, he had prepared lavish hors d'oeuvres for the *haut monde* in the Loire Valley. Later, during a stint at the Bristol Hotel in Paris, Diat had served *ris de veau financière* (sweetbreads with truffles and ox tongue) to King Leopold II of Belgium and the future British king, Edward VII, famous for his sophisticated palate. At the same hotel, he had prepared a braised leg of lamb falling off the bone for King Carlos of Portugal.[60]

And, of course, Diat was immensely proud of his ascendancy to the head chef's position at the Ritz and his achievements during a long tenure there. Nostalgically, he recalled such memorable events as the elaborate menu prepared for the opening of the hotel in 1910. Serving fifteen courses, each of which had to meet high standards, required a heroic effort on the part of the chefs; the diners, for their part, marshaled their appetites for a heroic effort of a different kind. Diat also spoke with pride of the approval he had received on several occasions from members of gourmet dining groups. Among them, André Simon extended his compliments for a spring lamb dinner served with seasonal dishes such as wild strawberries, while members of the Tastevin praised the Ritz dinner of May 3, 1948. (Even so, Diat confirmed Lucius Beebe's report that he suffered considerable anxiety on that occasion.)[61]

On many occasions, however, the head chef of one of the world's great hotels and the apprentice son of a Bourbonnais home cook dissolved into a single person. As Diat often insisted, the processes he learned from his mother were the foundation for all French cooking. He could use them to produce simple, delicious dishes for the family or, with some elaboration, the complicated fare of *haute cuisine*. Hence, while Diat's guests might have occupied the higher ranks of society, he could often prepare the food they enjoyed in a straightforward manner. Indeed, he braised the leg of lamb for King Carlos and roasted the chicken for Lord Beaverbrook precisely as his mother prepared them at home. *Hachi Bourbonnais* (Bourbonnais hash), a popular dish on the Ritz menu, was nothing more than ground, leftover *pot au feu*, which he had often eaten at home, while the Ritz's baked puddings were part of his mother's repertoire. Even the renowned *crème vichyssoise*, Diat's most famous creation, was a cold version of the leek and potato soup he had learned to cook from his mother as a small boy.[62]

It took Diat, aided by Helen Ridley, a number of years before he came to emphasize the teaching of kitchen fundamentals as the key to enabling American housewives to cook French dishes. In his first two cookbooks, there was very little attention to such techniques. Only after *Gourmet* hired him and more especially in the series entitled "Classes in Classic Cuisine," launched in January of 1955 and continuing until September of 1957, did Diat explain in detail the important processes in French cooking. By then, he had developed not only a warm, semi-feminine persona to put housewives at ease, but a pedagogical strategy designed specifically to impart the skills necessary to cook French recipes. Diat's great strength was to look at the teaching process from the point of view of the student. He lamented that cookbook writers and chef-instructors often took it for granted that "all readers know as much about this type of cooking as dedicated, experienced gourmet cooks." To make this assumption was itself a recipe for failure.[63]

Thus, Diat began the series on "Classic Cuisine" with the following suggestion to his audience: "You will be the apprentice and I the chef." He advised that, while reading the articles in this series, the readers should feel as if they were actually watching him work. However, he recognized that this advice would only be helpful if he, Diat, could put himself in their shoes. Happily, he remembered how M. Calondre, pastry chef at the Maison Calondre, had taught him and six other apprentices pastry-making techniques in a large room he called a "laboratory." Having saved the notes he had taken during this period, Diat consulted them in order to recall the techniques he had learned. Apparently, this exercise was not successful because, several months later, Diat borrowed a kitchen from an American friend, equipped with all the utensils he needed, including an electric beater. Next, he tried out various techniques as a way of recalling them. Then, "I knew that I could pass on to you my pupils, all the tricks . . . that mean success or failure in classic pastry making."[64]

Diat had a keen sense of the appropriate starting point for a series of lessons on French cooking. He would first teach the most basic techniques, those for making soups and sauces as he had learned them. And before even laying out the techniques for making soup, he remarked in the prefatory section of the soup chapter of the Gourmet's *Basic French Cook Book*, "As you learn to master these easy soups, you will be practicing many cooking skills and techniques that are used in other, more complicated cooking methods."[65]

However, it would first be necessary to learn how to make stocks, the foundation for both soups and sauces. Once his readers had mastered these techniques ("the hows and whys of the *roux*, the reduction, the finishing and so on"), they could apply them to making new soups and sauces with different ingredients. In the sauce category, home cooks should first learn the most basic white sauces, which would stand them in good stead as they studied the preparation of meat, poultry, and fish with which the sauces were often served. There would be no point, for example, in learning how to cook game without first having learned to make game marinades and sauces.[66]

The meat, poultry, and fish section of Gourmet's *Basic French Cookbook*, drawn from appropriate *Gourmet* articles, Diat entitled "Methods of Cooking." Instead of breaking this chapter down by types of meat (beef, pork, lamb, etc.), he explored braising, boiling, broiling, roasting, sautéing, and deep frying, six different ways of cooking animal flesh. In each section of the chapter he offered general instructions on a particular cooking method, followed by specific information for the preparation of particular dishes, including the kind and size of pan to be used, the liquid in which the flesh would be cooked, the proper heat to be applied, and the length of cooking time. The advantage of Diat's method of organization—quite similar to Escoffier's in the *Guide Culinaire*—was that once the cook had mastered the cooking process for a beef dish, she could apply it to pork, fish, or other meats with certain modifications. Following the meat, fish, and foul section, Diat moved on to other protein cooking (shellfish and game) and then to vegetables and desserts.[67]

After introducing readers to these kitchen fundamentals, Diat also emphasized the importance of practicing the steps in each process. In so doing, he drew once again on his experience as an apprentice, which forced him to master the techniques he learned through repetition until they were at his "finger tips." He reiterated the same point in discussing methods to make crêpes: "it takes practice to make good crêpes, but . . . once you master the technique you will not find it at all difficult."[68]

In some detail, Diat addressed such mundane, but important, topics as selecting the proper cooking equipment, the best ingredients, and appropriate dishes for a menu. To ignore these topics, as some cookbook writers did, would discourage the neophyte cook. And since the most basic food was soup, he insisted on the purchase of a large (6 quart) soup kettle; to prepare the ingredients for the soup, the cook would also need a thick cutting board and good paring knives. Because the *sauteuse* (frying pan) was still essential for frying meats and vegetables, he regretted that Americans were thoughtlessly throwing them away. In addition, he urged pastry makers to acquire a variety of heavy baking pans appropriate for their tasks, while recommending the electric beater to speed up the mixing process.[69]

One of Diat's constant refrains was to insist on choosing the best ingredients for any given recipe. Among other things, he would brook no substitute for butter; however, he recommended onions if leeks were not available. He also strongly advised hostesses to purchase fish in season and to check its freshness. Although Diat was quite impressed that out-of-season fruits and vegetables could be shipped long distances and were thus available year around, he doubted they could match the quality of seasonal produce raised locally. To ensure a source of fresh vegetables, whose potential for improving the taste and texture of their meals Americans rarely exploited, Diat found a retired French chef to grow what he needed near New York.[70]

On a related matter, Diat regretted the American custom of serving vegetables with the meat course, which diminished their culinary value within the larger menu. At the same time, by encouraging the consumption of wild mushrooms and greens, properly cooked and sauced, he hoped to exploit the increasing variety of vegetables to improve the American diet. On that subject, Diat, remembering Brillat-Savarin's prophesy to this effect, yearned to show his predecessor the splendid array of vegetables that were now available in Les Halles.[71]

To guide hostesses in choosing ingredients for a dinner, Diat offered advice in the series entitled "Menu Classique." First and foremost was to give priority to such seasonal items as oysters, partridge, and Brussels sprouts for a fall meal and lamb, shad/roe, asparagus, and sorrel in the spring. In addition, the hostess should seek a balance in the selection of menu items. It would be wrong, for example, to follow heavy hors d'oeuvres with a heavy soup or to repeat the same sauce for two dishes in the same meal. He also recommended that the meal planner select courses for the menu that would both contrast and harmonize with each other in taste and texture.[72]

To facilitate the task of the home cook, Diat simplified some cooking processes. Instead of having cooks weigh ingredients for pastry dough, as was common in France, he urged them to measure the ingredients by volume as was the practice in the American system. The change would enable American cooks to do without a kitchen scale. He also eliminated the use of potato and rice flour, often added to wheat flour in France, to simplify the preparation of pastry dough.[73]

In order to fully grasp the similarities and differences between Diat's and De Gouy's approaches to writing recipes, it is useful to conclude with a comparison of their bouillabaisse recipes. De Gouy devoted his topical article in the March 1942 issue of *Gourmet* to "La Bouillabaisse." In March 1948 Louis Diat launched his career as *Gourmet* chef with a "Bouillabaisse Ballet." The articles, virtually identical in format, each devoted about five columns to presenting five different recipes for bouillabaisse, including one for the Marseillaise variety. De Gouy's version ran thirty-five lines, while Diat's was shorter by two lines.[74]

Applying the criteria that I previously identified for judging the adequacy of these recipes as instructions to inexperienced cooks, it is notable that neither chef explained how to clean and dress the fish. In fact, De Gouy ignored this subject altogether, while Diat suggested that the cook might ask the fish dealer to take care of this matter.

Far more significant was the treatment of ingredients in the two recipes. De Gouy insisted on an exact duplication of the fish used in Marseilles, such as gurnard, turbot, conger eel, and John Dory, most or all of which were unavailable to Americans. Even experienced American cooks would not have been able to cook this version of the dish. By contrast, Diat, settling for an approximation of the "real thing," recommended red snapper, cod, and perch as substitutes for the Marseilles fish.

By specifying the number and size of the onions and leeks that would be incorporated in the dish, Diat provided a rough quantitative measure of these two items. De Gouy, instead, listed the quantities of these two ingredients in ounces, a more accurate way to measure, but one that would have required a kitchen scale.

As for the cooking itself, Diat gave several helpful pointers that were absent from De Gouy's recipe. He instructed readers to include in the soup the lobster shell with the meat, to place the lobster and fish on top of the other ingredients in the pot, and to cook the soup at a rolling boil in order to form an emulsion between the olive oil and the fish stock. De Gouy provided only for boiling the ingredients. Both recipes called for serving the soup on slices of bread, but Diat specified that they be one-fourth of an inch thick.

Equally revealing were the introductions to the recipes. De Gouy devoted al-most all of his five columns to recounting the charming myth of the origins of the soup. According to this story, bouillabaisse was the gift of the Sea God to two fishermen in recompense for their suffering at the hands of playful sea sprites who roughened the waters and drove them out to sea. For his part, Diat passed rapidly over the origins of bouillabaisse to establish its place in French cooking as a regional, rather than a national, dish. He noted that the ingredients changed from town to town according to the fish that were available, thus demonstrating that there were many local versions of bouillabaisse, which, in turn, justified substituting local fish when Americans prepared the soup in their homes. What was good for the goose was good for the gander. "With all of the fine fish and shellfish available in this country, isn't it a little ridiculous to say we can't make good bouillabaisse?" He added that many "homesick Frenchmen" enjoyed the soup that he cooked from the same recipe he was providing to *Gourmet* readers. Once again, Diat empowered his readers—this time to modify the original bouillabaisse from Marseilles, while insisting that they were making an authen-tic and tasty fish soup.[75]

In all likelihood, few upper-middle-class American women, the primary target of books and articles presenting gourmet recipes, actually learned to cook these dishes from either Diat or De Gouy. The obstacles to doing so, as is already evi-dent, were serious. Not until 1948 did the magazine have a *Gourmet* chef whose recipes would have been accessible to the novice housewife. No doubt, readers of *Gourmet* who were interested in learning French cuisine fared much better with Diat than De Gouy.

Unfortunately, I can give only circumstantial evidence for the claim that rela-tively few readers cooked from the *Gourmet* chefs' recipes. Certainly, the enthu-siasm that greeted Julia Child's *French Chef* in 1963 and the rapid expansion of her book sales after she launched the program suggest that previous efforts to explain French recipes to Americans had, at best, modest success. No doubt, live cooking lessons, when clearly presented, are more helpful to an audience of would-be cooks than reading recipes from a book.[76]

The failure to convert readers into cooks, however, does not mean that the publication of French recipes in cookbooks and *Gourmet* magazine articles was an exercise in futility. The fact that many subscribers read these recipes and the accompanying cultural commentary is an important event in its own right that raised readers' consciousness of French cuisine as part of a noble cultural enter-prise. Learning about this culture would prepare readers to participate in the good life through travel to France and/or to French restaurants in America's large cities. Their new knowledge and more worldly orientation, in turn, cemented their claims to social advancement.

It is important to note that the two French cookbooks that would have been most helpful to novice American housewives were both the products of collaboration between their authors, Joseph Donon and Louis Diat, and American food writers, who were women. These successes suggest that, in most cases, American cookbook authors needed help from expert French chefs to obtain a full understanding of French techniques and recipes, while the latter depended on American collaborators to rewrite these recipes and techniques in a form more accessible to an American audience. Even for chefs Diat and Donon, who were accomplished professionals and had lived for more than forty years in America, the reformulating of their recipes was a prerequisite for success. Especially noteworthy was the collaboration of Ridley and Diat in devising a strategy for reaching American women by presenting the master chef as the humble and fortunate heir to his mother's cooking. In addition, it is probable that editors Bakalar and Chamberlain helped Donon to lay out the basic processes of French cooking in a clear and logical fashion.

As will become evident, the successful collaborations between Diat and Ridley and among Donon, Chamberlain, and Bakalar created a model for transcending the cultural divide between France and America. These collaborations bridged not only the language gap but also the differences between the French culinary tradition and American foodways. In this sense, they provided a trial run for Julia Child's collaborative cookbook.

While the presentation of recipes was an attractive feature of *Gourmet*, the broad and inclusive approach of the magazine was its greatest asset in expanding circulation during the 1940s and 1950s. The magazine's readers could enlist in the gourmet movement from their armchairs, through their taste buds, as travelers, or, less frequently, as cooks, depending on their personal inclinations. By 1961, they could express their identities as gourmets by cooking or dining on not only French but increasingly American, Italian, and even British cuisine. All the same, the publisher and the staff, as well as most subscribers, understood that French cuisine was the standard by which gastronomers measured fine dining.

Although *Gourmet* built on the success of the dining societies, it offered a much wider array of options for Americans to help them assimilate elements of French culture and cuisine. The latter depended heavily on dinner and wine committees to educate their members. However, since the societies held their dinners from one to nine times a year, the exposure of society members was at best occasional and ephemeral. The magazine, by contrast, enabled interested subscribers to maintain a small reference library, which they could consult at any time. Even armchair gourmets, who read the monthly articles by the *Gourmet* chef, could develop an understanding of what it meant to dine in the French manner. Reading travelogues and descriptions of dinners and the settings for these occasions further enhanced their understanding of French culinary ways. Even so, the printed word could never convey the flavor and texture of French dishes and wines or the ambiance in which they were served as well as a gourmet society dinner.

The easiest route from the armchair to a gourmet dining experience was through *Gourmet*'s restaurant reviews, which familiarized readers with French restaurants in New York, in other regions of America, and abroad. Reviewers sought to persuade diners to try out the better restaurants. It was far easier, however, for readers who lived in or close to New York, New Orleans, and San Francisco to take this journey than those from small-town and rural America.

Travel writers, in turn, sought to convert their readers into travelers or, for those who had already been to France, to rekindle the travel bug through their articles in the magazine. There is no reason, however, to assume that all readers opted for the adventurous automobile tours that Chamberlain pioneered. Those who were hesitant about speaking a foreign language or inexperienced in overseas travel must have preferred a package tour or a trip along the beaten path. Many of these trips offered opportunities to experience different types of French restaurants on French soil and to put the dining experience into a larger context. In visits to local farms and vineyards and town and city markets, travelers witnessed firsthand the way the French produced and distributed the ingredients for their dinners. And they were able to try out artisanal food at local patisseries and charcuteries, while contrasting small regional restaurants and Parisian *haute cuisine*. With sufficient time and language skills, travelers also learned much about French daily life.

With the advent of jet travel, shorter trips, and cheaper fares, more *Gourmet* readers could afford to visit France. However, many of them returned to the United States with relatively little exposure to French cuisine. In two or three weeks, it was difficult for Americans to adopt the leisurely approach that Chamberlain recommended and, thus, to observe and interact with their hosts.

By mastering cooking processes and the manipulation of kitchen tools, as well as the vocabulary of French cuisine, Americans found another way to access the cuisine and the culture of France. Of course, the learning curve for mastering kitchen techniques varied with particular recipes, but it was especially daunting to the many *Gourmet* readers who possessed relatively weak kitchen skills. Those who persisted, however, acquired a "language" with which they could penetrate French culinary culture and better understand the high value Frenchmen put on the preparation and consumption of food. Ironically, the acquisition of this skill did not guarantee a full understanding of the dining culture or French daily life, unless it included a lengthy stay in France.

In its first two decades, *Gourmet* magazine transformed the gourmet dining scene in America. Building on the work of the gourmet dining societies, the magazine became a vehicle for spreading the word about fine dining beyond that small group to a largely upper-middle-class public of close to two hundred thousand readers. For liquor dealers, chefs, restaurant owners, travel agents, and hotel managers, *Gourmet* became a medium of communication that targeted their goods and services to a large, receptive audience and, in the process, helped to expand their businesses. At the same time, *Gourmet* readers not only became consumers of these goods and services but also embraced with varying degrees of enthusiasm the moral, aesthetic, and social agenda that the magazine advanced.

Chapter Eight

Julia and Simca

A Franco-American Culinary Alliance

It is a measure of Julia Child's impact on the American public that food writers, biographers, and historians began exploring her life and work while she was still alive. In addition to book reviews and articles, Julia has already been the subject of a full-scale biography and a biographical essay. These studies present a convincing portrait of a committed culinary artist and writer, who was also an exceptional human being. They illuminate the special mix of professional competence, exuberance, and generosity that deeply affected her readers and television spectators. Indeed, based on the evidence in the biographies, it is clear that Julia's cookbooks and television shows lured thousands of readers and viewers into the kitchen to prepare her French recipes.

Despite the thorough treatment of Julia's life and work, there is more to learn about her collaboration with Simca Beck on the first volume of *Mastering the Art of French Cooking*; that publication, which triggered her television shows, did more than any other event in the last half century to reshape the gourmet dining scene. In the cookbook, Julia and Simca worked out an approach to French cooking that enabled many Americans to prepare French dishes for the first time. To better understand the profound impact of their work on the gourmet movement, I will highlight four key issues that biographers have treated in passing or not at all: Julia's close ties to the existing gourmet movement; her careful attention to the size, class, and gender of her audience; the impact of wartime and postwar internationalism on the spread of gourmet dining; and the use of a collaborative approach in compiling the cookbook.

The partners' close connection to the gourmet movement was manifest in the preparation of *Mastering the Art of French Cooking*. Julia came of age professionally in 1951, more than a decade after the rise of the dining societies and *Gourmet* magazine. By that time, all three international gourmet societies were expanding across the United States. Meanwhile, with some fifty thousand subscribers, among them both Julia and Simca, *Gourmet* magazine was presenting

French recipes on a monthly basis, which augmented the recipe collections already published in more than a dozen French cookbooks.

The two women adopted without hesitation the movement's goal of advancing the pleasures of the table. Indeed, the correspondence between Julia and Simca almost always treated the taste of the dishes they cooked rather than vitamins, calories, and minerals that were the focus of recipes in the women's magazines. And while the women's magazines sought to liberate their readers from long hours toiling over the stove, Julia and Simca urged theirs to invest more time, as they saw it, in the noble and challenging art of cooking.[1]

As Julia came to realize, however, *Gourmet* and various cookbooks often presented recipes that were better suited to the needs of an audience comprised of middle-class French women with servants, a knowledge of French cooking processes, and access to markets with fresh produce. To address the novice American cook, Julia and Simca would have to rethink and rewrite French recipes with special attention to the social situation of their readers, most of whom were affluent, well educated, and familiar in varying degrees with France and French cuisine. In this way, the two authors learned from the failures, as well as the successes, of their predecessors in the gourmet movement.[2]

The unprecedented postwar Euro-American collaboration that brought Julia to Paris as the spouse of a United States Information Service (USIS) official and positioned her to meet Simca through a Marshall Plan official also shaped *Mastering the Art of French Cooking*. While the partners toiled together in one another's kitchens, American tourists flooded the continent; growing numbers of American scholars, soldiers, businessmen, and diplomats participated in a variety of projects with their European counterparts; and the American government promoted cultural exchanges through Fulbright scholarships and the funding of American libraries, lectures, and exhibitions in Europe. Such exchanges brought about greater contact between citizens of the two countries, but they were often accompanied by expressions of anti-Americanism from Communists and conservative Europeans who bristled at the perceived subordination of Europe to American ways.[3]

The collaboration of Julia and Simca was one of many cultural counterparts of the diplomatic and military alliance between the two countries and served, in a small way, to right the balance of power by promoting the spread of French culture to the United States. As France was joining the Marshall Plan and the Atlantic Alliance at the behest of the American government, Julia and Simca were teaching American home cooks French culinary practices and processes, and thus expanding their cultural horizons. They were also expanding the informal French culinary empire in America that Thomas Jefferson had helped to launch over a century and a half earlier.

Finally, the experience of collaboration shaped the cookbook in important ways. Julia and Simca worked out a division of labor in which both women selected and tested the recipes, while Julia, keeping in mind the special needs of novice American cooks, wrote them up. In this way, the partners took advantage of each others' strengths, while testing each recipe to make sure that it would satisfy their high standards. In evaluating this experience, however, Julia's biographers have given too much weight to her version of the story. My own account considers Julia's position as well as Simca's serious and legitimate reservations about certain facets of *Mastering the Art of French Cooking*; as such, it validates both authors' perspectives and views their conflict as a microcosm of Franco-American cultural relations in the early postwar period.

The impact of *Mastering* and the television cooking lessons that followed on the gender balance of the gourmet dining movement was dramatic. After all, dining societies and restaurants in men's clubs were run by men for men. Published by a man, *Gourmet*, nonetheless, opened the subject of gourmet dining to women. But *Mastering*, far more than *Gourmet*, enabled thousands of American home cooks, mostly women, to become gourmet cooks and thus to persuade their friends and family to become gourmet diners. As a counterpart to this change, hosts increasingly held gourmet occasions in the privacy of their upper-middle-class homes rather than in restaurants and at a much lower cost. In considering the production, as well as the consumption, of their dinners, these converts to French cuisine deepened their knowledge of gourmet dining.

Building a Partnership

Well before Julia Child entered the picture, Simca Beck was already collaborating with her friend Louisette Bertholle on a manuscript collection of French recipes intended for the American home cook. The cookbook idea grew out of a 1948 dinner featuring *boeuf à la mode* (beef marinated in white wine, cooked with a calf's foot, carrots, and onions) that Louisette prepared in the Grosse Point, Michigan, kitchen of her American friend, Lucille Tyree. Impressed with Louisette's culinary skills, Lucille persuaded her to publish a collection of French recipes for American home cooks. Louisette then invited Simca Beck, who was a fellow member of Le Cercle des Gourmettes, the only women's gourmet dining society in France, to become a partner in the project. Once the two women completed the manuscript, Louisette used family connections to obtain a book contract with Ives Washburn.

Ten years later, the lineal descendant of this manuscript, *Mastering the Art of French Cooking*, appeared to great acclaim, but only after Julia Child and Simca Beck thoroughly transformed it.[4]

As World War II broke out, Julia McWilliams was totally unprepared for the cookbook project she would undertake ten years later. With the exception of her years at Smith College and a brief stay in New York City, she had lived a protected life in the Pasadena, California, home of her affluent parents. Eager for adventure in the post–Pearl Harbor world, she landed a job as a clerk in the Office of Strategic Services (OSS) in Washington, D.C. In 1944, based on her excellent work in the OSS, Julia's bosses sent her briefly to India and then for a longer stay in Ceylon, where she worked with an intellectually vibrant community of officers. Among them was a mapmaker-artist named Paul Child, a worldly man who had lived in Paris in the 1920s and spoke fluent French. Following their assignment to Kunming, China, Paul and Julia often dined together in Chinese restaurants, where their discussions of the cuisine provided a segue for Paul's reflections on the French cuisine that he had grown to love. It was under Paul's tutelage that Julia developed her cosmopolitan aspirations.[5]

Two years after their 1946 marriage, the USIS, in an effort to convince a skeptical European public that Americans possessed the essential elements of a civilized society, sent Paul to Paris to curate exhibits of American art. With Paul's support, Julia decided to brush up her high school and college French (three courses at Smith College starting at the intermediate level) by taking lessons at Berlitz, where she "acquired a certain fluency." Already, a lunch in Rouen (*portugaises* [oysters], *sole meunière* [in a butter sauce], *salade*) on her first day in France had kindled a love affair with French food. To pursue her developing passion for French cuisine, she then enrolled in the professional track of the Cordon Bleu cooking school in 1949 with American GIs who were training to be chefs. Studying primarily under Max Bugnard, an Escoffier disciple, Julia developed skills that would qualify her to cook for a French family of the *haute bourgeoisie*.[6]

Julia's future partner, Simca, also grew up in privileged circumstances in Tocqueville en Caux, Normandy, where her family owned the Benedictine liqueur business. While she identified herself by her maiden name, Beck, on various cookbooks, in daily life she used Fischbacher, her second husband's name. In place of her given name, Simone, Jean Fischbacher had dubbed her Simca, after the small French car she drove despite her five-foot-eight-inch frame.[7]

Simca's father, Maurice Beck, learned the English language as a child from his English mother and arranged to have his children tutored in the language from an early age. He also entertained American business associates in his home, one of whom hosted Simca during her first trip to the United States. When Simca married Jean Fischbacher, who was himself fluent in English, she further solidified her connection to the Anglo-Saxon world. As early as 1933, moreover, Simca manifested her own interest in cooking by enrolling in the amateur track of the Cordon Bleu, after which she took lessons from one of France's greatest "chef-teachers," Henri-Paul Pellaprat. That activity qualified Simca to join the Cercle des Gourmettes, where she was among the most active members.[8]

Late in 1950, a Russian-born Marshall Plan official, George Artamanoff, who knew the Childs and friends of Simca, arranged their first meeting. Simca, in turn, introduced Julia to her friend Louisette, and the two French women arranged for Julia to join the Cercle des Gourmettes in February of 1951. Thus began an important chapter in Julia's culinary education, as well as an opportunity to bond with her future partners. She not only enjoyed the Gourmettes' specially prepared meals twice a month but, along with Simca and Louisette, bolstered her skills by assisting various chefs in selecting menus and doing the prep work for the dinners. This experience Julia considered "the real beginning of French gastronomical life for me."[9]

Shortly after joining the Gourmettes, she and Paul cemented the relationship with the Fischbachers and Bertholles by inviting them to their Paris apartment for a lunch that Julia prepared with her teacher, Max Bugnard (*crabe à la bretonne* [cream sauce with leeks, mushrooms, and celery], *poulet en waterzoië* [chicken and vegetables in cream], *crêpes suzettes*). As the collaboration with Julia developed, Simca also manifested a growing interest in American life. She welcomed Julia's help in understanding American culture and read books "to give me the feel of American life which I find exciting."[10]

With their partnership flourishing, Julia, Simca, and Louisette launched a cooking school called L'École des Trois Gourmandes. Julia preferred the name to "gourmet," which suggested an excessive refinement and snobbery in gastronomical matters. By contrast, gourmand, used interchangeably in France with gourmet, identified diners who recognized good food and drink but also possessed strong appetites. The three partners divided the teaching chores and instructed their students—mostly American women living in Paris—in the basic methods of French cooking. In their lessons, held in the Childs' Paris apartment, the three cooks used American measurements and ingredients as much as possible, thus setting the stage for a cookbook written from the perspective of the American home cook. The teaching experience strengthened the partnership and confirmed the accessibility of French cooking to Americans once their teachers explained basic processes.[11]

Meanwhile, in the fall of 1952, the Simca Beck–Louisette Bertholle cookbook project was at a standstill. Instead of revising the manuscript, submitted a year earlier, Herman Ripperger, the editor assigned to the task, wrote a short cookbook entitled *What's Cooking in France* (New York: Ives Washburn, 1952), based loosely on the recipes from the larger manuscript. Sales of the book were poor, largely because the publisher did little to promote it. Meanwhile, Ives Washburn sought to replace Ripperger as editor of the original manuscript, now entitled *French Home Cooking*, with an American editor who understood the situation of American home cooks. Quite naturally, the authors turned to Julia Child, who helped them to obtain a new contract with Houghton Mifflin.[12]

While Louisette was responsible for launching the cookbook project, she participated only sporadically in the revisions of *French Home Cooking*. Despite her great charm and excellent skills as a cook and host—Julia called her "everyone's dream of the perfect French woman"—her life was complicated. Unlike her partners, who were married but had no children, Louisette not only was preoccupied with her two daughters but cared for her elderly mother. Moreover, she was not cut out for the rigorous testing of the hundreds of recipes considered for inclusion in *Mastering*. Accordingly, the partners twice renegotiated their book contract and reduced Louisette's share of the royalties from one-third to one-fifth and eventually to 10 percent.[13]

The Cookbook Project

Taking account of Dorothy Canfield Fisher's critique of *French Home Cooking*, Julia and Simca sought to rewrite the recipes in a home-cook-friendly fashion. The revised book they regarded as a cooking school between covers that would provide instruction in basic cooking techniques and persuade the American woman, accustomed to efficient meal preparation, to work through some relatively complicated recipes. By "Americanizing" the home cook's labor through the use of familiar kitchen aids and some processed ingredients, the authors intended to make this extensive meal preparation more palatable without diminishing the French flavor of the dishes.[14]

Unlike Dorothy Canfield Fisher, Julia Child believed that the time was ripe for American women to become converts to the more challenging cooking experience that she and Simca advocated. In recent years, there had been a "great upsurge in 'doing it yourself,'" indicating that Americans often preferred to make things from scratch rather than buying them from a store. As a result, hobbies like carpentry and cooking were flourishing. These trends augured well for a cookbook that would require Americans to learn cooking skills and spend time in the kitchen using them.[15]

Julia and Simca's antagonism to the women's magazines' approach to cooking shaped their vision of the project. Julia bridled at the way the magazines protected the busy "housewife" from kitchen chores that might divert her from other household tasks, especially child care. Driven by an obsession with efficiency, she felt, the magazines sought to reduce the time required to prepare meals no matter how the reduction might affect the taste of the food. In response, Julia sought to revive the idea of the woman as a home cook, who was dedicated to producing tasty dinners as a labor of love. On weekends, moreover, the home cook would become "the cook/hostess," who prepared dinner parties without help from servants or the draconian shortcuts recommended by the magazines.[16]

To persuade publishers that their proposed book would serve the needs of the potential audience better than its competitors, Julia and Simca carefully reviewed French cookbooks to clarify the distinctiveness of their own. In their opinion, none of the books currently on the market—or published over the nine-year period during which they worked on the new cookbook—addressed the needs of the American home cook to master basic cooking processes. The "tragedy" was that "young brides will try out the recipes," with their inadequate instructions, and "conclude that only a genius can cook."[17]

Published just as the three partners were launching their project, Samuel Chamberlain's *Bouquet de France* (1952) was a perfect illustration of this problem. On the one hand, it was a "wonderful and beautiful book," combining information on travel in France with beautiful illustrations. However, the recipes were useless for the "novice." When Julia asked the Chamberlains, who were her friends and her competitors, where "they got all those wonderful recipes," they admitted to borrowing most of them from French cookbooks, sometimes without a trial run. As Julia perused the recipes, she discovered inaccuracies and a lack of clarity in the instructions that would confuse and discourage the home cook. As an example, she noted that the five-pound chicken recommended for *poulet à la Niçoise* (chicken in olives, garlic, anchovies, tomatoes, and green beans) should have been cooked for more than the one hour prescribed in the recipe. "I am being very mean about this book, but I think they are big competition for us, and I want ours to be way ahead of everything in accuracy and depth and perfection."[18]

Julia rendered similar verdicts on other competitors. She thought *The Gourmet Cookbook*, the first volume of which had appeared in 1950, "beautiful" but lacking in clarity: "I don't know what they are talking about in many instances." She dismissed Dione Lucas' *Cordon Bleu* for similar reasons, and when Lucas' more specialized *Meat and Poultry Cook Book* appeared in 1955, Julia announced, "Hers is 'Lucas cooking,' ours is classical French. Hers is a collection of recipes; ours is an attempt to teach the reader what in H. is going on and why." As an example of the inadequacy of the recipes, Julia noted that for the chicken galantine, Lucas never specified the type of chicken or sausage to be used. Hence, she concluded that, even though "the old Girl" is a "public drawing card," their own collaborative effort would produce a better book "if we live long enuf!"[19]

But the principal competition for the new cookbook came from monthly articles in *Gourmet*, which Julia and Simca followed with great interest and considerable anxiety. They had been unimpressed with the many recipes originally published in the magazine and republished in *The Gourmet Cookbook* and *Bouquet de France*. However, the *Gourmet* chef's series on soups and sauces by Louis Diat was an important exception, because Diat offered careful instruction in basic processes, much like Julia and Simca. Moreover, Diat and Helen Ridley were exploiting precisely the same partnership idea as Julia and Simca and, in so doing, confirmed the validity of that idea, while threatening their rivals' cooking project. Two years later, however, Julia breathed a sigh of relief: "Luckily for us, Diat just died the other day. (Horrid thing to say, though.)"[20]

After learning from the mistakes of their rivals how to properly construct recipes, Julia and Simca were confident that their cookbook would meet the needs of their readers. In revising the original Beck-Bertholle manuscript, they intended to simplify the learning process by making the steps in any given recipe so transparent that even a novice cook would be able to follow them from start to finish. In the cookbook, their master recipes presented explanations of necessary processes and ingredients, which were followed by variations on these recipes with references back to the ingredients and processes in the master recipe. The cookbook also included instructions on how to use American products and kitchen aids that shortened the cooking process, as well as definitions of French terms and a chart converting metric measurements to the English system. Happily, home cooks could apply the techniques they were learning to the preparation of dishes from other ethnic cuisines.[21]

A home-cook-centered approach required the authors to consider the social changes that had reshaped the world of the American cook-hostess over the previous twenty-five years. The new obligations of the mother to her children, as part of the "parent-chauffeur-den-mother syndrome," complicated the already-difficult task of cooking and entertaining at the same time. Of course, most American women had kept house and taken care of their children without the benefit of servants, but since World War II, as Julia noted, the "upper-middle-brow and upper-brow" classes were experiencing, for the first time, this servant-less world. Moreover, they were now purchasing their food at supermarkets. For that reason, Julia suggested *"French Cooking from the American Supermarket"* as a subtitle for *Mastering.*[22]

Given these changes, Julia identified the readers she and Simca hoped to reach as a "literate" audience that "LIKES TO COOK AND WANTS TO LEARN" in spite of the time constraints. In addition, among these upper-middle-brow women, the book would appeal especially to Americans who had traveled in France and experienced the joys of French cuisine. A select audience of this kind might not buy many books but could afford to pay more to cover the additional costs of high-quality paper and printing.[23]

Julia had nothing but contempt, however, for that part of the audience she dubbed "the fancy crowd." Nonetheless, she and her Houghton Mifflin editor, Dorothy de Santillana, agreed that this group, who regarded "gourmetude" as "only for the upper classes," might be useful in talking up the book. "Probably snob appeal helps. I am sure it pulls in the Gourmet, wine and food society crowd. And they do buy cookbooks." Even so, de Santillana expressed the hope that "we can push this book way past them into the hands of the housewife."[24]

Despite her misgivings, Julia took steps to appeal to this upper-crust crowd. As she explained to de Santillana, her contacts "in big-time gastronomy" through her French collaborators and the Cercle des Gourmettes were excellent. Indeed, in November of 1953, the three partners approached Paul Émile Cadilhac, a "respected" French wine writer, to gain entrée into the Confrérie des Chevaliers du Tastevin. Membership in this group would impress potential American buyers of their cookbook, who might not have heard of the authors, with their expertise in French cooking.[25]

Even so, Julia expressed a certain disdain for the "very commercial" aspect of the "TaddyVangs," as she and Paul referred to the Tastevin. "Someone who knows someone has gotten you in," although "the ordinary person in the U.S.

wouldn't know these sordid details." Indeed, Cadhilac, on their behalf, had approached Camille Rodier, one of the founders of the Tastevin, to secure their invitations to join the Society. Its reputation notwithstanding, Julia protested that the food and wine served at the induction ceremony were quite ordinary, although the ritual and the "fine old Cistercian hall" created a "Romantic" ambiance.[26]

As the publishing date for their cookbook approached, however, Julia sought to reach other social groups. Of course, she cultivated periodicals with a stylish readership, including *Vogue* and *Harper's Bazaar*; after all, "the American Vogue [*sic*] is always interested in elegant cooking recipes." In addition, she hoped to publish articles in *Woman's Day*, which she identified as a magazine for "lower income families," to appeal to its readers as potential buyers of the book. Earlier, she had spoken optimistically of reaching a "mass market" through Louisette's contacts with the American Federation of Women's Clubs. After reflecting on this idea, however, Julia changed her mind: "French cooking is not for the tv dinner and cake-mix set." Rather than approach mass-circulation magazines where "the majority of [the] readers would consider the French pre-occupation with detail a frank waste of time if not a form of insanity," she would find "a more sophisticated medium whose clientele has done some traveling about and knows about eating." Julia had in mind *House and Garden, House Beautiful,* and *Holiday.* In effect, the prime targets of the book would be the Julia Childs of America—the growing population of college-educated, upper- and upper-middle-class women who had traveled to France and experienced the delights of French cooking.[27]

Julia's strong commitment to the scientific ethos, for which Simca had less enthusiasm and Louisette none at all, nonetheless shaped the collaborative cookbook project. Julia took Louisette to task for espousing the Romantic idea of "born talent" that subverted the underlying assumption of the cookbook and penalized readers by failing to lay out the steps required to produce a particular dish. Once possessed of clear instructions, any cook, willing to work hard, would be able to prepare the recipes. A scientific approach was, thus, Julia's antidote to the conventional wisdom that French cooking was a mystery and good cooks were born, not made. In this respect, the partners were fortunate that Louisette had only a marginal role in writing the cookbook, whereas Julia and Simca, both "straight chef-type cooks," were perfectly suited to the project.[28]

In describing the scientific approach, Julia's rhetoric was reminiscent of mainstream nutritionists, although she emphatically rejected the latter's call for measuring diners' caloric and vitamin intake. Both Julia and the nutritionists hoped to disarm the preconceptions of male food authorities by presenting themselves as "scientific." And for Julia, this was more than posturing. She took genuine pride in the "laboratory" work she and Simca performed that set them apart from other French cookbook writers: "we are not merely three little old housewives who just love to cook; we are professionals . . . all the recipes and methods in the book are our own, worked out in our kitchen laboratories."[29]

This scientific process was laborious in the extreme. It required careful inquiry into the ingredients of each of the recipes, especially when Julia and Simca substituted American for French ingredients. For example, Julia checked with government authorities in both France and America to clarify the differences between American and French species of fish so that the cookbook would provide accurate information on how to cook them. One of Julia's guinea pig readers, who understood this scientific approach, insisted that there are "so many cookbooks on the market. None, however, that give the facts or the organization, and the science behind [*sic*] like yours."[30]

Consistent with the scientific method and with American practice, the partners insisted on accurate measurements for the ingredients of each recipe, as well as precise oven temperatures. French cookbooks, even Auguste Escoffier's, usually did not include such measurements, while, in the absence of thermostats in French ovens, temperatures were useless. For novice American cooks, the additional information could make the difference between success and failure in following a recipe. Thus, because Simca was not precise in her measurements, Julia worked out most of them, which required "a minute checking."[31]

Designating the book a scientific tome had clear implications for its style and tone. Julia had utter disdain for what she called the "charm school" of cookbook writing epitomized by *Bouquet de France*, with its nostalgia for traditional life in the French provinces and imprecise instructions for cooking the recipes. As a model for style and tone, she preferred *The Joy of Cooking*: "I adore it and always have . . . Somehow, old Mrs. Joy's [Rombauer] personality shines through her recipes too." What Julia strove for was the "comfortable and sensible note" of "wise and friendly advice from one cook to another" that Rombauer conveyed. This no-nonsense approach would also apply to illustrations and type. In place of the "sweetly sticky and girlish" images in many contemporary cookbooks, Julia preferred practical illustrations that would show the reader important techniques like how to cut with a knife. The book type would highlight methods and recipe titles.[32]

To preserve classical French cuisine, Simca and Julia systematically searched sources for recipes from the canon of French traditional cooking. They examined the standard cookbooks used by French housewives, including Escoffier, *Larousse Gastronomique*, Alibab, St. Ange, and Curnonski, along with recipes from such private sources as Simca's mother, Le Cercle des Gourmettes, and chefs they knew. The French cookbooks became the source of classical French recipes, also borrowed by their competitors; a distinguishing feature of their own volume were "good new recipes, always very French," drawn from family and friends.[33]

Once the partners decided that they should consider a particular dish for the cookbook, they checked at least three different versions of the recipe to determine which one they could present most clearly to American readers. In this process, it was Julia's task to determine the availability and cost of the ingredients in the United States, the preparation time, and then to write up the recipe. In Julia's words, Simca "feeds the recipes and I get them into shape." She was, in this sense, Simca's "American digestive tract."[34]

For the most part, the authors designed a testing process that would enable them to introduce traditional French cooking to Americans in an uncompromising fashion. However, recognizing the realities of the American culinary environment, Julia adjusted the recipes, the cooking process, and the menus to reduce the preparation time for housewives who had no servants. She advocated using the most advanced kitchen technology, including blenders, mixers, and automatic beaters, provided that they did not compromise the quality of the dish: "if something is not a French taste . . . we shall say so." To carry out their plan, the partners agreed to use some modern kitchen aids in preparing one of the three recipes they tested for inclusion in the cookbook. As she reflected on their absence from other French cookbooks then available to American housewives, Julia's enthusiasm for kitchen aids grew. "This whole field is wide open, that of using the electric aids for a lot of fancy French stuff . . . and we'll be presenting something entirely new. No sacred cows for us." However, if word got out, other cookbook writers might scoop them; accordingly, Julia wrote Simca as follows: "I think we must be careful not to mention our Waring mixer experiments to anyone . . . it would be a shame for some one else to beat us to it." In addition, she worried about having "any of this stuff stolen by Gourmet [magazine]."[35]

Among time-saving devices that Julia and Simca tried out, the pressure cooker yielded mixed results and received from her a guarded endorsement, while she successfully used the electric eggbeater for "experiments on yeast bread." With the Waring mixer, however, it was possible to prepare *mirepoix* (a mixture of diced vegetables used to enhance the flavor of meat), as well as *quenelles* (dumplings with spiced meat or fish forcemeat), more easily and with a great saving of time. When French guests praised the *quenelles* without realizing how they had been prepared, Julia considered this a true victory for the Waring mixer. As for the Waring blender, she and Simca used it to make shellfish butter that was superior to the version published in *Gourmet* (February 1956).[36]

Essential, but controversial, was the partners' willingness to substitute for French ingredients that were unavailable, too expensive at the American supermarket, or too time-consuming to cook. In principle, these substitutions were acceptable only when they maintained the French flavor of a dish, but the partners could not always abide by this rule, if they wanted American housewives to cook their recipes. The breadth of this problem was evident in a "List of Things to Investigate in the USA" that Julia sent to Simca shortly before she returned to America in 1954; a section of the list read as follows: "Flour (types of hard wheat, availability of soft wheat. What the whole grain, unprocessed wheat is like.) . . . Wild game. How much available, how important our game chapter should be. French *foie gras* available?"[37]

In considering the differences between French and American flour, butter, spices, and cooking oil, Julia and Simca encountered serious problems. Especially tricky was finding an equivalent for standard French flour made from soft wheat. For certain purposes, they could substitute American cake flour, the same density as French soft-wheat flour, for American hard wheat. Despite the fact that French butter was unsalted and had an "almost nutty flavor" quite different from its American counterpart, Julia insisted that for all cooking processes except cake frostings and some desserts, cooks should use salted American butter "interchangeably with the French." However, on the grounds that the French have a greater tolerance for butter than Americans, Simca suggested that Americans dilute butter with oil when preparing casserole roasted chicken. Meanwhile, Julia agreed to margarine as a substitute for olive oil, which was scarce. Other replacements included leeks or onions for shallots and spices from Spice Island.[38]

To avoid "scaring off" readers with modest food budgets, Julia limited the number of recipes that required foie gras and truffles or suggested options to them. Even though she acknowledged that canned truffles and foie gras were inferior to fresh, she condoned their use to reduce the cost, while suggesting the addition of Madeira to enhance the flavor of canned truffles. In fact, *Mastering* contained only four recipes incorporating foie gras and nine calling for truffles, and in several cases the authors listed these ingredients as optional.[39]

Simca and Julia both endorsed the discriminate use of canned and frozen ingredients. For Simca, it was important to combine these ingredients with others "treated in a French manner." Following an experiment using canned consommé to make a *gelée* (jelly) that her invited French guests found "succulent," Simca remarked, "An American dinner, but I was the only one to know it." Julia, in turn, endorsed the use of canned bouillon in *boeuf à la mode* and willingly used some frozen vegetables, but reported that a recent dinner prepared from frozen vegetables and frozen fish left her in despair: "It ain't French, it ain't good, and the hell with it." She was, moreover, adamantly opposed to frozen chicken, which she found "awful and tasteless and stringy." By contrast, certain American processed foods, including Minute Rice, pie crust mix, and powdered potatoes, were quite to her liking.[40]

In order to satisfy the needs of the chef/hostess, Julia and Simca flagged recipes that readers could cook in advance by placing an asterisk (*) in front of the last step to be completed before the company arrived. As Julia promised, there were "'make ahead' notes for everything," including such popular dishes as Burgundy beef and veal stew with onions and mushrooms. Julia also praised the *"poulet poêlé"* (braised chicken) and "covered roasting" methods as particularly well suited to cooking in advance. Even so, she acknowledged that dishes prepared before the guests arrived were rarely as tasty as those brought to the table directly from the oven. "But in modern life, one must adapt oneself . . . and if it is sometimes impossible to cook and eat, then one must cook ahead."[41]

The partners deliberately selected recipes for the cookbook that featured relatively quick preparations. Julia distinguished, for example, between the "quick method" and the "fancier method" for making *oeufs en gelée* (poached eggs in aspic). And she recommended using frozen *mirepoix* for pea soup because it would save thirty-three minutes of preparation time. In addition, she excluded recipes requiring lengthy preparations, as, for example, *mousseline de brochet dijonnaise* (pike mousse in mustard sauce), which appeared in *Bouquet de France,* on the grounds that American cooks would not have time to prepare them. Even in cases where the dishes were part of the French canon, Simca opted for simplification. "I am in complete agreement with getting rid of complicated recipes and perhaps to give more explanation to basic recipes."[42]

Even bolder was Julia's insistence that home cooks follow the American model of serving a single main course to include meat and sauce, potato and vegetable rather than presenting the latter as a separate course. Accordingly, *Mastering* suggested the appropriate vegetables to accompany each meat, fish, or fowl recipe. In discussing "quantities" in the foreword, Julia informed readers that the recipes in the book were designed "to serve six people with reasonably good appetites in an American-style menu of three courses." (Salad and dessert were the other two courses.) She contrasted that model with the French menu "comprising hors d'oeuvre, soup, main course [with garnishes], salad, cheese and dessert." Julia even encouraged the home cook to serve any vegetables and potatoes that harmonized with the meat dish, whether or not they were served in France. Broccoli was a case in point. "We have to remain French . . . but we should also indicate where something would be good as an accompaniment, although it is not a French practice to serve it."[43]

In short, Julia and Simca strove to duplicate French flavors in their recipes but deviated from this practice when, as in the case of cream, butter, and wheat, it was impossible for Americans to obtain the ingredients. In eliminating the hors d'oeuvre, soup, and cheese courses from the menu, however, the two women radically diminished the range of flavors that were basic to many French meals in order to enable the American housewife to more easily prepare the other three courses.

Squabbling Partners

In the wake of Louisette Bertholle's virtual withdrawal from the partnership, the success of the cookbook depended on the establishment of an effective working relationship between Julia Child and Simca Beck. The two women needed each other. Without Julia, Simca would have struggled to understand the perspective of the American home cook and to adapt the recipes accordingly. Without Simca, Julia would have had difficulty testing all the recipes and risked losing credibility with her American audience, as Paul Child acknowledged. The cookbook, he insisted, "must be by (or seem to be by)" French authors or Americans will not buy it.[44]

In the relationship between these two strong-minded women, cooperation was the dominant motif, although inevitably, in a nine-year partnership, conflicts developed. While Julia and Simca agreed, in principle, that they should adapt French recipes to the needs of American housewives, Simca could not shake her conviction that French dishes prepared from American ingredients would not have a true French flavor. Differences in personal style, shaped to some degree by the partners' respective French and American backgrounds, also figured in their conflicts. While both partners were hard workers, Julia's systematic approach to culinary matters clashed with Simca's intuitive bent. By virtue of her self-confidence and superior formal training in French cooking, Julia emerged as the dominant partner and was thus able to impose her views whenever disputes on important issues arose. Although Simca was stubborn, she was also at times deferential, as is evident in the following plaintive question, which she put to Julia after conducting a cooking lesson for NATO officers' wives: "Would my Julie be proud of me?"[45]

Just eighteen months into the revisions of the manuscript for *French Home Cooking*, an encounter in Marseilles clarified the dynamics of their working relationship. Following Paul's transfer to the USIS office there, Simca visited the Childs' new home for a weekend of testing various recipes. After Simca returned to Paris, Julia fired off a "harsh" (Julia's word) letter accusing Simca of failure to uphold the authenticity of the recipes for their book and then laying down four commandments designed to change her partner's behavior. Acknowledging that "on the whole . . . we work well together," Julia protested that Simca was "too modest, or too '*obéissante.*'" Of particular concern was a recipe for "*la fameuse sauce à la rouille*" (garlic, pimiento, olive oil, and chili pepper), which was traditionally served with *bouillabaisse*; Simca referred to the version they had prepared as a "*Rouille* Julia." This "SHOCKING remark," according to Julia, suggested that Simca would allow recipes that did not taste "French" to be misrepresented to American readers. By not confronting Julia directly and clarifying the problem, Simca had, in effect, abdicated her responsibility for monitoring all recipes to assure that they did not "depart from the French tradition to cater to American tastes." (Although details are lacking, it is likely that Simca objected to the substitution of American ingredients in the *rouille* such as Tabasco sauce for chili pepper and canned for fresh pimiento, the options listed in *Mastering*.)[46]

To remedy this problem in the future, Julia insisted that Simca assert herself "even if this is not in the tradition *française.*" Only if Simca expressed her views "as an equal partner in this enterprise" could they succeed in writing an authentic French cookbook. Julia also implored Simca to follow the "scientific method," which required thorough testing of all recipes, and to learn professional knife techniques. Somewhat prophetically, she added, "Who knows, we may end up on television." Julia completed her list of complaints by noting Simca's failure to clean the knives regularly and keep a clean work surface.[47]

In response, Simca wrote no less than three letters to Julia in the next week, one of them addressed to *ma chère déese de la cuisine* (my dear kitchen goddess). While the salutation has a sarcastic ring, the text of each letter conveyed Simca's genuine respect for her partner's prowess in the kitchen and commitment to the project, as well as a certain remorse for her own behavior. "As for your commandments," Simca agreed, "I will try to follow them as much as my conscience permits." Regarding Julia's complaint that she was too modest and obedient, Simca confessed to the latter, but not to the former. Julia, she pointed out, was more competent than she in culinary matters as evidenced by differences in

Julia Child and Simca Beck: Photograph by Paul Child, circa 1952, Paris, France.
Julia Child Foundation for Gastronomy and the Culinary Arts.

their training at the Cordon Bleu. (Although she said nothing, Simca must have known that Julia had earned a B.A., while she had never attended a university.) Not only was Julia better trained, but she also launched her refutations with "so many persuasive words that my personal conviction is shaken." Indeed, as a hard worker with a "certain practical intelligence," who was not an "intellectual," she found Julia's knowledge "intimidating." It was thus difficult for Simca to stand her ground. In any case, she promised never to repeat the "shocking remark" about "la Rouille Julia," although she did not retract her allegation that the *rouille* failed to measure up to the standard of *"goût français."* No doubt, as she suggested above, her "conscience" would not "permit" it.[48]

Regarding other commandments, Simca agreed that following the scientific method was essential to the completion of a "masterpiece," which was the partners' goal. Somewhat more sheepishly, she confessed to poor kitchen habits that she would try to remedy. However, there would be a price to pay for using proper knife techniques; the juice from sliced onions would leave "a detestable, strong odor" on her fingers.[49]

Both women then sought to mend the breech in their relationship. Simca denied that Julia's letter had been "harsh" and encouraged her partner's "direct way of exposing things" to handle future problems. Julia, in turn, provided a remedy for onion odors on the fingers and praise for the partnership: "We have both worked like dogs and who knows better than I, the recipient of all your work, what a remarkable girl you are!"[50]

While their confrontation arose over a disagreement about the substitution of American for French ingredients in French recipes, it was exacerbated by differences in cultural styles. The greater tendency in France to use irony or sarcasm in arguing a point contributed to turning the disagreement into an angry confrontation. Simca surely intended "La *Rouille* Julia" as an insult, and Julia took it that way. Julia's strong response, in turn, brought to the surface Simca's insecurity about playing her role as guardian of French taste in the recipes. In suggesting that the *tradition française* made it difficult for even a strong woman like Simca to confront someone who had been educated to a higher level, Julia was likely on the mark. Her insistence that she and Simca had a partnership of equals, however, was a case of protesting too much. Indeed, Simca could do no more than promise to try to overcome her sense of inferiority and speak up in the future for authentic French taste.

Arising early in their collaboration, the conflict between the two partners clarified their roles. Without question, Julia Child had taken the initiative by challenging Simca to defend the standards of classical French cuisine. Simca, in turn, applauded Julia's willingness to address problems directly and acknowledged her superior authority about kitchen matters. Simca clearly recognized her subordinate role in the project. The absence of similar confrontations during the next six years suggests that the problems in the working relationship had been put aside, but not necessarily resolved. Indeed, the collaboration was strained once again as the book neared publication in 1961.

Proofreading the final draft and reviewing the proofs, coinciding as they did with the publication of Trois Gourmandes recipes in *Cuisines et Vins de France* (CVF), the French *Gourmet*, reopened old wounds. Then, a testy exchange between Julia and Simca regarding the French generals' putsch that was intended to overturn the de Gaulle regime in April of 1961 exacerbated their differences.

In an April 24, 1961, letter to Avis DeVoto, their unpaid literary agent and friend, Julia issued a "long W*A*I*L from the far northland" (Oslo), where the USIS had sent Paul to head the office. At the last minute, Simca wished to correct certain recipes in the proofs, to which she and Julia had agreed in the final typed version of the manuscript, because they perpetrated a *"goût américain."* She thus appeared to be playing her role as monitor of *"goût français,"* although the timing was rather delicate. Among other things, Simca denied that bread rounds in soup should be sprinkled with beef drippings and insisted that cassoulet must be made with goose, although not all French culinary authorities agreed. The two women also quarreled about the spelling of Chateau d'Yquem. Most frustrating to Julia, however, was Simca's insistence on eliminating the slice of bread from pistou soup, which had originally been "HER SUGGESTION, god dammit." She added, parenthetically: "My god, I pity J.F. Kennedy trying to make any headway with de Gaulle. He's even worse than Simca, from all I've heard."[51]

Time constraints drove the resolution of these issues. The partners had a deadline to meet, so Julia once again wrote an insistent, somewhat patronizing letter to Simca ("as though to a child") clarifying the limited changes that the authors could make in the proofs. They could not, however, revisit matters that Simca had already approved "définitivement" in the final typescript. "If you now do not agree with what you formerly said, it is just—*malheureusement* (unfortunately)—too bad." After refuting point by point Simca's claims that errors had been made or that the version in the final manuscript had been changed in the galleys, Julia insisted that the book represented "GOUT SIMCA and there is no doubt about it. The only thing is that you have forgotten what your GOUT used to be!"[52]

In order to conclusively squash Simca's claim that the recipes introduced a *"goût américain,"* Julia rehearsed once again the procedure they had adopted to assure that all recipes would adhere to the standards of classical French cuisine, including consideration of recipes from "the great classic chefs" and then experiments to find the best recipe for each dish. This argument was no doubt persuasive, but Julia's concluding exhortation, assuming that authority derived as much from experience as from academic credentials, must have struck Simca as a foreign concept: "And you must not forget, either, that *you*, also, are an authority. You have had years of experience and training, you have read reams of authorities, and you know your business. Just try to remember that."[53]

Simca Beck experienced the conflict over the final stages of the book production from a different perspective and articulated her feelings in a less direct manner. While Simca's posture appears irrational as Julia described it, there were telltale signs that her resistance expressed a last-minute reluctance to put her name to a book that brought substantial changes, initiated by an American, to many of the traditional recipes in French classical cooking. From Julia's perspective as an American home cook, altering the recipes was essential to making the book accessible to the target audience. Simca, by contrast, periodically viewed these shifts as a violation of the French culinary tradition. To be sure, she had accepted many of these changes, sometimes with enthusiasm, as the partners prepared the final manuscript; however, at various points her conviction that French recipes must be made with French ingredients in order to have a French taste overcame her fear of facing Julia's forceful arguments. One of those points was the interval between the submission of the manuscript and the arrival of the proofs.

There is evidence to indicate that a crisis was building for a year before the proofs arrived. Simca was increasingly unhappy with Julia's behavior. In a spring 1960 letter to Avis DeVoto, with whom she had established a friendship, Simca praised Avis' "tenacious confidence" in the face of Houghton Mifflin's rejection of the cookbook manuscript. Far less worthy in Simca's eyes was "Julia's bitterness, which showed through her letters." Of course, Julia's mood since Knopf's agreement to publish the manuscript was "radiant."[54]

As for the cookbook itself, Simca never understood the importance that Julia placed on proofreading the final manuscript. For her, it was an essentially routine and repetitive task. "JJ [Judith Jones, the editor of *Mastering* at Knopf] has sent the corrected manuscript to the corrector and the latter will judge if this manuscript should be sent to be re-re-re corrected again." She was also disenchanted with the book title, which sounded pretentious in French. She would have preferred something more "personal and original," such as "La Cuisine des 3 gourmandes for American people."[55]

However, the event that precipitated Simca's efforts to revise the proofs was the commentary of her friends from the Cercle des Gourmettes on the publication of selected Trois Gourmandes recipes in *Cuisines et vins de France*. In publishing their recipes in a prestigious French cooking magazine, Julia and Simca expected to establish their credentials with the future buyers of their cookbook in the United States. However, they wrote the recipes in *CVF*, unlike those in their cookbook, in French for the French woman who was cooking overseas, especially in America. The recipes assumed a knowledge of French culinary methods on the reader's part, while explaining how she could find substitutes for French ingredients that were unavailable abroad.[56]

After reading the *CVF* recipes, Simca's friends protested that they would produce a *"goût américain,"* no doubt because they would be made with some American ingredients. The timing of these *"petits réflexions"* and a *"réflexion désagréable"* was critical. Simca relayed news of the Gourmettes' response to Julia just one week before writing the letter proposing the various changes in the proofs of *Mastering*. Meanwhile, based on her friends' comments, which she clearly endorsed, Simca recommended to Julia that they carefully monitor future recipes submitted to *CVF* to assure that there was no hint of *"goût américain."* Only after *CVF* launched an edition for Americans, which was supposedly in the planning stages, would recipes with a *"goût américain"* be acceptable.[57]

It is telling that so late in the project Simca and Julia understood the meaning of *"goût américain"* in quite different ways. Simca's view, which reflected her friends' approach, assumed that the use of American ingredients in a French recipe was bound to produce an American taste. Julia, by contrast, sought to determine through tasting whether the dish with the substitute ingredients actually had an American flavor. During the earlier testing of recipes, it is true that Simca often put aside her underlying conviction to prepare French recipes using American ingredients and serve them to French dinner guests without arousing their suspicions. However, Simca could never dismiss altogether the idea that American ingredients would alter the taste of a French recipe.

The comments of her Gourmettes friends about the recipes in *CVF* emboldened Simca to make a last stand for *"goût français"* in *Mastering*. In doing so, she revealed her frustration over the final manuscript version of recipes that she had supposedly accepted. On various occasions, Simca recounted, she had struggled to change her partner's mind about a recipe, but Julia would not budge. Exhausted in the face of Julia's counterarguments, Simca simply capitulated. No wonder, then, that when the final manuscript arrived after years of Julia's imposing her version of various recipes, Simca made no further effort to defend her point of view.[58]

Following Simca's last stand for *"goût français"* and Julia's defense of the recipes in the proofs as authentically French, Simca apologized for offending Julia (*"Je vous ai choqué"*) by expressing herself in "too vehement" a manner. The problem, Simca acknowledged, was that she was "too quick to react, rotten with defects" and "obstinate"; however, while admitting these character flaws, she refused to retract her claim that several recipes in the proofs yielded a *"goût américain."* Instead, she deferred to Julia's insistence that they get on with the project and so put off changes in the offending recipes for a new edition of *Mastering*.[59]

In the midst of this crisis, Julia made things worse. As the two women were arguing over the proofs of *Mastering*, French generals in Algeria attempted a putsch against the de Gaulle regime in order to block the movement toward Algerian independence. On April 24, 1961, Julia wrote to express her regrets about the emotional turmoil that Simca and others were experiencing; two days later, she commented casually, "I can't remember whether you would be for the Gen. Challe group (the rebels) or de Gaulle!" She added gratuitously, "We are for peace and calm!" Considering that the Fischbachers and the Childs had been close friends for eight years and had discussed current issues in French politics, Julia's remark was insensitive, as was evident in Simca's impatient response: "My political perspective is contrary to that of the Algerian rebels. I have been a Gaullist for twenty-one years." Julia never apologized, but agreed to a "moratorium on politics."[60]

The heated rhetoric subsided quickly, as time constraints drove the partners to complete their review of the proofs. Julia, in particular, had a strong incentive to heal the breech. With great insight, she wrote Avis DeVoto to express her concern that Simca and Jean "are going to trot around Paris" bad-mouthing the new book as "full of errors . . . I have had nothing at all to do with it; it's American taste." Such behavior on Simca's part would expose Julia and the book to criticism in America for not being authoritative and authentically French. That fear no doubt pushed her toward some compromises.[61]

As for Simca, she realized the impossibility of making substantial changes at the proof stage and focused on smaller revisions of great importance to her and her family. Among them was the prominent reference in the introductory section of the book to *soufflé au Grand Marnier* as a kind of classic French dish. With this recipe, Julia intended to appeal to her American audience, for whom the *soufflé* was a favorite in a collection of otherwise unfamiliar dishes. As owners of the Benedictine liqueur business, however, Simca's family regarded the reference to Grand Marnier so early in the book as free advertising for a competitor of the family enterprise. If the authors did not delete that reference, Simca was certain that the Benedictine salesmen would withdraw their pledge to promote the new cookbook. Even worse, Simca's mother would condemn (*"réprobation absolue"*) her for disloyalty to the family.[62]

To address this issue, Julia agreed to substitute in the introduction *"soufflé à la liqueur"* for *"soufflé au Grand Marnier,"* while, in the dessert section, the authors listed the recipe as *"soufflé à l'orange"* with two suggested versions: one using Grand Marnier, the other with Cointreau. So long as they buried these references in the dessert chapter, where neither her mother nor the Benedictine salesmen would notice them, Simca had no objection to naming the two liqueurs. As she remarked to Julia, "My intransigence goes only so far!" And Julia was satisfied that Americans would have a recipe for one of the few French dishes they knew.

The subject of wine also generated controversy. As early as 1954, Julia wrote Simca to report on the vast improvement in California wines, but she agreed that in the cookbook they would recommend only French wines by name. Two years later, however, Julia suggested that, wherever a "great wine is not called for," they should name both the French choice and a California equivalent, since French wines were often unavailable in smaller American cities. In the face of Simca's protests, no doubt driven by her eagerness to avoid any hint of *"goût américain,"* Julia agreed to mention only French wines by name.[63]

Even as she was criticizing Simca and the French, Julia praised both her partner's role in the project and certain character traits of the French. Of Simca's contribution, Julia said, "without her, this book would be nothing at all, as she has had the major suggestions for recipes, and the real French touch, and she works like a Trojan." Despite the imperious tone of her April 28, 1961, letter to Simca, Julia also understood that Simca's criticism of the final proofs reflected not only substantive issues but her personal situation. "Simca does too much, gets tired, is not in awfully good health, and is instinctive anyway." In light of their decade-long friendship, Julia could forget the frustrations of the moment. Indeed, she was determined that "there shall not be a break between us, as I am far too fond of the old goat, but it will take some delicate maneuvering to try and make her realize some of the truths of publishing." As for the French, they were "fun, gay, [and] affectionate."[64]

However, they were also "dogmatic." Indeed, the crisis over the proofs brought to the surface a long-standing emotional issue for Julia Child. Simca's reaction to the recipes in the proofs was yet another example, Julia believed, of the "tremendous dogmatism" that characterized her partner and many of her compatriots. The term seemed to account for the way Frenchmen adhered too strictly to techniques and recipes in the culinary repertoire. Eight years earlier, Julia had objected to the fact that "the real ways of doing things" had become "sacred cows." Particularly irritating to her was an incident involving Curnonski, who insisted that very few cooks were capable of making "white butter sauce" (*beurre blanc*) because they could only properly prepare it with "white shallots from

Lorraine and over a wood fire." She added, "but that is so damned typical . . . making a damned mystery out of perfectly simple things just to puff themselves up." Accordingly, she denounced Curnonski as a "dogmatic meatball."[65]

At its root, Julia believed, dogmatism was a strategy to reinforce the dominance of French male authorities, most notably chefs and writers. And even though they were amateurs, members of male gastronomical societies played an important role in turning ideas and practices into "sacred cows." Under these circumstances, the authorities refused to recognize either women or foreigners for their contribution to French cooking. However, Julia felt helpless to address these grievances, so she confined her protest to a letter: "being a foreigner I don't know anything anyway." In fact, she claimed to "know more than they do . . . which is so often the case with a foreigner. I suppose, cooking being a French preserve, they become dogmatic."[66]

As Julia presciently recognized, the conflict with Simca was more than a personal matter. Cultural differences that affected not only the culinary but also the political sphere shaped their confrontation. As other world powers increasingly eclipsed France, the French were becoming more sensitive to the possible erosion of their cultural traditions, including especially their language and cuisine. (In this regard, Julia's conflating the inflexibility of Simca and de Gaulle makes sense.) Working in such an environment, Simca must have hesitated to substitute American ingredients for such basic and critical items as cream and butter. And she must have wondered about the effect on *"goût français"* of reducing the French bourgeois dinner from six to three courses. Of course, Simca hurt her own cause by failing to clarify until the very last minute that she and her friends were attempting to protect the integrity of French cuisine. Had Simca raised the issues in a more timely and articulate fashion, she could have made a better case for resisting the inclusion of American ingredients in *Mastering*'s recipes.

Julia and Simca's partnership was an important experiment in bridging the gap between the French approach to cooking and the realities of supermarket foodways. With such an arrangement, the partners could give adequate attention to the two most important components in devising a successful French cookbook for Americans: knowledge of the recipes and cooking processes in the French culinary repertoire, and an understanding of the upper-middle-class, American home cook's lifestyle and approach to foodways. It was an arrangement, indeed, that Louis Diat and Helen Ridley had anticipated with much less fanfare but similar results a decade before Julia and Simca. Even so, the pairing of French and American nationals would only work if the partners were willing to persevere to assure that the recipes included in the cookbook achieved French taste through methods and ingredients that were accessible to the American cook. While the partnership created a setting for the partners to consider both components of a successful cookbook, it provided no guarantee that they would bridge the cultural gap.

The partnership between Julia and Simca reflected both the collaborative impulses of the postwar Atlantic community and the intensifying cultural conflict between French and American participants engaged in these projects. Overall, the Child-Beck-Bertholle cookbook ranks with other successful Franco-American collaborations in the postwar period and was one of several (for example, academic exchanges) that spread French ways to America. Both the character of the partners and the times in which they lived contributed to the success of these partnerships. Common languages and privileged backgrounds smoothed the path to collaboration for the cookbook authors, as did the favorable diplomatic climate. After all, Julia came to Paris as the wife of a USIS official and met Simca through the auspices of a Marshall Plan official.

Even so, the collaboration revealed areas of conflict that were difficult to negotiate. While Julia expressed her irritation with what she regarded as Simca's dogmatic approach to French cuisine, Simca must have found Julia's pragmatism worrisome. The stubbornness on both sides was reminiscent of diplomatic conflicts between the French and American governments over the NATO alliance. All the same, it is remarkable that the partnership, which required marathon cooking sessions and a voluminous correspondence at periodic intervals, should have persisted for ten years and then continued over another seven years, while the partners completed the second volume of their cookbook.

In assessing the impact of *Mastering the Art of French Cooking*, it is important to note the substantial sales of the book in the first two years, well beyond expectations for a French cookbook; equally interesting, however, was the increase in sales after Julia's appearance as "The French Chef" beginning in 1963 and on the *Time* magazine cover in 1966. Clearly, her dynamic personality was as important a factor in selling cookbooks as the quality of the product itself. That said, the opportunity to launch her cooking show grew out of the reputation she had established as an authority in culinary matters based on her role as coauthor of *Mastering*. The book, the television programs, and the media attention helped to awaken the upper-middle-class public to the joys of French cooking, while providing accessible instructions for cooking basic French dishes.

As Julia recognized, however, she and Simca succeeded, in part, because of the foundation laid by their predecessors. Asked by Narcisse Chamberlain to write a blurb for a new edition of her parents' wartime classic, *Clementine in the Kitchen* (1943), Julia explained that "French cooking for Americans was never the same after Clementine came into our kitchens over 40 years ago . . . She . . . taught us that we, too, could turn out a splendid home-style French meal in our very own American kitchens." In fact, Julia meant only half of what she said. Her earlier correspondence credited the Chamberlains with generating great enthusiasm for French culture and cuisine, while serving up recipes that were insufficiently instructive for novice home cooks. In both of those respects, Julia and Simca were beneficiaries. Julia learned from studying the Chamberlains' recipes how to do better, while she and Simca inherited members of the Chamberlains' audience who were still searching in 1961 for French recipes directed to the inexperienced home cook. In this way, the two authors built on the work of past pioneers to expand an already substantial French culinary empire in America.[67]

In so doing, they brought about a major shift in the orientation of the gourmet movement. Before *Mastering the Art of French Cooking*, a growing number of Americans read about the pleasures of the table in *Gourmet* and learned to enjoy French meals in restaurants at home and abroad. Organizing this restaurant activity was largely a task for men. With the publication of Julia and Simca's book, however, gourmet dining became increasingly a home-based activity featuring the production, as much as the consumption, of gourmet food. Moreover, most of the leaders and followers of this burgeoning sector of the movement were women.

Meanwhile, as women prepared French meals at home, the separation between the kitchen and the dining room narrowed. The cook, in fact, both presided over the kitchen and dined with her guests, thus bringing together consumers and the producer. That fact, as well as the lower cost of French dinners at home in comparison to restaurant meals, increased their accessibility to the upper-middle class and somewhat diminished their social cachet. Even so, as Harvey Levenstein has suggested, the gourmet movement was one factor in disrupting the relatively uniform diet of Americans across social classes from the Depression to 1960. From that point on, French meals provided an important social marker for members of the upper-middle class, who sought to distinguish themselves from the old middle class; meanwhile, the gap between the upper and upper-middle classes in America narrowed.[68]

The publication of Betty Friedan's *The Feminine Mystique* eight days after the launching of Julia's *French Chef* on WGBH-TV (February 1963) appeared to create a dilemma for these same home cooks, who were also the audience for *The Feminine Mystique*. Friedan, after all, was urging American women to find meaningful work mostly outside of the home, while Julia proposed creative work in the kitchen. At a deeper level, however, both women, who were Smith College graduates, advocated a more challenging life for women and men. By eliminating assigned sex roles so that members of either sex could seek work that engaged their passion and creativity, whether in the kitchen or in professions outside the home, they hoped to improve the lives of both men and women.[69]

Conclusion

The gourmet movement has had a substantial influence on the foodways of the growing professional and managerial classes in America. The dining societies and *Gourmet* raised the consciousness of these classes to the prospect of enjoying various ethnic cuisines, artisanal food and wine, the restaurants and shops where these products were available, and the home kitchens where gourmets could prepare their own dinners. Through its activities and publications, the movement also established a presence for gourmet dining that energized Julia Child, whose cooking lessons, in turn, attracted a much larger, yet still class-based, audience.

From the outset, however, the leaders of the gourmet dining movement were unclear about their goals. Early gourmet leaders and authors, including Earle MacAusland and André Simon, aspired to reach the masses as well as the classes by offering more traditional recipes for everyday meals to replace those published by the women's magazines. These leaders advocated substituting fresh produce for canned goods and taking advantage of the full range of edibles to provide a more varied diet. They also encouraged their audience to spend more time in the kitchen making basic stews and soups, and more time at the table enjoying them. In addition, gourmet leaders advocated the use of table wines for cooking and as beverages. In this way, they sought to provide a reasonably priced alternative to the foodways of mainstream Americans, who relied increasingly on the food establishment in preparing their meals.

However, Simon and MacAusland also advocated the planning, execution, and recording of elegant dinners prepared in restaurants and clubs, which were designed by gourmet societies to instruct diners on the principles of gastronomy. Cost and other factors limited attendance at the dinners and the number of subscribers to *Gourmet* to the relatively affluent. During the twenty-five-year period following repeal, the message was clear. Enjoying an elaborate meal, rather than the transformation of the everyday foodways of the American people, was the overwhelming priority of gourmet diners and leaders. Even Julia Child and Simone Beck addressed the chef hostess who "on occasion" could put aside time and money to make a special dinner, although the processes they taught were useful for everyday meals. It is important, however, to consider the way these two different approaches to gourmet dining have played out over the last half century.[1]

The most impressive activity in the realm of gourmet dining since 1961 has been the opening of a series of sophisticated restaurants, mostly in large American cities, by highly trained and talented professional chefs. As David Kamp has pointed out, many Americans would now find it difficult to even imagine "a world without celebrity chefs." Inspiration for this movement came from post–World War II New York, where Henri Soulé's Pavillon spawned a number of fine French restaurants in the 1950s. Following on the heels of Soulé and company, a new generation of chefs created restaurants of a different kind beginning in the late 1960s.[2]

Particularly notable was Alice Waters' launching of an American version of nouvelle cuisine at Chez Panisse, her restaurant in Berkeley, California. In important ways, James Beard laid the groundwork for Waters through his own early cookbooks, especially *The Fireside Cookbook* (1949), and his work with Restaurant Associates in New York. There he contributed to making "The Four Seasons" into a self-consciously American restaurant that used American ingredients and preparations. He then promoted this "American" approach in *James Beard's American Cookery* (1972).[3]

As a product of the 1960s' counterculture, Waters regarded dining as both an outgrowth of community solidarity and an opportunity to forge that solidarity by joining with friends in a leisurely fashion to share a meal and enjoy each other's company. Both Julia Child and Alice Waters admired French cooking, but Waters rejected *haute cuisine*, heavy sauces, the formal restaurant environment, and Julia's idea of enabling housewives to cook French dishes from supermarket ingredients. Waters preferred, instead, the French country cooking she discovered in Elizabeth David's cookbook by that name. Following David and the counterculture, she made arrangements with local farmers to supply her restaurant with fresh produce. Using local ingredients and offering California wines to her customers, she pioneered a California cuisine that provided a model for many other restaurateurs who wished to explore the possibilities of regional cooking in other parts of the country.[4]

Building on the work of Beard and Waters, a number of restaurateurs, most notably Larry Forgione, created a new American cuisine in the 1980s. At the River Café and An American Place, both in New York, Forgione served traditional American dishes such as spoon-bread griddlecakes, but with a new twist. The garnish in this case was a duck sausage. Regardless of the dish, Forgione insisted on fresh ingredients, including, for example, buffalo raised by a farmer in northern Michigan. Other chefs and restaurateurs narrowed the focus from America to a region, as Alice Waters had done, and created a southwestern, a Pacific Northwest, and a New World cuisine based in Florida that emphasized Caribbean ingredients.[5]

While restaurants featuring French and American cuisine dominated the upscale restaurant scene, the proliferation of ethnic restaurants, many of them modest, broadened dining options for urban Americans. Already in the 1960s, Chinese, Indian, Italian, and Japanese restaurants, as well as sushi bars, appeared with increasing regularity. After 1970, Mexican, Cuban, Thai, and Vietnamese restaurants exposed Americans to an even greater diversity of ingredients and flavors and also stimulated an interest in fusion cuisine.[6]

Almost as spectacular as the restaurant scene was the parallel proliferation of cookbooks that attempted to foster an interest in cooking the ethnic cuisines now available in restaurants. Particularly notable in launching this trend were four cookbooks that appeared in the early 1970s: Diane Kennedy, *The Cuisines of Mexico* (1972); Marcella Hazan, *The Classic Italian Cook Book* (1973); Wonona W. and Irving B. Chang, *The Northern Chinese Cookbook* (1974); and Madhur Jaffrey, *An Invitation to Indian Cooking* (1975). Inspired by Julia Child, their authors sought to teach home cooks, without access to the full array of indigenous ingredients, how to make authentic dishes from heretofore unfamiliar cuisines. In the process, the new cookbooks diverted some home cooks from their focus on French cooking. Once launched, the idea of using a cookbook to explore distant and exotic cuisines became increasingly popular, as evident in the deluge of such books, written by these authors and others over the last thirty years. While many home cooks must have read these manuals, it is quite likely that they prepared the recipes less frequently.[7]

Meanwhile, greater coverage of food news in periodicals, in restaurant guides, and on the Food Channel after 1993 has dramatically increased the visibility of various culinary enterprises. Based on the success of *Gourmet*, new periodicals such as *Bon Appetit, Food and Wine, Saveur,* and *Cook's Magazine* have established themselves as competitors for the burgeoning audience of gourmet diners.[8]

Of particular interest is the earliest of these publications. Launched in November of 1956, *Bon Appetit: A Magazine of Good Taste* demonstrated the success of *Gourmet* while clarifying its class-specific appeal. At the outset, mostly midwestern liquor dealers, subsidized by advertisers of alcoholic beverages, distributed the bimonthly periodical free of charge. Echoing *Gourmet*'s title with a simple French phrase, as well as Julia's signature greeting on *The French Chef*, and practically duplicating the subtitle, *Bon Appetit* featured cover photographs of seasonal food, paired with wine, and travelogues presenting adventurous dining episodes in distant lands. However, contrary to *Gourmet*, the magazine advocated "informal" fare served at home by cooks who exploited time-saving methods, as recommended in an article entitled "The Epicure and the Can Opener." Readers unable to afford *Gourmet* or its recipes could still pursue the good life through simpler recipes and learning how to drink wine. During its first five years, *Bon Appetit* thus illustrated Veblen's claim that those lower in the social order would imitate the leisure class—in this case by finding more affordable and efficient ways to consume exotic dishes in a somewhat less conspicuous manner.[9]

More surprising were developments in the realm of television. Of course, Julia Child's *The French Chef* and Graham Kerr's *The Galloping Gourmet* had already shown that a knowledgeable cook could educate large audiences by presenting gourmet cooking lessons in an appealing manner. Even so, it was difficult to imagine that Americans would support a channel broadcasting only food programs. To reach a larger audience, the Food Channel shifted the orientation of the programs from cooking as education to cooking as entertainment. This formula helps to explain the popularity of *Iron Chef*, a Japanese program that made cooking into a competition between two chefs, who were assigned to make dishes from a single ingredient in a limited time. Judges then evaluated the quality of the dishes.[10]

In short, since the publication of *Mastering the Art of French Cooking*, the American culinary scene has changed dramatically with the emergence of a vibrant restaurant scene, the publication of a variety of ethnic cookbooks accessible to home cooks, the proliferation of gourmet magazines, and the popularization of gourmet cooking shows on television. Taken together, these changes, much like the gourmet movement from which they sprang, delivered an implicit and sometimes explicit challenge to the food establishment by asserting the importance of fresh ingredients, as well as small-scale, labor-intensive kitchen work in the preparation of high-quality meals.

However, as David Kamp has argued, the chefs, restaurants, cookbooks, and the new media that comprise this culinary scene minister primarily to the appetites of affluent Americans without affecting significantly mainstream foodways. Privileged Americans are eating better, while most families are more vulnerable than ever to the strategies of the food establishment. That is particularly the case in single-parent households and families with two working spouses, where there is little time to prepare and eat nourishing dinners. In these families, gobbling fast food, deli takeout, or microwaved food on the run has become a daily reality. Such practices, in turn, help to account for the prevalence of eating disorders, obesity, and the obsession with dieting.[11]

Despite the opposition, in principle, of the now seventy-five-year-old gourmet movement to nutritionism, the food establishment is just as dominant a force in shaping current American foodways as it has been for the past century. Particularly notable has been its success in reorienting food products to suit the needs of Americans who eat in a hurry. The variety of frozen dinners from pizza to Lean Cuisine that appeal to a wide range of customers and even gesture, in some instances, toward gourmet dining reflect the inventiveness of these processors. Equally important has been the proliferation of snack foods and soft drinks that rely on sugar or salt to please their consumers' palates. And, of course, the fast food industry has excelled at satisfying the appetites of Americans from all walks of life.

The economic dominance of the food establishment is not its only source of power, however. Equally significant is the fact that even its many opponents analyze dietary issues in terms borrowed from nutritionism. As Michael Pollan has shown, Americans continue to calculate the micronutrients they consume as a measure of good health despite recent research that questions the benefits of micronutrients, especially when consumed as additives. Meanwhile, on the production side of the equation, food engineers continue to design more food products based on these same nutritional principles.[12]

Pollan's critique of nutritionism brings the discussion full circle to the early gourmet leaders' attack on the food establishment. Like his predecessors, Pollan has urged readers to reject many processed foods and return to traditional diets. And, among those diets, he has strongly endorsed French cuisine as a model, in part because it has a long track record of success. As he points out, however, that success may be based on a number of factors in addition to the nutrients contained in French dishes and wines. Among them are the leisurely pace of dining, the focus on the taste of food, and the enjoyment of human interactions at the table, all of which have been part of the larger French culinary culture. These practices, he suggests, may be more responsible for the relative immunity of French diners from problems associated with consuming large quantities of fat than the special nutrients found in red wine.[13]

Pollan's analysis also suggests that American foodways suffer from the impact of historical factors that preceded the rise of the food establishment. As he points out, France, in contrast to the United States, developed a national cuisine about two hundred years ago that improved both the health and welfare of the French people. It is pertinent, then, to note that the central themes of American history, including the overlapping traditions of individualism, Puritanism, the work ethic, and mobility, as well as ethnic diversity, served to fragment the society and block the creation of a national cuisine in the United States. Those living in diverse ethnic enclaves maintained inherited food traditions for a generation, or until they departed from their communities. Puritanism and the work ethic, which especially shaped the mind-set and behavior of old-stock, middle-class Americans, weakened the belief that food was anything more than a necessary fuel for the body; it was thus not a topic worth talking about. Furthermore, individualism discouraged the recognition of customs, traditions, and institutions, such as a national cuisine, that might shape the individual's choice of dietary options.

In this environment, cookbooks instructed middle-class Americans about appropriate dishes to serve on particular occasions and the best ways to prepare them. However, it was virtually impossible to have a conversation, written or oral, about the principles that normally underlie the creation of a national cuisine, such as the significance of food for individuals and groups or its role in promoting health, sensual enjoyment, and social interactions. As Sidney Mintz has argued, a cuisine is more than a "set of recipes" or "a series of particular foods." It "requires a population that eats that cuisine with sufficient frequency to consider themselves experts on it." Such a cuisine "has common social roots; it is the food of a community." In that sense, all members of a society share in creating, enjoying, and conversing about a cuisine as it develops gradually over time. However, unless the community assumes that food has a value beyond its function as fuel, a conversation about its significance would seem pointless.[14]

Given the grand themes of American history, it would have been difficult for citizens to agree on the underlying principles of a national cuisine. In its absence, the food establishment provided a powerful and convenient substitute that paid homage as well to the country's utilitarian notions. At the same time, the failure to create a national cuisine facilitated the work of privileged Americans in selectively appropriating French culinary ideas and practices to make their dinners more interesting and enjoyable. As Mintz points out, it is possible for a society, which has no cuisine of its own, to borrow an *haute cuisine* from another country. Many affluent and well-born Americans from Jefferson to the robber barons, who appropriated French cuisine, demonstrated the truth of his assertion. Clearly, twentieth-century gourmets took their cues from these precursors.[15]

The appeal of connoisseurship in the "land of equality," where class distinctions are not always easy to recognize, accounts in considerable measure for the success of the gourmet dining movement. At a gourmet dining function featuring *haute cuisine*, members could be sure that they were accruing cultural capital that would distinguish them from their mainstream compatriots. Accordingly, it made sense for the leaders of the gourmet dining movement, who wished to attract new members, to hold out in subtle ways the prospect of a higher place in the social order as a reward for participating in the movement. Such a prospect helped Simon lure some of his followers, who based their social activities in fine restaurants and exclusive men's clubs that served elaborate meals and high-priced wines. In this way, gourmet dining often resembled the kind of conspicuous consumption that Veblen described in *The Theory of the Leisure Class*.

The current restaurant scene appears to confirm Veblen's theory. It offers an opportunity for diners to engage in a quest to discover exotic flavors introduced by skilled chefs and winemakers, who turn out new dishes and wines at a pace that resembles the production of fashion designers in the clothing industry. Among other things, this productivity, which yields a growing repertoire of interesting dishes and wines from around the world, at once satisfies the senses and offers an opportunity for consumers to demonstrate a kind of connoisseurship that can be translated into social advancement. As Leslie Brennan argues, in recent years, food is undeniably "chic."[16]

However, by exploiting the artistry of the French chef to satisfy the palates of relatively few affluent customers, the gourmet movement has exacerbated a divide in American society that will be difficult to bridge. Leaders of the movement have routinely organized large, splashy events in order to attract the attention of the press and better educate affluent outsiders who are potential members. This strategy has brought many of these individuals into the fold but furthered the impression that only elegant dinners with complicated menus are appropriate for gourmet diners. In creating this impression, gourmet leaders have given little thought to their earlier claims that the movement should challenge the food establishment by offering mainstream Americans a healthier and tastier alternative. In the midst of the current food crisis in America, this preference for grandiose dinners seems hard to justify.

Despite these worrisome trends, it is also important to pay attention to some hopeful ventures, which, if properly nurtured, could be the harbingers of change. As Warren Belasco has shown, the counterculture and its allies in the late 1960s proposed a countercuisine that emphasized the consumption of homegrown produce as a healthy and tasty alternative to the products of the beef and food processing industries. Their support in 1977 for the efforts of the Senate Select Committee on Nutrition and Human Needs to reduce the meat and dairy component in dietary guidelines narrowly failed when last-minute lobbying by representatives of the industry deep-sixed the original guidelines.[17]

Continuing their efforts in a different way, the recent proponents of organic farming have scored some important victories against the food establishment. To supply farmers' markets, many local farmers now grow high-quality salad greens, peppers, and heirloom tomatoes. At the same time, the food establishment, ever mindful of the efficiencies of scale, has co-opted the marketing and sale of organic foods by establishing supermarket chains such as Whole Foods. Meanwhile, Alice Waters has tried valiantly to create a citizenry committed to a new food order through her Edible Schoolyard program in the public schools.[18]

On a somewhat different note, Josee Johnson and Shyon Baumann showcase the broad-minded approach of many gourmets, who reject the idea that only French cuisine is worthy of admiration. These new activists are eager to try exotic meats and produce, once scorned as "uncivilized," from all corners of the globe. While this trend initially promised to diminish the "snob" factor surrounding other cuisines, the high costs of hunting, shipping, and producing the global cuisine make it affordable only to relatively wealthy diners. In this way, the snob factor returns through the back door.[19]

One clear success story in broadening membership in the gourmet movement has been the admission of women to many gourmet societies. When gourmet leaders launched the movement in 1934, the gender exclusivity they preferred had governed the production of food since chefs ran the kitchens of the French monarchy, while women took charge of home cooking. Because gourmet societies in France, such as the Club des Cents, were open only to men, women founded Le Cercle des Gourmettes so that they too could enjoy fine cuisine on a separate, if not equal, basis. Not surprisingly, Americans institutionalized these practices in most of their own gourmet dining societies. However, the consequences of this division were greater in the United States than in France, where home cooks used recipe books written by the great chefs, while their American counterparts relied primarily on the food articles in women's magazines. Moreover, beginning in 1900, the regional cuisine movement in France gave recognition to home cooks who used their skills to cook for the public. By contrast, it was 1961 before Julia Child introduced French recipes that were accessible to American home cooks. In so doing, she not only brought American women into the production end of gourmet activity but also appealed to men who found this kind of challenge worthy of their time and efforts. In recent years, the barriers to women chefs in restaurants have begun to recede, and a number of gourmet societies now routinely admit women.

Despite these important successes, the task of rescuing America from the excesses of fast food and lavish dinners will not be a simple one. It is clear, however, that progress will only be possible if the food establishment and the gourmet dining movement play more socially constructive roles in the future. In its early days, the food establishment contributed to the welfare of Americans by supplying cheap food, while remedying problems of sanitation in the meatpacking industry and elsewhere. However, in the last half century these same food processors have become the single greatest threat to the health of the American people. So serious is this problem that it will surely require strong government regulation as one remedy. Over time, perhaps, food processors will be able to return to their original mission of supplying safe food at low prices.

In a similar fashion, gourmet leaders might consider returning to the vision of André Simon and Earle MacAusland that preceded their exclusive promotion of elegant and often extravagant dinners. Their claim that a simple peasant dinner could meet the standards of gourmet dining as well as or better than a sumptuous meal with a proliferation of dishes, sauces, and wines promised a more inclusive approach to dining. Using such a guideline for planning gourmet dinners would benefit rich and poor alike and thus bridge the gap between social classes in a way that seems appropriate to a democratic society. In addition, it would provide a welcome update to Brillat-Savarin's idea that a gourmet dinner should become the occasion for including diners from diverse backgrounds who would bond in the course of enjoying fine food and leisurely conversation.

To address the current problems of American foodways, the time is thus ripe for the leaders of the gourmet movement to take up the founders' cause and use their knowledge to propose dishes, cooking processes, and settings for dinners that are affordable, appealing to the palate, and conducive to greater social conviviality. They might take as their mission the restoration of appetite to eating, flavor to food, and pleasure to the dining experience not just for their members, but for all Americans.[20]

To accomplish this task, they would have to address the great confusion about dietary standards in virtually every segment of American society. This confusion has been sewn in part by the food establishment without significant opposition from members of dining societies. One response to this crisis is to launch a dialogue about the creation of an American cuisine. For starters, such a conversation would need to consider the kind of government regulation of the food industry that would alleviate the pollution of the land and of the digestive tracts of American citizens and focus that industry on producing cheaper, tastier, and healthier food.

Meanwhile, dining societies and gourmet magazines might consciously turn their energies to the creation of a healthy, appetizing dining culture in the United States. They could do so by modeling simpler meals based on fresh ingredients and modest wines that would be more accessible to middle-class Americans. They might also search for a more diverse membership or subscriber list and give more attention to the meal as a means to the end of social conviviality. These would be small steps that could, over time, contribute to changing the current dining scene.

In the end, the creation of a national cuisine would diminish the confusion that characterizes our culinary situation at present and increase the likelihood of finding a consensus that reflects the best judgments of the citizenry and food experts about the role of food in American society. Well-respected cooks, cookbook and food writers, grocers, nutritionists, and farmers could use the media to present their version of a national cuisine. A conversation about this subject would aim to reach a consensus about underlying principles, while socializing Americans to the idea that fine dining is beneficial far beyond its role in fueling the body for everyday purposes. The creation of such a cuisine would also address the limitations of nutritionism along with schemes for rapid weight reduction. Finally, once the underlying assumptions of fine dining have been addressed, experts might turn to helping citizens select and prepare recipes that would further the original goals of the gourmet dining movement.

Introduction

1. Clementine Paddleford wrote "All America Is Going Gourmet!" *Los Angeles Times*, Oct. 5, 1958, p. TW30; June 17, 1956, p. C9.

2. Grimod de la Reynière called his annual the *Almanach des Gourmands*; Brillat-Savarin, *The Physiology of Taste or Meditations on Transcendental Gastronomy*, trans. M. F. K. Fisher (New York: Alfred A. Knopf, 1972). See also "Author's Questionnaire Biography," Julia Child papers (JCP), Schlesinger Library (SL). Roy Brady, editor of *Wine World*, wrote in 1972 that "gourmet" "has been over-used, abused and debased until it is virtually useless." *The Brady Book* (Santa Rosa, CA: Nomis Press, 2003), p. xliii. On the meaning of "gourmet" and "gourmand," see *Trésor de la langue française: Dictionnaire de la langue du XIXième et XXième siècle (1789–1960)* (Paris: Éditions du Centre National de la Recherche Scientifique, 1981). On gastronomy, see Alain Drouard, "Chefs, Gourmets and Gourmandes: French Cuisine in the 19th and 20th Centuries," in *Food: The History of Taste*, ed. Paul Freedman (Berkeley and Los Angeles: University of California Press, 2007), p. 264.

3. Child, *Delicate Feasting* (New York: Harper and Brothers, 1890), pp. 78, 83; Griswold, *The Gourmet* (New York: Dutton, 1933), pp. 13–14. The 2001 edition of *Larousse Gastronomique* identifies increasing levels of connoisseurship from gourmand to friend (epicure), gourmet, and gastronomer; see p. 570.

4. Selmer Fougner, *Gourmet Dinners: A Book of Gastronomic Adventure, with the Menus of Great Meals and the Original Recipes of the Chefs Who Made Them So* (New York: M. Barrows, 1941); André Simon, *The Art of Good Living* (London: Constable, 1929), p. 17. Brillat-Savarin recommended satisfying the sense of taste "at least once every day." *The Physiology of Taste*, pp. 42–43. On the effects of turning "gourmet" into an adjective, see Alan Davidson, *The Oxford Companion to Food* (Oxford: Oxford University Press, 1999), p. 347.

5. See Bourdieu, *Distinction: A Social Critique of the Judgement of Taste*, trans. Richard Nice (Cambridge, MA: Harvard University Press, 1984), pp. 79, 177, 190.

6. *The Theory of the Leisure Class* (New York: Penguin Books, 1994 [1899]), pp. 69–73, 84; T. J. Jackson Lears, *No Place of Grace: Antimodernism and the Transformation of American Culture, 1880–1920* (New York: Pantheon Books, 1981); Kathy Peiss, *Cheap Amusements:*

Working Women and Leisure in Turn-of-the-Century New York (Philadelphia: Temple University Press, 1986).

7. Veblen could have had a field day considering "conspicuous waste" in the multicourse meals of the Gilded Age. Veblen, *The Theory of the Leisure Class*, pp. 69–73. On Veblen's sex life, see John P. Diggins, *The Bard of Savagery: Thorstein Veblen and Modern Social Theory* (New York: Seabury Press, 1978), p. 169.

8. Priscilla Parkhurst Ferguson, *Accounting for Taste: The Triumph of French Cuisine* (Chicago: University of Chicago Press, 2004), p, 153.

9. Brillat-Savarin, *The Physiology of Taste*, pp. 182–85; Rebecca Spang, *The Invention of the Restaurant: Paris and Modern Gastronomic Culture* (Cambridge, MA: Harvard University Press, 2000); Amy B. Trubek, *Haute Cuisine: How the French Invented the Culinary Profession* (Philadelphia: University of Pennsylvania Press, 2000); Jean-Robert Pitte, *French Gastronomy: The History and Geography of a Passion* (New York: Columbia University Press, 2002 [1991]); Joan DeJean, *The Essence of Style: How the French Invented High Fashion, Fine Food, Chic Cafés, Style, Sophistication, and Glamour* (New York: Free Press, 2005), pp. 112–13, 142–43.

10. Ferguson, *Accounting for Taste*, pp. 5, 33–34; Trubec, *Haute Cuisine*, pp. 42–43. Located in a few big cities, French restaurants in America were invisible to most Americans, who, in any case, rarely discussed even their own foodways.

11. Ferguson, *Accounting for Taste*, pp. 93, 154.

12. Elliott Shore, "Dining Out: The Development of the Restaurant," in *Food: The History of Taste*, ed. Paul Freedman, p. 318. Charles Ranhofer, Delmonico's head chef, wrote *The Epicurean: A Complete Treatise of Analytical and Practical Studies on the Culinary Art* (New York: C. Ranhofer, 1893) for private chefs hired to prepare French dishes.

13. Marcella Hazen, "No Chefs in My Kitchen." Op-ed, *New York Times*, Nov. 29, 2001, p. A21.

14. Pitte, *French Gastronomy*, pp. 51, 56.

15. Sidney Mintz, *Tasting Food, Tasting Freedom* (Boston: Beacon Press, 1996), p. 10; Jane and Michael Stern, *American Gourmet: Classic Recipes, Deluxe Delights, Flamboyant Favorites, and Swank "Company" Food from the '50s and '60s* (New York: HarperCollins, 1991), pp. 1–2.

16. David Kamp, *The United States of Arugula: How We Became a Gourmet Nation* (New York: Broadway Books, 2006), pp. 359–60.

Chapter 1 · Food Fights in Twentieth-Century America

1. On nutritionism, see Michael Pollan, *In Defense of Food: An Eater's Manifesto* (New York: Penguin Press, 2008), pp. 27–32.

2. Malcolm Cowley, *Exile's Return: A Literary Odyssey of the 1920s* (New York: Viking Press, 1934), pp. 60–61; and T. J. Jackson Lears, *No Place of Grace: Antimodernism and the Transformation of American Culture, 1880–1920* (New York: Pantheon Books, 1981).

3. All Fisher citations are from *The Art of Eating* compiled by Clifton Fadiman (New York: Macmillan, 1990 [1954]). *Serve It Forth* (1937), pp. 93–94; Jean Anthelme Brillat-Savarin, *The Physiology of Taste or Meditations on Transcendental Gastronomy*, trans.

Charles Monselet (New York: Horace Liveright, 1926), pp. xiii–xiv. A cult of Brillat-Savarin arose in mid-1920s Paris, much influenced by the gastronomer Curnonsky. See Pierre Varillon, "Grimod de La Reynière et La Physiologie du goût," *Revue des deux mondes*, June 1, 1955, pp. 503–10.

4. On Brillat-Savarin's life, see Giles MacDonogh, *Brillat-Savarin: The Judge and His Stomach* (Chicago: Ivan R. Dee, 1992), pp. 1–5, 74–75, 161–63, 207–10.

5. Brillat-Savarin, *The Physiology of Taste or Meditations on Transcendental Gastronomy*, trans. M. F. K. Fisher (New York: Alfred A. Knopf, 1972), pp. 20, 53.

6. Ibid., pp. 148–49, 180, 42. This theological justification for gourmandism was merely a restatement of Epicurus's position, which Brillat-Savarin later cited.

7. Ibid., pp. 51, 147–49.

8. Ibid., pp. 184–85, 182–83, 4, 152–53.

9. Ibid., p. 32.

10. Ibid., pp. 142–43, 90, 71, 86.

11. Ibid., pp. 77, 317.

12. Ibid., pp. 393, 160–63, 53.

13. Despite refusing to attend its meetings, Saintsbury was elected president in perpetuity of the Saintsbury Club. André Simon, *By Request: An Autobiography* (London: Wine and Food Society, 1957), pp. 80–84. A printed version of Oldmeadow's talk, entitled "The Saintsbury Succession," pp. 1–4, may be found in the Julian Street papers, Princeton University Archives (PUA). Among Saintsbury's American disciples, see Richardson Wright, *The Bed-Book of Eating and Drinking* (New York: J. B. Lippincott, 1943), p. 157; Street to Dexter, Oct. 21, 1933, Street papers, PUA. At its April 20, 1944, meeting, Oldmeadow remarked that "if there had been no Saintsbury—I mean no Wine-Saintsbury— we should have to invent one as a necessity of literature." Thomas Pinney has edited, annotated, and introduced a new edition of *Notes on a Cellar Book* (Berkeley and Los Angeles: University of California Press, 2008).

14. Edmund Wilson, "George Saintsbury: Gourmet and Glutton," in *Classics and Commercials: A Literary Chronicle of the Forties* (New York: Farrar, Straus and Giroux, 1950), pp. 367–68.

15. Simon, *Vintagewise: A Postscript to Saintsbury's "Notes on a Cellar-Book"* (London: Michael Joseph, 1945), pp. 6, 8; Saintsbury, *A Last Vintage: Essays and Papers*, ed. by John W. Oliver, Arthur Melville Clark, and Augustus Muir (London: Methuen, 1950), pp. 209–10.

16. Morrah, *André Simon: Gourmet and Wine Lover* (London: Constable, 1987), pp. 16, 64, 23–24, 40–42, 27–28, 48; Simon, *By Request*, pp. 35, 37, 71, 76.

17. Morrah, *André Simon*, pp. 100–101, 108; *Wine and Food: A Gastronomical Quarterly*, no. 1 (Spring 1934); Simon to Street, May 5, 1943, Street papers, PUA.

18. Saintsbury, *Notes*, pp. 208–27, 102.

19. Ibid., xiii–xiv.

20. Simon, *By Request*, p. 69.

21. Ibid., pp. 94, 126, 202–4, 157, 187, 228, xx, xiv.

22. *The Art of Good Living: A Contribution to the Better Understanding of Food and Drink together with a Gastronomic Vocabulary and a Wine Dictionary* (London: Constable,

1929), pp. 5, 14–16, 18–20, 111. A chapter entitled "The Art of Good Living" launched *André Simon's French Cook Book* (Boston: Little, Brown, 1938) nine years later (pp. 17, 29, 69).

23. *André Simon's French Cook Book*, pp. 5, 18; *The Art of Good Living*, pp. 69, 29–30.

24. *André Simon's French Cook Book*, pp. 5, 10–11, 119–20, 156–57, 180–81, 18–19; *The Art of Good Living*, pp. 19, 15, 111.

25. *André Simon's French Cook Book*, pp. 9–11.

26. Shapiro, *Perfection Salad: Women and Cooking* (New York: Farrar, Straus and Giroux, 1986); Levenstein, *Revolution at the Table: The Transformation of the American Diet* (New York: Oxford University Press, 1988); and *Paradox of Plenty: A Social History of Eating in Modern America* (New York: Oxford University Press, 1993).

27. See Donna R. Gabaccia, *We Are What We Eat: Ethnic Food and the Making of Americans* (Cambridge, MA: Harvard University Press, 1998), chap. 5.

28. Mary Ellen Zuckerman, *A History of Popular Women's Magazines in the United States* (Westport, CT: Greenwood Press, 1998), p. 108.

29. On Fisher, ibid., pp. 153–54; on Marsh, see *New York Times*, Mar. 1, 1942, p. R15; Feb. 6, 1973, p. 40. On MacFayden, see Jessamyn Neuhaus, *Manly Meals and Mom's Home Cooking: Cookbooks and Gender in Modern America* (Baltimore: Johns Hopkins University Press, 2003), pp. 75, 83.

30. On Batchelder, see *Ladies' Home Journal*, Aug. 1950, p. 33; Oct. 1935, p. 3; Aug. 1950, p. 8; on Taber, see Earle T. Walbridge, "Gladys Taber," *Wilson Library Bulletin*, Apr. 1952, p. 604; on Shouer, see her alumna file, Iowa State University archives.

31. On Johnston, see *New York Times*, Dec. 13, 1949, p. 46.

32. *Good Housekeeping*, Jan. 1941, p. 106.

33. *Better Homes and Gardens*, Mar. 1941, pp. 42–44, 96–97; May 1941, pp. 84, 86.

34. *Better Homes and Gardens*, May 1941, p. 84; *Good Housekeeping*, May 1941, pp. 14, 96. On vitamins and minerals, see also *Better Homes and Gardens*, Sept. 1941, pp. 46–47; Oct. 1941, pp. 46–47, 84–85, 94; *Ladies' Home Journal*, Feb. 1941, pp. 30–31; Aug. 1941, pp. 74–75; Oct. 1941, p. 116; *Good Housekeeping*, Feb. 1941, pp. 116, 122–23.

35. *Better Homes and Gardens*, Jan. 1941, pp. 42–43.

36. *Better Homes and Gardens*, May 1941, p. 84; Oct. 1941, pp. 84–85; *Ladies' Home Journal*, Mar. 1941, p. 106.

37. *Better Homes and Gardens*, July 1941, pp. 38–39; Jan. 1941, pp. 56–57, Apr. 1941, pp. 53–54.

38. *Good Housekeeping*, p. 117; *Ladies' Home Journal*, Dec. 1941, pp. 114–15.

39. *Good Housekeeping*, July 1941, p. 106; Aug. 1941, pp. 130, 138, 140–41; Sept. 1941, p. 117; Nov. 1941, pp. 139–41; *Ladies' Home Journal* printed the U.S. surgeon general's message in Aug. 1941, pp. 74–75, and Oct. 1941, p. 116.

40. *Better Homes and Gardens*, Jan. 1941, p. 49; May 1941, p. 48; June 1941, p. 48; July 1941, pp. 40–41, 49–50.

41. *Good Housekeeping*, Jan. 1941, p. 96; Oct. 1941, p. 120; Aug. 1941, p. 145; *Ladies' Home Journal*, Mar. 1941, p. 32; Apr. 1941, p. 36; May 1941, p. 34; June 1941, p. 32.

42. *Better Homes and Gardens*, May 1941, p. 86; Oct. 1941, pp. 84–85; Feb. 1941, p. 43; *Good Housekeeping*, Jan. 1941, p. 106; *Ladies' Home Journal*, Jan. 1941, p. 52.

43. *Ladies' Home Journal,* Mar. 1941, p. 106; July 1941, p. 89; Aug. 1941, pp. 74–75. Elizabeth Phillips considered "cooking timesavers" (*Good Housekeeping,* June 1941, p. 153), while Julia Hoover wrote on "Iced Drinks You Can Make in a Jiffy" (*Good Housekeeping,* July 1941, p. 100).

44. *Better Homes and Gardens,* Mar. 1941, p. 86; May 1941, p. 82; *Good Housekeeping,* June 1941, p. 102; *Ladies' Home Journal,* Feb. 1941, p. 100; Mar. 1941, pp. 30–31; Jan. 1941, p. 77.

45. *Better Homes and Gardens,* Sept. 1941, p. 48; Nov. 1941, p. 50; Feb. 1941, p. 44; articles also endorsed new and more spacious refrigerators, portable grills, and ice cream freezers: Apr. 1941, p. 132; May 1941, pp. 50–51; *Good Housekeeping,* Mar. 1941, p. 97; Apr. 1941, p. 138; July 1941, p. 96.

46. George Ellwanger, *The Pleasures of the Table: An Account of Gastronomy from Ancient Days to Present Times* (New York: Doubleday, Page, 1902), pp. 175–98 (197). Other turn-of-the-century advocates of French cuisine included Theodore Child, *Delicate Feasting* (New York: Harper and Brothers, 1890); Elizabeth Pennell, *The Feasts of Autolycus* (New York: Merriam, 1896); Henry T. Finck, *Food and Flavor: A Gastronomic Guide to Health and Good Living* (New York: Century, 1913), pp. 210–309.

47. Child, *Delicate Feasting,* pp. 110–11.

48. *American Mercury,* Oct. 1925, pp. 201–3; Apr. 1925, p. xxii. Mencken, who found *Notes on a Cellar-Book* "an amusing and mellow tome," remarked that "Poor Saintsbury, alas, is now an angel." *The Nation,* Feb. 4, 1934, p. 193.

49. *American Mercury,* Jan. 1925, pp. 69–70; July 1928, p. 296; Jan. 1926, pp. 8–9; July 1927, p. 276.

50. Ibid., Feb. 1927, p. 205; Oct. 1926, p. 196; July 1927, pp. 381–82; Feb. 1926, pp. 201–2; Oct. 1927, p. 159.

51. Knopf also published three books by Morton Shand, an erudite Francophile expatriate who disdained Anglo-Saxon food and drink: *A Book of French Wines* (1928), *A Book of Other Wines—than French* (1929), and *A Book of Food* (1928); Thomas Pinney, "The Wine List of Alfred A. Knopf," *Wayward Tendrils Quarterly* (Jan. 2003), pp. 1–13.

52. Knopf to Simon, Oct. 19, 1950, Knopf papers, University of Texas (UT). Knopf's wife, Blanche, a Francophile herself, oversaw the firm's list of modern French novels published in translation, for which she received the Chevalier de la Légion d'Honneur. See www.answers.com/topic/blanche-wolf-knopf; Wildman to Knopf, Aug. 17, 1960; Mencken dined with Knopf and the Van Vechtens on June 17, 1940. See "Meals 1940–1953," Knopf papers, UT; G. T. Hellman, "Portrait of a Publisher, III," *The New Yorker,* Dec. 4, 1948, pp. 42, 44, 46.

53. Hellman, "Portrait of a Publisher, III," pp. 42, 44, 46; Tastevin to Knopf, Oct. 12, 1962; Fernande Garvin to Commandeur, Jan. 23, 1964; Chaîne des Rotisseurs to members, June 5, 1963, Knopf papers, UT. Knopf belonged to La Confrérie des Chevaliers du Tastevin, the Commanderie du Bordeaux, and the Chaîne des Rotisseurs, among other gourmet groups.

54. Paul A. Bennett, ed., *Portrait of a Publisher, 1915–1965,* vol. 1 (New York: Typophiles, 1965), p. 289; *Hotel Monthly* (Jan. 1934), p. 65, recommended *Wines* as "the book of the year" for those who wanted a general knowledge of wine.

55. "What's the Matter with Food?" appeared in the Jan. 31 and Mar. 21, 1931, issues of the *Saturday Evening Post*. Simon to Street, Aug. 18, 1935, Street papers, PU. Street praised Saintsbury's display of "fine feeling" for wine, which provoked his friend, Henry Taft, brother of the president, to observe that Street matched Saintsbury's knowledge of wine and the "indulgence" necessary to acquire it. "What a lesson you and Saintsbury present to the world!" Taft to Street, Dec. 21, 1933, Street papers, PU. *Wines: Their Selection, Care and Service* (New York: Alfred A. Knopf, 1933), pp. 159, 36, 13, 65, 5, 91, 37, 18. Street wrote an essay on Brillat-Savarin in *Table Topics* (New York: Alfred A. Knopf, 1959), pp. 75–78; Oct. 21, 1934, Street memo, "Some Notes on the Matter of Differences between Bellows and Co., Inc., of New York, and former Senator Henry F. Hollis of Paris," Street papers, PUA.

56. "What's the Matter with Food?" Mar. 21, 1931, pp. 94, 11; *Wines*, pp. 173, 169, 174–94.

57. "What's the Matter with Food?" Mar. 21, 1931, pp. 94, 92; *Where Paris Dines*, pp. 2, 4, 142.

58. *Where Paris Dines*, pp. 67–68.

59. Ibid., pp. 2–4, 67–68, 107, 92–93, 99–100, 130, 202.

60. "What's the Matter with Food?" Jan. 31, 1931, pp. 14–15, 112; Mar. 21, 1931, pp. 10–11, 96, 94.

61. *Death in the Afternoon* (1932); *Wines*, pp. 3–4, 28.

62. Price to Street, Aug. 31, 1943, Street papers, PUA.

63. Price to Street, Aug. 31, 1943, Street papers, PUA. Joan Reardon, *Poet of the Appe-tites: The Lives and Loves of M. F. K. Fisher* (New York: North Point Press, 2004), pp. 164–66.

64. Brillat-Savarin, *The Physiology of Taste*, p. vi; *Westways*, Aug. 1937, pp. 41–42; Feb. 1935, pp. 18–19, 40. Fisher compiled a "Gastronomical Bibliography" for the Los Angeles Wine and Food Society, which exists only in manuscript form. Joan Reardon, *M. F. K. Fisher, Julia Child, and Alice Waters: Celebrating the Pleasures of the Table* (New York: Har-mony Books, 1994), p. 44. Salvatore Lucia, "Comment on the Wines Served at a Dinner Honoring Mrs. M. F. K. Fisher" (San Francisco: Bohemian Club, Nov. 29, 1944). Alfred Knopf, who regretted that *Serve It Forth* did not bear the Knopf imprimatur, published several of her later books. Fisher reported to him that she was "comforted and thankful that you may well publish my last one." Fisher to Knopf, Oct. 18, 1982, Knopf papers, UT.

65. *Consider the Oyster*, pp. 143, 150–51, 153, 167; *Gourmet*, Sept. 1941, pp. 14–15, 41; *Wine and Food: A Gastronomical Quarterly* (Winter 1944), pp. 60–64.

66. *Serve It Forth* (1937), p. 5; *The Gastronomical Me* (1943), p. 401; *Consider the Oyster* (1941), p. 171.

67. *How to Cook a Wolf* (1942), p. 320.

68. *Consider the Oyster*, pp. 133, 158–59, 170–71; *How to Cook a Wolf*, p. 311.

69. *Serve It Forth*, p. 43.

70. Ibid., pp. 40, 57; *Consider the Oyster*, pp. 154–55, 173; *How to Cook a Wolf*, pp. 320–21, 333.

71. *How to Cook a Wolf*, pp. 269, 271; *Consider the Oyster*, pp. 170–71; *Serve It Forth*, p. 19.

72. *Serve It Forth*, pp. 58–59; The Gastronomical Me, pp. 420, 456; *Consider the Oyster*, p. 181.

73. *Serve It Forth*, pp. 87, 27–28, 18; *Consider the Oyster*, p. 180; *How to Cook a Wolf*, p. 213. In *An Alphabet for Gourmets* (1949), she mocked readers for slavishly following recipes or joining wine and food clubs rather than following their own tastes (p. 589).

74. *Serve It Forth*, pp. 59, 9, 83, 92, 96.

75. Ibid., pp. 42, 44, 59.

76. Ibid., pp. 41, 42, 44.

77. *How to Cook a Wolf*, pp. 322, 249, 251; *The Gastronomical Me*, pp. 353, 477, 481.

78. *Serve It Forth*, p. 59.

Chapter 2 · Building a Foundation for Gourmet Dining in America

1. Harvey Levenstein, *We'll Always Have Paris: American Tourists in France since 1930* (Chicago: University of Chicago Press, 2004), pp. 3–24; *New York Times*, May 16, 1928, p. 7.

2. Kenneth D. Rose, *American Women and the Repeal of Prohibition* (New York: New York University, 1996), pp. 110–11.

3. Michèle Lamont, *Money, Morals and Manners: The Culture of the French and American Upper-Middle Class* (Chicago: University of Chicago Press, 1992); Paula S. Fass, *The Damned and the Beautiful: American Youth in the 1920s* (Oxford: Oxford University Press, 1977). The upper-middle resembles Russell Lynes' upper-middlebrows: civilized consumers, as opposed to creators, of culture. Michael Kammen, *American Culture, American Tastes: Social Change and the 20th Century* (New York: Alfred A. Knopf, 1999), p. 97.

4. Luxury lifestyle magazines were more expensive than the women's magazines. *Gourmet* was about 40% more expensive in 1943 than *Good Housekeeping, Better Homes and Gardens*, and *Ladies' Home Journal*; 25% more expensive in 1947; and 80% in 1952. Except for 1943, *Gourmet* sold at the same price as *House and Garden*.

5. Theodore Peterson, *Magazines in the Twentieth Century* (Urbana: University of Illinois Press, 1964), p. 264; Caroline Seebohm, *The Man Who Was Vogue: The Life and Times of Condé Nast* (New York: Viking Press, 1982), p. 31.

6. *Vanity Fair*, Jan. 1914, p. 13; Seebohm, *The Man Who Was Vogue*, p. 153.

7. Seebohm, *The Man Who Was Vogue*, p. 270; Bill Osgerby, *Playboys in Paradise: Maculinity, Youth and Leisure-Style in Modern America* (Oxford and New York: Berg, 2001), pp. 38–59.

8. *Magazines in the Twentieth Century*, pp. 248, 261.

9. *The Physiology of Taste or Meditations on Transcendental Gastronomy*, trans. Charles Monselet, foreword by Frank Crowninshield (New York: Horace Liveright, 1926), pp. x, xii–xiv; Joan DeJean, *The Essence of Style: How the French Invented High Fashion, Fine Food, Chic Cafes, Style, Sophistication, and Glamour* (New York: Free Press, 2005).

10. Ellsworth, *Much Depends on Dinner* (New York: Alfred A. Knopf, 1939), preface. On their European travels, see "S. H.," *New Yorker*, Mar. 7, 1964, p. 183; *June Platt's Party Book* (Boston: Houghton Mifflin, 1936), pp. xi–xiii; chap. 1 (Fisher); *New York Times*,

Apr. 10, 1957, p. 53 (Owen); Mary Frost Mabon, *The ABC of America's Wines* (New York: Alfred A. Knopf, 1942).

11. *Vogue*, July 1, 1933, pp. 15, 74; Dec. 15, 1933, p. 10; Nov. 15, 1933, pp. 64–65.

12. Leone B. Moats, "Putting Pleasure into Picnics," *House and Garden*, July 1932, p. 27; June Platt, "Lots of Ways to Cook Chicken," ibid., Nov. 1933, p. 50; Schoonmaker, "Prepare Your Cellar for Repeal," ibid., p. 33.

13. The first Hibben article, "What Every Young Cook Should Know," appeared in the Oct. 1934 *House Beautiful*, pp. 60–61; the first Ellsworth piece was "Bread as a Raw Material to Fill That Empty Place in the Menu," ibid., Feb. 1937, p. 62.

14. *New Yorker*, Mar. 15, 1930, p. 72.

15. Ross to Street, Apr. 17, 1930; Street to Ross, Apr. 18, 1930; Ross to Street, Apr. 21, 1930.

16. *New Yorker*, Mar. 7, 1964, p. 183.

17. Schoonmaker, "Wines and Liquors," May 19, 1934, pp. 62–64; GCS, "Restaurants," Oct. 8, 1938, p. 44.

18. Fisher, "I Was Really Very Hungry," *Atlantic Monthly*, June 1937, pp. 737–42; Simon, "Aesthetics of Eating," ibid., Nov. 1938, pp. 678–83; Codman, "Wine from Our Grapes," ibid., Feb. 1941, pp. 229–34; "California Grape Rush," ibid., June 1941, pp. 750–56.

19. *Time*, Oct. 9, 1933, p. 47.

20. Julian Street, *Table Talk*, 8, Jan.–Feb. 1944, p. 5; Wildman to Street, May 31, 1933, Street papers, PUA.

21. *New York Times*, Mar. 7, 1932, display ad, p. 12; Mar. 11, 1932, display ad, p. 4. Author interview with Julius Wile, Oct. 8–9, 2003, Scarsdale, NY; Penny Singer, "Julius Wile: Business and a Love of Wine," *New York Times*, June 4, 1995, p. WC10.

22. See www.bottlebooks.com/american%20medicinal%20spirits%20company/american_medicinal_spirits_compa.htm; *New York Times*, Aug. 28, 1924, p. 25; June 24, 1933, p. 22. National Distillers had a stock of aged whisky on hand that they used to lure investors to the company. *New York Times*, Aug. 15, 1932, p. 21; "Name Schenley, Age Three," *Fortune*, May 1936, pp. 98–104.

23. "Schenley Acquisition," *Business Week*, Jan. 13, 1934, p. 22; "Name Schenley," p. 99.

24. Pinney, *A History of Wine in America*, pp. 19–20. Other changes during Prohibition helped wine producers. The Grape Growers League of California pressured Congress to legalize wine while spawning the Wine Institute, which promoted wine. Ibid., pp. 31, 43, 50.

25. Ibid., pp. 26, 64, 78–79.

26. Ibid., pp. 57–58.

27. Ibid., pp. 64, 107.

28. Daniel Boorstin, *The Americans: The Democratic Experience* (New York: Vintage Books, 1973), pp. 316–31; *Letters of Rudyard Kipling*, vol. 5 (Iowa City: University of Iowa Press, 2004), p. 45; Evan Jones, *American Food*, p. 28.

29. Jones, *American Food*, pp. 94–96.

30. *Gourmet*, June 1956, p. 22.

31. Ibid., pp. 38–40, 68, 70, 72, 49–51, 118–20; Donna Gabaccia, *We Are What We Eat*, pp. 25–27, 29–30, 95–97.

32. *Gourmet*, June 1956, pp. 22, 32.

33. Neuhaus, *Manly Meals and Mom's Home Cooking*, pp. 23–25, 39.

34. Ibid., pp. 28, 32, 39. The Immigration Restriction Act introduced a quota on the number of immigrants who could enter the United States from various countries. Charles Ranhofer, *The Epicurean: A Complete Treatise of Analytical and Practical Studies on the Culinary Art* (New York: C. Ranhofer, 1893); Escoffier, *The Complete Guide to the Art of Modern Cookery* (New York: Mayflower Books, 1979 [1921]); Jan Langone, "Professor Blot and the First French Cooking School in New York," part 1, *Gastronomica: The Journal of Food and Culture*, Spring 2001, pp. 65–66.

35. See Martin T. Olliff, "Les Amis d'Escoffier and the Post-Depression Labor Market for Chefs de Cuisine in America," *Essays in Economic and Business History*, 19 (2001), pp. 185–87; G. Selmer Fougner, *Gourmet Dinners* (New York: M. Barrows, 1941), pp. viii, 11–12, 51–52.

36. See previous endnote.

37. In the next few years, colleagues supported Scotto's position. See *Culinary Review*, Nov. 1934, p. 12; Apr. 1935, pp. 20–21; "Cooking Schools," *The Oxford Encyclopedia of Food and Drink in America*, vol. 1, pp. 424–31; "What to Do about Apprentices for Our American Kitchens?" *Hotel Bulletin and Nation's Chefs*, June 1931.

38. *Culinary Review*, Nov. 1935, p. 10; Nov. 1936, pp. 29, 43.

39. Ibid., July 1941, pp. 13–17.

40. L. Timothy Ryan, "The Culinary Institute of America: A History," Dissertation in Higher Education Management, University of Pennsylvania, 2003, pp. 60, 63–64, 73; Herbert Mitgang, "How Chefs Are Made," *American Legion Magazine*, June 1954, pp. 22–23, 62.

41. For reviews of New York restaurants, see George S. Chappell, *The Restaurants of New York* (New York: Greenberg, 1925); Selmer Fougner, *Dining Out in New York and What to Order* (New York: H. C. Kinsey, 1939), pp. 3–7; George Rector, *Dining in New York with Rector: A Personal Guide to Good Eating* (New York: Prentice-Hall, 1939), pp. 63–64, 70–71. Duncan Hines' *Adventures in Good Eating* (New York: Duncan Hines, 1936) and *Gourmet's Guide to Good Eating* (New York: Gourmet, 1948) corroborate information in other sources for all six cities.

42. Iles Brody, *The Colony*, pp. 89–103. On Yves Ploneis, see *New York Times*, May 19, 1966, p. 47. *The Iron Gate of Jack and Charlie's "21"* (New York: Jack Kriendler Memorial Foundation, 1950), pp. 114–15.

43. See previous endnote.

44. *New York Times*, Feb. 12, 1933, p. 19; Mar. 18, 1934, p. 31; May 27, 1934, p. 18; July 1, 1934, p. 11; *New Yorker*, Nov. 10, 1934, p. 70. *Bloomingdale's* (New York: Harcourt Brace Jovanovich, 1980), pp. 43, 46. *New York Times*, Dec. 11, 1951, p. 19; Oct. 4, 1952, p. 13.

45. *The Letters of George Santayana, 1941–1947*, edited and with an introduction by William G. Holzberger (Cambridge: MIT, 2007), p. 7:358; *New Yorker*, May 5, 1934, p. 90; July 14, 1934, p. 44; Aug. 18, 1934, p. 58; Sept. 29, 1934, p. 70; May 19, 1934, p. 34; June 2,

1934, p. 60; July 28, 1934, p. 39; Sept. 15, 1934, p. 92; Dec. 29, 1934, pp. 44–46; Apr. 21, 1934, p. 72; Dec. 1, 1934, pp. 66–67; July 14, 1934, p. 44; *Catalogue. May 1937. Charles and Co.*, pp. 34, 11, 283–84.

46. See http://sherry-lehmann.com/about_us. The author is Michael Aaron, son of the founder. *New Yorker*, Jan. 12, 1935, pp. 48–49; Jan. 26, 1935, p. 56.

47. Natalie Scott and Caroline Merrick Jones, *Gourmet's Guide to New Orleans* (New Orleans: Scott and Jones Publishers, 1933); Scoop Kennedy, *Dining in New Orleans* (New Orleans: Bormon House, 1945); Roy Guste, Jr., *The Restaurants of New Orleans: A Cookbook* (New York: W. W. Norton, 1982); Roy Louis Alciatore, "Antoine's Wine List, 1840–1940" (1940), author's copy.

48. See previous endnote.

49. Guste, *The Restaurants of New Orleans*.

50. See http://findarticles.com/p/articles/mi_m3190/is_47_35/ai_80234743; Paddleford, "Food Flashes," *Gourmet*, May 1950, p. 54. *Good Things to Eat from All the World*: Solari's, New Orleans (New Orleans: The Firm, 1930).

51. Salvatore Lucia, "Eating in San Francisco," *Atlantic*, Mar. 1950, pp. 88–89; Clarence E. Edwords, *Bohemian San Francisco* (San Francisco: Silhouette Press, 1973 [1914]); Ruth Thompson and Chef Louis Hanges, *Eating around San Francisco* (San Francisco: Suttonhouse, 1937); Matty and Don Simmons, *On the House* (New York: Coward-McCann, 1955). See "Lucien Heyraud, renowned chef," *San Francisco Examiner*, May 8, 1975; "Funeral of Lucien Heyraud," *San Francisco Chronicle*, May 8, 1975; San Francisco History Center, Special Collections.

52. See previous endnote.

53. See http://content.cdlib.org/ark:/13030/hb6p3008cg/, http://books.google.com/boo ks?id=5YGE5HyDKcUC&pg=PA148&lpg=PA148&dq=GoldbergBowen&source=web&ots= dY3sO_aUm3&sig=uui28CerIK6t5CZ4soEIRhooMoc#PPA147,M1, and www.chowhound .com/topics/353176; *Los Angeles Times*, Dec. 15, 1933, p. 2. Sun Drug Co. advertised that it carried wines from Goldberg Bowen. Ibid., July 14, 1902, p. 4.

54. John Drury, *Dining in Chicago* (New York: John Day, 1931), no page numbers; Simmons, *On the House*, pp. 122, 134.

55. Drury, *Dining in Chicago*.

56. Ibid.

57. *Chicago Restaurant Association Buyer's Guide, 1945*; *Chicago Daily Tribune*, Feb. 12, 1934, p. 4; Nov. 24, 1934, p. 10; Sept. 8, 1983, p. B15, Sept. 8, 1983, p. D3.

58. Helen Ridley, *The Ritz-Carlton Cook Book and Guide to Home Entertaining* (Philadelphia: J. B. Lippincott, 1968), p. 121; Cellar Club menu collection, Boston Wine and Food Society Archives, Boston, MA. Joseph's was founded before 1943. See *Christian Science Monitor*, Mar. 8, 1943, p. 2. Locke Ober and Joseph's were still highly regarded in the early 1970s. "Boston: Flavor It Cosmopolitan," *Christian Science Monitor*, May 25, 1972, p. 12; Elliott Shore, "Dining Out: The Development of the Restaurant," *Food: The History of Taste*, ed. Paul Freedman (Berkeley and Los Angeles: University of California Press, 2007), p. 318.

59. "Boston's Loyalty to S.S. Pierce Survives a Century of Change," *Business Week*, June 3, 1931, pp. 26, 28; "S.S. Pierce: Growing with the Quality Trade," ibid., June 20, 1953,

pp. 132–334; "Decline of a Brahmin," ibid., Mar. 20, 1972, pp. 92–93; Nancy Hall, "Pierce's," *New Yorker*, Nov. 19, 1955, pp. 46–49.

60. "Menu Collection," Los Angeles Public Library. Jim Heimann, *Out with the Stars: Hollywood Nightlife in the Golden Era* (New York: Abeville, 1985). See www.latimemachines .com/new_page_23.htm. On Perino's, see *Wine and Food: A Gastronomical Quarterly*, Winter 1937, p. 88; Spring 1940, p. 87. "*Life* Goes to Mike Romanoff's Restaurant," *Life Magazine*, Oct. 29, 1945, pp. 141–45. Budd Schulberg, "See You at Dave's," *Holiday*, Apr. 1951, pp. 67–70, 135, 137–38.

61. See previous endnote.

62. *Los Angeles Times*, Dec. 25, 1932, p. H3; Feb. 3, 1933, p. A5; June 14, 1933, p. 4; Aug. 6, 1935, p. A2; Nov. 5, 1936, p. A6; Feb. 9, 1937, p. A6; Mar. 9, 1937, p. 7.

63. *Los Angeles Times*, June 30, 1948, p. A1. The Nov. 11, 1926, *Times* (p. A20) reported that Frank Vitale was arrested for manufacturing and selling alcohol. See also Dan Strehl, ed., *Tidbits from "Bohemian Life" as Seen by Savarin St. Sure* (Pasadena: Weather Bird Press, 2001).

64. "Farmer's Market Today," *Los Angeles Times*, May 27, 1934, p. 17; Aug. 8, 1950, p. 4. See www.farmersmarketla.com/history/marketfacts.html.

65. Jurgensen's promoted its products in a flyer called *Jurgensen's Palate Pointers*. Dan Strehl, ed., *The Epicurean: Excerpts from Jurgensen's Newsletter Written by Helen Evans Brown and Philip. S. Brown* (Pasadena: Weather Bird Press, 2001); www.larchmontchronicle .com/ArchiveDetail.asp?ArchiveID=358; *Bohemian Life*, 8, Apr. 1940, p. 4; 15, Nov. 1940, pp. 1–2.

66. Ibid.; Frederic Cople Jaher, *The Urban Establishment: Upper Strata in Boston, New York, Charleston, Chicago and Los Angeles* (Urbana: University of Illinois, 1982), pp. 277–78, 537, 681.

67. James M. Mayo, *The American Country Club: Its Origin and Development* (New Brunswick, NJ: Rutgers University Press, 1998), pp. 8–9; "New York's Dining Clubs," *New York Sun*, Feb. 18, 1893, no page numbers, as reprinted in *Records of the Zodiac as They Appear in the Minute Books, 1868–1915* (New York: Privately Printed, 1916). WEDA continued to meet at least until 1955. See New York Historical Society catalogue. *Records of the Zodiac*, pp. 10, 62, 331. See F. Gray Griswold, *The Gourmet* (New York: Duttons, 1933), dedication, p. 54; Herbert L. Satterlee, *J. Pierpont Morgan: An Intimate Portrait* (New York: Macmillan, 1939), pp. 406–7; *Gourmet*, June 1948, pp. 56–57.

68. *Vintage Dinners*, pp. 9, 91; Charles Codman, *Years and Years: Some Vintage Years in French Wines* (Boston: S.S. Pierce, 1935); Philip Dexter, *Notes on French Wines*, rev. ed. (Boston: Addison C. Getchell and Son, 1933); Theodora Codman, *Was It a Holiday* (Boston: Little, Brown, 1935). *By Request*, p. 112; Simon, *In the Twilight*, p. 68.

69. "By-Laws of Le Club des Arts Gastronomiques, 1941" (copy from the Boston Wine and Food Society).

70. Codman, *Vintage Dinners*, pp. 36, 59; *Wine and Food*, 5, p. 62.

71. *Wine and Food*, 13, pp. 56–57.

72. Ibid., 17, pp. 25–26. Simon obituary, *Boston Globe* (1970), in Boston Wine and Food Society archives, Boston, MA.

73. Oct. 19, 1939, menu, Cellar Club Menu collection, Boston Wine and Food Society archives, Boston, MA.

74. Theodore Zeldin, *France, 1848–1945: Intellect, Taste and Anxiety*, vol. 2 (Oxford: Clarendon Press, 1977), pp. 725, 745, 748, 755.

75. Ibid., pp. 715, 745, 748, 755.

Chapter 3 · Origins, Rituals, and Menus of Gourmet Dining Societies, 1934–1961

1. Veblen (p. 76) allows that "motives of conviviality and religion" also drive practices of consumer consumption. Thorstein Veblen, *The Theory of the Leisure Class* (New York: Penguin, 1994 [1899]), pp. 45, 70, 72–76, 84–85, 96; see Robert Lekachman's introduction in ibid., pp. v–xi; Jackson Lears, *Fables of Abundance: A Cultural History of Advertising in America* (New York: Basic Books, 1994), pp. 3, 63, 127–28, 240, 241, 255–56, 350–51.

2. Dining societies like Grimod de la Reynière's Société des Mercredis first appeared around 1800 but spread rapidly after 1918; barristers, musicians, and doctors formed clubs. Theodore Zeldin, *France, 1848–1945*, vol. 1, *Ambition, Love, and Politics* (Oxford: Clarendon Press, 1977), p. 747.

3. *New York Times*, Mar. 18, 1935, p. 18; Nov. 10, 1936, p. 27. Henry Taft to Julian Street, Mar. 1, 1937, Street papers, PUA.

4. *New York Times*, Aug. 3, 1924, p. SM11; Crahan, *The Wine and Food Society of Southern California: A History with a Bibliography of André L. Simon* (Los Angeles: Wine and Food Society of Southern California, 1957), p. 18.

5. *Wine and Food: A Gastronomical Quarterly*, 10, p. 1; André Simon favored the growth of small dining groups to complement the WFS.

6. Jessamyn Neuhaus, *Manly Meals and Mom's Home Cooking: Cookbooks and Gender in Modern America* (Baltimore: Johns Hopkins University Press, 2003), pp. 72–76; Lucius Beebe, "Crosby Gaige," *Bachelor*, May 1937, p. 25; Charles Browne, *The Gun Club Cookbook* (New York: Charles Scribner and Sons, 1930), pp. xiii–xiv; *New Yorker*, May 6, 1939, p. 11.

7. *By Request: An Autobiography* (London: Wine and Food Society, 1957), pp. 110–11; Morrah, *André Simon: Gourmet and Wine Lover* (London: Constable, 1987), pp. 108–10, 117–120; Street to Codman, Nov. 23, 1934, Street papers, PUA.

8. Among them was the Gourmet Society, organized in 1933 by public relations expert George Frederick, whose *Cooking as Men Like It* (New York: Business Bourse, 1930) denounced women for embracing nutritionism. The Society claimed to be "an Americanized version of the Club des Cents" but did not eat like one. Among various themed dinners were French, Eskimo, and the cuisine of the forty-eight states. Julian Street regarded the menus and wine lists as "very poor" and dismissed the society as a "personal, proprietary organization belonging to one man." *New York Times*, Oct. 21, 1935, p. 21; Mar. 23, 1936, p. 21; Mar. 1, 1937, p. 21; Apr. 5, 1937, p. 21; May 9, 1937, VIII, p. 20; June 25, 1937, p. 21; Oct. 18, 1937, p. 19. Street himself hatched a plan with backing from Henry Taft, the brother of the former president. Street to Taft, Mar. 8, 1937, Street papers, PUA. Wine merchants Frank Schoonmaker and Tom Marvel developed a prospectus for a "consumers' wine group" in 1934 that never materialized. Patrick Morrah, *André Simon*, pp. 121–23.

9. Street wanted to restrict membership in a dining society to fifty. Street to Wildman, Nov. 22, 1934; Street to Gaige, Nov. 10, 1934; Street to Taft, Nov. 13, 1934; Street to Wildman, Dec. 9, 1934; Simon to Street, Jan. 2, 1935; Wildman to Street, Street to Wildman, Nov. 27, 1934; Street to Hanna, Mar. 15, 1945; in a February 28, 1938, letter to Street, Simon remarked, "I shall never forget the wonderful help which you gave me at the beginning." Street papers, PUA.

10. Wildman to Street, May 31, 1933; Nov. 27, 1934; Nov. 21, 1935; see WFS Prospectus, Street papers, PUA; *Wine and Food: A Gastronomical Quarterly*, 9, pp. 58–59; 14, pp. 64–66; 15, p. 75; on Wildman's membership in WFS, see Laura Brown e-mail to author, Feb. 3, 2004, based on a search of Society ledgers.

11. Simon, *By Request*, pp. 69–70, 73–85, 112–15; "Chicago Branch—The Early Years" (produced by members of the WFS of Chicago), p. 7; "The Wine and Food Society's First Dinner," New Orleans, Chez Antoine, Feb. 11, 1935, Street papers, PUA; *Wine and Food*, 5, p. 75; Price to Howe, May 28, 1947; WFSSF menu collection. Simon had already met Los Angeles wine dealers William I. Converse, John S. C. Shaw, and Richard Day in England. Crahan, *The Wine and Food Society of Southern California*, pp. 8, 8b, 10.

12. *Wine and Food*, 11, pp. 55–56. Charles Browne arranged the dinner. Simon, *In the Twilight*, p. 68. Simon dined with the Zamaranos four days before the organizing luncheon of the WFSLA. Fred Alles, *Our First Forty Years!* (Los Angeles: Sunset Club, 1935); George E. Fullerton, *The First Half Century, 1928–1978* (Los Angeles: The Club, 1978). In 1954, Fred Herrington, a member of the Bohemian Club and the WFSSF, organized a Club "Dinner for Oenophiles and Gastronomes in the Manner of the Wine and Food Society" introducing seventy Bohemians to French cuisine. See www.lapl.org/resources/en/menu_collection.html.

13. Simon to Street, Feb. 28, 1938; Wildman to Street, Nov. 21, 1935; Street to Aliciatore, July 29, 1939, Street papers, PUA; *Culinary Review*, Feb. 1935, p. 20; Dec. 1936, p. 9; Fougner, "Obituary," *New York Times*, Apr. 3, 1941.

14. Lucius Beebe, "Heirs of Epicurus," *Culinary Review*, Dec. 1936, pp. 9, 35. Martin Olliff, "Les Amis d'Escoffier and the Post-Depression Labor Market for Chefs de Cuisine in America," *Essays in Economic and Business History* (2001), pp. 179–93.

15. *Wine and Food*, 10, pp. 64–65.

16. *Culinary Review*, May 1936, pp. 7–8; Dec. 1936, p. 8; Olliff, "Les Amis d'Escoffier," p. 8; *New York Times*, Mar. 18, 1935, p. 18; Street to Taft, Mar. 8, 1937; Simon to Street, Feb. 28, 1938, Street papers, PUA; *Washington Post*, Nov. 6, 1938, p. 15; Dec. 17, 1940, p. 21; *Boston Evening Transcript*, Nov. 30, 1937, p. 5.

17. John L. Sprague, *Confrérie des Chevaliers du Tastevin: History of the Commanderies d'Amérique* (Nuits St. Georges: Les éditions du Tastevin, 2002), pp. 15–16; Fougner, *Gourmet Dinners: A Book of Gastronomic Adventure, with the Menus of Great Meals and the Original Recipes of the Chefs Who Made Them So* (New York: M. Barrows), pp. 6–8; "Rapport de M. Jules Bohy," *Tastevin en main* (May 1946), p. 18.

18. Jean-Francois Bazin, *Confrérie des Chevaliers du Tastevin, 1934–1994* (Nuits St. Georges: Les éditions du Tastevin, 1994), p. 13; Sprague, *Confrérie*, p. 11.

19. Sprague, *Confrerie*, p. 13; see also Jacques Chevignard letter to author, Dec. 18, 2002.

20. The WFSLA and WFSSF held several dinners each year. Through the monthly *Bohemian Life*, edited by Hanna, a five-member War Food Council of the WFSLA provided recipes for nonrationed food such as marinated rabbit and sea bass. The WFSSF was more active. George Holl announced that "we . . . must do more than our part in upholding civilian morale . . . we too are soldiers and like soldiers march on our stomachs." Whiting to Hanna, Mar. 21, 1945; Hanna to Whiting, Mar. 22, 1945, Hanna papers, University of California, Los Angeles Archives (UCLAA); *Bohemian Life*, June 1940, p. 2; Feb. 1943, pp. 1–2; Sept. 1943, pp. 1–2. See copy of newspaper article on May 27, 1943, menu, WFSSF collection.

21. The "Code" was published in *Cooking as Men Like It* (1939), pp. ix–xv; "Statement of Operation of the Wine and Food Society—Los Angeles Chapter," p. 1, Hanna papers, UCLAA; "Constitution and By-Laws," *Culinary Review*, May 1936, p. 8; "The Wine and Food Society," Street papers, PUA; Wildman to Street, Nov. 26, 1934, Street papers, PUA.

22. "Statement of Operation of the Wine and Food Society—Los Angeles Chapter," p. 1, Hanna papers, UCLAA; "Constitution and By-Laws," *Culinary Review*, May 1936, p. 8; "The Wine and Food Society," Street papers, PUA; "Chicago Branch—the Early Years," p. 7; *New York Times*, Nov. 12, 1935, p. 18; "Rehearsal," *New Yorker*, Dec. 11, 1948, p. 28; *Chicago Daily Tribune*, Feb. 16, 1957, p. 14.

23. Beebe, *The Stork Club Bar Book* (New York: Rinehart, 1946), pp. xi, 91; Gibbs, "The Diamond Gardenia" (1), *New Yorker*, p. 24; Fougner, "Wines, Spirits, and Good Living," *Scribner's Magazine*, Sept. 1937, pp. 94–96.

24. *Bohemian Life*, Mar. 1944, p. 2; *Culinary Review*, Dec. 1936, p. 8; Olliff, "Les Amis d'Escoffier," p. 8; Alexander, "La Serviette au Cou," *New Yorker*, pp. 43, 46, 49, 50, 52; *Chicago Daily Tribune*, Dec. 6, 1935, p. 29; June 11, 1961, p. B24. The WFS of Chicago and WFSLA featured after-dinner lectures during their first year. "Chicago Branch—The Early Years," p. 8; *Wine and Food*, 7, p. 7; "Chicago Branch," p. 8; Crahan, *The Wine and Food Society of Southern California*, p. 15; *Chicago Daily Tribune*, Dec. 10, 1961, p. F6. *La vie à table à la fin du 19ième siècle* (1894), p. 12.

25. "Rehearsal," *New Yorker*, Dec. 11, 1948, p. 28; photographs in Sprague, *Confrérie*; Alexander, "La Serviette au Cou," pp. 46, 49; "Chicago Branch—The Early Years," p. 8; Crahan, *The Wine and Food Society of Southern California*, p. 14.

26. See "Proceedings" column, *Wine and Food*, 5, p. 116; Brown to Beebe, Nov. 6, 1947; Boitouzet, *Les Chevaliers du Tastevin*, p. 74; Georges Rozet, *La Confrérie des Chevaliers du Tastevin*, pp. 24, 51. The WFSNY substituted four wine tastings for six dinners. *New York Times*, Apr. 30, 1940, p. 24; Muscatine et al., *The University of California / Sotheby Book of California Wine*, pp. 347–48; Hanna to Street, Apr. 2, 1945, Street papers, PUA; Crahan, *The Wine and Food Society of Southern California*, pp. 37–47.

27. "The Gourmets Gather," *New York Sun*, Dec. 23, 1936, Women's Section, p. 8; *Wine and Food*, 13, pp. 86, 94; 14, p. 96; 23, p. 308; "Statement of Operations of the WFS—LA Chapter," pp. 1–2. When in 1936 demand exceeded space, the Escoffier Society considered ways to accommodate more guests. Supposedly, 650 diners sought places at the Hotel Lafayette dinner. *Culinary Review*, Dec. 1936, pp. 8–9; Jan. 1937, p. 9; Sept. 1937, p. 9; Feb. 1938, p. 9; Apr. 1938, p. 12; Alciatore to Street, Feb. 7, 1939, Street papers, PUA; *Boston Evening Transcript*, Nov. 11, 1937, p. 5; *Washington Post and Times Herald*, Nov. 27, 1956, p. D1; *Chicago Daily Tribune*, Feb. 21, 1939, p. 3.

28. *Chicago Daily Tribune*, Feb. 21, 1939, p. 3; *Washington Post*, Nov. 27, 1956, p. D1; Alexander, *"La Serviette au Cou,"* pp. 46, 49.

29. Nov. 14, 1935, menu, WFSNY, WFSNY archives; *Wine and Food*, 9, p. 79. While Robert Misch of the WFSNY praised the February 5, 1936, menu as "a real work of art," Julian Street protested the cost.

30. "Confrérie des Chevaliers du Tastevin" Script, 1940, 1947; Bohy to Rodier, Jan. 3, 1949; Alciatore to Bohy, Oct. 17, 1950; Brown to Alciatore, Dec. 9, 1947; "13th Chapter, Ritz-Carlton Hotel, May 3, 1948," Tastevin papers.

31. Beebe, "This New York," *Washington Post*, Dec. 21, 1941, p. SA5; "Rapport de M. Jules Bohy," *Tastevin-en-main* (May 1946), p. 18.

32. In 1949, the New York chapter made rehearsal dinners optional because of their expense ($30 per person). Brown to Carroll, Mar. 16, 1948; Bohy to Ortion, Feb. 24, 1949; Examination of Candidates, May 9, 1949; Mar. 9, 1949, Brown minutes; GCO to American members, July 20, 1949; Jan. 8, 1950, Brown minutes, Tastevin papers; *New York Times*, Feb. 20, 1953, p. 23; William Bird, *French Wines* (Paris: Havas, 1946).

33. *Chicago Daily Tribune*, Feb. 22, 1956, p. B10.

34. Lucius Beebe, "Heirs of Epicurus," *Culinary Review*, Dec. 1936, p. 9.

35. Hanna to Street, Mar. 26, 1945, Street papers, PUA.

36. Ibid.; *Roster of Membership* (WFSSF, Nov. 29, 1944), Street papers, PUA; Joseph C. Meyerstein, "Cercle de l'Union: A Retrospect"; Jeff Smith, "And Reminiscence," Jan. 29, 1962; Board of Governors, "History and Traditions of the WFS of SF," no date; Paul Scholten, "Salvatore Pablo Lucia," *Bulletin of the Society of Medical Friends of Wine* (Mar. 1993); Ronald Unzelman, "Thoughts on Leon Adams: The Man and His Mission, 1905–1995," *Wayward Tendrils Newsletter* (Jan. 1996). See also wine tours and tastings, WFSSF menu collection.

37. On Schoonmaker, see William Dieppe Interview, "Almaden is My Life," pp. 19–37; Maynard Amerine Interview, "Wine Bibliography and Taste Perception Studies," pp. 38–41, Oral History Collection, Bancroft Library, University of California, Berkeley; Marinacci, "Vinaceous Correspondents," *Wayward Tendrils Quarterly*, Jan. 2004, pp. 17–24; Amerine to Adams, May 29, 1939, Amerine papers, UCDA; "Antoine's Wine List, 1840–1940" (author's copy); May 16, 1939, menu, WFSSF collection; Pinney, *A History of Wine in America from Prohibition to the Present* (Berkeley and Los Angeles: University of California Press, 2005), pp. 120–23. While many wine producers criticized Schoonmaker, Phil Hanna and John Shaw supported him. Day to Shaw, May 23, 1935, Hanna papers, UCLAA; *Bohemian Life*, Sept. 1941, pp. 1–2.

38. May 16, 1939, dinner, WFSSF menu collection.

39. Ray invited WFSSF members to the celebration but did not attend. In 1944, the society honored Street for supporting the Masson wines. Street to Ray, Jan. 17, 1940; Street to Price, Mar. 11, 1940, Street papers, PUA; Marinacci, "Vinaceous Correspondents," *WTQ*, July 2003, pp. 13–14, 21; Mar. 26, 1940; July 17, 1940, menus, WFSSF collection. The WFSLA paid tribute to Herman Wente. Hanna to Wente and copy of tribute by Hanna, Apr. 16, 1941, Hanna papers, UCLAA.

40. Amerine to Adams, Oct. 12, 1938; Feb. 27, 1939; Adams to Amerine, Mar. 4, 1939, Amerine papers, UCDA. The SMFW held two dinners per year, often at restaurants

frequented by the WFSSF, but increased that number in 1956. Among after-dinner topics were Phil T. Hanna's "Good Wine Needs No Bush" and M. F. K. Fisher's "Wines and Foods."

41. Simon, *By Request*, pp. 106, 153; Simon to Street, Mar. 18, 1936; the Los Angeles and New York branches rejected donations of inferior products. Hanna to Street, Mar. 26, 1945, Street papers, PUA. "Minutes of the Executive Council, Jan. 21, 1942," WFSNY archives; *Wine and Food*, 21, p. 96; 13, p. 92; on wine cellars, see Muscatine et al., ed., *California Book of Wine*, p. 347. As an early member of the WFSNY, James Beard knew Julian Street, Richardson Wright, and Jeanne Owen, who arranged for Beard's Hors d'Oeuvres Inc. to cater a WFSNY wine tasting. Evan Jones, *Epicurean Delight: The Life and Times of James Beard* (New York: Alfred A. Knopf, 1990), p. 40n97.

42. Brown to Bohy, Feb. 20, 1946; Brown to Bohy, Apr. 19, 1946, Tastevin papers.

43. Brown to Bohy, Jan. 14, 1949; June 8, 1949; Bohy to Brown, Apr. 16, 1946, Tastevin papers.

44. After tasting thirty-five Clos de Vougeot wines, tasters eliminated Faiveley's. Bohy to Brown, Feb. 7, 1945. "Ordinances, Rules and Customs," trans. from French (undated but sent by Bohy, Apr. 6, 1946); May 18, 1949, minutes of the American Commandérie, Tastevin papers.

45. While Dreyfus, Ashby and Co. imported Confrérie wines, other importers shipped non-Confrérie Burgundy wines. Mar. 9, 1949, Minutes of GCA meeting; Bohy to Alciatore, Jan. 24, 1949; Jan. 6, 1950; Alciatore to Bohy; Howells to Bohy, May 29, 1951, Tastevin papers; "Antoine's: October 23, 1950," *New Orleans Times-Picayune*, Jan. 26, 1950, p. 1. In 1944, Camille Rodier ordered Bohy "to prepare the market for the sale of selected wines when the situation will permit." The GCA rejected Bohy's proposal to serve white and red Confrerie selections at each dinner but agreed to serve one such wine. Alciatore to Bohy, Nov. 13, 1940; Rodier to Bohy, Nov. 23, 1944; Bohy to Alciatore, Dec. 20, 1948; Bohy to Howells, Nov. 16, 1949; Howells to Bohy, Apr. 24, 1951; Bohy to Alciatore, Jan. 11, 1950; Sept. 6, 1950; Mar. 9, 1949, Brown minutes. For its tenth-anniversary dinner, Bohy urged Alciatore to serve the Confrérie Clos de Vougeot 1937; he served instead a 1943. Alciatore also ordered six dozen "Vougeot" glasses. Bohy to Alciatore, Jan. 9, 1950; Sept. 5, 1950; Alciatore to Bohy, Sept. 8, 1950, Tastevin papers.

46. On increasing French wine sales, see Richard de Rochemont, "The Bacchic Brotherhood, Part I," *Town and Country*, Oct. 1964, p. 46. Voluntary donations of wine by local dealers were common until the society created a wine cellar. Brown to Beebe, Nov. 6, 1947; Brown to Grieg, Feb. 13, 1948; Feb. 17, 1948; Howells to Bohy, May 29, 1951, Tastevin papers.

47. Among vegetable dishes were broccoli and cauliflower in a Mornay sauce (Bechamel with egg yolk and Gruyère), artichoke vinaigrette, and potatoes à la Parisien (with cream cheese, salt, paprika, lemon juice, and oil). These lists were compiled from the following menus: Keen's English Chop House, N.Y., July 3, 1938; The Ritz-Carlton Restaurant, N.Y., Apr. 29, 1942; Pierre's, San Francisco, Feb. 13, 1946; Palace Hotel, San Francisco, Apr. 28, 1934; Nov. 16, 1939; June 7, 1941; July 16, 1941; Oct. 25, 1945; Mar. 17, 1951; Apr. 24, 1953; May 14, 1946; St. Francis Hotel, July 4, 1928.

48. See WFSSF menu collection; "Proceedings," *Wine and Food*, 1934–1961; articles on the Tastevin and Escoffier Society dinners, *New York Times*, 1934–1961.

49. Francoz to members. See May 28, 1940, menu, WFSSF collection.

50. Lucius Beebe, "Heirs of Epicurus," *Culinary Review*, Dec. 1936, p. 35.

51. *Culinary Review*, Dec. 1936, p. 35; Fougner, *Gourmet Dinners*, pp. 30–31, 58–62, 80–86; *Wine and Food*, 13, p. 86; Alexander, "La Serviette au Cou," pp. 46, 49.

52. *New York Herald-Tribune*, May 4, 1948. The Escoffier Society called its four-member dinner committee, headed by Fougner, the Bonne Bouche (tasty mouthful). Alexander, "La Serviette au Cou," pp. 43–44; Fougner, *Gourmet Dining*, p. 183. See Beebe's account of WFS dinner planning in "Crosby Gaige," *Bachelor*, May 1937, pp. 24–25, 80.

53. Edouard Gros, "Report to the Wine Purveyors," Oct. 8, 1948; Bohy to Chevalier, Nov. 15, 1948, Tastevin papers.

54. Gordon Brown, "Memorandum of the Duties of a Dinner Committee Chairman, Dec. 7, 1948," Tastevin papers.

55. Brown to Stack, Mar. 31, 1948, Tastevin papers.

56. Brown to Stack, Apr. 6, 1948, Tastevin papers.

57. Brown to Bohy, May 16, 1947; "XIIIème Chapter: Ritz-Carlton Hotel, May 3, 1948," Tastevin papers.

58. At a previous dinner, Brown asked the hotel manager to keep waiters from sampling the wines. "XIIIème Chapter, Ritz-Carlton Hotel, May 3, 1948"; "13th Chapter," Ritz-Carlton Hotel, May 3, 1948"; Brown to Willy, Nov. 19, 1947; Dec. 3, 1947, Tastevin papers.

59. "XIIIème Chapter, Ritz-Carlton Hotel, May 3, 1948." See also "XIIème Chapter, Hotel Pierre, Dec. 8, 1947"; Brown to Bohy, May 16, 1947, Tastevin papers.

60. Brown to Beebe, Nov. 6, 1947; Brown to Bohy, Mar. 11, 1949, Tastevin papers. Diners at the Clos de Vougeot also imbibed with gusto. *Chicago Daily Tribune*, Dec. 1, 1952, p. B2. The *Tribune* (May 31, 1940, p. 12) reported similar behavior at a Chicago WFS dinner.

61. Beebe to Brown, Nov. 3, 1947; Brown to Beebe, Nov. 6, 1947; Brown to Willy, Dec. 3, 1947, Tastevin papers.

62. *Gourmet*, July 1949, pp. 6–7. See Jane Nickerson, "News of Food," *New York Times*, Mar. 28, 1950, p. 34.

63. Crahan, *The Wine and Food Society of Southern California*, p. 10d. Jan. 11, 1938; Dec. 17, 1936, WFSSF menu collection. The WFS chapters of New York and Boston tasted American wines in 1935 and 1939, respectively. *Wine and Food*, 6, p. 68; 8, pp. 77–78; 22, p. 206.

64. Phil Townsend Hanna, "California Vintage Tour," *Wine and Food*, 12, pp. 38–44; Dec. 9, 1936, menu, WFSSF collection; "Notes and Quotes: California Vintage Tour," *Wine and Food*, 24, pp. 388–91.

65. Hanna to Hammond, Dec. 28, 1936; John Shaw to Barney Van Der Steen, Apr. 9, 1935; Shaw to Hanna, no date (circa May 1935), Hanna papers, UCLAA; *WFS*, 87, pp. 192, 194; 86, p. 132; 110, pp. 147–48; 63, p. 220; 85, p. 70; Roy Brady, "American Branches of the Wine and Food Society," May 23, 1956, Roy Brady papers, UCDA.

66. Amerine to Gentlemen, Apr. 29, 1947; Amerine, "The Well-Tempered Winebibber" in "The 1955 Vintage Tour of the SF and LAWFS," Sept. 24–25, 1955; Jean Julliard,

"Comments and Anecdotes on Wine," St. Francis Hotel, Apr. 18, 1944; WFSSF Newsletter for Apr. 15, 1941, dinner. Rossi comments on the "World Cruise dinner," as quoted in Richard MacFarlane, "Wined, Dined," *San Francisco News*, Aug. 29, 1951, WFSSF menu collection; "Memorable Meals," *Wine and Food*, 87, pp. 171–72; Blanquie comments, Dec. 16, 1947, WFSSF menu collection. See also the thirty-seven "Memorable Meals" in *Wine and Food*, 1935–1961, the most for any American chapter; WFSSF menu collection.

67. Nora Martin, "Retired S.F. Doctor Lauds French Food, Eating Habits," *San Francisco Examiner*, Sept. 30, 1952. For later tastings, see menu collection, WFSSF archives. "Memorable Meals," *Wine and Food*, 96, pp. 236–37. In 1949, the WFSSF honored Knopf for endorsing Masson wines. The WFSSF promoted California wines less frequently after World War II. Mar. 9, 1949; Nov. 16, 1948; Sept. 26, 1949; Oct. 14, 1953; Aug. 9, 1949, menus, WFSSF collection; "Dinner on the S.S. President Wilson," radio script, unidentified station, Aug. 27, 1951.

68. *The Physiology of Taste or Meditations on Transcendental Gastronomy*, trans. M. F. K. Fisher (New York: Alfred A. Knopf, 1972 [1949]), pp. 3, 32, 153, 182, 184. Many members signed the 1942 Christmas menu. Years later, members wrote James Howe after an excursion to the Bohemian Grove. "It did lack you." Dec. 15, 1942; Sept. 10, 1958, menus, WFSSF collection.

69. On Price, see Joan Reardon, *Poet of the Appetites: The Lives and Loves of M. F. K. Fisher* (New York: North Point Press, 2004), pp. 163–66; on Weill, see telephone interview with James Hammond, Aug. 1, 2004; on Blanquie, see "Notes and Quotes: San Francisco's Silver Jubilee," *Wine and Food*, 106, pp. 114–16; on Howe, see Howe, "Notes and Quotes," *Wine and Food*, 79, pp. 191–92, and www.walnut-creek.org/about/visiting/history_of_howe_homestead_park_.asp; on Selleck, see Clark, "The Doctor Cooks Dinner," *Saturday Evening Post*, Dec. 16, 1944, pp. 26, 94–96; on Adams, see "Thoughts on Leon Adams: The Man and His Mission, 1905–1995, *Wayward Tendrils Newsletter* (Jan. 1996); on Lucia, see Paul Scholten, "Salvatore Pablo Lucia," *Bulletin of the Society of Medical Friends of Wine* (Mar. 1993); on Chaffee Hall, see www.scmwa.com/articles/kly_hlcrst.htm; on Smith, see Joseph Meyerstein, "Cercle de l'Union: A Retrospect," author's files; on Griffiths, see www.archive.org/stream/farnhamuniversitycalioogrifrich/farnhamuniversitycalioogrifrich_djvu.txt.

70. Street to Price, Mar. 11, 1940, Street papers, PUA; André Simon, *By Request* (London: Wine and Food Society, 1957), p. 114. Fougner regarded the WFSSF dinners as "magnificent beyond words." W. Selmer Fougner, *Gourmet Dinners*, p. 62; "Notes on Wines Served," Apr. 12, 1945. Chaffee Hall doubted whether ten Cheval Blancs "of outstanding years" could be found in any other American city. Hall to Howe, May 4, 1951, WFSSF menu collection; Neil Clark, "The Doctor Cooks Dinner," *Saturday Evening Post*, Dec. 16, 1944, pp. 26, 94–96.

71. For wild-game dinners, the Marshall family donated birds they had hunted. WFSSF menu collection; on Selleck, see Clark, "The Doctor Cooks Dinner," pp. 62–66; on Howe, see chap. 3, n71; on Blanquie, see Apr. 15, 1941, menu, WFSSF collection.

72. See Mar. 31, 1940; July 17, 1940; Dec. 5, 1944; Apr. 19, 1949; May 19, 1950; June 17, 1950; Mar. 12, 1957, menus, WFSSF collection. On Holl's menu collection, see *San Francisco Examiner*, Apr. 2, 1950, San Francisco History Center; Edan Hughes, *Artists in Cali-*

fornia, 1786–1940 (Sacramento, CA: Crocker Art Museum, 2002); Ruth Teiser, *Printing as a Performing Art* (San Francisco: Book Club of California, 1970); James D. Hart, *Fine Printing: The San Francisco Tradition* (Washington, D.C.: Library of Congress, 1985). Robert Grabhorn, part owner of the press, collected pithy gastronomical quotations from various sources over a forty-year period. To commemorate his death, his former colleague, Andrew Hoyem, published them in *A Commonplace Book of Cookery: A Collection of Proverbs, Anecdotes, Opinions and Obscure Facts on Food, Drink, Cooks, Cooking, Dining, Diners & Dieters, Dating from Ancient Times to the Present* (San Francisco: Arion Press, 1975) with an introduction by M. F. K. Fisher. Gourmets and art printers often shared an appreciation of fine food and special editions.

73. Mar. 31, 1940, menu, WFSSF collection; Clark, "The Doctor Cooks Dinner," p. 26. On Woollcott, see www.bbc.co.uk/dna/h2g2/alabaster/A662230.

74. May 5, 1948, menu, WFSSF collection; *I Wouldn't Have Missed It: Selected Poems of Ogden Nash*, ed. Linell Smith and Isabel Eberstadt (Boston: Little, Brown, 1975), p. 324.

75. *The Bent Elbow* caricatured Selleck shooting Novocain into a patient's mouth, while holding a tray of hors d'oeuvres. May 5, 1948, menu, WFSSF collection. "Memorable Meals," *Wine and Food*, 89, pp. 49–50. On a Selleck barbecue overlooking a canyon, see Clementine Paddleford, "I Found the Barbecue King," *Los Angeles Times*, June 19, 1949, p. G10.

76. James Howe, "Notes and Quotes," *Wine and Food*, 79, pp. 191–92; Aug. 3, 1956, menu, WFSSF collection.

77. Price to Street, May 9, 1942, Street papers, PUA; Codman to Price, Mar. 19, 1942; Apr. 6, 1942, Club des Arts Gastronomiques menu collection, WFS of Boston archives; May 5, 1942, menu, WFSSF collection. Chateau Cheval Blanc was a major theme at Society gatherings in 1939, 1947, and 1951; on Howe's cellar see Jan. 31, 1956, menu, WFSSF collection. May 2, 1951, menu.

78. Vintage Tour Committee to members, "The 1949 Vintage Tour of France," Mar. 31, 1949; Watt, "A Gastronomic Tour of France," *The Scotsman*, Nov. 10, 1949, p. 8; detailed tour account, untitled, pp. 1, 3, 4, 8, 14–15, WFSSF menu collection; Beard, "Vintage Tour—1949," *Gourmet*, Jan. 1950, pp. 8–9.

79. See MS version of "A Gastronomic Tour," p. 3; untitled MS, pp. 8, 14–15; Beard, "Vintage Tour—1949," *Gourmet*, Jan. 1950, pp. 26–28.

80. Untitled MS, pp. 20, 22–24; Beard, "Vintage Tour—1949," *Gourmet*, Feb. 1950, p. 25.

81. May 8, May 9, May 23, 1950, invitation and menus; Nate Hale, "Aristocrats Discourse on Wines," *San Francisco Chronicle*, May 9, 1952, p. 2.

82. In 1939, with Simon present, the WFSSF featured dishes from his 1938 cookbook. Jan. 26, 1939, menu, WFSSF collection. Members applied high standards to judging their food. Jan. 20, 1953, Oct. 25, 1952, menus, WFSSF collection; "Memorable Meals," *WFS*, 81, pp. 49–50; "Memorable Meals," *WFS*, 52, pp. 252–53; on the back of his October 17, 1951, menu, Price wrote, "a very badly planned dinner and one for gourmands, not gourmets." WFSSF menu collection.

83. Blanquie, "Notes and Quotes," *Wine and Food*, 106, pp. 114–16; Brillat-Savarin, *The Physiology of Taste*, pp. 184–85; Neuhaus, *Manly Meals and Mom's Home Cooking*, pp. 75–77. On ladies' nights, see WFSSF menu collection.

Chapter 4 · Selectivity and Publicity in the Gourmet Dining Movement

1. On Beebe's antics, see Wolcott Gibbs, "The Diamond Gardenia" (1), *New Yorker,* Nov. 20, 1937, p. 24.

2. *Social Register Locater* (1934, 1936); Jerry E. Patterson, *The Best Families: The Town and Country Social Directory, 1846–1896,* ed. Anthony T. Mazzolat and Frank Zachary (New York: Harry N. Abrahams, 1996), p. 26.

3. The *Wall Street Journal* noted an "uptrend" in fancy food sales and the "growth of *Gourmet."* *Gourmet,* Feb. 1957, pp. 10–11; the magazine claimed that more people were "paying more attention to what they eat" and actually eating good food. Ibid., Apr. 1951, p. 6; Jan. 1958, p. 8.

4. Crahan, *The Wine and Food Society of Southern California: A History with a Bibliography of André L. Simon Compiled by Marcus Crahan* (Los Angeles: Wine and Food Society of Southern California, 1957), p. 10; *Wine and Food: A Gastronomical Quarterly,* 10, pp. 64–65; Price to members of WFSSF, invitation to Dec. 10, 1940, dinner, Street papers, PUA.

5. *P.M. Boston Globe,* Apr. 13, 1959, *Boston Globe* library; Beebe to Brown, Nov. 3, 1947, Tastevin papers; Palace Hotel menu, July 16, 1941, menu collection, San Francisco History Center; *Washington Post,* Jan. 29, 1958, p. B3. Frederick and Alciatore's Code regarded gourmet dining as an activity for the affluent. It denounced the "food snob" but addressed restaurant goers who ate multicourse meals accompanied by wines. *Cooking as Men Like It* (New York: Business Bourse, 1939 [1930]), pp. ix–xv.

6. *Culinary Review,* May 1936, pp. 7–9.

7. Martin T. Olliff, "Les Amis d'Escoffier and the Post-Depression Labor Market for Chefs de Cuisine in America," *Essays in Economic and Business History,* 19 (2001), pp. 179–93; G. Selmer Fougner, *Gourmet Dinners* (New York: M. Barrows, 1941), pp. viii, 11–15, 51–53, 66–70, 102–4, 117–21, 149–50, 196–200, 202–3.

8. De Rochemont, "The Bacchic Brotherhood," part 1, *Town and Country,* Oct. 1964, p. 197.

9. The membership list for the Tastevin dates from 1965. There is no *Social Register* for Los Angeles. Among officers of the Chicago and Boston, but not the New York or San Francisco, chapters of WFS in the 1930s, a high proportion are in the *Register.* As for the Tastevin, many *grand officiers* and *officiers commandeurs* in the Washington (56%), Chicago (38%), and San Francisco (64%) branches are listed, but numbers are less conclusive for the chevaliers. Among national officers of Tastevin only 12% were listed. *Social Register Locater,* 1934, 1936, 1965. See also Simon, *By Request: An Autobiography* (London: Wine and Food Society, 1957), pp. 73–85; Hanna to Street, Mar. 26, 1945, Street papers, PUA.

10. *Wine and Food,* 15, pp. 1–2.

11. Simon, *In the Twilight* (London: Michael Joseph, 1969), p. 69; Simon, *By Request,* p. 113. Membership of the WFS of Chicago consisted of "club and hotel managers, but some of the Society's gourmets include Alfred P. Shaw and Willam C. Boyden." *Chicago Daily Tribune,* July 8, 1936, p. 17; "Report of Julian Street on Chicago and Detroit Activities," June 3, 1937, p. 2, Street papers, PUA; S. Dewey, *Wines for Those Who Have Forgotten and Those Who Want to Know* (Chicago: Lakeside Press, 1934). Suzette Dewey and her

husband Charles became leaders in the Washington branch of the Tastevin. *Washington Post*, Jan. 14, 1953, p. 14; Jan. 9, 1954, p. 9; Apr. 15, 1957, p. B4. In recognition of her role in founding the WFS of Washington, Simon presented Mrs. Dewey with a bottle of 134-year-old brandy. *Chicago Daily Tribune*, Mar. 3, 1947, p. 15. Julian Street insisted that the WFS of Chicago should include "a few names . . . representing the sinister money power, or social importance, or statesmanship." Street to Taft, May 2, 1935, Street papers, PUA.

12. Hanna to Shaw, June 12, 1935; Hanna to Street, Mar. 26, 1945; Whiting to Simon, Mar. 14, 1950; "Statement of Operations of the Wine and Food Society—Los Angeles Chapter," pp. 1–3; "1939 Applications for Membership," Hanna papers, UCLAA; Crahan, *The Wine and Food Society of Southern California*, pp. 18–22. As Alma Whitaker of the *Los Angeles Times* indicated, while the chapter admitted "any genuine bon vivant" regardless of social position who could afford the cost, "there is, in fact, a comfortable confidence that Epicureanism is synonymous with superior social standing." *Los Angeles Times*, Apr. 21, 1935, p. B6.

13. Whiting to Simon, Mar. 14, 1950, Hanna papers, UCLAA; Crahan, *The Wine and Food Society of Southern California*, p. 18; de Rochemont, "The Bacchic Brotherhood," *Town and Country*, Oct. 1964, p. 197; Sprague, *Confrérie des Chevaliers du Tastevin*, pp. 26–27, 31, 34.

14. "1939 Applications for Membership," Hanna papers, UCLAA; Jessamyn Neuhaus, *Manly Meals and Mom's Home Cooking: Cookbooks and Gender in Modern America* (Baltimore: Johns Hopkins University Press, 2003), pp. 75–77.

15. Benjamin Ichinose, presumably of Japanese ancestry, appeared on the list, but it is uncertain whether he joined before 1961. "Membership Roster: WFSSF."

For evidence of diversity, I have relied on surviving membership rosters, names listed in menus, newsletters, and capsule biographies. Reading ethnicity from names is problematic. Gentiles and Jews may have the same German name; mixed marriages can confuse the issue. In identifying someone as a Jew, I refer to ethnic heritage rather than religious practice.

My sources for the Escoffier and Tastevin societies date from the 1950s, for the WFS from the 1930s. Seating chart for the WFSNY dinner, Nov. 11, 1935. Crahan, *The Wine and Food Society of Southern California*, pp. 10–11; the full roster of the WFSSF (circa 1963) included eleven Italians, six of whom owned or managed wineries, and five Jews, one a wine dealer, another a wine expert, among 149 members; for early members of the WFSSF, see dinner committee lists, menu collection; "Roster of Membership" (WFSSF, Nov. 29, 1944); 1939 Board of Governors; *Boston Evening Transcript*, Dec. 3, 1936, p. 1; *Boston Evening American*, Dec. 4, 1936, p. 10.

The Escoffier Society had several Italian and French chefs in Boston and New York. German chefs were more numerous in Chicago, while the records are insufficient for Washington. Nov. 5, 1956, Escoffier menu, NYC; *A.M. Boston Globe*, Nov. 8, 1949; *Boston Globe* Library; phone interview with Charles Doulos, current president of the Boston chapter, Feb. 8, 2005; *Chicago Daily Tribune*, Dec. 8, 1936, p. 20.

There were no Italians on Tastevin rolls. The percentage of Jews, almost all wine dealers, journalists, and publicists, was as follows: New York (20), New Orleans (10), Chicago

(8), Los Angeles (4), Washington (0). The head of the Chicago chapter was Maury Ross, a wine dealer of Jewish extraction. Dec. 2, 1957, N.Y. Tastevin menu; Oct. 21, 1957, New Orleans Tastevin menu; "The History of the Sous-Commanderie de Los Angeles," p. 7 (founding members); Oct. 7, 1958, Chicago Tastevin menu; "Membership Roster, Sous-Commanderie de Washington," July 1, 1965.

16. Nov. 17, 1958, Escoffier menu; phone interviews with Lucille Giovino, Feb. 3, 2005; Ann Costa, Feb. 7, 2005; *A.M. Boston Globe*, Apr. 13, 1959; *P.M. Boston Globe*, Apr. 13, 1959; *P.M. Boston Globe*, Mar. 31, 1969, Boston Globe Library; Carol Eisen Rinzler, "Their Place Is in the Kitchen," *MS*, Nov. 1979, pp. 66–67.

17. *France-Amérique*, Apr. 16, 1950, p. 4; Lucien Boitouzot, *Les Chevaliers du Tastevin* (Nuits St. Georges: Société Bourguignonne de Propagande et Editions, 1984), p. 126; *Washington Post*, Jan. 9, 1954, p. 9; Feb. 26, 1967, p. F15; July 17, 1938, p. TT1; Dec. 20, 1957, p. C15; Richard de Rochemont, "The Bacchic Brotherhood," *Town and Country*, Oct. 1964, p. 126; Charles Codman, "Tastevin," *Town and Country*, Oct. 1937, pp. 68–69, 100.

18. On London, New York, and Boston, see Simon, *By Request*, pp. 106, 115, 147, 153, 155; *Wine and Food*, 24, p. 399; 25, p. 82; *Hotel Bulletin and Nation's Chefs*, Jan. 1935, p. 36. On women members in new chapters of the WFS, see "Proceedings," *Wine and Food*, pp. 88–112.

19. *Chicago Daily Tribune*, Mar. 21, 1961, p. A3. As early as 1936, ladies attended a dinner of the WFS of Chicago. See *Chicago Daily Tribune*, July 8, 1936, p. 17. Frederick's Gourmet Society encouraged women to join at the outset and hosted several women speakers. Taft to Street, Mar. 1, 1937; Street to Taft, Mar. 8, 1937; Street papers, PUA.

20. "Statement of Operations," p. 1; Hanna to Street, Mar. 26, 1945; *Los Angeles Times*, Apr. 21, 1935, p. B6; Crahan, *The Wine and Food Society of Southern California*, p. 10d. Hanna remarked that "cocktails for feminine consumption . . . must possess those attributes that are inherent in womankind herself . . . beguiling and dissembling." *Bohemian Life*, 15, Nov. 1940, pp. 3–4. One woman reporter, banned from a gourmet dinner by her sex, still printed recipes for the dishes, because they were "distinguished." *Los Angeles Times*, May 24, 1939.

21. *Washington Post*, Apr. 4, 1939, p. 3. Morrison Wood, columnist for the *Chicago Daily Tribune* and member of the WFS, described the "Delightful Gastronomical Experience" of a WFS dinner. "For Men Only!" Oct. 9, 1948, p. 12; Theodore Zeldin, *France, 1848–1945*, vol. 1, *Ambition, Love, and Politics* (Oxford: Clarendon Press, 1973), p. 747.

22. Simon to Street, May 10, 1936, Simon papers, PU.

23. Hanna to Elizabeth Stocker, Mar. 16, 1945; Simon to Hanna, Feb. 12, 1947; Whiting to Hanna, Feb. 5, 1947; Feb. 18, 1947, Hanna papers, UCLA.

24. Simon to Hanna, Feb. 26, 1947, Hanna papers, UCLA.

25. Whiting to Hanna, Feb. 5, 1947; Hanna to Simon, Apr. 3, 1947; Simon to Hanna, Feb. 12, 1947, enclosing a copy of Simon's letter to McCarthy, Jan. 28, 1947, Hanna papers, UCLA.

26. Hanna to Simon, Apr. 3, 1947, Hanna papers, UCLA. The Jewish actor Edward G. Robinson spoke to the Society on Sept. 4, 1935, when Jewish members would have been numerous. Crahan, *The Wine and Food Society of Southern California*, p. 12.

27. "Founding of the Westwood Wine and Food Society," Roy Brady papers, UCD. In *The Last Days of Haute Cuisine* (New York: Penguin Books, 2001), p. 83, Patric Kuh, citing James Beard, claims that the WFSSF rejected an applicant because he was Jewish.

28. Simon to Hanna, Feb. 12, 1947; Hanna to Simon, Feb. 19, 1947; Simon to Mrs. McCarthy, Jan. 28, 1947; Whiting to Hanna, Feb. 5, 1947, Hanna papers, UCLA.

29. "Minute and Resolution: Proposed Wine and Food Society of 'Hollywood,'" Mar. 26, 1947; Whiting to Hanna, Feb. 26, 1948; Whiting to Board of Governors, July 15, 1948, Hanna papers, UCLA.

30. Janns to Whiting, Feb. 24, 1948; Mauthe to Hanna, Mar. 4, 1948, Hanna papers, UCLA.

31. *Los Angeles Times*, Nov. 30, 1960, p. A1.

32. Dec. 1, 1948, Gordon Brown Memo; Mar. 9, 1949, Gordon Brown Minutes; Brown to Bohy, Mar. 11, 1949; Brown to Chevalier, Jan. 28, 1948. Roy Alicatore attributed the failure of a 1950 Tastevin dinner at Antoine's to the presence of too many diners and so opposed increasing chapter sizes. Peter Greig proposed that members, as with private clubs, maintain the "exclusive nature of the Confrérie" by requiring unanimous approval of society members. Grieg to Alciatore, Feb. 1, 1949, Tastevin papers.

Roy Alciatore criticized Tastevin officials for offering the title of "commander" to him for a price. Alciatore to Bohy, Nov. 28, 1950. Earlier Brown, protesting dictates from France, argued, "We can be French up to a certain point," but not when doing so alienated American members. If advice was always rejected, members would cease giving it. Brown to Bohy, Feb. 20, 1946; Bohy to Brown, Apr. 16, 1946; Brown to Bohy, Apr. 19, 1946; Bohy to Brown, Apr. 20, 1946; Brown to Bohy, Mar. 11, 1949; May 18, 1949; Brown to Bultinck, Dec. 14, 1948, Tastevin papers.

33. GCO to Brown, July 20, 1949, Tastevin papers.

34. Howells to Bohy, Jan. 4, 1950; May 29, 1950; Bohy to Howells, Jan. 6, 1950; Brown letter drafted for Bohy to members, Apr. 30, 1946. In 1950, the GCO recommended that each member pay $5 per year for Chateau upkeep. Bohy to Aschaffenburg, Jan. 23, 1951, Tastevin papers; de Rochemont, "The Bacchic Brotherhood," part 1, p. 195; "Rapport de M. Jules J. Bohy, *"Tastevin en main,"* May 1946, p. 19; Paul André, *Histoire du Tastevin* (Neuchatel: Editions Messeiller, 1974), pp. 220–21; Bohy to Brown, Apr. 16, 1946; Bohy to Alciatore, Jan. 24, 1949; July 28, 1949; July 6, 1950; Sept. 5, 1950. Bohy to Howells, Nov. 16, 1949, Tastevin papers.

35. Bohy, "Tastevin en main," pp. 20–21; *Washington Times-Herald*, May 29, 1946; Jan. 13, 1948. "In Vino Veritas," Howell's essay, which he circulated to government officials, endorsed Jefferson's belief that wine should be the national drink (pp. 2, 3, 7). Howells to Bohy, Nov. 8, 1949; Apr. 5, 1950, Tastevin papers.

36. Austine Cassini, "These Charming People," *Washington Times Herald*, Jan. 13, 1948; Jan. 9, 1948, menu, Tastevin papers.

37. Roux to Bohy, Jan. 21, 1948; Brown to Roux, Jan. 28, 1948, Tastevin papers.

38. Bohy to Howells, Jan. 22, 1948, Tastevin papers.

39. Howells to Brown, Oct. 15, 1948; Brown to Howells, Oct. 21, 1948; Howells to Brown, Oct. 15, 1948. Eisenhower and Bradley did not attend the Jan. 1948 dinner. Howells to Bohy, Dec. 31, 1947; Howells to Brown, Nov. 1, 1948.

40. Brown to Howells, Nov. 15, 1948; Howells to Brown, Nov. 29, 1948, Tastevin papers.

41. Howells to Bohy, Apr. 30, 1949; "By-Laws of the Washington Chapitre [*sic*]," Examination of Candidates, May 9, 1949; Bohy to Howells, Jan. 6, 1950, Tastevin papers.

42. Bohy to Howells, Apr. 1, 1950, Tastevin papers; *Washington Times Herald*, Mar. 20, 1950; *Washington Post*, Mar. 20, 1950, p. B1.

43. Howells to Bohy, Apr. 5, 1950, Tastevin papers.

44. "La Confrérie des Chevaliers du Tastevin Inventory—December 31, 1956"; Howells to Bohy, Jan. 5, 1951, Tastevin archives.

45. Fougner led a study "tour of good living" to Italy and France in 1936 that provided fodder for his column. Fougner, *Along the Wine Trail*, IV (New York: The Sun, 1936), pp. 7–9, 16–19, 22–23, 49, 61–62, 67. Hanna regarded Fougner as "perhaps the greatest single human influence in bettering the American table during the past decade." *Bohemian Life*, 22, June 1941, p. 4.

46. Nov. 15, 1935, p. 12; see also Street papers, PU.

47. Dec. 3, 1936, p. 1.

48. Dec. 4, 1936, p. 10.

49. *New York Herald Tribune*, Apr. 3, 1937, p. 3; Feb. 4, 1939, p. 14. Reporters treated a 1936 wine tasting at the Palace Hotel, attended by four thousand guests and sponsored by the WFSSF and the Wine Institute, as a society event. They paid close attention to the "fastidious hostesses seeking knowledge of wines to serve at social functions." *Wine and Food*, 12, p. 86; A. D. Hyman, "Tasters Learn about Wines," *San Francisco Examiner*, Oct. 16, 1936, p. 5.

50. Amerine wanted *Life* to cover instead the vintage tour planned by the Los Angeles and New York chapters. Maynard Amerine to Leon D. Adams, May 8, 1939, Amerine papers, UCD.

51. "Rapport de M. Jules J. Bohy," *Tastevin en Main*, May 1946, p. 17; Georges Rozet, *Tastevin en main* (Paris: Editions E.P.I.C., 1950), pp. 98–99.

52. Paul André, *Histoire du Tastevin: Confrérie bourguignonne et internationale* (Neuchatel: Editions Messeiller, 1974), p. 193.

53. *New York Times*, Dec. 25, 1938, p. 25.

54. *Los Angeles Times*, May 24, 1939, p. B3; May 27, 1949, p. B1; Oct. 24, 1936, p. I4; "With Champagne and Burgundy," *New York Times Sunday Magazine*, May 30, 1948, pp. 28–29.

55. Jack Alexander, "La Serviette au Cou," *New Yorker*, Mar. 20, 1937, p. 43.

56. Fougner, *Gourmet Dinners*, pp. 177, 171.

57. *Los Angeles Times*, Oct. 2, 1937, p. I4; May 19, 1939, p. A5; Mar. 2, 1941, p. H2; May 27, 1949, p. B1. Maury Ross of the WFS of Chicago was also featured for his expertise in cooking pressed duck. Genevieve Flavin, *Chicago Daily Tribune*, Feb. 3, 1954, p. A1.

58. *Westways*, Sept. 1938, pp. 24, 26; June 1938, pp. 22–23; Oct. 28, p. 26; Aug. 1937, pp. 41–42; Sept. 1938, pp. 18–19.

59. Armitage, *"Fit for a King": The Merle Armitage Book of Good Food* (New York: Duello, Sloan and Pearce Publishers, 1939), pp. xiii–xvi, 1–9. Rex Stout's mystery stories, first

published in 1934, featured a gourmet gumshoe, Nero Wolfe. "Too Many Cooks," *American Magazine*, Mar. 1938, pp. 12.

60. Street also wrote an essay on herbs that appeared in *Adventures in Good Cooking* in 1945 and worked for Hines as a "dinner detective," appraising restaurants for the guide. During the war, *Adventures in Good Eating* sold 3,500 copies per month, while sales rose to over five hundred thousand in the months after the war. Hines to Street, Jan. 30, 1945; Aug. 17, 1945; Street to Hines, Jan. 20, 1945; Feb. 20, 1945; Feb. 3, 1947; Hines to Street, Nov. 1, 1937; Hines to Street, Mar. 14, 1938, Street papers, PUA; Louis Hatchett, *Duncan Hines: The Man behind the Cake Mix* (Macon, GA: Mercer University Press, 2001), pp. 60–62, 145, 149.

61. Hines, *Adventures in Good Eating*, pp. v, xii, 142, 202–3; Hatchett, *Duncan Hines*, pp. 77, 137, 171, 237–38; Hines to Street, June 13, 1939; May 20, 1942, June 12, 1942; June 3, 1942, Street papers, PUA.

62. Feb. 1, 1941, p. 6. For other advertisements using gourmet societies to tout their products, see *New York Times*, May 5, 1937, p. 5; Dec. 8, 1959, p. 7; *Washington Post* display ad, Sept. 10, 1958, p. A9; *New York Times*, June 2, 1961, p. 34.

63. Eve Jochnowitz, "Feasting on the Future: Foods of the World of Tomorrow at the New York World's Fair of 1939–40," *Performance Research*, 4 (1), pp. 111, 112, 119.

64. Wine and Food, 22, p. 109; *Food at the Fair* (New York: Exposition Publications, 1939), pp. 6–7, 9; *New York Times*, Dec. 25, 1938, p. 17. The guide was formally endorsed by New York World's Fair authorities and recommended in *"Building the World of Tomorrow": Official Guide Book of the New York World's Fair, 1939*, p. 15.

65. Fougner, *Gourmet Dinners*, pp. 125–26. Among journalists who praised the Pavillon were Walter Lippmann, "A Day at the World's Fair," *Current History*, July 3, 1939, pp. 50–51; Sheila Hibben, "Around the Fair," *New Yorker*, May 20, 1939, p. 45; *Life*, July 3, 1939, p. 58.

66. *Wine and Food*, 24, pp. 391–93; *Vogue*, Feb. 1, 1939, pp. 162–63.

67. Alciatore to Street, Aug. 13, 1933; Dec. 10, 1933; Jan. 5, 1935; Dec. 12, 1936, Street papers, PUA.

68. Street to Alciatore, Sept. 7, 1934; Alciatore to Street, Apr. 6, 1940; June 2, 1940; Wildman to Street, July 8, 1940; Street to Wildman, July 20, 1940, Street papers, PUA.

69. Street to Alciatore, July 19, 1939; Alicatore to Street, July 17, 1939; Aug. 30, 1937; Street also recommended to no avail a publicist to secure more recognition for Antoine's and "a committee to include André Simon" to collect congratulatory messages. Feb. 7, 1939; July 29, 1939, Street papers, PUA.

70. Wright, *The Bed Book of Eating and Drinking* (New York: J. B. Lippincott, 1943), p. 42; Street to Lauryssen, May 28, 1938; Street to Lauryssen, Jan. 27, 1938; Feb. 8, 1938, Street papers, PUA; *Wine and Food*, 20, pp. 378, 383; Street to Lauryssen, Apr. 12, 1939; May 7, 1940; Lauryssen to Street, May 14, 1940, Street papers, PUA. Members of the WFSLA helped to "revise the wine lists of famous clubs and restaurants in the city." *Los Angeles Times*, Oct. 24, 1937, p. I4; June 12, 1958, p. A1.

71. Clark, "The Doctor Cooks a Dinner," *Saturday Evening Post*, Dec. 16, 1944, pp. 26, 91.

72. *Gourmet Dinners*, p. 62; Amerine to Adams, May 8, 1939, Amerine papers, UCDA; Clark, "The Doctor Cooks a Dinner," pp. 26, 91. Even less likely to jar wartime sensitivities was *The Bed-Book of Eating and Drinking* (New York: J. B. Lippincott, 1943). There Richardson Wright wrote a single entry for each day of the year mixing past gourmet events, recipes, and homage to Brillat-Savarin and current leaders of the WFSNY.

73. "Savarin Sure" (Hanna) wrote *Bohemian Life* for eighteen years. Robert Balzer started as a wine expert in Balzer's, the grocery store established by his father. Dan Strehl, ed., *The Epicurean* (Pasadena: Weather Bird Press, 2001). Street received a stipend for his work. Street to Greene, Jan. 15, 1943; Mar. 1, 1943; Jan. 21, 1945; Greene to Street, July 2, 1943; Street to Simon, June 4, 1944, Street papers, PUA; Koshland to Street, Sept. 24, 1959, Knopf papers, UT. After Street's death, his wife Margot (A.I.M.S.) gathered the pamphlets into *Table Topics*, published by Knopf in 1959. Newsletters distributed by wine dealers Peter Greig and Frank Schoonmaker were similar to "Table Topics."

74. "Tastevin," Oct. 1937, pp. 69, 100.

75. Brown to Trostler, Dec. 4, 1947; Brown to Alciatore, Dec. 9, 1947; Jane Nickerson, "With Champagne and Burgundy," *New York Times Magazine*, May 30, 1948, pp. 28–29; Clementine Paddleford, "Bit of Spice Peps Up Luncheon to Food Editors," *New York Herald Tribune*, May 4, 1948; Robert W. Dana, "Chevaliers Sample Burgundy," *New York World Telegram*, Dec. 8, 1947, Tastevin Archives. Diat later admitted that he worried about meeting the high standards of the Tastevin. *Gourmet*, May 1960, p. 22.

76. Brown to Roux, Jan. 28, 1948, Tastevin papers; Beebe to Brown, Nov. 3, 1947; Sawyer to Brown, Apr. 18, 1948; Brown to Bohy, Apr. 29, 1948, enclosing "Memorandum for Photographers," Tastevin papers; Charles Clegg and Duncan Emrich, eds., *The Lucius Beebe Reader* (Garden City, NY: Doubleday, 1967). Tastevin "struck out" with a *Life* photographer who photographed a dinner but never produced a story. Brown then courted Ted Patrick, editor of *Holiday*, to no avail. Brown to Bultinck, Dec. 14, 1948; Brown to Bohy, Mar. 11, 1949, Tastevin papers; *New Yorker*, Dec. 11, 1948, pp. 28–29.

77. "Tastevin," pp. 1–7; Script for Voice of America; Bohy to Rodier, Jan. 3, 1949, Tastevin papers.

78. *Life Magazine*, Dec. 9, 1946, p. 41. The writer credited Escoffier rather than Brillat-Savarin with the saying that "the inventor of a new dish confers more happiness than the discoverer of a new planet." Joseph Donon was the subject of a short piece in "Talk of the Town" and a lengthy profile on his relationship with the Vanderbilt heir, Mrs. McK. Twombly, who hired him as a private chef. *New Yorker*, Nov. 27, 1954, pp. 36–37; Mar. 10, 1962, pp. 47–78.

79. Jean Muir, "Cooking Is Like Making Love," *Saturday Evening Post*, Feb. 5, 1955, p. 89.

80. Brandy Brent, "Riding the Carrousel," *Los Angeles Times*, May 27, 1949, p. B1; May 26, 1940, p. 18; Apr. 13, 1947, p. E28; Oct. 24, 1937, p. I4.

81. *Los Angeles Times*, Dec. 12, 1957, p. A1; June 30, 1960, p. A1; Nov. 10, 1957, p. D16; Oct. 27, 1958, p. A1; Mar. 24, 1953, p. 19.

82. *Dining with My Friends: Adventures with Epicures* (New York: Crown Publishers, 1949), pp. 3–5, 12, 14, 64–68, 97, 130, 164, 179, 213, 263–64.

83. *New York Times*, Dec. 8, 1959, p. 7.

84. Bohy to Alciatore, July 28, 1939; Jan. 12, 1950, Tastevin papers; Beebe, "The Miracle of Antoine's," *Holiday*, Jan. 1953, pp. 57–59; see also Milton Lehman, "Gourmet's Paradise," *Collier's*, Nov. 8, 1947, pp. 84, 85, 87.

85. Frances Parkinson Keyes, *Dinner at Antoine's* (New York: J. Messner, 1948); Bohy to Alciatore, Sept. 30, 1949, Tastevin papers. Owen Brennan named his restaurant "Breakfast at Brennan's" to play off of Keyes' title. Debra C. Argen, "Brennan's Restaurant," www.luxuryweb.com/html/brennan_s.html. Brennan died Nov. 4, 1955, after attending a Tastevin dinner at Antoine's.

86. *Los Angeles Times*, Jan. 3, 1957, p. A1; Jan. 3, 1958, p. A1; Jan. 7, 1958, p. A1; Jan. 7, 1959, p. A1; Jan. 6, 1960, p. A1; Jan. 6, 1961, p. A1. On one occasion, the buffet table with trays of bluepoint oysters and a *filet de boeuf* provided the background for elegantly attired guests, including Florence Wellborne "in a net gown glistening with beaded fringe." Jan. 5, 1962, p. A1.

87. *Washington Post*, Mar. 20, 1950, p. B1; Apr. 5, 1955, p. 27; Apr. 20, 1955, p. 42; Jan. 29, 1958, p. B3.

88. Gibbs also mentioned the "handful of top-ranking food-and-wine lovers" in the Club des Arts Gastronomiques that she properly labeled the gourmet "elite." Angelica Gibbs, "Profiles: With Palette Knife and Skillet," *New Yorker*, May 28, 1949, pp. 34–48.

89. *Bohemian Life*, 71, July 1945, pp. 1–2.

90. *Wine and Food*, "Proceedings," 108, pp. 278, 280; 110, pp. 146, 148, 152. "U.S. Grows an Educated Palate," *Business Week*, Jan. 31, 1969, p. 30.

91. Virginia Stanton, "I Got the Whim Whams When I Was Asked to Do the Next Dinner for the Wine and Food Society," *House Beautiful*, Mar. 1959, pp. 140, 171–76.

92. *Bohemian Life*, 55, Mar. 1944, p. 3; Geoffrey T. Hellman, "Profiles: The Best of the Best," *New Yorker*, Mar. 10, 1962, p. 64. On Escoffier membership, see also *New York Times*, Jan. 2, 1961, p. 34; Dec. 10, 1951, p. 31; Dec. 9, 1952, p. 45; Mar. 2, 1955, p. 24; Jan. 23, 1956, p. 39; Nov. 17, 1958; Nov. 20, 1957, menus, Les Amis d'Escoffier menu collection; Craig Claiborne, "Menu Fit for 100 Gourmets," *New York Times*, Apr. 15, 1959, p. 36. After 1959, the *New York Times* ceased covering Escoffier events.

93. A.M. *Boston Globe*, Apr. 13, 1959, p. 7; Harold Banks, "Les Dames invite [sic] Les Amis," *Boston Herald*, Apr. 29, 1979, *Boston Globe* Library.

94. Sprague, *Confrérie des Chevaliers du Tastevin*, pp. 20–24.

95. *New Yorker*, Oct. 28, 1961, p. 45; Kate Lloyd, "Chef's Trial," *Vogue*, Apr. 15, 1964, pp. 114–15, 151, 153; Caskie Stinnett, "Dinner with the Big Boys," *Atlantic Monthly*, Apr. 1977, pp. 26–27; *Time*, Aug. 4, 1961, p. 38; Hellman, "Profiles," *New Yorker*, Mar. 10, 1962, p. 64.

96. Julius Wile, "Origin of the Commanderie de Bordeaux," rev. ed., July 23, 1996; "Charter Members (of the Commanderie), 1959"; Terry Robards, "Grand Master of Gastronomes," *New York Times Magazine*, Oct. 12, 1980, p. 115.

97. Wile, "Origins"; Craig Claiborne, "Food News: Wines," *New York Times*, Jan. 16, 1959, p. 32; *New Yorker*, Feb. 22, 1964, pp. 19–20; Jean V. Nevins, "About the Baillage," *Gastronome*, Millenium ed., p. 9; *New York Times*, Dec. 4, 1960, p. 14; Jan. 3, 1990, p. C1;

Jules Epstein telephone interview, Mar. 10, 2006; "Curnonsky," *Larousse Gastronomique*, pp. 386–87.

98. *Gourmet*, July 1943, p. 2; Dec. 1942, pp. 2–3.

99. *Chicago Daily Tribune*, Aug. 21, 1948, p. 12; *Gourmet*, May 1951, Mar. 1953, p. 1; Nov. 1960, pp. 9–11. Lucretia Cole announced that the "Friends of Food" from Los Angeles, devoted to "the pleasure of the table," had prepared a Greek dinner. *Gourmet*, May 1953, p. 2.

100. *Gourmet*, Aug. 1954, pp. 8–9; Aug. 1955, p. 2; Nov. 1955, p. 2; May 1956, p. 2; July 1959, p. 1.

Chapter 5 • Beating the Nazis with Truffles and Tripe

1. Riesman, *The Lonely Crowd: A Study of the Changing American Character* (New York: Doubleday, 1950), pp. 168–72.

2. Joseph Wechsberg, *Dining at the Pavillon* (Boston: Little, Brown, 1962); David Kamp, *The United States of Arugula: How We Became a Gourmet Nation* (New York: Broadway Books, 2006), p. 37; *Gourmet*, May 1955, p. 6.

3. Harvey Levenstein, *We'll Always Have Paris: American Tourists in France since 1930* (Chicago: University of Chicago Press, 2004), pp. 183–84.

4. "U.S. Grows an Educated Palate," *Business Week*, Aug. 23, 1958, p. 28; "Big Appetite for Gourmet Foods," *Business Week*, Aug. 23, 1958, pp. 55–59; see also *Gourmet*, Nov. 1958, p. 4; Nov. 1959, p. 8.

5. On Puritanism and gourmet dining, see Jane and Michael Stern, *American Gourmet: Classic Recipes. Deluxe Delights, Flamboyant Favorites and Swank "Company" Food from the '50s and '60s* (New York: HarperCollins, 1991), p. 2; Lucius Beebe, "Along the Boulevards," *Gourmet*, Feb. 1949, pp. 8–9.

6. Simon to Street, June 30, 1944, Street papers, PUA.

7. *Gourmet*, Sept. 1941, p. 2.

8. *Gourmet*, Jan. 1959, p. 6.

9. See, for example, *Gourmet*, Feb. 1944, pp. 2–3.

10. On MacAusland, see Leibenstein, "MacAusland and *Gourmet*," in Harlan Walker, ed., *Cooks and Other People: Proceedings of the Oxford Symposium on Food and Cookery* (Totnes, Devon, 1996), pp. 194–98; Anne Mendelson, *Stand Facing the Stove: The Story of the Women Who Gave America the Joy of Cooking* (New York: Scribner, 1996), p. 254; *New York Times* obituary, June 6, 1980, p. D15; Robert Clark, *James Beard: A Biography* (New York: HarperCollins, 1993), pp. 123–24, 126, 134–35, 236, 240; *Gourmet*, Feb. 1949, pp. 8–9; e-mail from Russell MacAusland, Oct. 18, 2005; *Gourmet*, Apr. 1949, p. 3.

11. On MacAusland's esteem for the *New Yorker*, see *Gourmet*, Jan. 1959, p. 6; author interview with Caroline Bates, Aug. 1, 2008.

12. *Gourmet*, Aug. 1941, p. 2; "Metzelthin, Pearl," *Current Biography*, 1942, pp. 587–88; Charles E. Planck, *Women with Wings* (New York: Harper and Brothers, 1942), pp. 200–202.

13. On De Gouy's life, see *New York Times* obituary, Nov. 15, 1947, p. 17; Robert Beddos, "Portrait of a Cook Book," *New York Times Sunday Magazine*, Oct. 17, 1948, p. 69; De Gouy, *Gourmet's Cook Book of Fish and Game*, vol. 1, Fish (New York: Gourmet, 1947), dust jacket.

14. Ralph Reinhold obituary, *New York Times*, Jan. 25, 1967, p. 42; telephone interviews with Victoria Reinhold and Cathy Farrell, granddaughters of Ralph Reinhold, Nov. 1, 2006; Leibenstein, "MacAusland and *Gourmet*," pp. 194–98.

15. Straus was also a council member of the New York State College of Home Economics (1943–46) and was appointed by Governor Thomas E. Dewey to the wartime Emergency Food Commission. Gladys Guggenheim Straus obituary, *New York Times*, Mar. 15, 1980, p. 24; John Davis, *The Guggenheims: An American Epic* (New York: Morrow, 1978), p. 368; Leibenstein, "MacAusland and *Gourmet*," p. 195. Evan Jones identified Straus as a "partner" of MacAusland. *Epicurean Delight: The Life and Times of James Beard* (New York: Alfred A. Knopf, 1990), p. 140.

16. Harkness was known for bringing the first giant panda from China back to the United States. Christensen authored numerous cookbooks, including *Voyage Gastronomique 1973* (New York: Hawthorn, 1973).

17. Coffin, a Pulitzer Prize–winning author, wrote forty books and taught at Bowdoin College, his alma mater. Longstreet wrote over one hundred books.

18. Also related to cooking were several series providing advice on specialized tasks such as "Gourmet's Herb Garden," "The ABC of Seasoning," "The Companionable Arts" (how to grow vegetables), "Frozen Assets," and "Freeze to Please" (how to freeze fresh meats and produce). Other series focused on "Chafing Dish Cookery," the "Well-Mannered Chafing Dish," and making "Patisserie."

19. The last of Stahlhut's covers appeared on the Nov. 1955 issue of *Gourmet*. See Dec. 1955 cover; Jan. 1958, p. 8; Jan. 1959, p. 4.

20. *Gourmet*, Apr. 1948, p. 2; June 1955, pp. 2–4; May 1947, pp. 2–3.

21. Ibid., June, 1955, pp. 2–4; Mar. 1956, pp. 3–4; June 1948, pp. 2–3; Jan. 1947, p. 4; Apr. 1949, pp. 3–4.

22. Ibid., Jan. 1941, pp. 5–6.

23. Ibid., Sept. 2001, p. 71. The Chamberlains' enthusiasm for their colonial Marblehead home, expressed in Narcissa's *Old Rooms for New Living* (Hastings House, 1953), balanced their love of France and reflected the prevailing ethos of the magazine.

24. Sinclair Lewis' critique of modern life in *Babbitt* (1922) articulates the views of many intellectuals; see pp. 52–58. *Gourmet*, Oct. 1944, p. 30. Gyorgy Scrinis' "On the Ideology of Nutritionism" echoes *Gourmet*'s attack on nutritionists. *Gastronomica*, Winter 2008, pp. 39–48.

25. *Gourmet*, Jan. 1941.

26. Ibid., Dec. 1945, p. 36; Mar. 1941, p. 3; Feb. 1943, p. 11.

27. Ibid., Jan. 1941, p. 4.

28. Ibid., Dec. 1942, pp. 8–10, 31–32.

29. Ibid., Nov. 1941, pp. 6–8, 36–37.

30. Ibid., Feb. 1941, p. 7.

31. Ibid., Jan. 1941, pp. 7–10.

32. Ibid., Jan. 1941, pp. 7–10; Feb. 1941, pp. 18–19, 40–41.

33. Leibenstein, "MacAusland and *Gourmet*," pp. 194–98. MacAusland sought to buy out early investors using the profits from the sale of the *Gourmet Cookbook* in 1950. Oct. 21, 2005, e-mail from Jon Carson; Nov. 21, 2006, telephone interview with Russell MacAusland, who claims that the investors were paid with Earle's inheritance from his friend John Clapp.

34. See publication facts for both books.

35. *Gourmet*, May 1946, pp. 2–3; Dec. 1946, p. 2; Oct. 1947, pp. 6–7; Nov. 1947, p. 2; Jane Nickerson, "News of Food," *New York Times*, July 4, 1947, p. 10.

36. *Gourmet*, Aug. 1953, pp. 4–5; Nov. 1953, pp. 4–5; Feb. 1954, p. 9; Mar. 1954, p. 11; Mar. 1956, p. 6. *Vanity Fair* offered travel services to readers in the 1920s through the Condé Nast Travel Bureau; see *Vanity Fair*, Jan. 1925, pp. 11–17.

37. *New York Times*, Nov. 19, 1954, p. 33; *Gourmet*, Oct. 1954, pp. 3, 13; Nov. 1954, p. 50; Apr. 1955, p. 47; May 1957, p. 67; Mar. 1957, p. 2; May 1957, p. 5. The last advertisement for the guide appeared in May 1957, p. 49.

38. The prevalence of whisky ads is clear from this random survey: three of the six full-page ads in the first issue (Jan. 1941) promoted distilled alcoholic beverages. In January 1947, four of the five full-page ads and five of the nine two-thirds-page ads endorsed whisky or brandy. By 1956 the proportion of full- and two-thirds-page ads for distilled alcohol beverages fell to about half (author's tabulations).

Frank Schoonmaker wrote thirty-four articles on wine, while forty-five more appeared under other bylines. On whisky/brandy, Don Summers wrote seven articles in 1941; between July 1942 and July 1950, Charles Baker, Jr., wrote forty articles. Other writers contributed an average of four articles a year containing recipes for summer and Christmas drinks incorporating whiskey from 1951 to 1961. On Bundschu, see Thomas Pinney, *A History of Wine in America from Prohibition to the Present* (Berkeley and Los Angeles: University of California Press, 2005), p. 406n22; *Gourmet*, June 1945, pp. 2–3. The California Wine Advisory Board also advertised by distributing free copies of the "Hostess Book of Favorite Wine Recipes" (1942) based on California wine.

39. *Gourmet*, Jan. 1952, p. 2.

40. Ibid.

41. Ibid., Sept. 1944, pp. 4–8; Oct. 1944, p. 30.

42. Ibid., Oct. 1959, p. 63; Nov. 1959, p. 63; Oct. 1961, p. 34.

43. Ibid., Apr. 1956, opposite p. 36 (pp. 1–4); Mar. 1957, p. 37.

44. Ibid., Dec. 1954, pp. 10–11.

45. John K. Jessup, ed., *The Ideas of Henry Luce* (New York: Atheneum, 1969), pp. 118–20, 113–14.

46. *Gourmet*, Apr. 1942, p. 47; Nov. 1941, p. 4; May 1941, p. 4; Oct. 1941, pp. 4–5; Sept. 1941, pp. 2–3; Feb. 1941, p. 35; May 1944, pp. 4–5; May 1941, p. 4.

47. Ibid., Mar. 1941, p. 28; Apr. 1941, pp. 2–4.

48. Ibid., Apr. 1941, p. 2; Mar. 1941, p. 3; Dec. 1941, p. 3.

49. Ibid., Mar. 1941, p. 3; Dec. 1941, p. 3; Feb. 1942, pp. 22–23; on war aims, see Mark Leff, "The Politics of Sacrifice on the American Home Front in World War II," *Journal of American History* (Mar. 1991), pp. 1296–1318.

50. *Gourmet*, June 1943, p. 2; Apr. 1942, p. 3; July 1942, pp. 2–3; Feb. 1943, p. 2.

51. Ibid., Sept. 1942, p. 21; May 1943, p. 7.

52. Amy Bentley, *Eating for Victory: Food Rationing and the Politics of Domesticity* (Urbana: University of Illinois Press, 1998); *Gourmet*, Sept. 1942, p. 21; Sept. 1941, pp. 2–3.

53. *Gourmet*, May 1943, p. 7; Sept. 1942, pp. 20–21; July 1943, p. 30; Feb. 1944, p. 2.

54. Ibid., Jan. 1944, p. 2; Mar. 1942, p. 34; Apr. 1943, p. 2; Mar. 1944, p. 44; Jan. 1943, p. 19; Mar. 1943, pp. 16–17.

55. Ibid., Aug. 1943, p. 1; Mar. 1943, p. 11.

56. Ibid., Mar. 1943, p. 3; Dec. 1943, p. 2.

57. Ibid., June 1943, p. 3.

58. Ibid., Jan. 1941, pp. 4–5.

59. Ibid., June 1941, p. 12; Feb. 1942, p. 34; "Best Cellars," Feb. to Sept. 1942.

60. Ibid., Nov. 1941, p. 32; Oct. 1943, inside back cover; Jan. 1943, back cover. Appeals to buy war bonds also appeared regularly: June 1943, inside cover, June 1945, cover.

61. Ibid., Oct. 1942, pp. 6–7, 28–30; July 1944, p. 64; Edward Dumbauld, *Thomas Jefferson: American Tourist* (Norman: University of Oklahoma Press, 1946), p. 199; Dumas Malone, *Jefferson and the Rights of Man* (Boston: Little, Brown, 1951), pp. 117–19.

62. *Gourmet*, May 1944, p. 44.

63. Ibid., Dec. 1946, pp. 72–73; Oct. 1946, p. 43.

64. Ibid., Mar. 1944, p. 59; Aug. 1942, p. 2. Samuel Chamberlain, *Etched in Sunlight: Fifty Years in the Graphic Arts* (Boston: Boston Public Library, 1968), pp. 110–12. Herman Smith, a New York clothes designer, wrote about his family's Alsatian cook in Michigan. Given the date of publication, he may have stolen the idea from Chamberlain. *Stina: The Story of a Cook* (New York: M. Barrows, 1942).

65. *Gourmet*, Feb. 1941, p. 14.

66. Ibid., Mar. 1941, p. 21; June 1941, p. 21.

67. Ibid., Aug. 1941, p. 3; Sept. 1941, pp. 16, 45; Nov. 1941, p. 28; Feb. 1942, p. 13; Aug. 1942, p. 43; Mar. 1942, pp. 10–11.

68. Ibid., May 1942, p. 16; June 1942, pp. 36–37; "Samuel Chamberlain's *Clementine in the Kitchen*," *Gastronomica: The Journal of Food and Culture*, Fall 2007, pp. 42–52.

69. *Gourmet*, Jan. 1945, p. 10; Apr. 1945, p. 14; June 1945, p. 14; Aug. 1945, p. 14; Sept. 1945, p. 16; Jan. 1946, p. 2; Dec. 1947, p. 2. *Katish: Our Russian Cook* (New York: Farrar, Straus and Giroux, 1947) was reprinted in 2001 in the Modern Library Food series edited by Ruth Reichl.

70. *Gourmet*, July 1942, p. 14. C. F. Kett wondered "what . . . will happen to those little restaurants of Paris under the 'new order of Europe.'" Aug. 1941, p. 18.

71. Ibid., Jan. 1944, pp. 18–19; Mar. 1942, p. 9; Dec. 1942, p. 40.

72. Ibid., May 1941, p. 6.

73. André Simon to Julian Street, June 4, 1944, Street papers, PUA; *Gourmet*, Mar. 1945, p. 30; Feb. 1944, p. 2. *Gourmet* offices were first located at 330 W. 42nd Street. *New York Times*, Sept. 23, 1940, p. 26.

Chapter 6 · Gourmet's Gastronomic Tours

1. *Bobos in Paradise: The New Upper Class and How They Got There* (New York: Simon and Schuster, 2000), pp. 203–10.

2. Ibid.; James Buzard, *The Beaten Track: European Tourism, Literature, and the Ways to 'Culture,' 1800–1918* (Oxford: Clarendon Press, 1993), pp. 5–7. While Brooks cites the Bohemian credo in Malcolm Cowley's *Exile's Return: A Literary Saga of the Nineteen Twenties* (New York: Viking Press, 1951 [1934]), pp. 59–61, 205, he ignores Cowley's account of returned exiles who worked nine to five, while perpetuating Bohemian lifestyles. Brooks and historians James Buzard and Harvey Levenstein want to eliminate the distinction between travel and tourism, so often used as a put-down of tourists. Underlying the snobbery, however, are two concepts that identify distinctive and legitimate approaches to travel. Tourists, in general, place decisions about itinerary, hotels, restaurants, etc., in the hands of others, while travelers make their own choices. Levenstein, *Seductive Journey: American Tourists in France from Jefferson to the Jazz Age* (Chicago: University of Chicago Press, 1998), pp. ix–xii.

3. Christopher Endy, *Cold War Holidays: American Tourism in France* (Chapel Hill: University of North Carolina Press, 2004), pp. 135–36.

4. Harvey Levenstein, *We'll Always Have Paris: American Tourists in France since 1930* (Chicago: University of Chicago Press, 2004), pp. 25–26, 29–30.

5. *Bouquet de France: An Epicurean Tour of the French Provinces* (New York: Gourmet Distributing Corp., 1952), p. vii. In 1957, Chamberlain sought to break his contract, which gave *Gourmet* exclusive rights to publish and market his books, and move to Knopf, but the legal complications were daunting. Chamberlain to Knopf, Jan. 25, 1957; Knopf to Chamberlain, Jan. 29, 1957; Chamberlain to MacAusland, Jan. 29, 1957 (copy of letter sent to Knopf); Narcissa Chamberlain to Knopf, Feb. 5, 1957, Knopf papers, UT. The Chamberlains also complained to Julia Child about MacAusland. Child to Avis DeVoto, Mar. 6, 1953, Child papers, SL.

6. The Chamberlains were listed in the 1934 and 1936 *Social Register Locators*, suggesting that they shared their readers' social ambitions.

7. *Etched in Sunlight: Fifty Years in the Graphic Arts* (Boston: Boston Public Library, 1968), p. 5; Richardson Wright, "The Iowan Discovers N.E.," *Saturday Review of Literature*, May 22, 1943, pp. 21–22; Cowley, *Exile's Return*, chap. 1.

8. *Etched in Sunlight*, pp. 6–7; *Bouquet de France*, p. 78.

9. *Etched in Sunlight*, pp. 10, 15, 18–19, 26, 40, 47, 49.

10. Ibid., p. 40. Warren Susman, "Pilgrimage to Paris: The Backgrounds of American Expatriation, 1920–1934," Ph.D. dissertation, University of Wisconsin, 1957, pp. 264–81.

11. *Etched in Sunlight*, pp. 63, 154.

12. Ibid., pp. 83, 86–89, 98–99, 108–10, 142.

13. Ibid., pp. 128–34; *Italian Bouquet: An Epicurean Tour of Italy* (New York: Gourmet Distributing Corp., 1958), pp. 378–79, 399; *Bouquet de France*, p. viii.

14. After 1945, Chamberlain published such photographic studies as "Behold Williamsburg" (1947) and *Boston Landmarks* (1947).

15. *Bouquet de France*, pp. xix, 84, 222, 99, 487.

16. *Antiques Magazine*, Sept. 1969, p. 697; Leslie R. Forester, "Talented Couple Invite Us to See Their 260-Year Old Home," *American Home*, Apr. 1959, p. 76.

17. *Italian Bouquet*, p. 90.

18. *Gourmet*, Mar. 1949, pp. 1–2.

19. Ibid., July 1951, pp. 8–9; Leslie R. Forester, "Talented Couple," *American Home*, p. 25. Chamberlain's recollections of such events as Lindbergh's 1927 landing in France revealed a long-standing association with Europe, shared with many of his readers, and emphasized Europe's link with America. *Bouquet de France*, p. 71; see also *British Bouquet*, pp. 81–82.

20. *British Bouquet*, p. 171.

21. For one reader, Clementine recalled Marie who cooked for him in Paris. Another felt "such nostalgia for France when reading 'Clementine.'" Sales reached fifty thousand by 1947. *Gourmet*, Feb. 1942, pp. 2–3; Aug. 1942, pp. 2–3; July 1943, pp. 2–3; Mar. 1942, pp. 2–3; May 1943, pp. 2–3; Dec. 1943, pp. 2–3; June 1947, p. 65. Mrs. John Williamson "reminisce[d] through the pages of your magazine." Apr. 1941, p. 2.

22. *Gourmet*, Aug. 1951, pp. 2–5; Feb. 1954, p. 1; Oct. 1953, pp. 2–3; July 1954, p. 2; Jan. 1954, pp. 1–2. In the *New York Times Book Review*, Charlotte Turgeon noted Chamberlain's capacity to "make the tourist think that he is meeting old friends." Privately, Julia Child called *Bouquet* "a wonderful and beautiful book. What fun it would be to travel with, and what fun they have had doing it together." Apr. 2, 1953, p. BR7; *Gourmet*, Jan. 1950, p. 2; Julia Child to Avis DeVoto, Jan. 5, 1952, Avis DeVoto papers, SL. Mort Lewis chose *Bouquet* over the *Guide Michelin*. "Your Bouquet," he wrote, "is worth its weight in *paté de foie gras!*" Ibid., July 1956, p. 2; Jan. 1959, p. 2.

23. *Gourmet*, Nov. 11, 1952, pp. 2–4; Aug. 1954, p. 1; *New York Times Book Review*, Nov. 30, 1958, p. BR30. For other reader comments on *Italian Bouquet*, see *Gourmet*, Jan. 1957, pp. 2–3; Mar. 1958, p. 2.

24. *Gourmet*, Jan. 1941, pp. 6–10; Mar. 1949, p. 11.

25. Ibid., Aug. 1953, pp. 4–5; Nov. 1953, pp. 4–5; May 1950, pp. 12–14, 36.

26. Only a page of advertising was given to the *Gourmet Cookbook*. Ibid., Feb. 1951, pp. 16–17; Nov. 1952, pp. 43–45; Oct. 1952, p. 44; Mar. 1954, p. 1.

27. Ibid., Oct. 1958, pp. 48–49; Dec. 1958, p. 80; May 1959, p. 61.

28. *Bouquet de France*, p. xix. The Chamberlains found recipes in cookbooks or obtained them from restaurants where they had eaten. Narcissa's favorite sources were *La France à Table*, a periodical devoted each month to one province, *Les belles recettes de provinces francaises*, and *La France gastronomique* (Curnonsky). Narcissa studied at the Cordon Bleu in Paris in 1950 and with Dione Lucas in 1947. See boxes 3 and 4, Chamberlain papers, SL.

29. In comparison to *Bouquet*, Fodor's *France in 1952* (New York: David McKay, 1952) was Paris focused.

30. "Prince of Gastronomes," *Atlantic Monthly*, June 1958, pp. 50–54; *Bouquet de France*, pp. 370, 431. On Curnonsky's eightieth birthday, celebrated by gourmets from all over France, Parisian restaurateurs promised to save a table for him whenever he chose to dine at one of their establishments.

31. "Prince of Gastronomes," pp. 50–54; *Bouquet de France*, p. xvi; *Italian Bouquet*, pp. viii, ix.

32. *Italian Bouquet*, pp. vii, 226, 158.

33. *Bouquet de France*, p. 335.

34. Ibid., pp. 158, 214.

35. *British Bouquet*, pp. 70, 122, 454. Chamberlain shunned most manifestations of modern life, including industry, motorcycles, and Victorian architecture. *Italian Bouquet*, pp. 3, 296; *Bouquet de France*, p. xvii.

36. *Italian Bouquet*, pp. 62, 196.

37. For Normandy, Chamberlain recommended Henry Adams' *Mont St. Michel and Chartres*. Guides, when necessary, ought to leave ample time for travelers to reflect on the site. *Italian Bouquet*, p. 443; *British Bouquet*, p. 116; *Bouquet de France*, pp. 370, 455.

38. *Bouquet de France*, p. 11.

39. *Italian Bouquet*, pp. 281, 284, 378–79, 286, 455.

40. Ibid., pp. 2, 371–72.

41. Chamberlain recommended the "ultramodern" Jolly Hotels in remote parts of Italy, rather than have Americans miss these areas for fear of suffering inconveniences. *Italian Bouquet*, pp. 92, ix; *British Bouquet*, pp. 105, 297, 240–41.

42. *Bouquet de France*, p. 533.

43. *Italian Bouquet*, pp. 23–24, 142.

44. *Italian Bouquet*, p. 308; *British Bouquet*, p. xi; *Bouquet de France*, pp. xviii, 228–29.

45. *British Bouquet*, p. 364; *Bouquet de France*, pp. 38–39. Chamberlain regretted that increasing numbers of American cyclists rode in Brittany and the Loire Valley, already overrun with tourists. Bus travel reminded him of packaged tours. *Bouquet de France*, pp. 383, 417.

46. *Italian Bouquet*, p. 58.

47. Ibid., pp. 57–58.

48. *Bouquet de France*, pp. 37, 40–42, 36, 44–45. The Place Saint-Lazare in Avallon was "an artist's subject which used to appear in the annual Paris Salon."

49. *British Bouquet*, p. 314.

50. *Italian Bouquet*, pp. 124–25.

51. *British Bouquet*, pp. 295, 297.

52. Stephen L. Harp, *Marketing Michelin: Advertising and Cultural Identity in Twentieth-Century France* (Baltimore: Johns Hopkins University Press, 2001), pp. 240–41, 265; Theodore Zeldin, *France, 1848–1945: Intellect, Taste and Anxiety*, II (Oxford: Clarendon Press, 1977).

53. *Bouquet de France*, p. 205.

54. Ibid., pp. 170, 103.

55. Ibid., pp. 33, 185.

56. Ibid., pp. 301, 120, 141, 253; *Italian Bouquet*, pp. 72, 180; *British Bouquet*, p. xvii.

57. Harp, *Marketing Michelin*, pp. 240–41.

58. *Bouquet de France*, pp. 301, 205.

59. Ibid., pp. 323, 589, 280.

60. Ibid., p. 205. In fact, the *Guide Michelin* treated regional and Parisian restaurants as separate categories. Until 1939, no regional restaurant was awarded three stars. Harp, *Marketing Michelin*, p. 250.

61. *Bouquet de France*, p. 66.

62. Ibid., p. 67. According to Julia Child, "Food was straight banquet food and nothing special, nor the wines, either." Child to DeVoto, Nov. 18, 1953, DeVoto papers, SL.

63. *British Bouquet*, pp. 510, 473, 110; *Bouquet de France*, pp. 97, 32, 205, 53.

64. *New York Times Sunday Magazine*, Aug. 3, 1924, p. SM11; *Bouquet de France*, pp. 356, 242, 370, 431, 506.

65. *Etched in Sunlight*, pp. 181–82.

66. *British Bouquet*, pp. xii, 378.

67. Ibid., pp. vii, 346, xiv, 80, 280, xvii.

68. Ibid., p. 502.

69. Ibid., pp. 505–22, 81–82, 91–92. Chamberlain recommended Ye Olde Bell in Hurley, whose Austrian chef cooked English and Continental dishes. *British Bouquet*, p. 84.

70. Ibid., p. 279. The Chamberlains celebrated remnants of French influence in Scotland, where a leg of mutton was called a "gigot." Ibid., p. 524.

71. *Italian Bouquet*, pp. 5, 168. There were 113 recipes in the text of *Bouquet de France* and 43 in *Italian Bouquet*. Daughter Narcisse noted that her parents were "less proficient in Italian" than French. Notation dated June 1988, Chamberlain papers, SL.

72. Ibid., pp. xi, 495.

73. Ibid., p. 495.

74. *Italian Bouquet*, p. vii; *Bouquet de France*, pp. 192, 235.

75. *Italian Bouquet*, pp. 95, 142.

76. *Bouquet de France*, pp. 540–41, 575.

77. *Italian Bouquet*, p. 497; *British Bouquet*, p. 551.

78. *Bouquet de France*, p. 260; *Italian Bouquet*, pp. 178, 498; *British Bouquet*, p. 523.

79. *Gourmet* covers reflected this shift. French and American dishes prevailed until 1957, after which more covers featured Indian, Italian, and Mexican cuisine.

80. By exaggerating the Bobos' quest for adventure, Brooks clarified their intention to use vacations to establish credentials for upward mobility. *Bobos in Paradise*, pp. 203–10.

Chapter 7 • *From Readers to Cooks?*

1. Street to Simon, June 4, 1944, Street papers, PUA. According to *Ulrich's International Periodical Directory*, *Gourmet*'s circulation was 190,000 in 1963. There is no figure for 1961; *Business Week* (Aug. 23, 1958, p. 55) reported the circulation at 130,000 for 1958 with an increase of 10% per year. That projects to 173,000 by 1961. *Gourmet* reprinted

volume 2 of Louis De Gouy's *The Derrydale Game and Fish Cook Book* (New York: Derry-dale Press, 1937). On sales, see *Gourmet*, July 1960, pp. 31–32.

2. Ann Vileisis, *Kitchen Literacy: How We Lost Knowledge of Where Food Comes from and Why We Need to Get It Back* (Washington: Island Press, 2008), chap. 6. Glenna Matthews highlights the role of home economists, especially Christine Frederick, in persuading women to buy brand names. *"Just a Housewife": The Rise and Fall of Domesticity in America* (New York: Oxford University Press, 1987), pp. 170–71.

3. Nineteenth-century cookbooks sometimes lacked a full list of ingredients and/or instructions in basic processes, but family and friends often helped the novice cook. See Neuhaus, *Manly Meals and Mom's Home Cooking: Cookbooks and Gender in Modern America* (Baltimore: Johns Hopkins University Press, 2003), p. 11.

4. *New York Times Magazine*, May 30, 1948, pp. 28–29; Apr. 16, 1950, pp. 52–53; *New York Times*, Dec. 9, 1952, p. 45.

5. *Gourmet*, Oct. 1954, pp. 4–5.

6. Ibid., Dec. 1948, pp. 2–3; Aug. 1952, p. 2; Nov. 1948, p. 2. In "You Asked for It" the most requested items were Lindy's cheesecake, soufflé potatoes, Caesar salad, and coq au vin. *Gourmet*, Jan. 1951, p. 51; Jan. 1954, p. 52.

7. *The* Gourmet *Cookbook*, vol. 1 (New York: Gourmet Distributing Corp., 1950), p. 7. In the introduction, MacAusland wrote that most of the recipes in volume 2 had been omitted from volume 1. In fact, *Gourmet* published many of them after 1950. Ibid.

8. Ibid., Oct. 1952, p. 5; Sept. 1948, p. 3.

9. Ibid., Oct. 1944, pp. 2–3; Jan. 1955, pp. 2–4; Oct. 1955, p. 4.

10. Ibid., Apr. 1959, p. 2; Nov. 1960, pp. 2–3; Jan. 1956, p. 2; Nov. 1948, p. 2.

11. Ibid., Apr. 1959, p. 5.

12. Elaine Tyler May, *Homeward Bound: American Families in the Cold War Era* (New York: Basic Books, 1988), chap. 1; Neuhaus, *Manly Meals and Mom's Home Cooking*, chap. 4.

13. *Gourmet*, Nov. 1948, p. 2. One veteran cook remarked that he could "reproduce or improve on [*Gourmet*'s Creole recipes] from memory with my eyes shut." Ibid., Sept. 1948, p. 3.

14. *Time* magazine, Nov. 25, 1966, pp. 74–80.

15. On Pellaprat, see Charlotte Turgeon, "Frenchmen in the Kitchen," *New York Times Book Review*, Oct. 14, 1941, p. 233. Mary Meade, the cooking editor of the *Chicago Daily Tribune*, considered *The Escoffier Cookbook* a tome for "chefs, epicures, and collectors" rather than housewives. *Chicago Daily Tribune*, Oct. 25, 1941, p. 17.

16. Toklas excluded basic dishes like boeuf à la mode and pot au feu.

17. On the inadequacies of *Mediterranean Food* and *French Country Cooking* for novice cooks see Charlotte Turgeon, *New York Times Book Review*, Oct. 19, 1952, p. 41; May 25, 1952, p. 30.

18. "The Soup is M. Diat's," *New York Times Book Review*, June 24, 1951, p. 181; Jane Nickerson, "News of Food," *New York Times*, May 7, 1949, p. 9; "News of Food," *New York Times*, Apr. 7, 1951, p. 15. Turgeon also translated *Tante Marie's French Pastry* (New York: Oxford University Press, 1954); see Max White, "Desserts à la Medici," *New York Times*

Book Review, Oct. 3, 1954, p. 16; Jane Nickerson, "News of Food," *New York Times*, May 29, 1948, p. 18.

19. *New York Times Book Review*, July 27, 1952, p. 12; Child to DeVoto and attachment, Dec. 30, 1952, JCP, SL.

20. Burton Lindheim, "Dione Lucas, TV Cooking Teacher, 62," *New York Times*, Dec. 19, 1971, p. 60; *Cordon Bleu Cook Book* (Boston: Little, Brown, 1947), p. viii; Angelica Gibbs, "Profiles: With Pallete Knife and Skillet," *New Yorker*, May 28, 1949, p. 34. For an American equivalent to the Cordon Bleu in Paris, *Gourmet* recommended Dione Lucas' classes. *Gourmet*, Feb. 1942, pp. 2–3.

21. *Cordon Bleu Cook Book*, pp. x, 3–4. Lucas referred to "sautéing" and "blanching" but never explained them; pp. 35, 59–60, 149–50. The fish chapter occupied nearly one-third of the book, twice the space she gave to meat and poultry. Lucas rectified this imbalance in *The Dione Lucas Meat and Poultry Cook Book* with Ann Roe Robbins (New York: Little, Brown, 1955). *The New York Times* claimed, "This is clearly not a book for kitchen novices." Sept. 13, 1955, p. 24.

22. Clark, *James Beard*, pp. 154, 173. There were recipes for Hollandaise and Mornay sauces, cream of potato and leek soup, and cassoulet. *The Fireside Cookbook* (New York: Simon and Schuster, 1949), pp. 230, 232, 45, 186.

23. Beard's Paris trip was supported by Sam and Jack Aaron in return for help in opening a Paris branch of Sherry's Wine and Spirits, Inc. Watt later became the food and wine correspondent for the *London Daily Telegraph*. Clark, *James Beard*, pp. 140–44; *Paris Cuisine* (Boston: Little, Brown, 1954), pp. xi–xv.

24. Charlotte Turgeon, "Parisian Dinners at Home," *New York Times Book Review*, June 29, 1952, p. 10; *Paris Cuisine*, pp. 8–11, 260, 104, 110; Jane Nickerson, "The Flavor of Paris," *New York Times Magazine*, May 19, 1952, p. 36.

25. *The Classic French Cuisine* (New York: Alfred A. Knopf, 1959). On Donon, see *New York Times* obituary, Mar. 20, 1982, p. 25; Geoffrey T. Hellman, "Profiles: The Best of the Best," *New Yorker*, Mar. 10, 1962, p. 47; *Culinary Review*, Mar. 1936, p. 15. Knopf twice rejected Donon's cookbook and accepted it only after Donon and the Vanderbilts agreed to pay $4,000 to subsidize production costs. Knopf wanted Narcissa Chamberlain's name on the title page, but Donon demurred. He then asked Bakalar, later an editor of *Gourmet* (from Apr. 1960), to finish the revisions. Internal Knopf memo #254.1, undated (circa Apr. 1958); Knopf to Donon, Dec. 27, 1957; Donon to Knopf, Dec. 29, 1957; Knopf to Narcissa Chamberlain, May 27, 1957; Apr. 1, 1958; Herbert Weinstock to Bakalar, Apr. 1, 1958; Weinstock to Knopf, Oct. 30, 1958, Knopf papers, UT; Craig Claiborne, "Chef Brings Classic Cuisine to Small Kitchen," *New York Times*, Sept. 17, 1959, p. 46. "It's All in the Knowing," *New York Times Book Review*, Sept. 13, 1959, p. 22. Turgeon praised the inclusion of recipes for traditional American dishes in Donon's book, while Julia Child's Houghton Mifflin editor, Dorothy de Santillana, objected strongly. De Santillana remarked that "compared to you chef Donon not only doesn't deserve the word classic, he doesn't even deserve the word French." We may surmise, however, that de Santillana's praise was intended to soften the blow that Houghton Mifflin was about to deliver by rejecting their manuscript. De Santillana to Child, Sept. 22, 1959; Paul Brooks to Child,

Nov. 6, 1959, Child papers, SL. See also Julia Child with Alex Prudhomme, *My Life in France* (New York: Alfred A. Knopf, 2006), p. 215.

26. *The Classic French Cuisine*, pp. v, vi, ix, 199, 39, 127, 229, 20, 316. Donon acquiesced in canned foie gras, escargots, and tomatoes but opposed canned soups for stock. Ibid., pp. 61, 99, 200, 245–48. Donon also balanced recipes for expensive and cheap cuts of meat. Ibid., pp. 6, 20, 248, 200, 141–85.

27. See the previous endnote. Knopf offered Tastevin members autographed copies of Donon's book if they placed orders before publication. Aug. 21, 1959, Knopf papers, UT.

28. Donon to Knopf, Jan. 7, 1958; Knopf to Donon, Jan. 10, 1958, Knopf papers, UT.

29. On De Gouy's life, see *New York Times* obituary, Nov. 15, 1947, p. 17; Robert Beddos, "Portrait of a Cook Book," *New York Times Sunday Magazine*, Oct. 17, 1948, p. 69; De Gouy, Gourmet*'s Cook Book of Fish and Game*, vol. 1, Fish (New York: Gourmet, Inc., 1947), dust jacket. Many of De Gouy's recipes appeared first in the magazine and then in either volume of *The Gourmet Cookbook*. The editors of *Gourmet* were infuriated that De Gouy republished his recipes from the magazine, slated to appear in *The Gourmet Cookbook*, Volume 1, in his own compendium, *The Gold Cook Book* (1947), which Simon Beck described as a "monument" more American than French. Author conversation with Anne Mendelson, June 24, 2008, New York, NY; Beck to Child, June 1953, SB papers, SL. *Gourmet*, July 1942, pp. 22–23; Oct. 1942, pp. 12–13; Nov. 1944, pp. 52–55.

30. See previous endnote; *Gourmet*, Feb. 1941, p. 46.

31. *New York Times* display ad, Oct. 17, 1948, p. BR15; *New York Times*, July 19, 1931, p. RE1. Neither De Gouy nor his Institute was listed in the *New York City Telephone Directory*, winter 1932–summer 1937, or mentioned in subsequent *New York Times* articles. *Publishers' Weekly* obituary, Nov. 29, 1947, p. 2479. See De Gouy, *The Derrydale Game Cook Book* (New York: Greenberg, 1950 [1937]), pp. v–vii.

32. *The Derrydale Game Cook Book*, p. 253; Gourmet*'s Cook Book of Fish and Game*, pp. 23–25.

33. *Gourmet*, Jan. 1941, pp. 18–19; Mar. 1942, pp. 22–23; Oct. 1942, p. 12.

34. Ibid., Feb. 1941, pp. 7–8; Mar. 1942, p. 24; Feb. 1946, pp. 18–19.

35. *The Derrydale Game Cookbook*, pp. 63–64, 69–70, 73, 83, 117–25, 237; Gourmet*'s Cook Book of Fish and Game*, pp. 106, 180, 152, 172; *Gourmet*, Jan. 1941, pp. 13–14; Oct. 1946, pp. 16–17, 44–47; Oct. 1947, pp. 80–83; Aug. 1941, pp. 14–16; Dec. 1941, pp. 14–15; Oct. 1942, pp. 12–13; Nov. 1943, pp. 14–15; May 1941, pp. 19–20; Oct. 1943, pp. 43–44; Sept. 1941, pp. 20–21; May 1943, pp. 16–17; July 1945, pp. 20–21.

36. Ibid., Jan. 1941, p. 13; Jan. 1944, pp. 18–19.

37. *Gourmet*, Jan. 1944, p. 16.

38. Ibid., Feb. 1946, p. 17.

39. Ibid., Dec. 1946, p. 34.

40. Ibid., July 1942, pp. 22–23.

41. Ibid., July 1942, p. 18; Jan. 1941, p. 38.

42. Ibid., Feb. 1946, p. 53; Jan. 1941, p. 38; June 1944, p. 21; Jan. 1944, p. 18.

43. Ibid., Mar. 1942, pp. 22, 28; Feb. 1946, p. 52.

44. Ibid., Mar. 1942, pp. 22–23; July 1942, p. 19; Feb. 1946, p. 49; Dec. 1946, pp. 77, 80, 83; July 1942, p. 43.

45. Ibid., Apr. 1946, pp. 22–25; May 1946, pp. 18–19, 22–23; Feb. 1941, p. 13; Nov. 1944, p. 22; Dec. 1946, p. 34; Feb. 1947, p. 30; Nov. 1943, pp. 18–19; Jan. 1941, p. 18; Dec. 1941, pp. 20–21.

46. Ibid., Oct. 1944, pp. 22–23; Feb. 1942, pp. 18–19; Nov. 1944, pp. 52–54; Aug. 1947, p. 24; June 1944, p. 20.

47. Turgeon, "A Lot of Good Things to Eat," *New York Times Book Review*, Feb. 25, 1951, p. 223.

48. *Gourmet*, Feb. 1955, p. 22; Aug. 1955, p. 17. On Ritz menus, see Diat, *Cooking à la Ritz* (Philadelphia: J. B. Lippincott, 1941), p. xiii; Helen Ridley, *The Ritz-Carlton Cook Book and Guide to Home Entertaining* (Philadelphia: J. B. Lippincott, 1968), pp. 51, 344; *Gourmet*, Jan. 1956, p. 19; Mar. 1957, p. 42; *New York Times*, Aug. 30, 1957, p. 19.

49. De Gouy obituary, *New York Times*, Nov. 15, 1947, p. 17.

50. Helen Ridley was married to William Friedburg, the son of her chemistry professor. "How Well Do You Know Your JWT-ers? Thumb-Nail Sketch No. 39," *Helen Ridley*, Dec. 31, 1964, Helen Friedburg Ridley biographical file, J. Walter Thompson papers, Duke University.

51. *Cooking à la Ritz*, p. 20; *Louis Diat's Home Cookbook: French Cooking for Americans: La Cuisine de Ma Mère* (Philadelphia: J. B. Lippincott, 1946), p. vi; Gourmet's *Basic French Cookbook*, pp. 9–11.

52. *Good Housekeeping*, Oct. 1950, pp. 185–86, 340–45; July 1938, pp. 72–73; *Sauces French and Famous* (New York: Dover, 1978 [1948]), p. 7; Jane Nickerson, "News of Food," *New York Times*, May 19, 1953, p. 34; Louis Diat, "Mon Pays, the Bourbonnais," *Gourmet*, Sept. 1953, pp. 21–22; Gourmet's *Basic French Cookbook*, pp. 9–11. On the reception of *Sauces*, see Mary Poore, "The Soup is M. Diat's," *New York Times Book Review*, June 24, 1951, p. 181. Evan Jones reported that Ridley was a "constant companion" of Diat's. *Epicurean Delight: The Life and Times of James Beard* (New York: Alfred A. Knopf, 1990), pp. 142–43.

53. *Louis Diat's Home Cook Book*, pp. v, xiii–xiv.

54. Ibid., pp. xiii–xiv, p. 292; *Gourmet*, May 1952, p. 23; *Cooking à la Ritz*, p. xiii.

55. *Sauces French and Famous*, p. 14; *Gourmet*, Nov. 1948, p. 96; May 1952, p. 22.

56. *Gourmet*, Nov. 1948, p. 96; May 1956, p. 68.

57. Gourmet's *Basic French Cookbook*, p. 403; *Gourmet*, Oct. 1956, p. 44; July 1956, p. 22.

58. *Gourmet*, Aug. 1948, p. 30; Mar. 1956, p. 38.

59. Ibid., Feb. 1953, p. 22; Nov. 1952, p. 24; *Louis Diat's Home Cook Book*, p. 283.

60. *Gourmet*, Apr. 1948, p. 16; Mar. 1953, p. 22; Feb. 1952, p. 18.

61. Ibid., Jan 1951, p. 10; Apr. 1951, pp. 29, 54; Jan. 1954, pp. 24–25; Aug. 1954, p. 24; May 1952, p. 60; May 1960, pp. 37–44.

62. Ibid., Jan. 1953, p. 20; June 1954, p. 26; Gourmet's *Basic French Cookbook*, p. 27.

63. *Gourmet*, Oct. 1957, p. 26.

64. Ibid., Jan. 1955, p. 26; June 1955, p. 22; May 1956, p. 21.

65. Gourmet's *Basic French Cookbook*, pp. 29; see also *Gourmet*, Oct. 1956, p. 26.

66. Gourmet's *Basic French Cookbook*, pp. 27, 29; *Gourmet*, Sept. 1955, pp. 20–25; Nov. 1955, pp. 26–33; Dec. 1955, p. 29; *Sauces: French and Famous*, pp. 14–15.

67. Gourmet's *Basic French Cookbook*, pp. 99–234.

68. *Gourmet*, Feb. 1955, p. 36; Mar. 1955, p. 26; Feb. 1957, p. 22.

69. Ibid., Oct. 1957, pp. 52–53; May 1956, p. 21.

70. Ibid., July 1955, p. 22; May 1954, p. 24; June 1956, p. 22.

71. Ibid., June 1956, p. 22; June 1948, pp. 18–19; May 1957, p. 24; Sept. 1957, p. 32; Jan. 1953, pp. 26–31.

72. Ibid., June 1954, p. 26; Oct. 1953, pp. 15, 72–73.

73. Ibid., May 1956, pp. 21, 68; Gourmet's *Basic French Cookbook*, p. 588. *Gourmet* printed little reader response to Diat's articles. However, a December 1948 (p. 2) letter from Mrs. E. H. Cannahan praised Diat's sauce articles for their clarity, while Mrs. James M. Cass was pleased with Diat's recipe for bouillabaisse. Ibid., July 1948, p. 2. Caroline Bates, former editor of *Gourmet*, preferred Diat's recipes to Julia Child's. Telephone interview with author, Aug. 1, 2008.

74. *Gourmet*, Mar. 1942, pp. 24–25, 45–47; Mar. 1948, pp. 18–19, 60–63.

75. *Gourmet*, Mar. 1948, p. 60.

76. Kamp, *The United States of Arugula*, pp. 96–97.

Chapter 8 · *Julia and Simca*

1. Child to Beck, July 18, 1957, JCP, SL.

2. As Patric Kuh explained, Julia was repositioning "ethnic food outside the immigrant experience." Kuh, *The Last Days of Haute Cuisine* (New York: Penguin Books, 2001), p. 179; *The Gourmet Cookbook*, vol. 1 (New York: Gourmet Distributing Corp., 1950), p. 7; *Gourmet*, Oct. 1944, pp. 2–3; Apr. 1959, p. 2; Nov. 1948, p. 2; Child to DeVoto, Jan. 19, 1953, JCP, SL.

3. Richard Pells, *Not Like Us: How Europeans Have Loved, Hated, and Transformed American Culture since World War II* (New York: Basic Books, 1996); David Strauss, *Menace in the West: The Rise of French Anti-Americanism in Modern Times* (Westport, CT: Greenwood Press, 1978).

4. Louisette met with the American Federation of Women's Clubs and Ida Bailey Allen, the well-known cookbook writer and former host of a radio show on cooking, who endorsed the cookbook project. "Louisette Bertholle," Author Questionnaire, Knopf papers, UT; Bertholle to Child, Nov. 29, 1957. Louisette entertained Corning Glass officials and gave a demonstration/luncheon to U.S. Air Force Officers' wives in her 16th arrondissement apartment in Paris. The Americans invited her as guest of honor to their Orly base. Feb. 13, 1955, JCP, SL.

5. Fitch, *Appetite for Life: The Biography of Julia Child* (New York: Doubleday, 1997), pp. 16–17, 42; chaps. 5–7, especially pp. 114–16.

6. Ibid., pp. 114–15, 155; list of Julia's classes provided by Smith College Archives; "Cooking Biography of Julia Child" (undated), p. 5, Avis DeVoto Papers (ADP), SL; Child to Fski, Apr. 7, 1951, JCP, SL.

7. Beck, with Suzanne Patterson, *Food and Friends: Recipes and Memories from Simca's Cuisine* (New York: Viking, 1991), p. 91.

8. Beck, *Food and Friends*, pp. 6–8, 91–92, 141, 160, 192, 248. The Women's Club Interallié invited Simca in February 1961 to Fontainebleau to give a cooking lesson to the wives of NATO officers, followed by a tea for which Simca premade two hundred madeleines with Swans Down cake flour; 185 wives attended. Beck to Child, Feb. 21, 1961; Beck to Child, June 24, 1953; Aug. 30, 1954, JCP, SL.

9. "Cooking Biography of Julia Child," pp. 6–7.

10. Beck, *Food and Friends*, pp. 151–59; Fitch, *Appetite for Life*, pp. 187–88; "Le Cercle des Gourmettes, 1952" (roster of members with addresses); Bugnard to Child, Apr. 3, 1951, JCP, SL.

11. "Ecole des Trois Gourmandes. Paris: July 1, 1952," Simone Beck Papers (SBP), SL; "Cooking Biography of Julia Child," pp. 7–9, ADP, SL.

12. Child to DeVoto, Enclosure 1, Dec. 30, 1952, JCP, SL.

13. Child to Beck, Dec. 13, 1954; Child to DeVoto, Dec. 20, 1952, JCP, SL; Child to DeVoto, Aug. 20, 1960, ADP, SL.

14. Beck, *Food and Friends*, pp. 160–61; Fitch, *Appetite for Life*, pp. 196–97. Fischer was a personal friend of the Fischbacher family.

15. Child query, no date; Child to Beck, Aug. 23, 1954, JCP, SL.

16. Fitch, *Appetite for Life*, pp. 307, 323–35; Child to DeVoto, Jan. 19, 1953, Child papers, SL.

17. Child to Putnam, Nov. 30, 1952; Child to DeVoto, Jan. 5, 1952; Child to Beck, Dec. 20, 1957, JCP, SL. On the older cookbooks still in print, see chap. 7.

18. Child to DeVoto, Jan. 5, 1952; Mar. 6, 1953.

19. Child to Beck, Dec. 20, 1957; Child to Putnam, Nov. 30, 1952; Child to de Santillana, Dec. 13, 1955; Beck to Child, Jan. 13, 1956, JCP, SL. One of Julia's students found Lucas' teaching "adept" but not "scientific." Child to Fski, Feb. 4, 1952, JCP, SL.

20. Child to Beck, Mar. 23, 1955; Dec. 4, 1957, JCP, SL.

21. Child to DeVoto, Jan. 8, 1953, JCP, SL.

22. "Ecole des Trois Gourmands"; Child to DeVoto, Jan. 19, 1953, JCP, SL; Child to DeVoto, Jan. 20, 1953, ADP, SL; Child to Beck, Feb. 1, 1955, JCP, SL; Child to de Santillana, Feb. 22, 1953, ADP, SL; *Mastering the Art of French Cooking* (New York: Alfred A. Knopf, 1961), pp. vii, ix.

23. See previous endnote.

24. Child to Sheeline, Mar. 2, 1953; de Santillana to Child, Feb. 11, 1953, JCP, SL.

25. Child to de Santillana, Feb. 7, 1953.

26. Child to DeVoto, Nov. 18, 1953; Apr. 16, 1953, JCP, SL; Rodier to Child, Nov. 10, 1953, Child papers.

27. Child to Beck, Sept. 28, 1955; Sept. 27, 1954; Aug. 19, 1957; Child to Bertholle, Mar. 1, 1953; Child to Leggett, Feb. 10, 1958, JCP, SL.

28. Child to Beck, June 24, 1953; Child to Bertholle, June 19, 1953; Child to Beck, July 18, 1957, JCP, SL; Fitch, *Appetite for Life*, p. 191.

29. Child to Putnam, Dec. 10, 1952.

30. Child to de Santillana, Feb. 7, 1953, JCP, SL; "Guinea Pig Response to Sauce Chapter. No. 1," Jan. 20, 1953, ADP, SL.

31. Child to Beck, Feb. 11, 1954; Mar. 10, 1954, JCP, SL; Child to DeVoto, Jan. 25, 1954; Child to DeVoto, Feb. 16, 1954; Dec. 29, 1960, ADP, SL.

32. Child to Putnam, Nov. 30, 1952; Child to DeVoto, Jan. 5, 1953; Feb. 12, 1953; Child to Beck, June 29, 1953; Child to Putnam, Dec. 10, 1952, JCP, SL; DeVoto to Child, Jan. 22, 1953; according to Julia's Houghton Mifflin editor, Dorothy de Santillana, an early draft of the soup chapter struck precisely the right tone in addressing readers. Child to de Santillana, Feb. 22, 1953; "Guinea Pig Response to Sauce Chapter. No. 1," Jan. 20, 1953, ADP, SL.

33. Beck, *Food and Friends*, p. 160; Child to Beck, May 7, 1954; no date (circa 1954); Auguste Escoffier, *Le guide culinaire: aide-mémoire de cuisine pratique* (Paris: E. Flammarion, 1921); Prosper Montagné, *Larousse gastronomique* (Paris: Larousse, 1938); Ali-Bab, *Gastronomie pratique: études culinaires* (Paris: E. Flammarion, 1928); *La bonne cuisine de Madame E. Saint-Ange* (Paris: Larousse, 1927).

34. Child to Putnam, Dec. 10, 1952; Child to DeVoto, Jan. 8, 1953; Child to Beck, Mar. 2, 1954; Dec. 27, 1955, JCP, SL; Child to DeVoto, Dec. 29, 1960, ADP, SL.

35. Child to DeVoto, Jan. 8, 1953; Child to Beck, no date (circa May 1953), JCP, SL; Child to DeVoto, Jan. 19, 1953; Child to de Santillana, Feb. 7, 1953. Julia worked without servants in Europe while Simca did so on occasion—with Julia's sympathy: "it will put you in the proper mood for U.S. cooking. Mais pénible, ma chère!" (But painful, my dear!) Child to DeVoto, Feb. 12, 1953; Child to Beck and Bertholle, Aug. 4, 1953, JCP, SL.

36. Child to DeVoto, Jan. 5, 1953; Child to de Santillana, Sept. 24, 1953; Child to Beck, no date; Child to DeVoto, Jan. 5, 1953; Child to Beck, Feb. 28, 1956, JCP, SL.

37. Child to Beck, Jan. 1954; Child to Beck, 1954 (rest of date unclear), July 18, 1957, JCP, SL.

38. *Mastering*, pp. 14, 17–18, 249–50; Child to DeVoto, Jan. 5, 1953; Beck to Child, June 3, 1954; Child to DeVoto, Mar. 6, 1953, JCP, SL.

39. Child to Beck, Mar. 2, 1954, JCP, SL; *Mastering*, pp. 19, 284, 548.

40. Child to DeVoto, Jan. 5, 1953; Jan. 30, 1953; Child to Beck, July 1, 1953; Aug. 23, 1954; Mar. 6, 1953; Mar. 4, 1954; Child to DeVoto, Jan. 25, 1954, JCP, SBP, SL. Simca suggested that the Trois Gourmands become partners in a business offering "*une excellent qualité* 'frozen food.' " Beck to Child, Oct. 30, 1953; Child to Beck, Nov. 11, 1957; Beck to Child, Jan. 13, 1956, JCP, SL; Child to DeVoto, Jan. 30, 1953, ADP, SL.

41. Ecole des Trois Gourmands, SBP, SL; Beck to Child, June 3, 1954; Aug. 30, 1954; Child to Beck, date unclear; Child to DeVoto, Jan. 8, 1953, JCP, SL; Child to DeVoto, Jan. 19, 1953, ADP, SL. Julia's Smith College classmate Charlotte Turgeon (with Charles Turgeon) presented recipes that could be prepared in advance in "*The Saturday Evening Post*" *Time to Entertain Cookbook* (1954).

42. Child to DeVoto, Jan. 19, 1953; Mar. 6, 1953; Beck to Child, Aug. 30, 1954, JCP, SL.

43. *Mastering*, pp. ix, 455; Child to Bertholle, Jan. 13, 1956, JCP, SL.

44. Pski Diaries, Jan. 29, 1961, JCP, SL.

45. Beck to Child, Feb. 21, 1961, JCP, SL.

46. Child to Beck, May 3, 1954, JCP, SL; see *Mastering*, p. 53.

47. Child to Beck, May 3, 1954, JCP, SL.

48. Beck to Child, Oct. 30, 1953; May 4, 1954; May 5, 1954; May 11, 1954, JCP, SL.

49. Beck to Child, May 5, 1954, JCP, SL.

50. Beck to Child, May 11, 1954; Child to Beck, May 7, 1954; Mar. 8, 1954, JCP, SL.

51. Child to DeVoto, May 24, 1960; Apr. 24, 1961; Apr. 28, 1961, ADP, SL.

52. Child to Beck, Apr. 28, 1961; Child to DeVoto, Apr. 28, 1961, ADP, SL.

53. Child to Beck, Apr. 28, 1961, ADP, SL.

54. Beck to DeVoto, May 13, 1960, ADP, SL.

55. Beck to DeVoto, Aug. 27, 1960, Jan. 27, 1961, ADP, SL.

56. *CVF* had a circulation of 45,000 in France and only 100 in the United States. Beck to Child, Apr. 18, 1961; Apr. 28, 1961, JCP, SL.

57. Ibid.

58. Beck to Child, Apr. 29, 1961; May 3, 1961, JCP, SL.

59. Beck to Child, Apr. 28, 1961, JCP, SL.

60. Child to Beck, Apr. 24, 1961; Apr. 26, 1961; May 3, 1961; Beck to Child, May 5, 1961, JCP, SL.

61. Child to DeVoto, Apr. 28, 1961, ADP, SL.

62. Beck to Child, Apr. 29, 1961; Beck to Child, May 3, 1961; Child to Beck, May 5, 1961, JCP, SL.

63. Julia also agreed to Jean Fischbacher's correction of the term *vin ordinaire* (a blend of inferior wines), which was replaced by *vin du pays* (regional wine). Beck to Child, May 5, 1961; Child to Beck, May 6, 1961; Child to Beck, Aug. 23, 1954; Child to Bertholle, Jan. 3, 1956, JCP, SL; *Mastering*, pp. 31–34.

64. Child to DeVoto, Apr. 24, 1961; Apr. 28, 1961; Nov. 16, 1960, ADP, SL; Fitch, *Appetite for Life*, pp. 327–30.

65. Child to DeVoto, Jan. 8, 1953; Feb. 12, 1953, JCP, SL.

66. Ibid. Art Buchwald satirized French dogmatism about food in "What Noble Cuisine!" *Washington Post*, Apr. 20, 1958, p. B2.

67. Julia Child to Narcisse Chamberlain, July 15, 1987; Child to Devoto, Mar. 6, 1953, JCP, SL.

68. Harvey Levenstein, *Paradox of Plenty: A Social History of Eating in Modern America* (New York: Oxford University Press, 1993), pp. 117, 138–49, 220–23.

69. Laura Shapiro, *Something from the Oven: Reinventing Dinner in 1950's America* (New York: Viking, 2004), pp. 147–48.

Conclusion

1. *Mastering the Art of French Cooking* (New York: Alfred A. Knopf, 1967 [1961]), p. vii.

2. David Kamp, *The United States of Arugula: How We Became a Gourmet Nation* (New York: Broadway Books, 2006), p. 3.

3. Patric Kuh, *The Last Days of Haute Cuisine* (New York: Penguin Books, 2001), pp. 56–60.

4. Ibid., pp. 134–46; Warren Belasco, *Appetite for Change: How the Counterculture Took on the Food Industry* (Ithaca, NY: Cornell University Press, 1993), pp. 4, 46, 51, 64–65; David, *French Country Cooking* (London: John Lehmann, 1951).

5. Evan Jones, *Epicurean Delight: The Life and Times of James Beard* (New York: Alfred A. Knopf, 1990), pp. 209, 283–84, 286–87; Kamp, *The United States of Arugula*, pp. 282–83, 305–6; Leslie Brenner, *American Appetite: The Coming of Age of a Cuisine* (New York: Avon Books, 1999), pp. 208–11.

6. Kamp, *The United States of Arugula*, pp. 309–14; Brenner, *American Appetite*, pp. 108–16.

7. Kuh, *The Last Days of Haute Cuisine*, pp. 180–82; Kamp, *The United States of Arugula*, pp. 221–29; Brennan, *American Appetite*, pp. 2–3.

8. Deidre Carmody, "New Flavors for Readers of Food Magazines," *New York Times*, May 23, 1994, p. D9.

9. "Keep Those Home Fires Burning" and "Informal Fare for a Midsummer's Eve," July–Aug. 1957; Nov.–Dec. 1956, pp. 4–6, 8. Mrs. J. R. remarked, "I like your magazine's style. It's informative in a friendly way without being all fired chi-chi about it." Regarding meals prepared without a trip to the supermarket, see Sept.–Oct. 1959, pp. 4–7; Mar.–Apr. 1959, p. 9. On similarities between *Bon Appetit* and *Gourmet*, see July–Aug. 1957, p. 3; Mar.–Apr. 1958, p. 11. "The Epicure and the Can Opener," Sept.–Oct. 1959; Poppy Cannon, "What's New to Eat and Drink," Jan.–Feb. 1958, pp. 4–5; Veblen, *The Theory of the Leisure Class* (New York: Penguin Books, 1979 [1899]), pp. 84–85.

10. Kamp, *The United States of Arugula*, pp. 110–12, 344–50; Brenner, *American Appetite*, pp. 77–78; Krishnendu Ray, "Domesticating Cuisine: Food and Aesthetics on American Television," *Gastronomica*, 7, 1 (Winter 2007): pp. 50–64.

11. Kamp, *The United States of Arugula*, pp. 359–60.

12. Pollan, "Unhappy Meals," *New York Times Magazine*, Jan. 28, 2007, p. 38 (L). For more details, see *In Defense of Food* (New York: Penguin Press, 2008), pp. 27–32.

13. Pollan, *In Defense of Food*, pp. 27–32.

14. Sidney Mintz, *Tasting Food, Tasting Freedom: Excursions into Eating, Culture, and the Past* (Boston: Beacon Press, 1996), p. 96. Raymond Sokolov argues that a vernacular cuisine can only develop in a society with a peasant class and a court. *Why We Eat*, p. 233. Leslie Brenner links gourmet dining to a leisurely disposition at the table. *American Appetite*, p. 324.

15. *Tasting Food, Tasting Freedom*, p. 101.

16. Brenner, *American Appetite*, pp. 172–74; Peggy Steiner, "Food and Fashion in United States Society: The Mass-Culturalization of Gourmet Cookery," Ph.D. dissertation, Washington University, St. Louis, MO, 1986.

17. Belasco, *Appetite for Change*, p. 149.

18. Ibid., pp. 111–12, 231, 233; Sokolov, *Why We Eat What We Eat: How the Encounter between the New World and the Old Changed the Way Everyone on the Planet Eats* (New York: Simon and Schuster, 1991), p. 233. Richard Pillsbury claims that Americans change diets more easily than eating habits. *No Foreign Food: The American Diet in Time and Place* (Boulder: Westview Press, 1998), pp. 8–9; *American Appetite*, p. 321.

19. "Democracy versus Distinction: A Study of Omnivorousness in Gourmet Food Writing," *American Journal of Sociology*, July 2007, pp. 165–204. See especially pp. 166, 173, 177, 179, 183, 188, 189, 193, 195.

20. Brenner, *American Appetite*, pp. 6–7.

The student of gourmet dining in America faces a number of challenges in locating materials on the topic. Among the most serious is the absence of a *Gourmet* magazine archive, which, according to *Gourmet* author and historian Anne Mendelson (letter to the author, Dec. 2, 2001), was "variously misplaced, burned, or deep-sixed" years ago. To compound the problem, the researcher must also overcome the haphazard documentation of gourmet dining society activities and the spotty treatment of gourmet restaurants and their chefs. Moreover, of the three international gourmet societies that emerged in the 1930s, only the Confrérie des Chevaliers du Tastevin actually maintained an archive, and that for only a five-year period. Despite these problems, there is happily no dearth of primary material, located in manuscript and menu collections, as well as in various periodicals and the heads of gourmet practitioners, on which to base a history of the subject.

Manuscript Collections

The Julian Street papers at Princeton University are particularly valuable. They include letters to and from Julian Street that document the activities of his correspondents, including André Simon, Frederick Wildman, and Roy Alciatore, all key leaders of the gourmet dining movement in the 1930s. The Alfred Knopf papers at the University of Texas clarify his role in persuading knowledgeable food writers to publish their books in the series "For Wine Lovers and Gourmets" that Knopf launched during Prohibition and sustained for many years. Invaluable as well are the Julia Child, Simone Beck, and Avis DeVoto papers at the Schlesinger Library, particularly for understanding the interactions between those three women during their work on *Mastering the Art of French Cooking*. I have also used the M. F. K. Fisher and Samuel and Narcissa Chamberlain papers at the Schlesinger.

Somewhat more narrowly focused are the collections devoted to three California leaders of gourmet dining. The Phil T. Hanna papers at UCLA shed light on the activities of the Los Angeles chapter of the Wine and Food Society during its first two decades, while the Maynard Amerine and Roy Brady collections at the University of California, Davis, treat the wine industry of California and the activities of the Los Angeles and San

Francisco chapters of the WFS. As for the private archives of the Tastevin, they contain correspondence, menus, and photographs, which document conflicts between the parent organization and the American branches, as well as the latter's dinner committees during the society's formative years from 1945 to 1950.

Menus

A valuable record detailing gourmet activity in the quarter century after repeal, menus both for gourmet society events and for restaurants serving French food comprise an essential component of this study. However, these items have been preserved somewhat randomly. The nearly complete set of the San Francisco Wine and Food Society menus presents a relatively full history of its gastronomic activity. While the Boston chapter of the WFS has preserved few of its own menus, it has been the custodian of a virtually complete collection of those of its predecessor, Le Club des Arts Gastronomiques. As for the New Orleans and Washington, D.C., branches of the Tastevin, members of both societies have maintained helpful archives of their menus. Moreover, accounts of gourmet events in various periodicals, most of which contain at least lists of dishes and wines served on these occasions, provide a useful supplement to the menu collections (see "Periodicals Devoted to Gourmet Dining" under "Printed Sources").

To compare the cuisine of the gourmet societies to that of the best French restaurants in large American cities, I have also used the menu collections from the Culinary Institute of America, the Los Angeles Public Library (online collection), the New-York Historical Society, the New York Public Library, and the San Francisco Center for History.

Interviews

While very few gourmet activists from the 1930s are still alive, dozens of individuals who knew them shared their memories by telephone on the subjects identified below. These recollections I have used to supplement documentation from the archives and from secondary sources. In addition, I have found helpful material in the Bancroft Library's oral history collection.

Julia Child

Susy Davidson, Julia Child Foundation Coordinator, Apr. 29, 2005
Judith Jones, Julia's Knopf editor, May 15, 2005
Henry Morgenthau, friend of Julia's, Apr. 13, 2005
Patricia Pratt, friend of Julia's, Apr. 13, 2005
Marian Schlesinger, friend of Julia's, Mar. 14, 2005

Gourmet Magazine

Caroline Bates, former editor, *Gourmet*, Aug. 1, 2008
Jon Carson, son of former editor, *Gourmet*, Oct. 21, 2005
Russell MacAusland, former business manager and grandnephew of *Gourmet's* founder, Earle, Oct. 18, 2005

La Confrérie des Chevaliers du Tastevin

Marion Baumann, Tastevin National Office, Feb. 15, 2005
Harold Block, New Orleans chapter, Dec. 6, 2004
Millard Cohen, St. Louis chapter, Feb. 9, 2005
Paul C. P. McIlhenny, New Orleans chapter, Feb. 9, 2005
James H. Pipkin, Washington, D.C., chapter, Feb. 8, 2005
Henry Ravenel, Washington, D.C., chapter, Feb. 8, 2005
Jules Stiffel, Chicago chapter, Feb. 3, 2005
Edward Weihman, Fairfield, CT, chapter, Feb. 17, 2005

Les Amis d'Escoffier

John Dorman, New York chapter, Feb. 2004
Charles Doulos, Boston chapter, Feb. 8, 2005
Harry Heinz Hoffstadt, Chicago chapter, Nov. 2004
John Kauffmann, Chicago chapter, Nov. 2004
Gus Saunders, Boston chapter, Feb. 14, 2005

Les Dames des Amis d'Escoffier

Ann Costa, Boston chapter, Feb. 7, 2005
Lucille Giovino, Boston chapter, Feb. 3, 2005

California Wine Industry

Dan Turrentine, former manager, Wine Advisory Board, June 9, 2003
Robert Zerkowitz, librarian, Wine Institute, June 9, 2003

Oral History Collection, Bancroft Library, University of California, Berkeley—
    Maynard Amerine Interview, "Wine Bibliography and Taste Perception Studies,"
    pp. 38–41.
    William Dieppe Interview, "Almaden is My Life" (on Frank Schoonmaker), pp. 19–37

Printed Sources

Periodicals Devoted to Gourmet Dining

Essential to this project are the complete runs of two serials through 1961: *Wine and Food: A Gastronomical Quarterly* (1934–1961) and *Gourmet: The Magazine of Good Living* (1941–1961). The former, addressed to members of the Wine and Food Society, published "Proceedings" for each chapter that chose to report them to the editor. Through their regular accounts, the San Francisco, Los Angeles, and New York chapters left a reasonably complete record of their dinners for this period; entries for the Chicago chapter are complete for the postwar period, while the WFS of Boston recorded relatively few events. The *Quarterly* also published detailed descriptions of "Memorable Meals," which included both private dinner parties and regularly scheduled chapter events. Moreover, in each issue, editor André Simon addressed both society concerns and current food issues in Europe, America, and Australia, where WFS chapters were located.

In the absence of an archive, the *Gourmet* staff's responses to letters to the editor, as well as its choice of authors and topics of magazine articles, its determination of advertising policies, and its treatment of public issues, provide useful evidence for assessing the motives and goals of the publisher and editors and the interests and motives of subscribers. In addition, a small secondary literature partially illuminates the origins and early history of the magazine. Particularly useful is Anne Mendelson, "60th Anniversary," *Gourmet*, Sept. 2001, pp. 71, 110–11, 113, 133, 153, 203, 219; other studies include Carolyn Voight, "You Are What You Eat: Contemplations on Civilizing the Palate with *Gourmet*," M.A. thesis, Graduate Program in Communications, McGill University, Montreal, Quebec, Dec. 1996; Margaret Leibenstein, "MacAusland and *Gourmet: The Magazine of Good Living*," in Harlan Walker, ed., *Cooks and Other People: Proceedings of the Oxford Symposium on Food and Cookery* (Totnes, Devon, 1996), pp. 194–98. Studies devoted to other topics also shed light on *Gourmet*. See, for example, Anne Mendelson, *Stand Facing the Stove: The Story of the Women Who Gave America the* Joy of Cooking (New York: Scribner, 1996) and Robert Clark, *James Beard: A Biography* (New York: HarperCollins, 1993).

Several wine dealers published and distributed free of charge to their customers monthly newsletters that were informative about gourmet dining. Among them were Phil T. Hanna's *Bohemian Life* (1939–1957) and Julian Street's *Table Topics* (1943–1947), both of which reviewed books on gastronomy, published recipes for gourmet dishes, and discussed notable activities of gourmet diners, past and present.

The *Culinary Review* (1930–1945), the monthly publication of the American Culinary Federation, followed the activities of professional chefs and of Les Amis d'Escoffier, the dining society they helped to create.

The *Bulletin of the Society of Medical Friends of Wine* (1956, 1960–2007), a biannual publication of a San Francisco–based wine and food society, included news of society events, a print version of the talks delivered after the society dinners, and biographical sketches of the society's founders.

The *Hotel Monthly* (1934–1935) offered advice to food professionals, especially in the Chicago area, on menus and wine pairings.

Other Newspapers and Magazines

Reports on gourmet dining events in widely circulated periodicals were essential to achieving the societies' goal of informing the larger public about its activities. To check the frequency and content of these communications in the *Chicago Daily Tribune*, the *New York Times*, the *Washington Post*, and the *Los Angeles Times*, I have used the ProQuest Historical Newspapers program. In addition, all of Lucius Beebe's weekly "This New York" columns, published in the *New York Herald-Tribune*, and many of the republished columns from Selmer Fougner's daily "Along the Wine Trail," collected from the *New York Sun*, are available. Newspaper clippings in the Tastevin papers, the Hanna papers, the *Boston Globe* Library, and the San Francisco History Center also clarify the reaction to gourmet events in the following dailies: the *A.M. and P.M. Boston Globe, Boston Evening Transcript, Boston Evening American, New Orleans Times-Picayune, New York Herald Tribune, San Francisco Examiner, Washington Times-Herald, Washington Star*. In addition,

The Readers' Guide to Periodical Literature provided citations to a number of articles that appeared in *Saturday Evening Post, Town and Country, Colliers,* and other magazines.

Central Themes: Primary and Secondary Sources

Gourmets versus Nutritionists

Treatment of the controversy between gourmets and nutritionists in the twentieth century must begin with the texts on gastronomy from the seminal work of Brillat-Savarin to the writings of his successors in England and the United States; rarely mentioned by scholars, the latter updated Brillat-Savarin's work for twentieth-century audiences, while maintaining his emphasis on satisfying the sense of taste. The contrasting stance of women journalists, who focused on maintaining the health of their readers, emerges clearly in their monthly recipes in *Better Homes and Gardens, Good Housekeeping,* and *Ladies' Home Journal.*

The new food columns in luxury lifestyle magazines following the end of Prohibition also challenged the approach of food writers in the women's magazines, as is evident in *House and Garden, House Beautiful, New Yorker, Town and Country,* and *Vogue.* The authors of these columns, often familiar with the tradition of gastronomy, enthusiastically promoted the gourmet ethos rather than nutritionism. Collections of their recipes, originally published in magazine articles, later appeared as cookbooks.

Several recent scholarly works shed light on the origins and nature of the French culinary culture that Brillat-Savarin helped to define. Among them are Amy B. Trubeck's *Haute Cuisine: How the French Invented the Culinary Profession* (Philadelphia: University of Pennsylvania Press, 2000), which explores the production side of gourmet dining; and Priscilla Parkhurst Ferguson's *Accounting for Taste: The Triumph of French Cuisine* (Chicago: University of Chicago Press, 2004), which emphasizes the consumer's approach to this activity. Other important works are Jean-Robert Pitte, *French Gastronomy: The History and Geography of a Passion,* trans. Jody Gladding (New York: Columbia University Press, 2002); and Rebecca L. Spang, *The Invention of the Restaurant: Paris and Modern Gastronomic Culture* (Cambridge, MA: Harvard University Press, 2000).

Meanwhile, scholarship on the rise of a nutritionist ethos in dietary matters as promoted in the women's magazines has demonstrated the centrality of this issue in shaping Americans' approach to foodways. The origins of this ethos, as Laura Shapiro has shown in her *Perfection Salad: Women and Cooking* (New York: Farrar, Straus and Giroux, 1986), lie in the work of the Boston Cooking School; meanwhile, Harvey A. Levenstein's two volumes, *Revolution at the Table: The Transformation of the American Diet* (New York: Oxford University Press, 1988) and *Paradox of Plenty: A Social History of Eating in Modern America* (New York: Oxford University Press, 1993), focus on the later development of a food establishment based in part on the nutritionist approach. For the application of nutritional ideas in wartime, see Amy Bentley, *Eating for Victory: Food Rationing and the Politics of Domesticity* (Champagne: University of Illinois Press, 1998). On the role of women's magazines, so central to the formation of a food establishment, I have drawn on Mary Ellen Zuckerman, *A History of Popular Women's Magazines in the United States* (Westport, CT: Greenwood Press, 1998).

Social Class, Luxury Consumption, and Men's Clubs

In *The Theory of the Leisure Class* (New York: Penguin Books, 1979 [1899]) Thorstein Veblen convincingly portrayed luxury consumption as an upper-class strategy to secure its social ambitions. Over the last century, this claim has set the agenda for scholars considering upper-class culture and has received at least partial confirmation in recent years. For Veblen's "conspicuous consumption" Pierre Bourdieu has substituted the notion of "cultural capital" as an engine for achieving higher status; see *Distinction: A Social Critique of the Judgment of Taste*, trans. Richard Nice (Cambridge, MA: Harvard University Press, 1984). Other works that stress the efficacy of luxury consumption in promoting social mobility include David Brooks, *Bobos in Paradise: The New Upper Class and How They Got There* (New York: Simon and Schuster, 2000); Peggy Steiner Ratcheson, "Food and Fashion in United States Society: The Mass-Culturalization of Gourmet Cookery," Ph.D. dissertation, Washington University, St. Louis, MO, 1986; and Nathalie Jordi, "Samuel Chamberlain's *Clementine in the Kitchen*," *Gastronomica*, Fall 2007, pp. 42–52. From evidence secured in a series of interviews, Michele Lamont concludes that culture is only one factor in enabling the middle class to climb the social ladder; see *Money, Morals and Manners: The Culture of the French and American Upper-Middle Class* (Chicago: University of Chicago Press, 1992). In an earlier work, T. J. Jackson Lears regards the cultural transformation of the upper-class establishment as a desperate response to the ravages of the industrial revolution that required a regeneration of class values; see *No Place of Grace: Antimodernism and the Transformation of American Culture, 1880–1920* (New York: Pantheon Books, 1981).

To better understand the gourmet dining society, it is essential to examine the primary and secondary literature on the operation of upper-class organizations over the past century. In *Members Only: Elite Clubs and the Process of Exclusion* (Lanham, MD: Rowman & Littlefield, 2008), Diane Kendall offers an update on how the exclusivity of contemporary clubs empowers members in dealing with outsiders; William Domhoff makes a similar argument in *The Bohemian Grove and Other Retreats: A Study in Ruling-Class Cohesiveness* (New York: Harper & Row, 1974). On the origins of the country club, see James M. Mayo, *The American Country Club: Its Origins and Development* (New Brunswick, NJ: Rutgers University Press, 1998); see also James Nowland, *Glory, Darkness, Light: A History of the Union League Club of Chicago* (Evanston, IL: Northwestern University, 2004).

Histories of clubs, which served as feeders for the gourmet dining societies, include Fred Alles, *Our First Forty Years!* (Los Angeles: Sunset Club, 1935); George E. Fullerton, *The First Half Century, 1928–1978* (Los Angeles: The Club, 1978); Joseph C. Meyerstein, "Cercle de l'Union: A Retrospect"; and Jeff Smith, "And Reminiscence," Jan. 19, 1962 (author's copy).

Among earlier studies of urban elites, all of which treat their subjects' approach to business, educational, charitable, and social activities, I have examined Frederic Cople Jaher, *The Urban Establishment: Upper Strata in Boston, New York, Charleston, Chicago and Los Angeles* (Urbana: University of Illinois, 1982); E. Digby Baltzell, *Puritan Boston and Quaker Philadelphia: Two Protestant Ethics and the Spirit of Capitalism* (Boston: Beacon Press, 1979); and Cleveland Amory, *The Proper Bostonians* (New York: E. P. Dutton, 1947).

Members of gourmet dining societies and men's clubs have written most of the accounts of their group's activities. One exception is "New York's Dining Clubs," *New York Sun*, Feb. 18, 1893, no page numbers, as reprinted in *Records of the Zodiac as They Appear in the Minute Books, 1868–1915* (New York: privately printed, 1916); for an account of dinners arranged by knowledgeable oenophiles, see Russell Codman, *Vintage Dinners* (Boston: Anchor Linotype Printing, 1937) and "By-Laws of Le Club des Arts Gastronomiques, 1941" (copy from the Boston Wine and Food Society archive).

Of the several Tastevin histories, John Sprague's *Confrérie des Chevaliers du Tastevin: History of the Commanderies d'Amérique* (Nuits St. Georges: Les éditions du Tastevin, 2002) focuses on the American chapters; for an illustrated history of the Confrérie in Burgundy, see Lucien Boitouzet, *Les Chevaliers du Tastevin* (Nuits St. Georges: Société Bourguignonne de Propagande et Editions, 1984); illustrations also accompany the text of Georges Rozet, *La Confrérie des Chevaliers du Tastevin* (Paris: Editions E.P.I.C., 1950); more analytical are works by Jean-Francois Bazin, *La Confrérie des Chevaliers du Tastevin, 1934–1994* (Nuits St. Georges: Les éditions du Tastevin, 1994); and Paul André, *Histoire du Tastevin: Confrérie bourguignonne et internationale* (Neuchatel: Editions Messeiller, 1974).

André Simon has devoted parts of his two autobiographies to the Wine and Food Society: *By Request: An Autobiography* (London: Wine and Food Society, 1957) and *In the Twilight* (London: Michael Joseph, 1969); his biographer, Patrick Morrah, also comments on Simon's role in the WFS in *André Simon: Gourmet and Wine Lover* (London: Constable, 1987); on the first two decades of the Los Angeles chapter of the WFS, see Marcus Crahan, *The Wine and Food Society of Southern California: A History with a Bibliography of André L. Simon* (Los Angeles: Wine and Food Society of Southern California, 1957).

Aside from the following rosters, menu credits to members who served on dining committees provide the best evidence of membership in a dining society. See also Membership Roster, Confrérie des Chevaliers du Tastevin, July 1, 1965; *Roster of Membership* (WFSSF, Nov. 29, 1944); Membership Roster, WFSSF (1963).

Travel and Gourmet Dining

Samuel Chamberlain often treated gourmet dining as an integral part of a vacation tour in Europe, although his first *Gourmet* articles, depicting "Clementine in the Kitchen," portrayed a Burgundian cook's experience in America. The book-length collection of these articles, first published in 1943, appeared in a Penguin edition (2001) edited by Ruth Reichl and was the subject of Nathalie Jordi's "Samuel Chamberlain's *Clementine in the Kitchen*," *Gastronomica: The Journal of Food and Culture*, Fall 2007, pp. 42–52. By contrast, Chamberlain's *Bouquet de France* (1952), *Italian Bouquet* (1958), and *British Bouquet* (1963) have been ignored in recent years but were popular among *Gourmet* readers from 1949 through the 1960s. They offer helpful insights into the central role of travel and gourmet dining in shaping the upper-middle-class lifestyle. To assess Chamberlain's guidebooks in relation to his competitors, I have also examined *Fielding's Travel Guide to Europe* (New York: William Sloane Associates, 1952) and Arthur Frommer, *Europe on 5 Dollars a Day* (1957).

On the cultural dimensions of travel, Chamberlain's autobiography, *Etched in Sunlight* (Boston Public Library, 1968), occupies a special niche. So does Malcolm Cowley's *Exile's Return: A Literary Saga of the Nineteen Twenties* (New York: Viking Press, 1951 [1934]), which treats the exile experience of Chamberlain's generation. Invaluable as well are Harvey Levenstein's two volumes: *Seductive Journey: American Tourists in France from Jefferson to the Jazz Age* (Chicago: University of Chicago Press, 1998) and *We'll Always Have Paris: American Tourists in France since 1930* (Chicago: University of Chicago Press, 2004). Among other topics, they give some attention to the dining habits of American tourists. On the impact of political, social, and cultural factors on travel, see also James Buzard, *The Beaten Track: European Tourism, Literature, and the Ways to 'Culture,' 1800–1918* (Oxford: Clarendon Press, 1993); Christopher Endy, *Cold War Holidays: American Tourism in France* (Chapel Hill: University of North Carolina Press, 2004); and Stephen L. Harp, *Marketing Michelin: Advertising and Cultural Identity in Twentieth-Century France* (Baltimore: Johns Hopkins University Press, 2001).

Food, Wine, and Restaurants

In the absence of published accounts of resources available in the mid-1930s to support gourmet dining, I have attempted to identify these resources and assess their adequacy to the movement. There are useful studies of wine production in America, but no comprehensive account of the resumption of wine imports, the establishment of wine dealerships, and the adequacy of imported foodstuffs. To document the availability of wine and foodstuffs, I have used food and wine catalogues and periodical advertisements. As for restaurants, the only comprehensive accounts for this period are restaurant guides by Duncan Hines: *Adventures in Good Eating* (New York: Duncan Hines, 1936) and *Gourmet's Guide to Good Eating* (New York: Gourmet, 1948). Among the most useful local guides are Natalie Scott and Caroline Merrick Jones, *Gourmet's Guide to New Orleans* (New Orleans: Peerless Printing, 1933); Ruth Thompson and Chef Louis Hanges, *Eating around San Francisco* (San Francisco: Suttonhouse, 1937); John Drury, *Dining in Chicago* (New York: John Day, 1931); and George Rector, *Dining in New York with Rector: A Personal Guide to Good Eating* (New York: Prentice-Hall, 1939).

On wine production, see the thorough account by Thomas Pinney, *A History of Wine in America from Prohibition to the Present* (Berkeley and Los Angeles: University of California Press, 2005); in addition, there is *The University of California / Sotheby Book of California Wine*, ed. Doris Muscatine, Maynard A. Amerine, and Bob Thompson (Berkeley and Los Angeles: University of California Press / Sotheby Publications, 1984); an older history of wine production by Leon Adams: *The Wines of America* (Boston: Houghton Mifflin, 1973); and articles in *Wayward Tendrils Quarterly* (1996–2003).

On food in America, see Evan Jones, *American Food: The Gastronomic Story* (New York: E. P. Dutton, 1975). Donna Gabaccia's *We Are What We Eat: Ethnic Food and the Making of Americans* (Cambridge, MA: Harvard University Press, 1998) treats the food scene as a melting pot. Also useful are *The Taste of American Place: A Reader on Regional and Ethnic Roots*, ed. Barbara G. and James R. Shortridge (Lanham: Rowman & Littlefield, 1998); and Richard J. Hooker, *Food and Drink in America: A History* (Indianapolis: Bobbs-Merrill, 1981).

Gourmet Cooking

Between 1941 and 1961, *Gourmet* chefs Louis De Gouy and Louis Diat published many of the French recipes that were reliable for and accessible to novice American home cooks. Their articles and cookbooks thus provide evidence of the state of the art, as well as social and cultural messages to readers, whether or not they cooked the recipes. Most useful among the cookbooks are De Gouy's *The Gold Cook Book* (New York: Greenberg, 1947) and Diat's *Gourmet's Basic French Cookbook: Techniques of French Cuisine* (New York: Gourmet Books, 1961). Scholars who have interpreted the class, ethnic, and gender implications of these messages include Sherrie Inness, *Dinner Roles: American Women and Culinary Culture* (Iowa City: University of Iowa Press, 2001); Jessamyn Neuhaus, *Manly Meals and Mom's Home Cooking: Cookbooks and Gender in Modern America* (Baltimore: Johns Hopkins University Press, 2003); Janet Theophano, *Eat My Words: Reading Women's Lives through the Cookbooks They Wrote* (New York: Palgrave, 2002); and Erika Anne Endrijonas, "No Experience Required: American Middle-Class Families and Their Cookbooks, 1945–1960," Ph.D. dissertation, University of Southern California, 1996.

Mastering the Art of French Cooking contains its own set of messages, which the Julia Child papers and her autobiography, written with Alex Prud'homme, *My Life in France* (New York: Alfred A. Knopf, 2006), help to unravel; also helpful are two biographies: Noel Riley Fitch, *Appetite for Life: The Biography of Julia Child* (New York: Doubleday, 1997); and Laura Shapiro, *Julia Child* (New York: Penguin Group, 2007). Shapiro's *Something from the Oven: Reinventing Dinner in 1950s America* (New York: Viking, 1960) offers helpful reflections on the gender implications of the work of Julia and her contemporary Betty Friedan, while Joan Reardon's *M. F. K. Fisher, Julia Child and Alice Waters: Celebrating the Pleasures of the Table* (New York: Harmony Books, 1994) considers the interactions and mutual influences of three major players in the rise of gourmet dining. For articles on and remembrances of Julia Child, see the summer 2005 issue of *Gastronomica: The Journal of Food and Culture.*

239–42; and École des Trois Gourmands, 2, 225, 240; and *The French Chef*, 1, 245, 251; on goût français / gout américain, 236, 239, 241–44; impact of, on gourmet movement, 1–2, 221, 246; impact of internationalism on, 221–22; as mentor to ethnic cookbook writers, 250; ties to gourmet movement of, 221; and *Time* article, 245. See also *Mastering the Art of French Cooking*

Child, Paul, 224–25

Child, Theodore, 2, 28–29

"Christmas on Paradise" (Coffin), 144

Claiborne, Craig, 9; *New York Times Cookbook*, 195

"Classes in Classic Cuisine" (Diat), 207, 213

Classic Italian Cook Book, The (Hazen), 250

"Clementine in the Kitchen" (Chamberlain), 158–59, 161, 196

Clovelly, England, 175

Club des Arts Gastronomiques, 65–67; photo of table setting for, 65

Club des Cents, 71, 182, 255

Codman, Charles, 48, 64, 66, 115, 124

Codman, Russell Sturgis, 64–66, 97

Codman, Theodora, 105–7

Coffin, Robert, "Christmas on Paradise," 144

College Inn restaurant, Sherman Hotel, Chicago, 61

Colony restaurant, New York City, 57

Commandérie de Bordeaux, 130

Concise Encyclopedia of Gastronomy, A (Simon), 196

Confrérie des Chevaliers du Tastevin, 72–73, 76–77, 181–82; as advocates of French cuisine, 73, 85; appeal of ritual to, 73, 80–81, 99; debate over expansion of, 111, 129; examinations for, 81; hierarchy in, 80–81; influence of, on Chamberlain, 182; and local control, 111–12, 281n32; members' behavior in, 89; photo of serving suckling pig for, 90; and planning for May 1948 dinner, 87–89; and promotion of Burgundy wines, 84–85, 120, 123–26, 274n45; selection of members for, 104, 106–7, 111–15, 279n15

connoisseur. See gourmet, definition of

conspicuous consumption / leisure. See luxury consumption

constitution and bylaws, Escoffier Society, 78

cookbooks: *Gourmet*, 189–90; gourmet, 195–99, 250. See also specific books

Cooking à la Ritz (Diat), 208–10

Cook's Magazine, 250

Cordon Bleu Cookbook, The (Lucas), 198

Cordon Bleu cooking school, 224

cost, of gourmet dinners, 103

Coste, Pierre, 59

Côte Basque restaurant, New York City, 134

Crowninshield, Frank, 14, 45–46, 260n3

cuisine bourgeoise, 7

cuisine régionale, 179–81

Cuisines et Vins de France (CVF), 239–41

Cuisines of Mexico, The (Kennedy), 250

Culinary Institute of America, 55

Culinary Review, The, 55, 76

cultural capital / social status, 6, 70–71, 163, 165, 168, 187, 190, 223, 252, 254

Curnonsky (Maurice-Edmond Sailland), 130, 172, 179, 243–44, 292n30

Curnonsky and Rouff, Marcel, *La France Gastronomique* (28 vols.), 172

Dames des Amis d'Escoffier, 106, 129

Dave Chasen's Southern Pit Barbecue, Los Angeles, 62

David, Elizabeth, 183, 195, 249; *French Country Cooking*, 196; *French Provincial Cooking*, 196; *Mediterranean Food*, 196; *Summer Cooking*, 196

De Gouy, Louis P.: biography of, 200–201, 295n29; "La Bouillabaisse," 216–17; *The Derrydale Game and Fish Book*, 201–2; "Gastronomie sans argent," 200, 206–7; and gender-coded recipes, 190, 200–205; as *Gourmet*'s first chef, 139; interest in Creole and game dishes of, 202; "Mardi Gras," 144–45; and reasons for hiring, 199–200; recipe by, 203

Delmonico's restaurant, New York City, 7, 11, 32, 34

de Rochemont, Richard, 124

Devizes, England, 175

DeVoto, Avis, 239, 242

Dewey, Suzette, 105, 278n11

Dexter, Philip, 64